THE
FREEDOM
TRANSMISSIONS

THE
FREEDOM
TRANSMISSIONS

A PATHWAY TO PEACE

YESHUA

AS CHANNELED BY
CARISSA SCHUMACHER

HarperOne
An Imprint of HarperCollinsPublishers

HarperCollins books may be purchased for educational, business, or sales promotional use. For information, please email the Special Markets Department at SPsales@harpercollins.com.

FIRST HARPERCOLLINS PAPERBACK PUBLISHED IN 2023

Designed by Joy O'Meara @ Creative Joy Designs

Library of Congress Cataloging-in-Publication Data is available upon request.

ISBN 978-0-06-309857-2

23 24 25 26 27 LBC 5 4 3 2 1

To the Beloved

Our birth is but a sleep and a forgetting:
The Soul that rises with us, our life's Star,
Hath had elsewhere its setting,
And cometh from afar:
Not in entire forgetfulness,
And not in utter nakedness,
But trailing clouds of glory do we come
From God, who is our home.

—WILLIAM WORDSWORTH

Contents

Introduction

Hello, Beautiful Spirit. I'm Carissa. I am one of Yeshua's channels. It is my greatest joy to lend my body, my heart, my spirit to serve as an anchor and vessel for Yeshua in the channeling of the Freedom Transmissions. That is my only presence and purpose here. The rest of the journey is between you and Him.

It does not matter when you are finding these Transmissions or how—the energy behind the Transmissions of Divine Spirit knows no time.

If you felt the call to read or listen to this book, you were drawn to it for reasons beyond the mind. The "why" does not matter. Let it be. The mind often cannot comprehend the ways of the Divine. If you found your way here it is because Spirit put out a call to you and you answered that call. Or you put out a call to Spirit and Spirit answered your call. The incredible Grace and Wisdom of Yeshua is for those truly ready to transform, illuminate, and evolve in consciousness and embodiment of Light in a very direct way.

Before you begin the Freedom Transmissions, I will share with you how I came to be a vessel, channel, and anchor for Yeshua, as well as a few important things to understand about the power of Yeshua's Presence and Love.

You may be wondering, "Who and what IS Yeshua?" I will simply say: Yeshua is Christ. Yeshua is Divine Father, Christ, and the Holy Spirit or Divine Mother. I was told of His name long ago and identified Him as the Presence or Logos many refer to as Jesus. When He "birthed" in my channel, meaning came to and through me for the first time, He was clear that His name was Yeshua. I asked, "Why am I not to call you Jesus?" He answered, "Because that was not My name."

His name in Aramaic, the language spoken by Christ at the time of Christ in Judea, was Yeshua. While the pronunciation of His name in Aramaic was Ye-*shu*-a, He expressed that *Yesh*-ua is perfectly fine and interchangeable. If you resonate with the name Jesus you are free to call Him that or whatever you wish, but He was clear that Jesus carries a ladle of some deep imbalances and misunderstandings with regard to who He is. So, to me, He wished to be called Yeshua. It is important to note that Yeshua's Presence in the way He comes through my channel is far greater than His representations in many religious texts or even accounts of His one Life. Yeshua is far, far "older" than His one Life.

Many times over these Transmissions, which are His Offerings and the energy behind them, He will remind you to see Him "not as He was but as He is." For God evolves progressively as we progress in evolution and consciousness as individuals and a collective.

While He/She carries both masculine and feminine energy just as all souls do, I am referring to Him as a "Him" for Simplicity. However, His Light is carried in all things and all people and thus He is all genders, races, colors, and lenses of consciousness. Whatever resonates for you in your experience of Him is what is right for you even if another person has a completely different perception and experience with Him. Allow your perception of Him to evolve, transform, and shift as you do.

You can call Him a Her, an It, or anything that resonates for you. If you relate more to the Divine or Yeshua as Jesus, Christ, Hamaschiach, Messiah, Hashem, Allah, Gaia, Divine Mother, Buddha, Moses, Shiva, Archangel Michael, Kali, Pele, or Elmo, that is wonderful. The Divine is One God. Thus, Yeshua speaks for and as All Sacred Be-ings. Whatever resonates for you, or not, is what's right.

Thus, while you may have associations of Yeshua from the past that you are bringing to the present, please allow for His Presence in the now. For He speaks of things important to your illumination in the present world not from a place of the past but from a place of today.

What that means to you is unique to you. Some experience Yeshua as God; some as an Ascended Master; some as a Prophet; some as a mortal man who existed long ago; others deny His existence altogether. There are no rights or wrongs. One of the greatest gifts of His unique Divine Presence is His unconditional Love, Forgiveness, nonjudgment, and inclusivity of all people and all life . . . not just those who worship Him or receive Him in a certain way. Yeshua is not just for some people, Yeshua is for all people.

It is important to note that, regardless of name, Yeshua is the Presence of Peace. Not just the feeling of Peace but the very Essence and energy of Peace itself. Yeshua IS Peace. Peace IS Yeshua. There is no difference. Thus, if you are so inclined, you can replace "Yeshua" with "Peace" altogether. For those of you that might have some resistance to receiving the Transmissions from Yeshua, just reframe the Transmissions as Grace flowing to you from the energy of Peace.

Simply allow for Peace, the Voice of Peace, to speak to you from within you throughout the Transmissions. Having an intimate experience and conversation with Peace is the same thing as having an intimate experience and conversation with Yeshua. Many people have experienced a first connection or whole new relationship with Yeshua as a result of shifting perception of Him from a religious figure to that of pure, simple Peace. That is how I experience Him, as well.

Yeshua/Peace brings calm, Light, wisdom, and relief to any and every heart even in the darkest of storms. When you come to a sudden moment of calm, Presence, and Peace, you are in the Presence of Yeshua, of Consciousness.

Even if you don't know Yeshua, you do know Peace, even if it feels like it is lost in certain moments. Yeshua Offers you Pathways to the Heart of Peace and thus to His Heart, through your own. The more you embody Peace, the more you too become an anchor, channel, and conduit for Yeshua, for Peace on Earth. This is the realization of your Divine/Yeshua/Peace self.

In past Transmissions, Yeshua has defined this realization as our purpose in coming to a human life. He has said that we are here to know self as Divine through being human, to accept what we come to know and experience, and to come to Peace with self as a result. It is a nonlinear process with no beginning and end. There is no metric or finish line. Only a refinement and restoration of the Divine self, Yeshua self, that comes as a by-product. The rewards for this process are not about what "you will get," and approaching the Transmissions with an expectation that these will guarantee you a fast track to money, relationships, success, power, or fame is a setup for disappointment.

While those might come as a by-product of your transformation, they are far less significant than what you do "get" through commitment to the process, not just through reading or listening to this book but through the whole of your life. What you "get" is a communion and intimacy with the very essence of Divine Love that makes the darkest storm Light. What you "get" is yourself—your Freedom, your joy, your Peace on the inside. And, as a by-product, a fluidity of showering your soul's Light into the world through your very Presence.

The way Yeshua illuminates this Pathway to Peace is quite surreal at times. He is a consciousness and intelligence so far beyond the comprehension of the human mind, it is astounding. His Offerings create a Pathway to realize Peace within whatever way density, stress, despair, anger, anxieties, doubt, grief, dis-ease, etc. is showing up for you: addictions, restlessness, emotional swings, mind chatter, or worries about children, parents, relationships, finances, technology, jobs, politics, health, and other trappings of human life.

He understands what it is to be human. He cannot solve your every issue; that is your journey. Nor does He take sides or assert opinions. He provides insight as to how to realize Peace no matter what you are experiencing. In a sense, He knows you better than you know yourself and Loves you unconditionally no matter what. Surrendering to that allows you to receive His support, wisdom, and strength in a way that brings deep relief.

While Yeshua's Presence is very, very Powerful, His humility, kindness, compassion, and patience allow for the process with Him to be personal, intimate, and co-creative. With Yeshua you are always seen, heard, and Loved. There is nothing you can do that could cause Him not to Love you. It's almost maddening at times. There have been many moments I have said, "Yeshua, we can be so cruel to one another and to ourselves as human be-ings. Why do You still Love us?" His response is always simple and pure: "Because you ARE."

Yeshua's Transmissions are not structured to conflict with your beliefs. He is not here to change your beliefs. He is here to expand your consciousness, unburden you from the imbalances of the mind that lead to unnecessary suffering, strengthen your Faith and sense of worth, and, overall, to evolve and restore Balance and joy to your spirit. So that you can live from your true essence.

You do not have to believe in Yeshua to receive the incredible gifts of Love, Truth, and Peace He offers. His Transmissions are to augment your Faith and personal communion with the Divine. By Faith I mean true Faith, the unwavering constant within you, no matter what beliefs and changes come to your life, mind, or heart.

Just as He did not come to the world centuries ago to undo or tear down Judaic law but instead to fulfill, restore, and evolve it, He is not one to undo or tear down the mindsets you have about God, self, and world. He simply serves to fulfill, restore, and evolve you more deeply into your natural essence of be-ing. Yeshua is so pure in Balance between Truth and Love to create Peace that He can mirror to you many aspects of self that you didn't even know were out of Balance. Yeshua leaves no stone left unturned, so to speak!

To restore Balance within you, Yeshua can bring forth a lot of polarities that can sometimes be challenging to work through. To bring unity, He can bring forth the experience of two seemingly opposite feelings, tendencies, or beliefs from within you. Flip sides of the same coin. For example, a healthy polarity is a positive and negative charge—opposing "forces" that serve the whole of the function. Another example: To guide you to deeper trust (light polarity), you may need to experience the opposite shadow polarity: doubt. One moment you can experience total Peace and the next minute feel conflicted. Then back to Peace. This can conjure strong emotional feelings and even frustrations. Those are for you to work through with kindness, curiosity, and patience.

Yeshua is not narrow-minded in focus. Your soul is interested in all experiences and emotions. Thus Yeshua brings you through a range of feelings. It is not a one-food supper He Offers. There is an abundant cornucopia of nourishment He provides even in moments He is supporting you through uprooting some polarities. Sometimes when reading or listening, you can feel a Love so strong that you just begin to cry or even feel a sense of grief. He is helping you to remember that grief and Love are One. One highlights the other. Sometimes you might feel a moment of resistance or irritation well up for seemingly no reason. In such moments, He is helping to bring your shadow into the Light so that it can be witnessed, processed, integrated, and Balanced. If you flow with this movement, a profound liberation and newfound sense of Peace can come in an instant.

He helps to show you unhealthy polarities like unhealthy internal dominance and suppression structures by showing you the Balance that two healthy polarities, like yin and yang, can create. This will come through the Transmissions, as well as what comes to you in your life before, during, and after listening or reading. Yeshua moves energy powerfully through the whole of your be-ing as you receive His Offerings, even if you only ever read one paragraph. The movement of energy is only ever to restore Balance and Peace.

That restoration sometimes requires really looking at, feeling, transforming, and releasing all that isn't Peaceful or Balanced. Sometimes that means looking at the Truth. But Yeshua always brings forth your inner imbalanced polarities with such Love that His Presence somehow makes it feel safe and even joyful to look at some of the things you didn't want to look at before. He is the essence of humility and non-judgment.

His Presence makes it easier to work through your internal dissonance to restore the organic flow to your be-ing and life. All Yeshua asks of you is to be honest (since He sees all parts of you anyway). And to reclaim your Divine essence by taking responsibility for your own dissonance instead of seeking who to blame for it. Your path with Yeshua, if you allow for it, is one of unconditional support, partnership, and friendship. He knows what it is to be human and to become Divine through your humanness.

Yeshua, Peace, is the "Child" of Truth and Love. Peace is the best of both worlds in a sense. Yeshua's Peace is a ruthless Peace; nothing can shatter it. Thus, it takes a lot of humility and a warrior heart to understand the deep Love and Truth He Offers you through Peace. He likes to go straight to the core of your judgments and limitations of perception to illuminate, uproot, and rebalance them.

So, if you stumble upon words that are in conflict with your beliefs or do not resonate, just let it be. Again, certain things He says can trigger some old things within you, and some resistance can bubble up. Be patient. Everything can make sense in an instant. It is truly Miraculous how right He is just at the moment you decide He is wrong. I have been through that myself.

The resistance makes sense. Yeshua is a very polarized figure in the world. It is rare to find a single human be-ing on the planet who does not have some opinion of who they think He is—or a wound from what was indoctrinated in them through institutions that stoked fear about a harsh and judgmental God, Gods, Yeshua, or Divine Father (even Divine Mother in certain institutions). Nowadays, some people with a strong relationship with Yeshua even fear speaking about their relationship with Him to others. As the world has changed, there are those who mock Yeshua and those with an open spiritual connection to Him. Many persecutions and even crimes have been committed under His Name through the ages even though such actions are the antithesis to Yeshua's essence, Peace and humility.

Yeshua triggers a lot of very diverse and even defensive feelings within people just through the collective perceptions and misperceptions of His historical representations. The Truth of His Life then may never and probably can never be known. But He Offers the Truth of His Eternal Life to you now in a new, yet familiar and consistent way.

There is no indoctrination of dogma inherent to His Transmissions. He is never fussy, punitive, shaming, authoritarian, or technical. However, what He Offers, often through humor, is very original and can challenge old belief systems—including those made in His Name, hundreds of years after He lived, by those who did not know Him. The word *Church* did not exist at the time of His Life. Yeshua did not create a "Church," He created a "Community" available to all willing to receive, live, and serve through Truth, Love, and Peace in alignment with simplified Divine Law. Including the Golden Rule. The old Semitic word for Church is actually a legal term that means "a place to gather together for the purpose of testifying."

Yeshua's "Ministry," "Temple," or "Church" is a nondenominational community available to all those who have the humility to live in alignment with the simple tenets of Divine Balance. All people are members. No one is excluded or unworthy in the community of the Heart of Peace, Yeshua's Sacred Heart. When you offer words of Prayer for all people, especially those you do not like or perceive as "wrong," serve through joy, Forgive trespasses, take accountability through humility for your own trespasses, choose resolution through Love over wrath and judgment, move deeper into Balance, and practice gratitude, you are testifying. When inspired by the words of another that fill your spirit with Grace, support, and inspiration, you are receiving testimony. That is Yeshua's Church, the Coming of Unity, which is the Second Coming.

While membership in a Church, Temple, Mosque, Kiva, Inipi, Alcoholics Anonymous, or any other organized place of gathering can be wonderful if it is rooted in equality, community, embracing, honesty, and support, membership in Yeshua's community does not require you to be part of one to connect to and be served by Him. As a matter of fact, when you embody Peace, you become the essence of Peace, itself. That is what it is to live from and as your Divine self, Yeshua self, true self. As you do, you naturally hold the Light for others to awaken to such within themselves.

Through the stories told of Him through oral and some written traditions such as the Bible, which is nearly all we have to know Him in His physical life prior to now, He was a Truth-giver then and now. The wisdom and Grace He Offered two thousand years ago was shocking for that time, for it challenged many of the engrained belief-sets of the time. He is no different now. What He Offers is original though it goes slightly against the grain of current collective mindsets, even when He makes reference to words He said in the past.

In many ways, through His Transmissions, I feel He Offers us a restoration to the Truth of His past teachings in a way that is applicable to the now. Who knows? That is up to you to explore. I am not a historian, philosopher, psychologist, or religious scholar, and I will confess I do not have more than a rudimentary understanding of almost any religious literature. But that is what makes Yeshua so accessible to all people: It doesn't matter. He is here for you and all of creation here and now. He is just who He is, always has been, and always will be: the Light beyond Light. A Savior then and now even if all He saves you from is all the ways you do not Love yourself or all the ways you withhold your true self from the world.

I was really surprised by Yeshua's essence and Words when He came through my channel for the first time because I expected Him to be solemn and didactic. He is anything but! If anything, through the lens of Yeshua that comes through my channel, He is grounded, funny, Loving, and always completely honest. His Transmissions make the experience of Divinity in human daily life so much simpler. Some parts may resonate deeply, others may not. These Transmissions are a guidepost, not a dictation, as He said from the very beginning. He guides, suggests, presents, uncovers, weeds, uproots, Balances, soothes, triggers, nourishes, shakes up, plants, seeds, connects, constructs, deconstructs, and illuminates with an effortless perfection and ease. It is an adventure and an exploration. If anything, an experience.

He is far more than the Words He Offers. The energy He moves within you matters far more. Even if you read one word and throw out this book, He will still move energy in your life. The Light always moves energy through your spirit, but through this particular channel to Yeshua, there is a deeper communion and flow of Grace that occurs in very specific ways. The more open you are, the more patient, and the more committed, the deeper the Miracles that can come. I have witnessed this countless times in those who have sat with Him or received His Transmissions.

The Transmissions are for you to explore and know yourself as One with God, not to become confused, frustrated, and then to go into judgment. You are co-creating the Transmission WITH the Divine through this experience. Thus, you are fulfilling, restoring, evolving, and serving as a vessel and anchor for the Divine in participating in this process.

If you come to the Transmissions from a space of bias and defensiveness, looking for flaws, holes, and inconsistencies, you will miss out on the incredible experience of His Grace and wisdom—and all that it Offers to you in transformation and realization of Freedom. He is not here to change your mind, He is here to shift your consciousness and illuminate new possibilities in your experience of self and world. If you come into this open, it can bring a new wholeness to your relationship with the Divine, and your ability to embody the Light. Though it is up to you (the Divine will never override your Free will), consider sparing judgment until you have read or listened to the Freedom Transmissions a few times.

I offer this advice because I have now lived this experience. I was not born into a religious family; in fact, I majored in neuroscience at Brown because I wanted to understand if there was a scientific explanation for how I have experienced the world since I was a young child. I was a child empath who was born with strong psychic and mediumship abilities, abilities that were substantiated more and more as each year of my life went on. As a "grounded" person, I spent years of my life trying to discredit my own self. In some ways, since no one could explain why I could see and hear what I did, I was a self-skeptic despite strong proof of the accuracy of my visions and intuitions. I have realized since then that questioning and "checking" one's own sense of self isn't the worst thing in the world. Doing so has allowed me to maintain humility and to continuously strive for deeper understanding of self and Spirit beyond asking "why."

Nature always felt like "Temple" and true "Community" to me more than any other place. The beauty of Mother Earth/Gaia is that, even when you're alone within Her, She invites you into her community of crickets, worms, and trees. I always felt a natural draw to indigenous and Native American energy, which I was lucky to learn a bit about from my parents. The first song I ever learned was a Native American song. It was about the Spirit alive in all things and people. My parents encouraged time in nature and also WORK in nature from the time I was young. They taught me that there is almost no human be-ing that nature cannot make whole. And that we do not take from the Earth without giving back to Her in equality. They taught me that life is Balance and, if that Balance is disturbed, the entire ecosystem falls into burden. As do we as members of the ecosystem.

Thus, they never allowed me to become entitled. They told me that we own nothing but who it is that we are in the inside; everything else is ephemeral. Service was a given in my family. Almost every weekend was spent in service to others or reflection in nature. Yeshua was not spoken of often in our household. However, knowing almost nothing of Him, I felt His Presence from the very beginning. And at age seven was told by a Presence in Spirit, an angelic Presence of energy and Light, that I would come to serve as one of Yeshua's channels.

As a young girl, He was my friend and I would often bury boxes that I labeled "God boxes" all over the property in secret. These boxes contained toys, cookies, and all things I felt I needed to share with God. In many ways, it was early on that I learned trust in my relationship with Spirit. Trust in human be-ings was harder, given the judgment and ostracism I faced for being a child empath and medium. But growing trust in human relationships became far easier once I accepted my own self.

I felt a kinship with Yeshua but never completely understood His Essence and Power until He began His Transmissions, despite having known my whole life I would be one of His channels. As a deeply discerning person, it was not until He birthed in my channel and I experienced His direct Presence that I even began to understand the Grace, wisdom, and unconditional Love that Yeshua holds and illuminates.

As I am a full-body or "trance" channel and do not know what is said when Yeshua is giving a Transmission, when Yeshua first birthed in my channel and I listened back to His Offerings via the sound files, every inflexible belief I had about self and world was called up into question. That is true even when I listen now after I volunteer my body for Him to come through. There have been many moments when I've had resistance and even anger about things He said. However, through humility and allowing for the process, I realized that what Yeshua Offers is not just about me. When He gives a Transmission, He is introducing new energies and healthy polarities into the individual AND the collective. He is not just giving energy to you, though your relationship with Him is very personal. He is moving energy through you to anchor and illuminate deeper consciousness and Light into the world.

Most of the time, I found that the things that provoked me were the very areas I did not want to look at in my own life. The very areas in which I was resisting change, stuck in self-righteousness, or afraid to let go of a belief due to fear of the unknown. As He dissolved more of my old identity to make more space for His Presence in my channel, a lot of fear surfaced, as well as doubt. Some beliefs, even about who Yeshua was or is "supposed to be," even beliefs about who I am or am "supposed to be," were so engrained that I had never taken the time to look at them. As His Light and wisdom flooded into my be-ing, all of that shadow became highlighted. I needed to explore, blend, and integrate it.

Through Faith, surrendering to Faith and the higher wisdom of the Divine, each time I let go of or brought awareness to my doubt, vast liberation, clarity, and joy came to take its place. Often within an instant. In what I received on the inside and often from the external world too. Though all that came from the external world was just icing on the cake. The true gift Yeshua brings is the liberation on the inside. I realized quickly in my first few months as His channel that Yeshua wasn't trying to change me. Yeshua was giving me what I needed to work through shadow and unhealthy resistance. Yeshua was changing all the aspects of me that were not authentic to the true me. He didn't just show me how to Love, He showed me how to BE Love to self and others.

Through His Transmissions, He will show you how to BE your Yeshua self, which just means your best self, true self, natural self instead of the illusion self, the fabrication of the imbalanced ego. It is a process. Every day is a day of humility, humor, and Surrender with Yeshua. He will accelerate and enrich your process of enlightenment profoundly if you are open and allowing. There are no rights and wrongs with Him, only allowing for evolution, change, and what IS within the moment.

As a lifelong channel and medium, I guess I'm a convenient vessel for Him because I'm able to get "myself out of the way" to let Him through. I also have the discipline to maintain a "clear" or "pure" channel by adhering to a simple, humble life structure with lengthy daily meditations, time in Prayer and solitude, healthy diet, regular exercise, and immersion in nature. If my channel is fuzzy and diluted, it impacts the purity and quality of the Transmissions and/or my private sessions with individuals. Maintaining a clear channel is an absolute necessity and responsibility I take quite seriously. Luckily, it's one that brings me joy.

Again, I am not conscious of anything that is said when He is "coming through" until I "come back to" and listen to the Transmissions after. He has full access to and control over my body. That said, He allows me complete control over how, when, and where He comes through. He is respectful of my boundaries, so I feel safe and honored in the process. I serve Him when He needs to come through and He respects and serves my needs completely.

I am not special or better because I am one of Yeshua's channels. The Divine made that clear very early on. I am NOT Yeshua, nor do I get to project my personal feelings, opinions, or biases into what is channeled. While I try to just live by witnessing, I am human and do have my own thoughts on things. None of that gets to enter when I channel Him; He is not here to serve my puny, ignorant opinions. He is here to Offer what YOU need to transform. Thus, no "me" gets to be inserted into His Transmissions. His time with you is for you.

As you move through these Transmissions, especially if you are new to this and coming into this with heavy discernment or even outright judgment, I might suggest approaching it like attending a "Thanks-giving" dinner. When at a "Thanks-giving" dinner, if someone offers you brussels sprouts and you do not like brussels sprouts, just say no thank you and pass the dish along to those that do. Instead of throwing the plate across the room, ridiculing the host for serving brussels sprouts, shaming those that like brussels sprouts, and leaving in a big stinky huff.

Just pass on the brussels sprouts if you don't like them and maybe the next dish offered to you through the Transmissions will be something you do like and can partake in, savor, and be nourished by. Maybe you don't like any of the food but then just come to sit, listen, share, and commune out of curiosity to explore new things . . . because you were invited and said yes. Even if you never return to the table again.

Yeshua is the Host of this Supper. This is His invitation to you. I am just the servant and secretary. There is something for everyone at this Supper. Nourishment for the world. Even if just through the energy alone. Or the humor, Love, tears, and Miracle of the incredible journey of your life that has brought you to this place. Or even the absurdity you may feel in reading or listening to these Transmissions that feels wrongly right . . . or even rightly wrong. Whatever. This may feel wacky at times. I can assure you that, as a pretty grounded person who likes science and rational explanations, having Yeshua come through my body has struck me as wacky at times too. But that's the Divine for you!

There is no need to rush, and no "getting there" when it comes to Yeshua. Through His Grace, He moves you to deeper layers through His honesty, humor, and deep, deep Love. The more you allow, accept, and discern what resonates and what does not, the more you will receive. Including a Divine Sacred Love and connection within self of a magnitude that makes all that happens in the outer world less scary, hooking, and provoking.

Yeshua makes Forgiveness possible by showing you the areas where you need to Forgive self or other. He makes Love possible by showing you the aspects of self you do not Love. He makes Truth possible by showing you the areas that make you feel like you have to hide and pretend. And He does it through Light, awareness, and consciousness by helping you to become more grounded, anchored, and present in your own Yeshua self, Divine self, or God-self.

In many ways, by moving through the Pathway to Peace He Offers, He is showing you the way to Freedom. He helps you not only to know and feel self as One with God, but to serve as a result of that. To serve through joy as a Light-holder and vessel of Peace, Balance, and Presence. Thus, welcome. It is such a gift to serve alongside you on this special journey.

A few final suggestions to note:

1.   It is very common to experience a massive burst within your creative life-force (known as Shakti) as a result of these Transmissions. Sometimes this takes place throughout the whole process; sometimes it is in the days and weeks after as the energy integrates within you.

The pure Light Yeshua Offers ignites and illuminates whole new aspects of your creativity and Divine Feminine. As you gestate the energy of the Transmissions through your Divine Feminine and it moves out through your Divine Masculine, it is not uncommon to experience huge bursts of connection that can feel like you are downright channeling the Divine yourself. Because you are. He will open the chords within you as needed at the right time.

2.   As you access more of your Yeshua self, the Light will shine

through you. For every surge of resistance you work through, a blessing comes externally or, better yet, internally. Thus, please do yourself the favor of having a pen and journal handy during, and in the weeks after, reading or listening to this. Keep them close every time you read or listen.

3.   Also note that He is not separate from you or speaking to or at you. He is speaking from within you, which is why it is so important to take what serves you and make that the focus. In the entire structure of these Transmissions, He Offers many Pathways to Peace. Each Transmission is a new Pathway with many trails to explore within it through your internal experience as well as what you attract in your outer life.

For this reason, I recommend reading or listening to His Words numerous times. Each time you listen and move through the process, especially the meditations and written exercises, you will uncover new Truths and moments of self-realization. Each time you listen, what you receive will evolve exponentially. You may find a specific reso-nance with only one sentence or Transmission. Even one sentence that resonates, if you read it, sit with it, and embody it, can carry the key to your entire awakening of consciousness.

4.   He often says things multiple times. He is not being redundant. Some things He says can seem to contradict other things. As a bit of a contrarian by nature, when He first birthed in my channel, my limited human self Loved to say, "HAHA, caught you, Yeshua, you just said something that contradicted what you said in a past Transmission." Silly, silly me. Keep listening, as He always reveals the path for two Truths to unite as He goes. If you look beneath the surface, you will see how He does this. Over time. In all aspects of your life. Where the Truth inter-sects is your path to discover over time and is, frankly, part of the fun.

He presents specific energies and concepts in a vast number of ways through multiple lenses. The avenues in which these weave, emerge, and intersect in your consciousness can be quite different at various times and stages of your life. What can be confusing or seem irrelevant one day can be resonant and deeply illuminating the next. What can rock the core of your be-ing one day can seem commonplace and obvious the next. He is a Divine Master. Again, as the Divine, He AND She knows you better than you know yourself.

There are infinite ways He expresses things and infinite ways to interpret His Offerings, even in one simple sentence He shares. The experience of utilizing your creative and intuitive energies to interpret meaning for yourself is part of the joy. He will inspire new realizations even if the realization comes through disagreeing with something He said. Why not? This is again a co-creative process between you and Him.

When He is saying something several different times, He is opening and illuminating a new energy cord. Or seeding something more deeply into your consciousness. He can sometimes say one thing numerous times. For example, He often closes Transmissions by saying the word "Pace" (pronounced *Pah-chay*) three times. Though I am not certain why He does this, I believe it is because He is transmitting a Blessing to you from each emanation of the Trinity. He also often says, "Walk with Me" over and over. Each time that He says it, He is inviting you to walk with Him energetically, because He is seeding, or aligning, or transforming, a new energy within you, in co-creation with your spirit and your soul.

5. Yeshua's Transmissions are almost always in vocal or audio format. In order to create this book, the sound files needed to be transcribed, then edited, which was quite a process. The written Word is quite powerful. However, I deeply recommend listening in audio format, as well, especially for the meditations. The written format can illuminate things the audio doesn't and vice versa. He transmits sound codes through voice. It strengthens the intimacy to hear how directly He speaks to and through you.

6. It is important to take care of your body throughout the Transmissions. There is a huge amount of detox of your mental, emotional,

and even physical pain bodies that can occur. The whole of your be-ing transforms through the course of the Transmissions. Taking some extra time to be in nature, meditation, and reflection can deeply augment your ability to process and receive greater benefit.

7.   Likewise, I recommend refraining from consumption of a lot of sugar, caffeine, alcohol, and marijuana throughout the Transmissions. Overconsumption of these substances will make it harder for you to integrate, which can flare up imbalanced resistance and polarity. Through the meditations, which are probably the most important aspect, a lot of energy will be moving through you. You may have some powerful dreams or manifestations that come while reading or listening. Moving your body, exercising, and deep breathing are deeply helpful as you raise your vibration.

Give yourself the space to immerse. It can help to set some extra boundaries with those around you while reading so that you have the space to truly immerse. It can also help to ask for support from someone you can share the process with, such as an open-minded friend or family member. Throughout listening and/or reading, it helps to create a "sacred space" like an altar, place in nature, or room in your house to relax and reflect. The Light energy that spills into your home space and all those within it can be deeply rejuvenating.

8.   Do not expect others to understand or even get on board with the shifts that come as a result of moving through this process. Allow for your own process and have compassion for those around you who may be in a different place on their journey. If they judge you, do not internalize. Change is scary for everyone. The changes, big or small, that come through can sometimes elicit some resistance from others. Let it be and trust that whatever aligns will be just right. You are deeply held through this process.

As you are welcomed into the Heart of Yeshua, Heart of God through your own heart, it is my deepest Prayer that the Freedom

Transmissions bring you joy, Balance, and Peace. Then and now, Yeshua provides us a Pathway to remember the Truth of what and who we really are: Love. Love in all of its different facets, faces, and emanations, shadow and Light. Regardless of beliefs, Yeshua shows us how to look beyond and within ourselves to rediscover the incredible Grace and Light we all hold. And the Miracles we are capable of through kindness, courage, compassion, and Love.

Through His own example, He guides us to the deep place within that is humble, pure, and timeless. He doesn't tell us what or who to be. He shows us how to be through His raw, pure, simple Essence. He is the Divine within Humanity and Humanity within Divinity. His Power of Peace guides us to find, feel, act, and live from that Power of Peace within self every day more and more.

With a deep breath of humility, reverence, and gratitude, I now surrender the Freedom Transmissions and Yeshua to you. So, for the remainder of this text, there is no "me" here. There is only Him . . . and you.

Please enjoy the Freedom Transmissions and this sacred time of reunion and communion with Yeshua. He is with you and within you. Thank you for the gift of your courage, curiosity, intuition, and Presence. Have a beautiful and blessed journey. I'll see you on the other side. Namaste.

PART ONE

THE SACRED HEART TRANSMISSIONS

1

....

I AM Yeshua

(Originally channeled December 12 and 14, 2019, January 12 and 27, 2020)

YESHUA MEDITATION

Hello, Beloved One. Let us begin with meditation. Eyes closed, sitting up, spine straight, heart open.

Begin to draw deep breaths of air and Light into your body. Turning the lens inward to the space of Stillness, the space of Peace, the space of vast infinite Light within the present moment. Bring yourself into this moment as this moment brings itself into you. Nowhere to go. Nothing to be apart from that which you are. Release all thoughts of the external world—events, circumstances, people.

All that you need is present for you within this moment. Your need from self, from Divine—to BE-loved. You are the Be-loved. Allow for this Offering of the Divine Seed of Consciousness to stream and weave into your be-ing. Resurrecting you to your authentic Presence as and of Peace. Your receiving of this Divine Grace is your offering of Love to Us in return.

This BE-ing, this receiving within the Present, IS your service to this world. Your Presence is enough. Your Presence of Peace IS your purpose. Your life is a co-creation, hand in Hand with God.

This is YOUR moment. The moment you have been waiting for has arrived. To see, feel, and know yourself as whole, seen, heard, understood, and Loved. We have heard the call of your soul to embody and live the Song of your spirit, the Prayer of your soul. And so now too, within this moment, you are answering the call of My Prayer for you: to allow Me to Shepherd you, the vessel that you are, into your awakening and embodiment of the Seed of Consciousness, Presence, and Light. The Seed that I, Yeshua, Divine Father and Divine Mother, as One, planted within you, breathed into you long, long ago.

Let us breathe again together now. Allow your inhale to become Our exhale. As you inhale, breathe in the energy of Light and communion. Allow your exhale to become Our inhale. Oh, Sacred Vessel, Holy Tree. You are of the Tree of Life.

Begin to breathe deeply into the roots of your tree. Connecting deeply with Gaia, Mother Earth, your ancestors, the Web of Life. Breathe into your roots.

Feel the Light, the Consciousness present in every cell in your body, begin to vibrate through your legs, through your hips, through your organs, through your spine, through your throat, through your brain. Breathe into the center of your be-ing, your sacred heart. Feel the Balance of the Light weaving through your breath: creation, destruction, rebirth.

Open your heart to the energy of Light. And remember. All the suffering your heart has carried through the crosses of imbalance . . . as of this moment you are Free. Through your exhale give over the doubt, the war, the struggle, the crosses, the burdens. LET IT GO. And breathe into your Free heart, open mind.

Settle your heart into My Garden; plant the seed of your Presence within it. Feel the Sacred Fire of the Holy Spirit alive within you. A Holy Peace rippling from your soul through your spirit body, the strings that connect you to the external world. Within this Garden of One, breathe into the four chambers of your sacred heart.

First the energy of Simplicity. Breathe in the Light of Simplicity to the sacred space of your sacred heart. Feel the Simplicity inherent to your heart, essence, and breath. Now breathe into the chamber of Stability. Feel the Stability within your body, the vessel that carries you through this life. Feel the Stability of the present moment and My Presence within it.

Now breathe into the chamber of Surrender. Surrender before yourself. Surrender your burdens and crosses to Me, as I dissolve them and clear the Path for Peace. My Light to your Light. One Light. Surrender to My embrace.

Now breathe into the chamber of Stillness. Still mind, still heart. The silent space in which you can hear beyond the din of the world to remember what and who it is that you are: Peace.

From above, feel the energy of Divine Masculine, Truth, spilling into your body. Receiving the Truth of your Absolution. Now feel the energy of Divine Feminine, Love, creation and destruction, through the rise and fall of your breath.

As these two energies, Truth and Love, intersect, feel them braid and weave through you. Intertwining, consummating. These energies coexist and are the fluidity of Consciousness you are One with and birthed from. As these energies of Truth and Love flow through you, upward from Mother Earth and downward from the heavens, with humility, allow them to Balance within your sacred heart, the seat of your soul.

And feel the Child created: PEACE.

THIS is God. Breathe into the space of Peace within you. The space beneath the suffering, crosses, grief, burdens, worries. It is your consciousness, your Grace united with Mine. When you have found the space of Peace within, you have found the space in which there is NO DEATH, no pain, no time. It is the timeless space of Light.

Breathe deeper into this space. When you have found this space of Stillness and Peace, you have found the essence of your be-ing. And the Essence of Be-ing itself. You have found the narrow gate that leads you to the Kingdom and Garden of God. You have found Me, Yeshua, within you. You have found your true self.

I am your guide to Truth and Love through Peace. The only way to the Divine Father, Truth, is through Me, Peace. The only way to the Divine Mother, Love, is through Me, Peace. The only way to Me is through Them, equally, as Creator and Creation.

Your evolution is a co-creative Pathway to Peace, equally masculine and feminine. It is through the consciousness, the awareness of self as One with these energies that **exist within you,** that you flow more deeply into this co-creation, this Resurrection.

Exhale whatever you are ready to Surrender that needs to die so that you can be Resurrected to the space of Eternal Life, Consciousness, Peace. For this space is also the essence of Freedom. Are you ready to come Home? To be Free?

Our journey is the Pathway to Peace and Freedom within you. The Resurrection and Deliverance of your Christ self, Yeshua self, Balanced and One in Truth and Love, masculine and feminine. Thereby, the Ark of the New Covenant lies within you.

You have asked for millennia, what I AM. Who IS Yeshua?

I, Yeshua, Divine Father manifest through Son of God, Truth and Love,

I, Yeshua, AM your PEACE.

I AM PEACE, the Essence of your Be-ing. I created and create you, nourished and nourish you, fertilized and fertilize you, seeded and seed you. When you choose the infinite, omnipotent Power of Peace, you choose God. You choose Me. You choose your true self. I AM your Peace. I AM Peace. I AM the Word. And so too are you.

Breathe into this space; roam within this space Free of death. This is your immortal self. This is your Yeshua self. Now, allow the energy of Passion to rise, ignite, and illuminate from this Peace.

Mine was and is a Passion fulfilled through Peace. Allow Peace to move through your spirit, aligning, weaving, stitching, braiding your passion into realization. Faith over fear, Forgiveness over blame, Freedom over suppression. A Passion through Peace IS the Pathway of authentic service. Allow the Passion of the Light to spill into you, through you, and out into the world with Radial Balance, Grace, and Love. You are the Light of the world.

As this Starlight streams through you, now allow it to integrate into your body. You are nothing more than a Presence, an entity, Spirit in form. Allow the Light to integrate and settle into your body, your vessel, your ark.

Place your hands over your heart, honoring yourself for your choice to be present here today. Feel the rightness. Feel the Peace. When you are ready, place your hands together at heart center, palms pressed together. Smile a big smile. And simply say, "Thank you." When you are ready, only if possible, get down on your hands and knees, place your forehead to the Earth, and ground your energy deeply into Her Presence.

When you feel complete, please sit up and open your eyes.

I have been calling to you, Beloved One. As you have been calling to Me. Now we move deeper into the Heart of Freedom. And so it is.

Om Nami Maia. Om Namah Sananda. Om Nami Yeshua. Sancti, Sancti, Sancti. Pace, Pace, Pace. Amein.

YESHUA TEACHING

Welcome, Beloved One. It is My joy to be Present with you today. Please know that you do not need to believe in Me or have Faith in Me or even to understand Me to receive My Grace. My Grace is available to all Freely and works through you equally no matter what you perceive or believe in.

You do not even have to receive Me to know Me. As I Am you. I

AM all that you are and you are all that I AM. Our Journey together begins today in a new way, else you would not have found your way here. I am your true self and you are My True Self when all the rest is stripped away. I am here to assist you in feeling and living the essence of Peace every day more.

There will be days you feel Me in every cell of your be-ing. Other days I will feel so far away that you cry out, "Why hast thou forsaken me, God?!" I know that story well, Beloved. But the Truth is, I am never far. In fact, I am always here. In the moment. As you are here. In this moment. And in this moment, We are here together. I am your Be-loved and you are mine. This is OUR moment. This is our time no matter the form in which you experience or understand Me.

And why has this moment come? Well, in Truth, it has always been this moment, this dreaming, this dream. However, there is a collective call emerging on your planet for Peace. Equal in worth, equal in Love, you are all My sons and daughters, brothers and sisters, finding your way to that Path. The call you feel requires courage, for you are the pioneers ushering in this Era of Balance, Transparency, and Peace. Balance is Peace and Peace is Balance. **That cannot come to you until you come to it. And that is why I come to you now.**

Over the past decades, centuries, even millennia, there has been a vast movement of energy shifting for the coming of this Era. The times in the aftermath of your year 2020 is a gateway of Revelation and a period of change inherent to you and every other vessel of energy that is present in your world. Responsibility for choices past and present is coming to the surface. Many of you have been reevaluating who and what is of worth to you.

For you, I carried the Cross so that you could be Free of burdens. But you must set your judgments down. Of self, of others, of God. I carried your burdens then and now. Your burdens cannot hurt Me. They are Mine to carry so that you can be Free. What will you choose? To carry the suffering and cross, which is to deny My Presence and

Offering of Truth? Or to give your burdens and crosses over to Me so that we may walk together in Peace?

Lower the bar on the cross that keeps you suspended in disappointment, imbalance, and regret. Stop raising the bar in favor of more, more, more—more money, more attention, more fillers, more "followers," more following, more seeking. If each of you reached for Balance and lowered the bar of expectations of self and world, you would experience far more Freedom and Peace. You will need to learn to shift your focus from the be-coming to coming to BE.

For none of the Second Coming of your Yeshua self is about be-coming more or less than what you already are. Coming to BE is your journey of realizing that what you already are is enough. Your Presence is what the world needs, not what you think, what you do, and how hard you do or do not try. Embodying that Presence is, however, a deep responsibility that all human be-ings are accountable for as individuals within the collective.

If you devoted as much time to Simplicity, Stability, Surrender, and Stillness as you do to complexity, busyness, control, and dominance, you would find that all of your needs would be met and beyond. Balance is your process, not "too much" or "too little." The "just right" comes when you accept self and allow for what is within the coming of each moment, each breath.

Allow your new cross to be the Balanced cross, Balanced with all life. The Medicine Wheel, the circle of life. I gave My Life to set you Free. When you choose the Balance of your heart over the complexity of your mind, thoughts, and ego, you choose Me, you find Me in Simplicity, joy, and Freedom. Where will you stand? Perched above on the crucifix as the judge and judged, betrayer and betrayed? Or at center, in Faith, Forgiveness, and Freedom? That is our journey together then, now, and beyond.

Will you choose the Pathway to and of Peace? Or the struggle on the inside that keeps you separate and at war in the external world? I

Freed you then and I come again to you now to set you Free. To receive and embody the Truth of, not the Story of Love, but the essence of Love. Your true essence and state of be-ing. You ARE a child of God. Equal with all others. You are a child Yeshua. Learning what it is to walk in Balance, humility, and Peace with, of, and as God.

A call has come, a horn has sounded within you and within your world. A call for more Balance, more space, and deeper realignment and communion with your Earth Mother, Gaia. Within Gaia, be it in Her fire of desert, earth of grasses, forests, and fields, waters of oceans, streams, and rivers, or air of mountains and plains, you are held, you are One. You can feel and hear all of Spirit within Her. As the Divine calls to you from the wellspring within you, so too does Gaia. We, the Divine, are One with Gaia for she is of the Dreamer and the Dreaming. As We call out to you, "Come Home, Beloved," so too does She.

There is a hunger, a thirst, a call moving from the wellspring of your Divine soul in all of its humanity and glory, to move closer to the Heart of God. For you were created as and of God, Consciousness. From the clay of Gaia to the clay of the body created from Her, you were molded by the Hands of the Divine. Which is how and why We hold your hand and you hold Ours at all times. The Hands of the energy of Love. Your true longing is to come Home to the Divine, to the Heart of Freedom. To come back into your true self. This realignment is the Truth and real meaning of the Second Coming.

The Heart of God is One Heart, One collective Breath, the Breath of the Divine to which your soul and heart pulse in rhythm. The Second Coming is realigning with that pulse and Breath. The Breath IS the Word. And was from the beginning. You breathe and thus Speak with Me at all times in co-creation. The breath I speak of is your soul's breath, which extends far beyond death. It is the breath of consciousness, continuously expanding, creating, dissolving, and evolving. As you do. This breath, this Word, is the essence of the Sacred Heart.

In the hearing, feeling, and accepting of this call to be present and come home to self, there is also a tremendous amount of confusion you may feel, even conflict, especially when what your soul is asking of you does not make sense to your mind or you are afraid of what you might lose in the process of the change you feel welling within you. Confusion about how to dig out from the weight and density holding you back from Peace. Confusion regarding what Peace even is or feels like on a sustainable basis. How to find it, recognize it, embody it, and live in it.

The call of the Second Coming, the coming Home to your true essence, may have begun as a quiet voice in the background, your intuition saying "slow down," "reduce commitments," "use discernment," "this is not sustainable," "I am not happy." But often the voice is suppressed through the clamor of the mind and all of the external expectations and responsibilities you face as a human be-ing. Yet, the voice will not disappear. And now, as a matter of fact, it has grown louder. For your soul wishes to be suppressed no longer.

You have heard this call as an individual. Some of you heard it long ago and are just remembering it. Some of you heard it more recently. Some have committed to the path of exploring that call for years or a whole lifetime. Some are still trying to ignore or suppress it.

It is the call of the soul, the call of the spirit. The soul that is the Seed of Consciousness within you. The spirit that extends from your soul, connecting you to the external world and Web of Life. It is the call, the cry of Gaia, Mother Earth. And Spirit's call to you from within you. It is the call for Peace and for Freedom. It is the soul's call for the Freedom to live its purpose. The soul's purpose, not the mind's expectation of what that purpose should be.

Throughout the next months and years on your planet, We, the Divine, are bringing to you the change and Truth necessary to Resurrect Balance, which sometimes may come in ways that are uncomfortable or unexpected to your mind. Individually and collectively. In the beginning, the Path to Balance may appear like chaos to your mind, even to your heart. The more you Surrender to what you cannot control or understand and reach for the strength of the Light within you, the more you will see, hear, and realize the wonder of the Pathway to Peace unfurling.

As a collective you have chosen to begin this Era of Consciousness, Transparency, and Masculine/Feminine Balance. This momentum, this Revelation, this Second Coming, is a process that cannot be reversed. Nor would you want it to be. These shifts are occurring and will be occurring whether your mind gets on board with them or not. Hence the changes that have occurred and are about to occur within your world.

You are evolving rapidly, and the only thing holding you back is fear. Fear of loss of control. That is why I am here, Beloved. To shine the Light for you to walk through those doubts, those fears, with support and Love. To bring you the wisdom and clarity you need to leap into deeper Faith, deeper Forgiveness, deeper Freedom.

I will hold your hand through this process and you will hold Mine. Through the course of our time together, we will simply be creating a bit more room for the true self through the dismantling of the illusion self and all of the imbalances, complexity, and stress that the "supposed to" self creates for you.

This is simple, Beloved One. Your minds are what complicate everything. Evolution of consciousness is not about communicating with Spirit guides, psychic abilities, crystals, or other tools that can awaken deeper unity with Spirit. Those can be wonderful to inspire your Faith. However, until you can come to Peace in mind, heart, and spirit regardless of the outer influences sucking you out—even family, spouses, work, children—and learn how to quiet emotions and thoughts and live presently, you will miss the point of what Spirit is, what you ARE, and how We work through you.

Oneness cannot be created on the outside until it is created internally within each vessel, each person. Many of you have already begun on this Path, or else you would not have found your way to the wisdom and energy that is Offered to you through these Transmissions. You are not a Light-worker. You are a Light-holder or Light-anchor. Through your movement to deeper Balance and Peace, you hold the Light, inspire, and liberate others to move deeper into their own. That is the service of your Yeshua self. I set the Path for you long ago. Your Path is Mine and My Path is yours. That is why we will walk this Path together. Walk with Me.

Ohm nami Yeshua. Sancti. Pace. Amein.

2

....

The Three Veils and Seven
Imbalances of the Mind

(Originally channeled February 9, 2020)

YESHUA TEACHING

Hello, Beloved One. It is a joy to be present with you today, on this Pathway to Free you of your crosses, burdens, and suffering. Let us live in this moment, within the Simplicity of Truth. The crosses you have carried are crosses of your mind but carried on your heart. The gateway to God opens more through the giving over of those crosses. To live clear-hearted. That is what it is to know Freedom.

The Free heart is Balanced—an exhale, an inhale, a birth, a death, destruction, creation. There is a rightness and Simplicity within the order of your breath. The same order to the flow that allows for the sun to hold its center within its orbit. The same order that allows the flowing out and the flowing in of the tides.

In the origin of your soul's inception, you were created in Balance, as the One is Balanced. Your world and universe were designed in Balance. You were Seeded with Consciousness. You became self-aware and, in becoming aware of the self, the "I," you became aware of choice. In a rudimentary sense, that is the basis for Free Will. You have the choice to be separate or the choice to be One.

You have the choice to align your will with the Divine Will or take matters into your own hands and make imbalanced choices that go against Divine Will. Mainly choices of the separate self that are not for the greater good of All.

Alignment is never "a line" as your perception of linear time is. Alignment is nonlinear—you weave here, unthread here, tie here. Your life is more a journey of realignment than it is of alignment. Realigning with the wholeness you are. Realigning your Will with the Divine Will is realigning yourself with Balance and reweaving yourself back into Balance.

Through choices of separateness throughout time, Seven Imbalances of the Mind were created. These imbalances were not created by the Divine, they were created by the human fragmented perception and construct of identity. Thus, to rebalance them, to transcend your need to come to body, to form, and move into Transcendence, you must dissolve the fragmented construct of self and "reality" through awakening the Seed of Consciousness that lies within you. As that Seed grows, you become aware of self-awareness and conscious of Consciousness. The separate self is replaced by the self that knows and experiences itself as whole and One with all that is. That is what it is to live in Presence and Transcendence. When you are in true conscious Presence, you are in the Presence of God.

Some in your world speak of the "Seven Sins." Oh the burden misunderstanding the misuse of this word, *sin*, has created. It is time for us to set that burden down. In My Life, the word *sin* simply meant "missing the mark," NOT Eternal damnation and shame. That does not occur within My Garden, Beloved. Only in yours, when you allow the imbalances of the mind to consume you. And even that is transient. Imbalances of the mind are areas where you "miss the mark" in embodying your Peace, Divinity, and Yeshua self.

Most in your world are familiar with the teachings I gave in My Life. However, after My Death, there were many more Offerings I gave. I came to the vessel that is the Magdalene after My Death as I appeared to several others, including many of you at various times in various ways. To Her, I brought forth Transmissions, many of which never reached the Light of day until more recently in your world as you moved toward this gateway to the Era of Masculine and Feminine Balance.

I spoke of the Seven Imbalances of the Mind to many people before and after My Resurrection. **The Seven Imbalances are the ego's distortions in perceptions, actions, projections, and behaviors. They are what contribute to and create the illusion self, the "supposed to" self, the "story of self" that causes you to see yourself through a lens of distortions, which you then project onto others and the world.**

Statements such as "The world is out to get me" or "I have been wronged by the world and thus I am entitled to take and steal from others" or "I always fail, so why bother?" or "This person or group of people is to blame for my issues. I am going to punish them for that" are perfect examples of thought constructs that come from these distortions. These are ghost stories, Beloved One. When you live by them, you become a ghost, a shadow, a fragment, a shade of yourself. Instead of the Presence that you are—in, as, and of My Presence.

It is important to note that what you attribute to the "Seven Sins"—pride, greed, lust, envy, gluttony, wrath, and sloth—are present in each of the Seven Imbalances of the Mind. For example, greed can be found in all Seven Imbalances of the Mind. If and how that is manifest is unique to each person.

Some struggle with certain imbalances more than others. Certain people may struggle mainly with only two imbalances of the mind but all seven of the "sins" can manifest within them. Or a person can struggle with all of the seven imbalances but only one or two of the "sins" are expressed within them.

You all have struggled with all of the imbalances at various times, as individuals and a collective. Those who say they do not struggle or possess any of these imbalances and distortions are usually the very ones who struggle with them the most and do not even realize that they are.

However, do not fear, Beloved One; this Offering is not about judgment or humiliation. It is simply an Offering of Truth. As long as you are in form, aspects of the imbalances will always be there. Thus, please do not judge yourself if you recognize or uncover one within you. Humility, willingness, and even having a sense of humor can truly save the day. Becoming conscious of the imbalances and where they hide within you is the very moment you begin to transform these distortions and illusions.

I caution you against attempting to ascribe imbalances to others. Even if you think you recognize some of the qualities of a particular imbalance in someone you know, that is on the basis of your opinion. It is hard enough to look at or understand your own imbalances and impossible for you to know what another experiences. Have humility and compassion for yourself and others as you come to understand these more deeply. As such, these are also certainly never to be used as a weapon.

The more you give over and Surrender the distortions and burdens these seven imbalances create through awareness, courage, and Love, the more they clear. As they do, immense Peace is restored to the whole of your be-ing. Thus, I am bringing you through these in an invitation to give them over to Me, so that you can be Free. This is the process we will share together with Love, tears, laughter, patience, honesty, and deep communion.

The first imbalance of the mind or ego is the perception of darkness or separation. This imbalance is feeling and experiencing self as separate from the Light, Divine, or your world, including the ecosystem. It includes consistently and deeply feeling the energies of separation: guilt, shame, blame, fear of failure, despair, overwhelm, unworthiness; doubting self; doubting the Divine; doubt in its deepest shadow form—depression or despair; comparing of self to others; paranoia; delusion; skepticism; internalization of trauma; wallowing in trauma; victim-consciousness; self-criticism; chronic apologizing for who you are; isolation of self; secrecy; obsession with "dark" or shadow energies attacking you; interest or dabbling in "dark" energy to cause harm to another; insecurity; feelings of deep disconnect; feeling like a displaced ghost or shade; and/or feeling silenced—that what you say does not matter—which results in suppression of voice.

This imbalance can also make you feel like an imposter to the world, fraudulent and undeserving. It impedes you from even realizing the joys of your own triumphs. The mind convinces you others are better and that you are not deserving. It rationalizes successes and reduces everything you do to ash. The distorted ego and fear-based primitive mind assumes dominance and power, deepening the chasm between your human and Divine self. It chains you to standards of perfection that are unattainable, and strips you of your ability to feel that you deserve joy . . . or deserve anything at all. In separation, it can feel as though nothing you do is right, good enough, or that you are not right. There is deep shame or feeling of isolation that can be internalized as a result.

In robust manifestation, this ego distortion can cause you to feel that you are not from your Earth or that you do not want to be on Earth, in body. There is little room for joy and engagement when you feel like an outcast or pariah. There is also little room for gratitude in this defeatist myth-state of the mind. It makes you feel "less than," yet also continuously pushes you to "do better." And not in a way that inspires you to evolve and grow, but in a way that forces you to keep trying to prove it wrong.

This imbalance can move into deep shadow and unconsciousness when it elicits the perception that you are unworthy of God and thus unworthy of Love in general. The perception that you are flawed and have been sent into body as a punishment. While the imbalance of separation, as all of the imbalances of the mind, leads to distortions that cause you to perceive yourself as flawed, separate, and lesser-than, this specific imbalance carries the burden of overwhelm and fear of failure.

Such thoughts as "Since I am already flawed, why even bother?," self-flagellation, and self-shaming or self-loathing are rich within this imbalance. There is a punitive quality to it, as though you need to serve out a sentence in this life. And that if you fail to "please" God, you have failed not only as a person, but as a soul. That you will be cast out of the Garden completely. This, Beloved One, is not possible, but the mind in this imbalance governs your actions, self-esteem, and fear through telling you so.

This can lead to punitive behaviors toward self, such as with-holding, depriving yourself of Love, obsessive rituals to appease some angry judgmental God, over-giving to overcompensate for lack and un-worthiness, shaming or blaming yourself, internalizing guilt, suffering alone through your issues because you feel you are unworthy of Love and support, hiding, or setting higher and higher standards for success due to fear of failure. This results in unsustainable stress—the kind that leads to addictions, abusive relationships, depression, and even suicidal thoughts. It is no more than a pain cycle, but the depth of the pain cycle can consume and suck tremendous amounts of energy from your soul, spirit, and life force, as well as devour years and decades of your life.

This imbalance is one of the deepest impaling spears, not only to the sacred heart but also to the mind. It leaves a gaping hole or a Void that leaves you susceptible to fear prisons and dissonant thoughts. It keeps you separate and isolated. It is hard for Me to reach you in such places because you are walking through the valley of the shadow of death in fear instead of Faith. The fear of judgment or shadow keeps you locked into shadow. Thus, some with this imbalance act in shadow and judgment. Others continuously martyr themselves, and give and give to feel One with others again. They give, but less from a space of abundance and more from a space of overcompensating for a deficit or disconnection they are struggling to reconcile. The toll of this imbalance is heavy on the body, mind, and emotions.

Only God can walk with you through the rebalance of this, for you need support to walk through the shadow until you have the strength, humility, and Faith to remember your inherent worth and Light. To transcend this imbalance, you must reach for something that is greater than yourself. And release the expectations of what God is, how life should be, and who you are supposed to be.

This can come through standing beneath the stars, before the vastness of the sea, before a forest of trees that are alive and part of an ecosystem that you are a part of too. Breathing with the stars, breathing with yourself, meditating, and exploring new aspects of life you once feared are essential to seeing the Light in all things again. Engage deeply with a cause you are passionate about without focusing on outcome. Share for the sake of sharing.

And have compassion for yourself. Honor yourself, for the imbalance of separation signifies a deep desire for connection. It is not that the connection is not there; you have just been blinded to the existence of it through the density of form and distortions of the mind. There is a desire for God, Consciousness, community, connection, and intimacy inherent to this imbalance that is important. Allow that to govern.

Channel your beautiful essence into caring for something that needs your unique Grace and Love. Caring for another life, be it an animal, a child, an elder, a tree, or those within your community, can elicit a deep communion. And then you can begin to see God in all things and to Let there Be Light. Shining to you, through you, and from you in the garden of the world.

The second imbalance of the mind or ego is tyrannical

desire and lustful greed. This imbalance is responsible for many of the most imbalanced, unnatural dominance and suppression hierarchies in your world that have existed and exist today. The root of this imbalance lies in greed and lack of integrity. It spawns from separation and the sense of needing to "get mine" and take more to the detriment of another or others.

This includes: insatiable desire for power and dominance; greed; lack of integrity and authenticity; lack of transparency as to motives and agendas; doing things for the "I" instead of thinking of the "We"; imbalanced giving and receiving; desire for fame, power, worship from others, "specialness," and validation; elitism; dominance in general but especially in relationships; sexual manipulation; prostitution; hypersexuality and/or objectification of others for purposes of conquest and lust; the need to be right; overthinking; desire for power no matter the harm it creates others to get it; emotional blackmail; lying; fraudulence; betraying another's trust for self-serving gain; breaking commitments with those deemed less important or worthy; throwing another under the bus to achieve personal gain; and lack of almost any actual remorse, accountability, or empathy for the hurt caused to others as a result.

Despite popular perception in your world, this imbalance is not always driven by the greed that is about material abundance. A person with this imbalance can actually tend to withhold at times on such things because this imbalance is foremost about power. The imbalanced ego's drive in this is for dominance and power.

Thus, when this imbalance is central and a person is leading a mind-based life, the person is enslaved by greed, lust, and power and does not even realize it. Those with this imbalance have pathologically convinced themselves that if they had the power, everything would be all right. Control is a big part of this imbalance. It plays out in big ways and small ways in individual life.

When this imbalance is strong, a person will do whatever needs to be done to achieve the desired agenda, even if he or she needs to crucify others to do so. It is a deep self-absorption and energy of lack. A desire to be the king or queen, the main guru, the most powerful, instead of serving as a guide to others through honoring others' individual Sovereignty and Rights.

Greed spawned from the imbalance of desire is a disease of addiction to power that is unquenchable. Often those with it Love to recruit those in lower places to do their dirty work by making false promises to them. Those in greed and desire see others as disposable and pawns to achieve their agenda. They are playing a game of chess with life. Winning is everything. There is a psychosis of pathological lying that accompanies this imbalance, in which people can actually convince themselves they are doing what is right by stomping upon the Freedom and Rights of others.

This imbalance has led to rape, war, and people trying to assume roles of power, often under the auspices of "higher service" that do not serve the greatest good of all. There are even many spiritual "gurus" throughout the ages who indoctrinate others through aggrandizement of themselves instead of through humility. Meaning that they overassert and project their "superior spiritual wisdom" in a way that mitigates their own authenticity.

That is hypocrisy. And hypocrisy is apostasy to the Truth of equality inherent to Divinity. There is a deep unconscious insecurity and doubt held within such projections, which is why, especially when manifest in "spiritual," academic, and political landscapes, those with this imbalance can do great harm. They feel they have been "chosen by God" in a special way and have the liberty to thereby bypass the rules that apply to others. There is no "other" in this imbalance. There is only the "I," the feeding of the "I," praise for those who praise their "I," and shaming or isolating those who do not acknowledge their "I" as superior.

The "I" in this instance is completely interchangeable with "I"deology.

Those with this imbalance are in the "I"dea of "I," not the actual true "I." They are predominantly defined by ideological constructs, many of which are fed to them through the external world or through their own egos. Thus, those with this imbalance tend to be quite aggressive about their ideological agendas because that is what constitutes the majority of the "I" for them to varying levels and degrees.

Many with this imbalance are in pride or hubris. They believe they are "superior" and thus feel entitled to project their will onto others. As this imbalance builds and is fed, they will do whatever they need to tear down any voice of dissent or challenge. This is not service; it is systematic silencing of those with differing opinions to preserve the superiority and dominance.

There is no room for co-creation, Balance, and equality. Entitlement and equality have not, do not, and will not ever go hand in hand. Many leaders of your world then and now, including those in political, financial, and even some religious systems, have or have had this imbalance, which is why, in My lifetime, I preferred to sit in the back of the temple, not the front.

This imbalance leads to crimes of opportunity, taking advantage of situations with little regard or empathy for others' feelings, boundaries, best interests, or even safety. There is an inherent lack of integrity that the disillusioned ego tries to rationalize in a multitude of ways. It will do whatever is in its power to avoid being caught, including lying, cheating, and stealing. The justification and rationalization aspect of this imbalance is the ego's way of perpetuating its own illusion. It does not care about the Truth; it cares about sustaining its own illusion and opinion of the Truth.

There is a fragility in the face of temptation to which a person with this imbalance is susceptible. Thus, betrayal and disloyalty are strong tendencies at varying levels. In the face of temptation, all human beings struggle with honoring integrity versus "getting mine" or "staying safe."

You all have moments of deep alignment with right action and kindness, as well as moments where you take advantage, and write it off as "Well, this isn't so bad compared to what other people do" or "Anyone in my shoes would do this" or "The system works against me, so I am justified in taking more to get my share even if it hurts others" or "I will take this because I can do good with it." The impulse is there within all of you. It is a betrayal to self foremost. Which is the part of this imbalance that hurts the most and that the ego wishes to bury the most. This is why it is important to have compassion and Forgiveness to stop the cycle of this imbalance.

The more the greed and power feed the ego, the more those with this imbalance struggle. It can lead to deep guilt, shame, and self-sabotage cycles, as well as hurt for others. When someone shames you or you shame another for actions of desire or greed, it only feeds the energy more. Forgiveness, service, compassion, integrity, discipline, and construction of new boundaries are essential for alleviation of the crosses and burdens of this imbalance.

Rebalance from this requires commitment to service in ways that do not lead to personal gain in the areas of sex, money, and power. It requires having the humility and integrity to finally put closure on past relationships left in ruin, if even just through a simple apology. It requires resetting and converting a metric of success based in "getting mine" to the joy experienced in true giving, kindness, and service. As well as opening the heart to compassion, to gratitude, to Grace. Those with this imbalance suffer deeply from feeling that if they are not powerful or important, they will be irrelevant. Thus, defining Faith and connecting to a cause or a God beyond self is essential. That is what restores the integrity and respect for the diversity and yet also uni-versality and equality of all life.

The third imbalance is ignorance, denial, or complacency. This imbalance is the ego distortion most prevalent in your world. In many ways you all have it to some extent, because you are in limited consciousness and can only grow and evolve into the Truth over time. However, this imbalance can tip into pain cycles that affect both those with it and those around them deeply.

This imbalance is often likened to sloth, yet the Truth is that it carries a deep quality of agitation and avoidance within it. The endless sea of complaints and whining that stem from this imbalance can fill the entire galaxy of self if left in unconsciousness. Especially when you need to answer to a Truth that you turned a blind eye to. Within this imbalance is a blindness—a denial of and inability to accept the Truth. Those with this imbalance often deflect Truth by avoiding conflict, change, or life altogether. In attempting to avoid, deny, or ignore problems or confrontations, they often wind up creating more for themselves and others. They often assume others know what they are thinking or feeling but do not communicate it, which creates confusion for others.

This imbalance includes resisting change; wallowing; blind Faith and allowing others to govern your fear and emotions; lack of Truth; abdication of responsibility; allowing other people's teachings and opinions of you to dictate your worth, including those of parents, spouses, and peers; procrastination; drug or alcohol use (most addictions fall into this imbalance); naiveté; causing a mess and leaving someone else to clean it up; and denial (very important). There is a huge amount of laziness inherent to it. Those in this imbalance tend to want all of the fruits of the labor others receive through hard work . . . without having to do any of the work.

Thus, there is an interesting quality to this imbalance. Many with this imbalance believe equality to mean that, even though doing no work, they deserve exactly the same amount as another person who has worked hard. This is a form of entitlement. Very often those with this imbalance struggle with unworthiness or fear of conflict. **However, people with unworthiness issues can simultaneously feel entitled.**

For example, their unworthiness may express itself through complacency, procrastination, and avoiding work because they feel they do not deserve success. However, this can actually exacerbate their sense of entitlement to receive things so that they can continue to take the easy road instead of confront their fears and the source of the unworthiness. They expect others to clean their diapers and support them emotionally, financially, etc., while remaining in complete denial or even becoming agitated or volatile if confronted with responsibility. Many of them fancy themselves to be givers but actually take more than they give, in energy and in resources.

Those with this imbalance can even feel entitled to project opinions onto others from a place of ignorance or denial of the full picture. They are not interested in exploring the Truth or even seeing the Truth. They are interested in maintaining the status quo or "getting mine." They cannot see what they are not willing to look at and they will not be ready to see it until they are ready, and not a moment before. Trying to argue or reason with someone in ignorance, self-righteousness, complacency, and denial is futile and exhausting. What your world refers to as gaslighting or even compulsive lying is not often done consciously by those with this imbalance. They can cause those around them to question their reality or sanity, especially when those with this imbalance are so fervent in their limited beliefs and understandings.

This third imbalance is allowing the outer to dictate the inner. Or for the inner to project a lens of delusion onto the outer. This imbalance includes allowing yourself to be indoctrinated by others' interpretation of God instead of defining, allowing for, and celebrating your own unique relationship with God. It is an abdication of responsibility for your role in imbalance, which can lead to blame or shame when your thoughts or feelings are rejected by the external world. This imbalance also includes doing things the way others do instead of honoring originality and authentic creative process.

This imbalance represents an overexertion or underexertion of worth. It is resisting transformation and evolution. It is an inability to cope with life in the sense of continuously feeling overwhelmed or underwhelmed. There is an equal self-righteousness and judgment essence to this imbalance. It is either apathy, allowing for others to violate boundaries or mitigate your worth, or it is a defense strategy similar to an ostrich burying its head in the sand. This imbalance is "looking away" from things that require change or shift. Trying to pretend they are not there. Procrastination can thus be a behavioral manifestation of this imbalance. Continuously putting things off or trying to will away what your intuition and soul continues to draw your attention to.

This imbalance can lead to chaos. Projects started and left unfinished. Waiting another day. Giving up when something becomes difficult instead of honoring discipline and devotion to create what you wish for your life and the world.

Realignment of this imbalance requires courage in allowing for discomfort. It requires flowing with your resistance and accepting your shadow. It also requires listening to your discernment. And taking action to create your own reality and dreams instead of waiting or expecting another to do it for you. Humility and acceptance of Truth, as well as taking the responsibility and accountability to look at the uncomfortable, limiting beliefs and behaviors that keep you stuck, is the gateway to Freedom from this imbalance. As is communicating, even when it feels hard or impossible to communicate your thoughts and feelings. Clear communication and embracing instead of denying change is an essential. As is listening. Many with this imbalance listen selectively. Listening fully to others as you would wish others to listen to you can open many new paths, friendships, and connections that were not possible before.

There are words that have been spoken: "Many will trade their Freedom for the illusion of safety." Rebalancing this distortion requires examining the illusions, taking some leaps of Faith to move into deeper passion and resolution of issues long ignored, and taking the steps to open the door to your own Freedom. It requires nurturing your inner child but not as a child, instead as Divine Parent to yourself. This is simpler when you allow Faith to govern and structure a deeper relationship with the Divine.

The fourth imbalance is excitement over death or endings, or enslavement to the flesh. This imbalance represents both a fear of and a gravitation toward or obsession with death, destruction, and endings. It goes beyond the inquiry of "What happens when I die?" and into the realm of paranoid preoccupation with survival, safety, and personal longevity. It is fearing the exhale and even fearing the inhale because then the exhale is inevitable. In many ways it is simply a fear of the Void or the unknown. Those with this imbalance never want to put closure on anything and thus can leave others they have been in relation with confused or resentful. They go to great lengths to avoid or exert control over the possibility of loss, which in turn creates deeper fear, loss, and paralysis of the heart and spirit.

Preoccupation with health and personal safety, whether in the form of obsession about body, illness, germs, other people's germs, physical risks, or the like, is deeply reflected in this imbalance. A person with this ego distortion is prone to victimhood, defensiveness, and self-absorption. It is the mindset of "The awful, scary world is out to get me and I must protect and defend myself."

What is fascinating is that, in trying to escape death, loss, or harm, a person can become quite infatuated with death and destruction. That can come in the form of consciously or subconsciously seeking out morbid things that feed and deepen the imbalance and fear. For example, those with irrational fears surrounding their health and what "could happen" may seek out information sources that feed the fear instead of the reality. Or even surround themselves with others who feed their stories and distorted perceptions.

This imbalance can present itself in perpetual fear of illusions such as "darkness" and "evil," as well as a robust fear of death and abandonment. It is a fascination and continuous preoccupation with potential loss and shadow that can consume a person's whole be-ing with morbid fear or morbidity in general. This shuts down the person's access to Balance and Light. Very often there is either a paralyzing anxiety or smothering depression that results from it. This lens of the imbalance creates exhaustion and the feeling of already being dead on the inside.

It can also present itself in someone choosing behaviors of deep risk, or what your world calls "flirting with death." Often this is accompanied with the imbalance of foolish wisdom in which people think "nothing will happen to me—maybe to others, not to me." This goes beyond a mild curiosity and sense of adventure. It comes from a devaluation of life and addiction to risk and the possibility of destruction. When the destruction doesn't come and they evade death or harm, they receive a rush. Sustaining the rush requires deeper and deeper pushing of boundaries.

This also occurs in cases of deep unconsciousness when a person is aroused or excited by the power of harming, killing, or destroying another. There is an inherent lack of compassion, empathy, and humanity within this imbalance.

One cannot fear death without fearing life. Thus, within this imbalance, the fear of mortal death blinds the eye of the soul from seeing the Light, and Surrendering to what is. Including Surrendering to the unknown. It is the imbalance that stems less from separation and more from doubt.

This imbalance is dangerously rampant within your world at this time. There is an emphasis placed on life, life, life. Let us create more and more and never let go of anything. Let us abolish death . . . "Death to death!" This has led to more and more consumption, more and more in general. Which leads to imbalance in the body, the emotions, and the ecosystem. For death and destruction, like the exhale, is equally important to birth and creation. One cannot exist without the other. When this imbalance becomes engrained in collective ideology and personal beliefs, there is a constipation that emerges.

The constipation creates discomfort. And the ego must fight harder to maintain and feed its identity. Things in life then bottle up. Feelings left unfelt build and build and are stuffed down more and more. Thus, an identity culture emerges that is limiting because it leaves little room for the collective identity to shift and move. This results in more pushing, asserting, clutter, and hanging on to things of the past, instead of letting the past die with reverence and appreciation so that you can inhale the new moment and dawn.

To rebalance this ego distortion and the captivity of fear and doubt that it keeps you in, there must be a reengagement with life. A celebration of mortality as well as a celebration of Divinity. The imbalance is a focus on or excitement over death, while the reality is that you are not only in life as a soul in form, you are made of the fabric of Consciousness and of Eternal Life. Your ability to awaken more deeply to this was one of the central purposes of My Life, Sacrifice, and Resurrection: to create a more conscious Path for you to walk with God through your Divine Self. This imbalance causes the opposite: a perception of the death of the Divine self.

To Resurrect that self means accepting that there may be things you will never know, could not know, and will never understand. However, that is where Faith is essential in the restoration of Balance to this illusion of death as finite. Faith gives you the ability to walk in the Light despite the unknown or unseen. Faith is a deeper knowing of self as Eternal: Seen by the unseen. Known by the unknown. Faith sets you Free from fearing death, living in a perpetual valley of the shadow of death, so that you may reengage with life, joy, and Peace.

Remembering that your life is of value simply through your Presence in a body sets you Free. Free to embrace that you ARE life, you ARE death, you are mortal, yet you are also timeless. You have the power to create through your Divine essence. You have the power to destroy that which no longer serves you. You have control over your perceptions, as well as the power to shift your perceptions.

Such is the power of Faith, acceptance, and releasing attachment to one polarity over another.

The fifth imbalance is the imbalance of human want and lust, or desires of the flesh. This imbalance, more than greed, is about wanting. It is a wanting of things to be other than what they are. Wanting a relationship, wanting sex, wanting more attention, wanting more money. It is a state of entitlement steeped in the illusion of desirability. It is about what you think you should have instead of what you do have.

It is a preoccupation with external image, which is why the creation of a strong illusion self is so strong within this imbalance, as is projecting the false image of self onto the world. There is a lack of authenticity inherent to it. Often the image a person with this imbalance projects is not the reality going on beneath the surface. There is a tremendous amount of low self-esteem and lack of confidence at the root of this on a subconscious level, as well as a high degree of self-absorption and narcissism.

It is an imbalance of "I want it and I want it now" and furthermore, "If I don't get it now, I am going to kick and scream and take what I want or burden others with my discomfort." It is thus an imbalance that leads to addictive tendencies and gluttony. This imbalance requires constant feeding from the external world. More money, clothes, houses, cars, sex, food, sugar, alcohol, technology, dopamine . . . whatever can soothe and comfort the lack within.

This imbalance is seeking external nourishment in the exact form you want it to come in a way that does not nourish you or anyone at the end of the day. This imbalance is a fear of the Void, a fear of the unknown, and a fear of looking at what the real lack within self stems from. Thus, people with this imbalance tend to seek and seek, want and want, eat and eat, and are never full. They go from one thing to the next, amassing more things, more knowledge, more attention, more achievements, hungry, hungry, never full.

One of the most unfortunate aspects of the imbalance of desires of the flesh, like the imbalance of ignorance of complacency, is that there is very little originality about it. Inherent to it, the ego desires what others have and wants to do what others do. It is about "want" and "fitting in" by the trappings of the primitive animal self as opposed to the Divine self. You were designed to be completely yourself, completely original. Originality stems from a purity of essence. You cannot be pure in Divine essence and thus original in thought, feeling, behavior, and creativity when focused on outer agendas and being who you are not.

It is often easier to do things the way others do. There can be a great deal of fear of rejection and judgment that results from originality. Thus, this imbalance often couples with complacency or denial. Parroting of others' words, mimicry of others' actions, doing things the way others have done them to achieve status, fans, and followings is one of the many ways this imbalance manifests.

Sadly, since this imbalance causes the mind to focus so much on the external, it can render a person susceptible to those who wish to dictate their worth or capitalize upon it. Many fad diets, clothing companies, social media companies, even credit card companies prey on those with this imbalance deeply, which has created quite a mess for your world. "If you look like this, if you have these things, you will be happy and if you do not, you will not be happy." Or healthy, or abundant. That is the story you are told either directly or indirectly.

Nearly every human be-ing on the planet, given your current collective focus on want and quantity over quality, struggles with this imbalance. Even those who wish to be original feel that they must use the current technologies and strategies to be relevant and have a voice. For example, a wonderful speaker may feel that he or she needs to be on social media with many followers in order to be heard or seen. He or she may loathe social media and feel dissonance and internal conflict while using it. However, there is the fear that deviating from the mold will cause him or her to fail. Or not be accepted or heard.

The feeling of lack of integrity to the true self, coupled with the repression that comes from not expressing your Divine originality, can be deeply stifling. It can move into shame and deepen the imbalance of separation. Many with this imbalance are not aware of the burdens it causes self and others to carry it. Always needing more things, more "food" to fill in the hole of what is missing on the inside: a robust connection to the Divine self and Essence of Be-ing.

The more those with this imbalance amass, including people, the more they tend to hoard. There is little reciprocity between giving and receiving. They work harder and harder and are less and less fulfilled. Some of the core aspects of this imbalance are fear of loss of possessions, wealth, and status; constant seeking of validation in outer world structures; defining worth in self and others through money, prestige, physical appearance, status, social relationships, and so on. Comparing self to others is a constant in this imbalance.

It can also be continuously seeking romantic relationships on an attachment basis. Or, in general, needing something or someone else to define your worth or complete you, which strips you of your power because you are leaving it up to another person, people, substance, boss, or the like to decide your value for you. That is a disempowering and even dangerous way of be-ing that can lead to pain cycles, imbalanced or even abusive relationships, and co-dependency.

Rebalancing this ego distortion requires restoration of Simplicity, releasing of attachments and narrow-minded expectations, remembering that you are already complete, worthy, and whole regardless of anything or anyone in your external reality, and, most importantly, refining wants versus needs. This includes converting to new metrics of what truly nourishes you. For example, replacing focus on money or number of followers with moments of joy and reciprocity can completely reset your sense of value, worth, and equilibrium. And, interestingly, beget more natural, organic fluidity in relationships and service.

The sixth imbalance is foolish wisdom or not aligning with Divine Will. This imbalance of the mind or ego distortion stems from a lack of humility, elitism, self-righteousness, and a propensity toward assumptions. There is an arrogant quality to it despite its absurdity that leads to judgment and belittling of others deemed "lesser than." There can be a mocking or dismissal of those deemed to have "less knowledge," "less prestige," or "less importance."

Stereotyping and labeling of others in a condescending manner is common with this imbalance. It is often accompanied by cynical, presumptuous, sweeping generalizations or patronizing behaviors, including prejudging something or someone based on assumptions. For example, assuming those on a Faith-based or "spiritual" path are, as you say, "woo woo," assuming that someone who did not graduate high school is incapable, or assuming that someone who is blessed with beauty, wealth, intelligence, or status looks down on others as a result . . . or has not struggled just as much as anyone else.

Those with this imbalance tend to adhere to an "us versus them" or "me versus world" haughty mentality, be it in politics, social issues, or even on the home front or work front. It is an assumption of moral, intellectual, or other superiority. Most with this imbalance project it tactically and passive aggressively, whether they are conscious of it or not. This distortion of the ego is very much about judgment.

In its foundations, this imbalance is assuming that you know better or that you are right. That if you read enough books and have enough knowledge, you are wiser than and intellectually superior to others. And therefore, justified to assert your thoughts, perspectives, and opinions. Or to dismiss or judge the thoughts, perspectives, and opinions of others you perceive to be ignorant. This can lead to patronization of others and the tendency to smirk and "pat on the head"

those who "know" less than you, or who do not have the same credentials or body of experience. As if the credentials and titles of your
human hierarchies have any bearing in My Garden of Equality.

It is wonderful to have knowledge and experience with many
things, for purposes of learning, teaching, relating, writing, growing,
and exploring. But when you feel righteous and adhere strictly to the
domains of your knowledge set, there is little room to evolve and grow.
The moment you decide you are right and another is wrong is the
moment fragmentation and disconnection occurs, which severs the
beautiful energy of co-creation possible in every moment.

Those with this imbalance have little tolerance for perspectives
that deviate from their own. They often selectively pick and choose
what serves their ideology and bias and reject all else. The illusion self
the ego creates from this imbalance enjoys focusing on minutiae and
bickering over anything that threatens its ideology. There is a preachy
and didactic quality to it that includes the tendency to assert opinions
over others, including how another or others should be and what they
should do.

If a person with different beliefs on the "opposing side" counters
them, those in foolish wisdom will often shame them for it, even if it
means pleading the victim or attempting to silence them. There is a
censorship energy to this that can become quite harmful to the equality of expression.

As a human be-ing it is hard enough to even know what you need.
Assuming to know what others need, and then projecting that onto
them in an unsolicited way, is a kind of madness. Dispensing your
well-intentioned but often biased or misguided opinions to others
when they did not ask you to is invasive of boundaries. And creates a
disconnect and lack of trust.

As human be-ings, though you share this world, your perceptions
of reality are completely unique. No one person perceives reality the
same way. You are not here as a human be-ing to tear down another's

reality because it differs from your own. Or inconveniences you. Or because you are jealous of another's achievements and happiness. You are not here to question and judge another's reality no matter how limited or ignorant you presume it to be. You do not have the Right to do so. Nor do others have the Right to do so to you. You ARE here to explore, experience, expand, and evolve your consciousness of reality to include the All, not the "some." For you are One with all people and all things. Thus instead of being on a "Mission from God," why not be on a "Mission to God"?

Restoration of Balance from this ego distortion requires humility—deep humility—to disrupt the grips of pride. While it is wonderful to feel your worth and to be proud of your accomplishments, when your ego is so delicate that any bruise to its pride feels like a personal assault, then it has moved into imbalance. It is important to allow yourself to have your beliefs, but even more important to be open to changes in those beliefs. For true wisdom comes from admitting that you do not know. Rebalance from this imbalance requires letting go of the need to be right . . . letting GO of the assumption church of self that is a church of one.

The only thing to assume in this imbalance is responsibility for realigning your will with the Divine Will, which is rooted in humility and kindness. It is easier to do so by disengaging from activities, behaviors, "platforms" (or irreverent pulpits, as I call the majority of them), and people that tend to feed and provoke egoic, childish, suspicious, foolish reactions within you.

More than anything else, humor is what truly saves the day in rebalancing from foolish wisdom . . . being able to laugh at yourself. Laughter is connection. I understand that many things matter to you that you take very seriously. However, laughter brings you to the heart of joy, Simplicity, and closer to the Divine heart of the matter. Which is what really matters: equality, exploration, inclusion, and Love. As you embody that more and feel the humble joy of your

Yeshua self more, the foolish aspect drops away and then you stand in wisdom.

The seventh imbalance of the mind is wrathful wisdom or judgment. While this imbalance can often be synonymous with foolish wisdom, its essence is completely unique and often of a deeper level of shadow and consequence. In fact, wrathful wisdom stems more from the imbalance of separation. The deeper the separation a person feels, the more that person is in fear. Anger, rage, and wrath are energies that mask fear. When not processed and transmuted to grief or channeled in a passionate, mindful way, a person in separation projects these distortions onto others. This creates further division between self and other. The pain and disconnection experienced festers into resentment.

As the resentment grows and builds, it combusts into a reaction stemming from judgment. Feeling judged and judging is the result. The separation imbalance can cause a person to feel isolated, rejected, judged, and angry. While many with separation imbalance fall into despair and depression, others cry out through rage. Reactions of wrathful wisdom are about ascribing blame onto whoever the person feels is deserving of punishment. Often, after the rage is exercised, a regret ensues, which deepens the separation wound.

However, other times, the reaction can bring a rush, a sense of vindication, false power, and false control. An example of this would be a child who is bullied and ostracized or believes as such regardless of whether it is true. If the child is not supported by family, school, or friends and does not have the coping skills and self-esteem to feel his or her worth, he or she can withdraw and suffer deeply. The child begins to obsess about what is wrong with him or her, how to prove others wrong, or how to get attention even if it means through harm.

The child can begin to write mental stories based in delusion, which can even include developing obsessive and paranoid projections about certain individuals. The stories can evolve into a plot for vindication and revenge. Most with wrathful wisdom do not act on the stories. However, there are times, increasingly so in your world, when the child begins acting on the plot. This has led to many of the acts of the deepest levels of unconsciousness in your world over time, from animal and child abuse, to rape, to the shootings in school systems, to riots, to bombings of temples, churches, or mosques, and even to holocausts and genocides.

Though "plots" developed through this imbalance can be calculated, strategic, and even somewhat diabolically creative, there is very little or no rational, coherent, and evidence-based rationale for the violent execution, be it in actual violence, shaming, judging, bullying, silencing, or even just aggression and volatility disrespectful of others' boundaries. In a sense, it is a person's retaliation from suppression to shove his or her dominance down the throat of others—most often, the innocent and least able to defend themselves. It is the imbalance of the most primitive human animal nature. Thereby, it is also the imbalance in which repressed sexual energy is exercised in violent OR secretive ways the most.

This thought distortion is a convenient way for the ego to stay in power. It keeps blame directed "out there" to avoid sitting with the feelings of discomfort "in here." Thus, a person with it never processes and releases the enormous burden of the latent grief carried within.

In certain cases, when strongly coupled with the imbalance of separation, wrathful wisdom can also be inflicted on self. It is a common imbalance in those who constantly berate themselves over their every mistake and flaw. And, in extreme circumstances, those who inflict self-harm through behaviors such as cutting, unsafe sexual activity, addictions, eating disorders, or even tolerating mental, emotional, and physical abuse.

Wrathful wisdom is most widely manifest in those who "live" in a state of deep emotional and mental polarity and unconsciousness who decide to take the law into their own hands by cutting off the hand of another . . . or their own hand. There is little empathy or seeking of understanding in this imbalance. It is about bullying and ascribing justice in a limited human way instead of allowing Us, the Divine, to restore Balance through Love.

It is the imbalance of the mob—the mob of the mind. When a culture or society is absorbed by the ego as the dominant force, collective mobs gather and persecutions occur, as well as crucifixions. This ascription and imbalanced judgment of guilt leaves holes, wounds, and scars that require a long time to heal. Especially when the Truth is revealed of the lambs killed in the blinding rage of hatred. In many ways, you are all still healing from times others have tried to crucify you or you have tried to crucify others.

I gave My Life to end this cycle. And return to you now to complete what began long, long ago, so that you may be Free within your heart. Those who cast stones will know stones. For it is they in their wrathful and foolish wisdom that contribute to the burden, the beast of burden. And they must face that burden themselves, for they live in burden already. My Hand is always stretched out to any who wish to take it. Your burdens are safe within My Hands, My Heart, where, through Forgiveness, they are transformed into Miracles. The Miracle of Peace that comes from embracing and be-ing embraced. Such is the embrace of Forgiveness. All arrive to this embrace someday. Why not allow someday to be today?

This connection to Divinity is what rebalances wrathful wisdom. The drunken blindness of hate cannot stand in the Light of joy, connection, and Love. Rebalance requires reconnecting to life, including nature. Reconnection to others, including those who can support through the processing of grief or anger lingering from past abuse, trauma, or rejection. Reconnecting to patience, gratitude, and the power of the Light within. And, above all, reconnecting to Love.

The only Pathway to Peace from this imbalance, and all imbalances really, is through Love. Those whom you judge, Love them.

Those who judge you, Love them more. Love as God Loves you, unconditionally and without need for reason and purpose. Love can unburden you from all that is imbalanced. Love is the counterbalance to fear in your reality structure of duality. Wrathful wisdom stems from fear and separation. Thus, only Love can Light the way. For Love is My essence, as well as the Truth of yours. With Love all things are possible. For it is Love that made you possible in the first place.

Behold, I have Offered you this Truth of the Seven Imbalances with Love. So that you can move deeper into the Truth of My Heart and your own. So that you can know My Grace, My Peace, through the experience and embodiment of it within you. All that you have and need to transform and transcend already lies within you. For I Seeded it there long, long ago. And now the Revelation of your Truth as Love is moving deeper into the luminous essence of your true Divine self.

To complete this Truth I wish to Offer, prior to bringing you deeply into realization of the Sacred Heart, it is essential for Me to share with you the root or origins of the Seven Imbalances of the Mind. For these will give you deeper insight as to how the imbalances developed, as well as how to restore them to Balance:

The Seven Imbalances are distorted lenses of perception created by the Three Veils that come as a by-product of your current existence in form, in body. The Three Veils are the Logos of separation or, as you say, "the fall" that came in the awakening of consciousness that gives you the perception of the "I," the ego, Free will, and choice. The Veils, like the imbalances, can be thick to those in deep unconsciousness, or nearly transparent to those whose shadow and Light are blended and integrated in a Balanced way. The thicker the Veils, the deeper the distortions of the Seven Imbalances.

First, the Veil of Separation: Like the mind or ego imbalance of separation, the first Veil is similar but flows far deeper: perceiving self or world as separate from the Divine. This Veil creates dissonant thoughts and unhealthy fear or rejection of shadow. This leads to the tendency to isolate, hide, and suffer in silence. Shame can thus be an engrained tool the mind uses against you to keep you in a withdrawn and unworthy state.

Many institutions throughout time, including external structures and systems, have utilized this Veil to instill fear and deeper separation to assume dominance over you. And to coerce you into giving up your power and Freedom as a Sovereign individual through controlling your mind.

This Veil is an illusion, for you cannot be separate from God as you were created of God, of Consciousness, of Light. In form, as a human be-ing, you also have shadow. The shadow is your attachment to form, to identity as human, flesh only. This attachment to form identity instead of energetic identity is what has gotten you and your world into trouble for millennia. Yet the shadow is essential, because it is what gives room for possibilities, pace of evolution, and revelation. **The shadow is nothing more than space waiting to be filled with Light.**

The Veil of Separation is not shadow. It is division. Not recognizing the I as One with the We. Longing to stand in the Light of God yet never feeling One with God. Detachment from Presence, which is what connects you most deeply to the Presence of the Light. This Veil is the original Source wound that came and comes as a by-product of coming into body as a conscious be-ing with an individual identity. It is what creates your experience of grief, mourning, longing, and even mortality. When this Veil is thick, there is less creativity, motivation, and inspiration and far more fear, anxiety, doubt, and despair that can feel inescapable and incapacitating.

This Veil is the original Source wound and thus causes you to simultaneously miss and mourn the Light—despite always standing in it. However, realization of the latter only comes through reopening your true soul eye to the unseen essence of the Divine.

The separateness is what creates the deepest pain and fear of rejec-tion. Or feelings of unworthiness. Or the perception of failure—that you can fail God, fail yourself, and be cast into the darkness or shame-ful fire of Gehanna eternally. Beloved, you are always One with Us. For there to even BE fire, that means the Light is present. Your jour-ney is realizing that in a deep internal way. You will remain in form as long as you are attached to form, which is what is easy. Your brain wants to keep you safe through seeking externally and focusing on whatever transient problem you are experiencing in the moment. And that is not even close to the reality of what you are.

When you release the attachment to limited identity based on the "seen" and known, you come to feel and know yourself as One from the deep space of consciousness that is the unseen. And thus, feel deeply seen in a new way: seen with the Divine eye within self. The number of those on your planet who profess to stand in utter Oneness, Consciousness, and wisdom is large. The number of those who actually do is very, very small. Their Presence is what holds the Light for all of those finding their way through the lifting of this Veil.

Second, the Veil of Polarity: This Veil, also an illusion, is the by-product of a binary mind based in duality. A mind that perceives things as black and white, good and bad, right and wrong. A mind that needs to be able to judge or discern when making choices. Like the Veil of Separation can only be lifted through embracing the gift it gives you of both individuality and Divinity, the Veil of Polarity can only be lifted through coming to Balance, Peace, and appreciation for the experience of one energy in two different forms.

What I mean by this is that there are healthy polarities. These are necessary, essential, and maintain Balance in your universe. For example, a positive and negative charge are both of equal value. One cannot exist without the other. They are opposite yet they complete one another, and hold the Balance for one another. Another example are emotions that seem different because the emotions they pro-voke are different—but really they are One. Such as doubt and Trust. Doubt is simply the shadow form of Trust. Trust is the Light form of doubt. One cannot exist without the other.

Acceptance of polarities allows a person to witness both ends of the spectrum free of judgment. Thus, a person able to witness and experience either shadow or Light polarity with appreciation tends not to be polarized by them. And thereby gets to experience the full spec-trum of every shade and color in between in a way that is joyful.

A person who is not conscious of this Veil tends to be charged, ag-gressive, and polarized. Emotional outbursts or swings between joy and depression are common when this Veil is thick. Polarized thoughts and emotions result in impulsivity, defensiveness, dissonance, and judgment. There can even be an addiction to polarity, where, if things are calm, the person seeks out polarized, even dangerous situations. Or provokes and instigates them. It is an addiction to the rush of the high, and the bar keeps getting higher and higher when the lows that come from the crash of withdrawal are felt.

This Veil is combustible and reactionary to those in fear or ego, which is why wrathful wisdom and/or desires of the flesh imbalances are often magnified when this Veil is thick. It can be accompanied by paranoia, the feeling that others are blaming, shaming, and attacking you when they are not. Often the one feeling paranoid tends to blame, shame, judge, and hurt others from this fear state.

Animals understand polarity. There are times when it is winter and food is scarce. There are times of abundance in the summer. In the choice of separateness, especially nowadays, human be-ings have lost touch with the cycles of polarity within nature, which has perpet-uated further imbalance. Your Mother Earth is very polarized, in that She actually has poles, in a way that is Balanced. It is you who have disrupted that Balance by focusing on imbalanced polarities. This Veil can cause you to feel that, when unexpected or polarizing things happen that you do not like or understand, especially in the case of natural "disasters," God is doing something TO you.

I promise you, Beloved, it isn't personal. The Divine simply created and maintains the Order to the flow. It is not until you come back to wholeness as a human be-ing, and rebalance the Seven Imbalances of the ego/mind, that you can truly lift these Veils, come to deeper embodiment, and synchronize with the natural rhythm of the ecosystem. As these things occur, your purpose and service are expressed more fluidly and organically. Through witnessing before reacting or judging, this Veil lifts and thereby you experience a more Balanced, Peaceful, and Grace-full Path through life.

Third, the Veil of Complacency: Like the imbalance of ignorance, this Veil, also an illusion, is an avoidance of the Truth. It is a sloth and laziness that halts the soul's evolution and leads to boredom, stuckness, and malaise. There is a fear of loss built into it. The sense that "well, my life is not so bad compared to other people's, so I will just stick with where I am" even when the heart is crying for new life, creativity, and change.

There is also the fear that if you pursue your dream, or make a change, you will not get what you need. The ego and critical self make up stories to keep you in complacency by telling you things like, "Why bother?" or "You're not good enough." Or, that it will be a "waste of time." "You will be rejected and lose everything." It makes up scary stories to keep you safe and small, stuck in a false sense of safety.

Foolish wisdom stems largely from this Veil, which is ultimately about fear, sometimes glossed over with arrogance and elitism. "Well, I know better" is a wonderful way to stifle the totality of your experience as the Divine in form. The Divine is the All. So, when you are arrogant and elitist, you are caged in the prison of your own beliefs. Again, that does not mean you have to resonate with everything. But openness to new perspectives and exploring new ways of be-ing helps you to better know self. And you will be surprised by the humility and joy that comes as a result.

The Veil of Complacency is a resistance to change, when change is a central aspect to the flow of creation and manifestation, feminine and masculine. This is why many times, when people do not change, they experience pain. If a tree's roots outgrow its pot and it is not put into a bigger pot or open soil, it begins to suffer and die. You are the ever-evolving Tree of Life. The Veil of Complacency is waiting for the suffering before making a change. Or waiting for someone else to give you your bigger pot. If no one does, you either wallow and suffer or become angry. This is the "arrogant victim" in grand manifestation.

Lifting this Veil is understanding that change is going to occur and you have a need for it to occur. You are progressively evolving alongside the universe and Consciousness itself. Lifting this Veil does not mean smashing through change or trying to do it all at once. It is bringing awareness to the areas where you are feeling burdened and actively participating in the process of transformation. This includes asking Me to support and assist you through the process. The inner energetic change is what makes the external changes and shifts in behavior possible.

Allow the Light and Grace I strengthen you with to bring you to the Faith that you are held and One no matter what change is occurring in your life. Lifting this Veil requires the energy of both creation and destruction. Valuing both creation and destruction thins this Veil and allows you to manifest more organically in the ways designed and aligned for you. Lifting this Veil is about accepting change and facing what needs to be faced for the Miracle of your liberation to occur.

All three of the Veils are about fear. They are illusions of fear and limited consciousness, which is why it requires Faith to lift them. It also requires honoring an original path rarely

taken in the world instead of the one the outer world tells you will make you happy.

YESHUA HOMEWORK

Beloved One, I recommend you take several moments, even hours, over the next days to write about which imbalances you recognize within yourself. And how the Veils interact with the imbalances. You will begin to see some patterns. Which of the Veils tend to be the strongest for you? Which of the imbalances tend to be the strongest? What behaviors exacerbate and feed them? How have the Veils dissolved for you through different experiences in life?

Once you have done this writing, I ask that you place it by your bedside for as long as it needs to be there. And each day before sleep or waking, please call in My Presence. And ask Me to assist you in the transformation of the imbalances and lifting of the Veils. Breathe in My Grace, Peace, and Light. And know that I already see you as perfect, Balanced, and whole. Through this writing and process, I will be helping you to open and live from your Divine eye instead of your human eyes alone. So that you can see yourself as the Love you are within this world.

In your nakedness and humility, YOU are the power, YOU are the glory, YOU are the Kingdom, for you are your true self, your Divine self. In this space, all that I AM is all that you are. And all that you are is all that I AM. I walk with you each day, as you walk with Me. Allow My step to strengthen yours. With every step we walk together. Sancti. Pace. Amein.

3

....

The Chambers of the Sacred Heart

(Originally channeled February 9, March 8, and March 18, 2020)

YESHUA TEACHING

Behold, Behold. Coming into Peace is an internal journey. I promise you, Beloved, if you are in a war zone in the external world and you are at Peace in the internal, there is nothing about the chaos that disconnects you. For a heart at Peace renders you immune from all that is of separateness and war.

Peace is a union, a marriage of Truth and Love. It is a blending of your shadow and Light, masculine and feminine. It is a resonance of flow connected to Divine within self and thus all life. Feeling worthy, abundant, aware, present, and accepting of all things, no matter how you perceive them, as gifts and opportunities for service.

Peace is a Faith that no matter what you perceive, you are connected and whole. Always have been, always will be. That is connected through the Now. All things are occurring within the Now. All of your past lives, future lives, are occurring within the Now, within this present moment. This should help bring more Peace to your heart. You have already been born, and died, and reborn. What you are to experience tomorrow has already occurred, so why worry about it? You know exactly what to do when you are present. Always.

As such, just because you are not at Peace with a situation does not mean you cannot still be at Peace with yourself. *You* are not the situation. Situations should have no bearing on your Peace . . . unless you allow them to. You did not come to this world for situational Peace. Peace does not need a modifier. You came to this world to come to Peace with yourself and, as a result, to serve from that Peace through your Divine essence.

Faith is an energy that emerges from Peace. Faith is a constant. It is the only constant and thus it is immune from polarity. Faith is the acknowledgment of your Divinity. No matter how tough things are, no matter how great things are, it is a fire inside you that knows that everything will be all right no matter what—because you are Divine.

When you illuminate within your Faith, and there is that level of connection and communion, We can speak to you and through you. Thus, when you have Divine Faith, all things in the human, all things that you used to worry about, almost become silly and easier to manage. No longer do your imbalances set off a chain of burdens for you and others. No longer are you as triggered by others' imbalances that set off a chain of burdens for you. Because you are able to use healthy separation between reality and distortion. That restores Peace and ends your self-imposed sentence of suffering.

Pain is not suffering. Pain is a sacred emotion that cleanses you. It is the shadow form of Love alongside grief for as long as you are in human form. Without it, the Light aspect of Love would not be possible or felt. Pain is simply a death or loss. A perceived loss of Freedom or identity. The pain is never really the issue. It is the fear of the pain or the pain of the pain that creates the deeper suffering. Even in the case of physical pain. It is an inconvenience, a perceived limitation on your Freedom to do what you wish to do. Thus, when in pain, it is easy to become frustrated and to wallow in self-pity or resentment.

When, if you look beyond the surface, there is a journey of deep Love beneath it. A Freedom to explore your strength and all the possibilities held within it. It is the fighting of the pain, the hatred of the pain, that deepens the pain and leaves you in the shadow.

Predominantly, when you experience pain or grief surrounding a loss, what you are ultimately mourning is a loss of identity—part of your story has left. A person has died, a relationship has ended that was once a part of your story. It was part of your mind, your ego's story, your heart's story—part of the story of your life. When that story, belief, or construct dissolves, there is mourning created, rooted in the Veil of Separation.

Pain is a sacred emotion that is rooted in honesty, and vulnerability, and humility, and Truth. Thus, pain brings deeper Oneness, provided it is honored as a part of your journey but not the only part. Addictions to pain speak to other imbalances, especially excitement or fear of death and endings. Coming to Balance with pain allows it to be processed naturally. And, over time, as the grips of your ego identity transform and enlighten, the emotions and thoughts dissipate more and more. Thus, pain is processed more quickly. Or witnessed and experienced without judgment and attachment. And that, Beloved One, is the Freedom of Peace.

There are four Elements of Peace that create the Balanced Sacred Heart. The heart is not the heart you know as the emotional self. The heart's center is the center of your be-ing that rests at the zero point space, the center space of your be-ing. The Sacred Heart is the great Void from which you move into and out of form. The Sacred Heart is the Center, your center, united with the Center of Gaia, of the sun, of the universe, and of God. It is the intersection of the dreaming and dreamer, creation and creator, subconscious and conscious, seen and unseen.

There are four chambers to the Sacred Heart. Often it takes what you all call a "heartbreak" or a piercing to more deeply open the chambers within it. Which is why grief is such a strong gateway for your movement deeper into Spirit and awakening.

There are four chambers of the Sacred Heart of Peace, which originate from the union of Divine Mother, Love, and Divine Father, Truth. When these unite in your sacred heart through all four chambers, you naturally come to embody your Yeshua self over time.

The Four Elements of Balance and Peace in
the Chambers of the Sacred Heart:

- **Simplicity**
- **Stability**
- **Surrender**
- **Stillness**

These four energies complete the Sacred Heart. Through these four energies, the Pathway to Peace becomes clear, for these are the four chambers of My Heart, the Heart of the Divine Father, and the Heart of the Divine Mother. When you embody these four energies, your sacred heart is in Balance and Peace.

These four energies lead you to the narrow gate of the Divine. To the space where there is no pain, suffering, or death. This space exists within you at all times, but you must choose to find and illuminate it.

You were birthed into the world, created as a soul and as a person through these four energies. You thereby carry these four energies within you. The death of the identity or form self to Resurrect in your Yeshua self, the Conscious self, cannot occur without these four energies.

Sadly, these are not energies highly valued, focused on, or priori-tized within your world. Your world is increasingly complex, volatile, unstable, controlling, and cacophonous. It has become a world focused on expectations, entitlement, arrogance, image, victim-ideology, and ownership. A world so demanding and noisy that it dulls your senses, including your intuition and discernment if you do not have the disci-pline and discernment to know when you need to take time away. A world so addicted to anxiety, chaos, and substances that it can make you feel like everything is spiraling out of control. In some ways, it is. Which is why these four simple energies, if you are willing to prioritize them, can restore your Peace, even if you are the only one on the block who resets inner values to honor them.

It is rare when someone focuses on these four energies, and yet those who do experience the most joy and connection no matter the external reality they live within. Were these four energies to be the central currencies for success, your world would be a different place. The rarest be-ings on your planet, the Lightest, are really the most Balanced. They radiate from the center and emanate a Peace that is simple, stable, surrendered, and still.

For these four energies are not only the image of the Divine. These four energies *are* the Divine. Your access to them comes from your Divine self, your soul. They are what actually create and bring the most abundance, nourishment, joy, and flow to your life. Because they not only create Balance, they Balance each other and, in Truth, are the essence of Balance, itself.

Thus, to realize your Divine Yeshua self, focusing, creating, and bringing awareness to these four energies can restore equilibrium to the whole of your spirit, including your internal and external reality. The more you reach for, embody, and prioritize these energies in your life, the easier it is for the Divine, including your own spirit, to bring your needs with fluidity just when and how they need to come.

If all be-ings in human bodies on your planet, or even just a hand-ful more of you, focused daily on streaming and weaving these ener-gies into your heart, body, mind, choices, and behaviors, there would be far fewer problems and burdens for you all to carry. And far less of a burden for Gaia to carry as a result. The four are as follows:

Simplicity. Simplicity is one of the most central aspects of Peace and thus one of the central aspects of realizing the Me in you and the you in Me. Simplicity is the root, seed, and branches of the Tree of Life. Infinite in vastness and dimension yet also raw, natural, naked, empowered, and strong. Simplicity is letting go of all that feels burden-some and disturbing to your Peace.

Breathe in a breath of Simplicity. And ask: What are the aspects of my life that continuously feel chaotic, polarized, overly complicated, and volatile? Am I willing to participate in the process of simplifying my life? Even if it means working less/more, taking better care of my body, decluttering, and taking the time I need to do the things I have been putting off that keep piling up and causing stress? Every breath of Simplicity you draw into your life will bring you Peace, Light, relief, and certainly JOY.

Stability. Stability is essential to understanding and embodying the Divine. A stable foundation for your soul, your Presence, your consciousness IN body means spending more time in the present, in your body, instead of in your mind, your illusion self, and the future or past. Stability is all about examining and, with patience, exploring the structures of your life, including relationships, career, and behav-iors. It is creating trustworthy, strong, reliable, consistent, honest, and transparent structures conducive to evolution and Love. It is building your house on the rock of Faith instead of the sand of complacency.

Ask: What feels unstable in my life? What anxiety and impa-tience does that bring? What is unsustainable? Am I willing to par-ticipate in the process of bringing more Stability to my life? Even if it means asking for support, taking back control over debt, bills that I have been putting off? Even if it means leaving volatile relationships with emotionally imbalanced or overly dramatic people behind? Even if it means structuring deeper boundaries? Every breath of Stability you draw into your life will bring you Peace, Light, relief, and certainly JOY.

Surrender. Surrender is a necessity to Love in alignment with the Divine Will. Some view Surrender as a weakness; others view it as a virtue and even profess to live in Surrender. However, they pick and choose what they will Surrender and how much. Surrender is neither throwing up your hands and saying, "You do it, God" nor "Here, God, deal with this and I will allow for what You bring, but only within my very narrow set of parameters." You cannot selectively Surrender, Beloved One. It is a state of be-ing rooted in humility, discipline, integrity, and devotion in a way that can sometimes require effort, but never in a way that creates more burdens.

Ask: Where in my life do I fear Surrender? What do I fear Surrendering and what is it that I am Surrendering to? Where in my life do I continue to exert control? Where do I tend to try to force or manipulate outcomes the most and with whom? Am I willing to participate in the process of bringing more Surrender to my life? Even if it means fully giving over with Faith that everything will be all right no matter the outcome? Am I willing to stop playing tug-of-war with Yeshua with my burdens and Surrender not only my burdens but my whole self? Every breath of Surrender you draw into your life will bring you Peace, Light, relief, and certainly JOY.

Stillness. Stillness is the most lyrical and nourishing aspect of the Sacred Heart. In fact, it is the essence of the Sacred Heart, which may sound odd since the heart is never still. It carries a harmony and melody in One—it echoes out and echoes in at once. It is the gateway to giving and receiving Divine Grace. Stillness requires Presence and unwavering devotion to looking beyond the noise and chatter to hear what Spirit is echoing, streaming, and weaving into you.

In a world that focuses on talking and talking in circles, talking in a bloviated way that contradicts its own utility, embodying Stillness of heart and mind allows the echo of your spirit to thunder tremendous Light into the collective. There is a great confidence, compassion, and trust in Stillness. Those who can come to Stillness have often mastered the Veil of Polarity. They are comfortable with silence and communicate more powerfully through Presence and energy than words alone. For Stillness is the language of the Light. By Surrendering to Stillness, you are able to listen to, hear, and be heard by the Divine all at once. Please note that Stillness is not just about quiet. It is about separating from the things, behaviors, people, and stimuli that create dissonance.

Ask: What areas of my life lack Stillness? What feels like a cacophony that I am obligated to engage with and participate in? How does my mind sabotage the Peace in my heart? Where do I feel Stillness and when? Does Stillness make me nervous? If so, what am I afraid I will hear within the Stillness? What am I running away from in my restlessness and external seeking? Am I afraid to be alone with myself and my own thoughts and feelings? If so, why?

Am I afraid of Stillness and the productivity I might lose through taking the space to come to quiet and Peace? Am I worthy of Stillness? Am I willing to participate in the process of bringing more Stillness to my mind and heart? Even if it means turning off all the temptations of these outer voices and stimuli? Even if it means committing to a practice of meditation, being in nature more, or turning off my television, cell phone, and computer to take a bath in candlelight? Even if it means setting and enforcing boundaries and/ or removing those from my life who are grating, self-absorbed, and needy? Even if it means I need to be less self-absorbed so that I can be absolved and dissolved into the Light of Divine Equality? Every breath of Stillness you draw into your life will bring you Peace, Light, relief, and certainly JOY.

Breathe into these energies of My Peace. Breathe into the possibility of a life of Simplicity. Not scarcity. Simplicity. Exhale all that feels complicated, burdensome, and chaotic to Me. Now inhale Simplicity again. Notice how that feels. And allow Me to bring you all that you need to realize this energy more every day.

Now breathe into the possibility of a life of Stability. Not rigidity. Stability. Exhale all that feels volatile, overwhelming, and unsustainable. Now inhale Stability again. Notice how that feels. And allow Me to bring you all that you need to realize this energy more every day.

Now breathe into the possibility of a life of Surrender. Not giving up. Surrender. Exhale all that feels controlling, pushing, and impatient. Now inhale Surrender again. Notice how that feels. And allow Me to bring you all that you need to realize this energy more every day.

Now breathe into the possibility of a life with Stillness. Not isolation. Stillness. Exhale all that feels screeching, grating, and dissonant. Now inhale Stillness again. Notice how that feels. And allow Me to bring you all that you need to realize this energy more every day.

Breathe into the possibility that all of these energies are not to-do's. You already have them within you right now and in every moment. They are your true state of be-ing. For they are the foundation of your true heart and the heart of your authentic self. Feel the Peace they bring echoing within you through the breath of Divine Grace and Balance.

Your sacred heart is the gateway that connects you to your Yeshua Self. You were designed for Simplicity of realization, Stability of foundation, Surrender in transformation, and Stillness in invocation.

These are the four chambers of the Sacred Heart. This is the foundation and structure for the Pathway to Peace. The center point of the Sacred Heart, the Medicine Wheel, where these energies intersect, IS the space of Freedom.

The Offerings of My Heart throughout these Transmissions guide you to this space, the space where I reside, where Peace is found, and where the Light beyond the Light that you know exists. It is My joy to walk with you through your realization of Freedom.

You are the brightest of rays to My Heart, Beloved One. In many ways that is a responsibility but never a burden. The golden Eye and Ray of God is upon you. No one in this world could understand you the way I do. Within Me, you are seen, heard, understood, and deeply, deeply Loved. May the gates of your heart open every day more to this knowing.

It has been My honor to have served you on this day. Peace be with and within you.

Om Nami Maia. Om Namah Sananda. Om Nami Yeshua. Sancti, Sancti, Sancti. Pace, Pace, Pace. Namaste.

PART TWO

THE FREEDOM TRANSMISSIONS

(Originally channeled August 21, 2020–September 1, 2020)

The Weaving of Spirit upon the Web of Life

1

....

The Thread and Stitching of the Dreaming

YESHUA MEDITATION

Good evening, Beloved One. I would ask that within this moment of Peace and of joy, you please take a moment to close your eyes and to begin to draw deep breaths into your body, breathing in My Presence, My Light, through your own Presence and Light. Settling your awareness into the whole of your be-ing.

As you breathe, begin to unstitch yourself from any thoughts of tomorrow, of yesterday. Begin to unstitch, unhook, unthread from issues with others, from your worries, from your beliefs. Unstitching yourself, peeling yourself away from all that keeps you heavy and bound. Feel yourself unstitching, unthreading, and unweaving any tension in your body, breathing through any knots. Filling your body, liberating your body, your Tree of Life—branches, trunk, and roots—with Freedom. Allowing the doubts within yourself, others, the Divine, to be unthreaded and released with Forgiveness, with Faith.

As you unstitch from these love-nots, begin to open to the healthy Love knots of your soul, your natural essence, stitched to your body, the Body of the Earth, and the Body of the Divine. Feel the flow of the Light move through your body as you breathe in Love, breathe in Truth, breathe in Peace. And exhale the same. From above, through the branches of your tree, feel the **Strand of the Divine Vine of Faith,** your Divinity, flowing through your tree, branches to roots.

Feel the **Strand of the Divine Vine of Forgiveness** flowing through you, branches to roots. Now feel the **Strand of the Divine Vine of Freedom** flowing through your tree, branches to roots, unraveling you from all of the braids and knots that keep you bound to dissonance and stress. Feel as these three energies, Faith, Forgiveness, and Freedom, weave and braid through you in abundance, harmony, and Grace. As they weave and braid through you, continue to breathe.

Om Mani Hu, Om Mani Ma, Om Mani Hu, Om Mani Ma, Om Nomani Hu, Om Nomani Ma, Om Nomani Hu, Om Nomani Ma (keep breathing as you braid), Om Homani Hu, Om Homani Ma, Om Homani Hu, Om Homani Ma, Om Domine Hu, Om Domine Ma, Om Domine Hu, Om Domine Ma, Hu Omni Ma, Ma Omni Hu, Hu Omni Ma, Ma Omni Hu, Om, Om, Om . . .

Now allow these energies to rest and settle within the whole of your be-ing. Place one hand on your heart, and the other on your womb for women or your hara for men. Take a deep breath, and smile. Place your hands together at heart center in the mudra of Prayer. With a deep breath, simply say, "Thank you." Open your eyes.

Beloved One, know Me not as I was, but as I AM. As I, Yeshua, AM all things, including you. I AM your Faith, and you are Mine. I AM your breath, and you are Mine. I AM your tears, and you are Mine. I AM your joy, and you are Mine. I AM your friend, and you are Mine. I AM all things, and no things, as you are all things, and no things. You are My dreaming and I AM yours. You are My dreamer and I AM yours. You exist. You are not of life, or in life, you ARE life. That is all you need to know of the Light.

YESHUA TEACHING

Beloved, nature is the common thread that unites you all. By nature, I do not simply mean Gaia, Mother Earth, human nature—it is the nature of the essence of your soul, the nature of the essence of your Consciousness, Creator in Creation; Creation in Creator. In coming to a body, your soul is weaved and stitched into matter, into form, which gives you the perception of an identity that is the self. In this life, your soul has chosen to be woven into a body through your DNA, through your chakras, through your bones, through your blood, through your heart, through your spirit.

While your soul resides within body, alongside heart, mind, and physical body—call it your spider—your spirit body is the space all around you, the strings, threads, energy that connects you to the Web of Life. The spirit body is what connects you to the external world in seen and unseen ways. When you are in a soul-based life, a present life, your soul orchestrates in harmony with God, in alignment with Divine Will. When you are in a mind-based life with the ego imbalances and lack of humility and awareness, you are a dissonant orchestra of fear, control, and imbalance. An orchestra of one instrument playing out of tune without even realizing that it is. Because it does not realize it is even playing in an orchestra, a community of many spirits in bodies, human and other in this life.

Sadly, playing out of tune has become the attunement of your world. Thus, lack of attunement to the humble, simple harmony of your essence is often rewarded in your world and by your ego. Your world often rewards you for playing along to the tunes of money, status, success, prestige, and influence above Simplicity, Stability, Surrender, and Stillness. The imbalanced ego's solution is always: keep playing louder. More noise, more stress, more money, more power and I will get to where I need to be.

I promise you, Beloved One, none of this do you take with you. Never in your spirit, your sacred heart, will you remember posts, news reports, games, intimate moments with wine and sugar, or quests for money, sex, and power when you cross over. You do not carry with you that which is not real and dulls you to the full experience, joy and pain, of sensory experience. You do not carry with you the empty casks of consumption.

You are here to consume experiences, memories of value found in gardens and streams, in moments you say hello and good-bye to Loved ones, to strangers. You carry with you those moments when others see you and you see them. You carry with you moments of connection and communion, not the dull, numb fear-stitches and strings of suppression. You are here to play in tune with your natural self in co-creation with the orchestra of Life. You are here to weave, braid, and know God through all experiences, foremost in the experience of knowing yourself as Divine in human form. And, with humility, allowing your soul to co-create with your spirit in alignment with the Divine.

What you carry with you are the moments of intimacy and Forgiveness, when one soul lets go and Forgives the other. You carry with you the moments you choose Faith over fear and reach for the courage to honor what is right for you instead of what others tell you. You are here for the Freedom of being a "part of," yet also allowing this life to be your individual journey with God in a way that no other can control or understand. It is time for you to unstitch from all that keeps you out of tune and to begin weaving yourself back into your organic essence and the Tapestry of Life, including the Earth.

I am using threading or stitching, but really it is vibrations, waves. Those are the threads—the spectrum of the elements that make you, well, YOU. The elements of your water, fire, air, earth, and space. Each person with a unique recipe and vibration.

The ecosystem you weave with extends far beyond your planet and reality and into the Sacred Heart of the universe. There is a perfection within this ecosystem between death and life, creation and destruction—that is Love, that is Truth, that is the order to the chaos that I have spoken of before. Thus, when it is said that you are Love, it is not just your soul or body—the entire stitching and threading of the vibration that you are is OF the fabric of Love.

You are also stitched in "love-nots" to ancestral family and personal karma, which is in part what creates your distortions and imbalances of ego. Part of your Journey is unstitching from those distortions to restore your clear vision of what you are: Spirit, Light, One with God. Love-nots are knots of "nots." The "nots" that leave you knotted up inside with regret, disappointment, and resentment.

You often speak of "tying the knot" within your world as an expression of Loving commitment. On our Journey together, we will untie the knots that are not rooted in Love. The knots of "nots" rooted in warped perception of self and world. So that you are Free to weave, braid, stitch, and dance with self, Divine, and world in a co-creative tapestry.

Oftentimes with knots or wounds, because they are ugly, they can take a long time to heal. They can cause you to feel that sometimes these tightly bound stitches, be they perfectionism, judgment, despair, rage, control, unworthiness, or victim identity, are more like nails. Nails binding you to a cross or burden of worry, anger, fear, doubt, and isolating behaviors.

Because they are not pretty to you and because the social structures of your world cause you to feel shame surrounding them, you all often spend much time trying to hide them. Or to stitch up these stigmata on your own. By applying any number of different salves that ultimately do not heal the wound or the dissonant knot/not, but that patch it up and in so doing make it worse because it is left hidden—it cannot breathe.

These wounds are not wounds that can heal simply through the external topical resolution because they cannot be healed through the mind—your "knowledge," "wisdom," and human ego identity construct. They cannot even be healed through your heart, which is the greatest bearer of some of the nails that you have felt. They require your soul, the conscious dreamer within you; not the ego lost in the dreaming. They require not only your soul, but your Presence, your spirit, your consciousness, AND Ours—the Divine, the Divine Dreamer, Creator of the dreaming you call your reality.

This is why many of the times that you feel the deepest nails, and stress, and burdens, and crosses, are very often some of the moments that We reach to you the most, or your soul reaches to Us the most. That is important for you, Beloved One, because it is one of the reasons that your world is experiencing the shifts that it is right now.

There was a call within the collective for you to unstitch from some of the oppression, repression, suppression—not just on the external, but on the internal as well. These past years and coming years are not to cause more burdens for you, Beloved. They have come to set you Free, as well as Gaia and your ecosystem, from the burdens that were keeping you asleep. It is sometimes uncomfortable to wake from a blissful dream-state of false safety, assumptions, and denial. Often, when a Truth is revealed that brings discomfort or change, We hear you say, "I wish to go back to sleep."

It can be uncomfortable to wake up after a time of slumber, loss, or complacency. As a world, you are waking up now. The power structures that are the least transparent want you to be asleep so that you will behave as they wish for you to behave. They are very afraid that you will wake up and thus unstitch, unhook, unweave from them, and take your power back on the inside. This can even include certain friends, Lovers, family members, media, financial systems, employers, or politicians.

They will show you illusions that create fear, shame, and none of the illusions they show you are real. They are projecting their fear onto you. Do not feed that fear for, when you do, it becomes your own.

Your liberation can never come on the outside until you are able to find liberation, through humility and reconnection, on the inside. This is not to cause you doubt and skepticism in your relationships. It is to help you to remember discernment and who is or is not authentically supportive of your deeper movement into your authentic self. Do not assume that you know. What I am speaking to here is the importance of exploring and appreciating your individual Sovereignty, given unto you by God. If you take these words for granted, you will never understand the power of your essence and worth. And then all Freedom is lost to you internally and in the external world.

Unstitching from a mind-based, "make-up" life of external focus can be quite a challenge when many things are unraveling all at once and things are changing very rapidly. It can be overwhelming when much change, revelation, AND accountability comes all at once. But your soul is ready. Your spirit is ready. Even your heart. Your ego is the only one whining and in dissatisfaction. Let it go. Exhale.

These years on your Earth are an invitation to receive Love—not just Love in the form of wants and happiness. Love in the form of Truth. This can be very painful because your souls are becoming Lighter and thus there is shadow that surfaces to be blended and integrated. And illusions of what and who you think you are that are being dissolved. You are being shown reality, the authentic self. This, as opposed to the illusion of safety and security that you have known in the past where there was some communion with Love, but also a part of you that felt as though it was separate from this energy. You are not interested in being separate anymore, at least not those of you who are here now.

Kundalini is rising. Shakti is rising. Kundalini is an unthreading of many love-nots all at once. It is not just practiced through the uncoiling of energy in the spine. Kundalini or Shakti rising means an unbridling of any things that have kept your vibration, your consciousness, your behavior, weighted down. It is an unthreading to clear past density, past trauma from within the power of the present. In many ways, it is a death. Perhaps not a physical death but a death to all that makes you feel dead inside so that you can mourn, release, and move forward feeling Lighter and more Free.

Actual physical death is an unthreading from the body entirely. In this Divine Gateway and collective shift, there may be slightly more be-ings choosing to leave their bodies than usual. Including your Elders. Which is why it is essential to honor and cherish them as much as you can. They may have added to your burdens at times, but they have also shown you what you need to evolve and grow. They have survived storms far worse than you have ever known and could ever imagine. Do not blame them for the past. Listen to them. Love them. They gave you life, all of them. The discarding of Elders is not something you can escape from. As someday you will be an Elder, too. Treat them as you wish to be treated when you are as such.

Over these years, refrain from trying to understand in your mind why certain things are happening and comparing yourself to others. That is not relevant to your process. Love may not always come in the form that you wish it would, but it always comes in the form that helps you to evolve the most in your embodiment of it and service through it.

Incarnation is a threading to body and form. As you evolve as a soul in form, as you en-Lighten, warps and knots/nots that have kept you bound often for a long time, even since childhood and beyond, need to rise. These suppressed parts of self need to rise up to your consciousness so that they can be healed by the Light, through the Light—dissolved and integrated. While this can happen in an instant, most often it requires time and many different experiences or "pass throughs" to fully dissolve and integrate. That journey is unique unto you.

Prior to even going somewhere, anywhere, your soul and spirit have already stitched you to the place and people there, and they to you. It is a co-creative choice to weave and flow with others that happens on a level far beyond the mind's comprehension. It does not matter whether you like the people or not, whether you are stitched to them while walking past them once on a sidewalk, whether you are woven with them on one simple plane ride, or whether you stitch to them for a lifetime.

This is a period in your life in which you will find yourself reevaluating who you wish to be stitched to, who you wish to "untie the knot" from, and who you wish to weave and braid with in a way that is more aligned with your natural, simple essence. Some within your world, still asleep, may be stitching to even more density, more stress.

Thus, there is a period of polarization occurring with regard to who is choosing transparency, Faith, and Forgiveness, and who is choosing fear, rage, distortions, and blame. It is an individual choice and, together, the choice of Light or shadow will dictate the path of the collective as this new Era progresses. These changes and reevaluations are the main reason why so many changes are coming in your relationships, living locations, careers, and even identity.

Your spirit cannot undo the imbalanced threads and knots. While your spirit works co-creatively with your soul, the choice to release and process a knot or tangled thread must come from your soul. Your brain is an incredible, astounding gift and tool. However, the imbalanced ego mind does like to keep you stitched to more dense things, behaviors, people—anything that perpetuates its story of self. It prefers to keep you stitched to what you know, even when you are unhappy. The mind is in limited consciousness and does not have the humility to know that your soul, which is One with the Divine, your consciousness, and Presence, knows far better.

Through our time together, through My Words, your soul, your Light self, your Presence, your vibration will be rising. Your choice to be here in this moment with Me means that you are ready to rise from the crosses, burdens, and nails that the imbalanced ego and illusion self keep you exhaustively bound to. Thereby, you are also saying yes to the natural rethreading of your joyful, simple, need-based, Divine essence within the ecosystem.

Sit for a moment and feel into the stitching of your life. The stitching to your land, home, family, animals. And now feel if there are any stitches that feel more like love-nots. Which feel more like the healthy Love knots that stitch you into Gaia, your bodies, the ecosystem, and those you Love? Which feel more like the love-nots, which bring anxiety and doubt? What behaviors are you "not-ted to"? Who are you stitched to? Do you wish to be stitched to these things? To sugar? To social media? To fixation on money, media, and politics? Do you wish to be stitched to hatred and despair? Who is your Savior? The flesh or Spirit? The question is whether you will choose flesh and your human impulses like many other animal species . . . or Spirit, the fabric of your existence.

We, the Divine, do not choose this for you, Beloved One. It is your choice. What We serve is all that you were designed to be, no matter what you experience in your life. What We serve is the Love grounded in Truth, transparency, and Freedom that is your Sovereign gift as a conscious be-ing. We always honor your Free will. If you wish to stitch to things and places and people that are not in alignment (no matter how much you thought they were), that is your choice. However, as it is the path of every soul to enlighten to the degree it no longer needs to come into matter or form, We always bring you what you need to come Home to yourself.

The higher you raise your vibration, when you unstitch from thought, emotion, trauma, and density, the Lighter you become. The amount of credence that you give to the thoughts, biases, fears, expectations, assumptions, and emotions you stitch to is what weighs you down.

Incredible Peace flows when you are able to unstitch, unhook from your emotions. For these are often triggered and manipulated by your mind far more than you know. Emotions are simply vibrations that need to be expressed, moved, processed, held, and brought back into Balance. Not through projecting them onto others or even needing to know where they came from and why, but expressed through movement, creativity, laughter, tears, courage, vulnerability, and allowing. Peace comes when you are able to allow some of those emotions—those tears, that anger—to be experienced and given over to Me to hold so that you can reclaim your piece of Peace. That is an unthreading from a love-not. There is no one to blame for it; there is no one to judge for it.

Take a moment, a breath, to unstitch from your thoughts right now. Pause, observe, and exhale. Center in the Peace of this present moment. Once again, pause, observe, and exhale. Wonderful.

Love-nots are thought forms, stitching you to the primitive fears and behaviors of your primal animal self, not your Divine Spirit self. When you stitch to a thought, the funny thing about it is that it tends to keep you stitched to the next thought, to the next thought, to the next thought. It becomes almost a shadow form of Jacob's Ladder—a spiral—in which, from one minor thought or trigger, you can think your way into rage, or revenge, or resentment, or blame. Then that "not" knot festers. It has been brought into you, sucked into your being as foreign matter—an outside thought form has stitched into your brain (you have allowed it to) and it stitches to your emotions and causes illness, dis-ease, and negativity.

Unstitch from your thoughts. When you are thinking your thoughts, at least become aware—*I am stitching to a thought*—*is this a resonant thought? Is it a dissonant thought?* Even just that awareness can restore you to the present and bring Light. If it is a resonant thought such as sharing, offering a meal, going for a walk, communing in your garden, wonderful. If it brings you Peace and Presence, you are in Surrender. If the thought brings fear and resentment, reaction, or regret, stay with it, exhale it in full trust to the Divine. And We will lift it. Even if it takes a minute, hour, day, week, or year for you to do so in full. Let it GO. And I will bring all you need in the process of release.

If your ego, your "I," even the healthy "I" that allows you to participate as an individual within the collective, wishes to keep you stitched to fear, have Faith that your child Yeshua self, your Divine self, knows what resonance is. By bringing your awareness to areas of dissonance and fear, We, the Divine, working with your spirit, can bring you what you need to transcend the dissonance and restore the resonance. Work with your own Divine Presence not in judgment but in allowing. Call in My Presence and, together, we will dissolve and resolve the love-nots through Love to weave and braid you into the Tapestry of Life in the way most aligned for your Balance and joy.

At a certain moment when you are ready, you will even have moments of unstitching from the concept of be-ing an "I." To become the I AM. And the We. The One. That is the journey. That is the journey of why you come to body, to remember the All that you are a part of, no matter what. It will take you far longer to return Home to this space of unity when you fight your own self and the flow of Spirit from your doubt, endless dissatisfaction, and seeking. I exist within you. So why don't you start there and leave the rest up to Me?

Moving forward, be cautious of where you stitch, and what and who you allow to stitch in you. As I have said many times, this includes finding Balance with your technologies. While your technologies can be wonderful tools, when imbalanced, your technologies enslave you, heart, mind, and spirit. You are a Free spirit, not a slave. Why choose slavery with your addiction to and imbalance with these things?

Allow the Web of Life to be a wave that you are of and witness to simultaneously. If there is any unstitching that you want to do, or wish to do—tell Us. Within the next years of Voids, deaths of old identity, and restoration of Balance for you as an individual and as a world, I will bring to you all that you need for completion and rebirth.

All that is needed for you to unbraid yourself from that which keeps you in doubt, in anger, and avoidance of processing latent grief is awareness and consciousness. Bringing awareness to a love-not allows the thread of Love to flow into it. It is your role to allow Us to transform that: take the time in nature, in quiet, to unstitch from these things. I promise you that in that process, Love will bring you what you need to have more space, more Freedom, more joy. And stitch you to what is right and aligned for you. What you need will come to you when it is time, and not a moment before.

This is an unthreading year for you, as are the coming years. You will be unthreading from and held responsible and accountable for your own greed, bias, ingratitude, arrogance, and numbing either consciously within self, the simpler path—or unconsciously through what your spirit brings you in experiences. Humility, integrity, and kindness will allow the process to flow forth with Grace. These are three of the most powerful qualities of your Yeshua self and yet often the least valued and incubated in your world. Braiding humility, integrity, and kindness into every breath and stitch of your life brings consciousness and prevents "not" knots from forming in the first place.

Your soul in its liberation needs to trust that the moment that it is unstitched from one relationship, or pattern, or mindset, or pain cycle, it has the space it needs to move the essence of your be-ing into a passion of Peace. Your soul and spirit need to trust that, when the revelation of your passion comes, you are not going to go right back into projecting and restitching yourself into a predominantly self-imposed suppressive structure resulting from your abdication of personal responsibility and accountability for your own joy and Peace.

Your soul wishes to enlighten and to remain Light. That is why it is Freeing you from so many things during this time. Even if your mind tells you that it is scary, trust your soul—the Holy Spirit that is in and upon you will Free you of those burdens. Choose Faith over fear.

For as you do, your tapestry of self will be restored to the beautiful, Balanced shroud it was designed to be. With patience, compassion, allowing, Forgiveness, resilience, and Love come Miracles, Beloved One—foremost, the realization of the Miracle that you are. That Miracle catalyzes many more in its wake.

When your soul or vibration rises, oftentimes stitches can burst. As I said, major change can come as a result, and that can be painful at times. In some cultures and Faiths, they call this the rising of samskaras or soul wounds. These are covered-over, suppressed love-nots that need to be embraced, nurtured, and healed. This can sometimes require grief, pain, and discomfort to surface. Stale thought bubbles can surface; old resentments can surface. In this process, fear not.

And trust that through holding yourself through these risings, sometimes catalyzed by external events such as a loss, sometimes just coming from nowhere, changes to your perception of your external reality can occur as well. You may feel less interest in engaging or participating in dissonant behaviors. You may feel triggered. Let it rise and it will transform. Every time you allow for a death in any form it comes, process the change, and accept the change, a great, vast relief will come. And joy. Joy, Freedom, and wisdom are the outcome, the Miracle.

Do not project your own thought bubbles and rising traumas and resentments onto others. Bring them to Me. Give them to Me. I can take it. Others cannot. Whatever hatred you have, work it out with Me, not your fellow soul mates of this Earth, no matter what they have done or how much you hate them. Give Me your hate and I will transform it so that you can be Free to Forgive and to Love. Hatred, arrogance, pride, and impatience are some of the heaviest crosses to carry and you must set them down. For it is YOU who carries the burden of these energies within YOU when you feel or project them.

Gaia, Mother Earth, welcomes you to give your crosses to Her too. Your crosses, not your contempt and egoic dominance. She Loves when you include Her in your process of excavation and serves you well in grounding your energy. She is the cool clay of God and in belonging to God, longing to be with God, you too belong to Her, the Dreaming, within this life. Do not dismiss or reject Her in this process. You cannot. Which is why nature is your Greatest Temple or Church. She and I are old, old friends and Lovers. She is yours, as well, for She is the origins of the Dreaming—your experience of reality.

What I speak of now is the rebalancing that needs to occur within your life and your world. This is not a prudent time to be focusing the majority of your time and energy on external issues. Each of you who are on this planet at this time have come to a body to take the narrow gate, the gate to Spirit within self. Whether you take that opportunity is to be determined by you. The higher your vibration, the more powerful your passion through Peace will be in times to come. The more Balanced you are, the more fluid and malleable your stitching will be in the Tapestry of the ecosystem and Web of Life. That stitching anchors and grounds you into greater fulfillment of your purpose and service through joy as a Light-holder. The knots of this Tapestry are the healthy knots.

The Love knots and healthy stitching of your soul/spirit into matter grounds you and brings Spirit deeper into every cell of your be-ing. We imparted and stitched the Love knots within you through your chakras, your design long before your conception. And no matter what the world tells you, you are perfect. Always. When in Balance, allowing for the Love knots to stitch you in Surrender, commitment, and Faith, you are threading, braiding, and weaving deeper into the Web of Light. The rest unfurls from there. I AM your Thread. Gaia is your loom. You are the conscious creator. And together, we can illuminate the beauty of your tapestry within THE Tapestry of Consciousness and Divinity.

Your spirit's thread is My Light, Gaia's as well. We are THE Beloved. In every moment She is calling to you, weaving through you to set you Free, as She set Me Free. And I am setting Her Free now too. Thus, there will be even more natural rebalances and shifts occurring that will not end until you come back home to Her and to yourself. Those that move deeper into their natural essence and passion through Peace are the Divine Vines that are working in co-creation to set Her Free, through anchoring Grace, kindness, and compassion upon this Earth. As you refashion healthy Love knots of communion and Balance with Gaia and untie the love-nots born of disconnection from Her, you will find deeper Freedom, as well. This is a journey, a river of Freedom. Let go of the old shore. The time is now.

When I have spoken of separating the wheat from the chaff as an analogy, a story, it in part means separating the healthy stitches and nourishing braids from the love-nots in your life. However, like many things I speak of, there are many meanings for you to draw. Separating the wheat from the chaff is also a reference to death, when soul and spirit unstitch from body. Death is an unstitching from form so that you can be One with God in Spirit.

Separating the wheat from the chaff also means separating from the parts of you stitched into density—unconscious thoughts, patterns, pain cycles, and behaviors that are devoid of Light—such as rage, and judgment, and the imbalances of the ego. **Separating the wheat from the chaff within yourself is unstitching yourself from the isolation of victimhood, stagnancy, shame, and inertia and restitching yourself into the realm of infinite possibilities, Presence, and Spirit. That is weaving upon the Web of Light. That is your mind as loyal servant, your heart as your guide, and your soul as the sacred master of self, working with your spirit body to call in your true needs as opposed to just your ephemeral, insatiable wants. It is a state of equilibrium.**

Spirit serves needs, not wants. Remember that you are Spirit too. Serve needs, not wants. In self and to others. Serving others' wants and expectations is fussy and complicated. Serving needs is quite effortless and joyful.

Separating the wheat from the chaff also means separating the worthless from the valuable to you. This does not mean judging whose worth is greater and lesser and who is right and wrong. None of you are right or wrong. Separating wheat from chaff is separating the aspects of you that feel unworthy, separate, nailed to the human thought forms and dense emotions of anxiety and fear, as well as your own tendencies toward judgment, denial, and withholding, and imprisonment of your joy.

It is to separate those aspects of self that no longer serve the beautiful golden threads of your tapestry and weaving upon the Web of Life, including those who weigh you down and mitigate your worth. Separating the wheat from the chaff is, in its deepest echo, a remembrance of this,

The Prostration Prayer:

Your worth is equal to mine, beloved,
    my worth is equal to yours, beloved.
Those who blame, or I have blamed,
    your worth is equal to mine, beloved,
    my worth is equal to yours, beloved.
Those who shame, or I have shamed,
    your worth is equal to mine, beloved,
    my worth is equal to yours, beloved.
Those who guilt, or I have guilted,
    your worth is equal to mine, beloved,
    my worth is equal to yours, beloved.
Those who judge, or I have judged,
    your worth is equal to mine, beloved,
    my worth is equal to yours, beloved.

Those who have failed me, or I have failed,
  your worth is equal to mine, beloved,
  my worth is equal to yours, beloved.
  You are the Beloved, as am I.
  I am the Beloved, as are you.
  We are One in Divine Grace,
  Divine Power, Divine Truth, Divine Love.
  Om Nami Yeshua. Amein.

The Prostration Prayer is an act and offering of humility and devotion to the Divine, as well as a deep reverence for all life as equal in worth. Even if what you value may not be the same as another. Even when someone devalues your worth. The Prostration Prayer is a Prayer of equality of worth. Through the Word, Eyes, and Consciousness of the Divine.

Separating the wheat from the chaff is a separation, or unstitching, or unbraiding, from the imbalances of the mind and the three Veils. **In essence, to separate the wheat from the chaff is *separating from separation.*** The chaff is in many ways the body—the body returns to the Earth in the end. Your soul, the wheat, your Light, returns to the One. Energy cannot be created nor destroyed, but the physical body, and things that are of matter, and separateness, and imbalance, can be created and destroyed in the sense of ashes to ashes, dust to dust. What you wish to focus on, seen and transient through the lens of the chaff, or unseen and timeless through the lens of the wheat, is up to you.

Focusing exclusively on chaff, external life, mind, thoughts, and wants will keep you bound to the primal animal self, the flesh of ash and dust. Focusing on wheat will Free and liberate your spirit, no matter what your external circumstance is. But your focus is a choice. And here is the interesting part: Focusing on the chaff as your dominant self can bring you happiness, but often at the cost of another's. Chaff-focused life requires so much work and effort even just to get to the moments of fleeting happiness or ephemeral security. It isn't living life in Freedom, it is enduring life, toiling through life. Focusing on chaff, you may do many things, but you never really evolve beyond a few tiny steps.

Focusing on the chaff does not necessarily move you deeper into the wheat. However, focusing on the wheat, the spirit, the inner self in giving over the armor and burdens, DOES augment your experience of the chaff exponentially. While essential to your evolution, the chaff limits you. The wheat Frees you to a deeper, richer experience of BOTH. Meaning, focus on the external does not always or even often augment the internal Peace. Focus on the internal with humility and Love DOES shift and transform your external reality. You cannot singlehandedly transform the world, the external. But you can transform your inner world and that transforms your external reality in time, as well.

Your soul cannot be created nor destroyed. It simply is. Your soul is what has value foremost. Your body may be the chaff, and your body is deeply important to the tapestry, but it is your soul, your Light self, that is the wheat. That is My Bread, that is My Wine for you to eat and drink from, and Gaia's as well. You cannot fully realize the wheat without the chaff, which is why your human reality construct of this life is so important. In your current human experience, the chaff is just as valuable as wheat, as it is the vessel for wheat, like your body is your vessel or temple. It is the body, the chaff that allows the Seed, the stitches of your Yeshua self, to grow.

That being said, the unfurling, echoing, and service of your wheat, your soul and spirit, unto the world is the greatest calling you could answer. For what you are called to now that is the most valuable to you and all IS your Freedom, your joy, your Peace. NOT "getting mine," which is what the ego wants. Thus, question any and all things that keep you separate from your Balance, including your fears of loss or pain. When you fear such things, you are biased toward them, so even when things are going fine, you wind up self-sabotaging or creating your own pain. Unstitch from that which does not bring you space, Balance, kindness, Freedom, and Peace.

And do so without demanding certain terms be met first. "If I get a job, THEN I will focus on my Peace." No. If you focus on the Peace, the job will flow in when and if it needs to. The same with relationships and resolution to other matters. Stop delaying. Stop taking little sips of your spirit only when you have a convenient break from the episodes of the lack-of-reality series called your perception of human life. It is a choice. Take the time. Advocate for your wheat, your soul, not your mind that wants to compartmentalize and dictate what is "more important" than your Prayer, Surrender, and communion with the Divine, with Me, Yeshua. When you spend more time embodying the Me within you and the you within Me, I tend the field of the dreaming with you in co-creation, harmony, and partnership. So that you can BE.

Resolve in these next months. Not your external issues alone. Resolve in your heart if you are willing to Love yourself enough to take the time for your Balance. Resolve whether you will say yes to change. Resolve if you are willing to move into Surrender within instead of setting the terms to feel safe enough to do so. Leap, Beloved One. Leap. Resolve. And commit.

Ask Us for resolution when you cannot see the Way. This is what We are bringing you now. Ask Me for resolution to the things that keep you out of joy, out of Freedom, and out of Peace, and out of space. That I can gladly serve as I AM the Son, the Divine Father, and the Divine Mother in One. Ask and you will receive. That is well within the embrace of the Divine for you are inviting Us into your process instead of trying to do it all on your own.

While We are all-embracing, it would behoove you to also respect the awe of God. Those who do not resolve to commit more to their inner process and choices of Forgiveness, Faith, allowing, and kindness will be brought to their knees in the times to come. Through their own choices. This is not a wise time to rest in complacency, polarity, and separation. For the ensuing years are the years of "you reap what you sow" as individuals and a collective. Those who plant seeds of Love will know Love. Those who plant seeds of blame will know blame. Thus, your choices now are of a bit more magnified importance than ever before.

I AM your Creator and we co-create now together as we have since the first moment I gave the Breath and Word of Consciousness to you, long before you entered this life. You were not just made to be in life. You were made OF life. Do not deny yourself the joy of living. You are not here to fear, you are here to Love. As you choose Love over the violence that is fear and cease your feeble arrogant judgments, all of you, you will receive the same. THAT is how you change the world. Through the inner self, before any progress can be made in your external reality.

As you move through the looming Voids and this period of Truth and revelation, which will come unexpectedly and bring you through the process of grief into the process of change, do not try to rush, Beloved. Like Love, grief is not an energy that enjoys being controlled. Nor can it be. Trying to rush through your grief prolongs it and creates deeper suffering for you and others. As does putting it off for later. Grief, like Love, as they are ONE energy, enjoys movement. It flows in and out and is a glorious catalyst for change.

Grief is an energy that has been and will be very important through the next period because it is the very energy of the letting go and the final internal processing of the unstitching. That is grief. Grief is what lies beneath the crosses and burdens. Now that you are letting the burdens and crosses go to Me, who can carry them for you, you may feel the fatigue, depression, and releasing beneath it all. Let it be. Take the time.

Grief comes the moment when there has been a change, expected or unexpected. You are vulnerable. Out of nowhere, no matter how much you have prepared, there is the trauma, the reality that something is being let go. No matter what catalyzed it, when grief comes it can feel as though it has befallen you. Nothing befalls you that you have not chosen, Beloved One. It is important for you to recognize this.

There is a deeply Sacred process that comes as a result of a change, a trauma, a void, or a loss of any kind. It leads to the denial, and then to the bargaining, and then to the anger and the rage. In reality, everything right now is about letting go. Whether it is moving energy, density, out of your body or feeling what it is that you need to feel, without judgment. Grief is important.

You are all grieving in various levels of your processing because you cannot let go of an old stitch that you have carried, participated in, identified with, for a long time—until there is a mourning, and acknowledgment of the importance of what that stitch brought to keep you safe. An unstitching is a good-bye to an old story, and it is not until you accept that that you are able to begin the new. Whether you are unstitching from body or a Beloved in your life, leaving a relationship or career, picking up the pieces from a loss, healing from an illness, or processing an old wound, there is a mourning, and through the mourning comes the new dawn of clarity, compassion, humanity, and rebirth.

Certain stitches are not meant to be healed until the exact moment that they are ready. Same as wounds. You cannot take a bandage off until it is time. Sometimes, when letting go, you realize a sudden liberation that there was actually no wound, the perceived wound healed long ago, and you feel Free. Almost guilty to feel so Free when you "should be" grieving. According to whom? Certainly not God. In such moments you realize you never needed to put that bandage on in the first place.

Other times, not. The stitching is deep and visceral and requires time with Me, Spirit, not just the external world to transcend it. No one can completely understand how deep your stitching is. Only Us. Thus, in such moments, you need to come Home within yourself, to the Stillness, and sit with Me.

Grief is a change to your story. It is a loss of identity that you actually never had, despite your perception, but believed that you did. It is about an attachment to your story. Or a story that is taught to you, that you take into the fabric of self, a story from the outside that is stitched into you by another, by the collective. In detachment from that story, there is a feeling of loss, even betrayal. It can make you angry. The deeper the attachment to that identity construct, that story, the deeper the grief will be.

The deeper the Love that you felt for someone, the deeper the grief can be when you lose that person. That is Love. Grief is Love. Thus, know that in moments of grief, you have never been closer to Love.

You all have various things, at various levels, that you are grieving right now. Whose is worse, who is the worst victim or perpetrator, and other such comparisons are utterly irrelevant and contrary to the point. Have some compassion for yourself and one another. Any comparing of whose grief is worse will ultimately prolong your grief. Whining about your grief is not grieving—it is talking about the grievance instead of taking the personal responsibility to process the grief and let it go. No matter what was done to you, and by whom, in the past, continuing to whine about it does not move it. Only Love can.

The energy of denial, denial of grief, or not allowing things to shift is a deep cross within your world. Grief/Love requires change, and you all resist change and would rather create solutions to numb it or prolong it than accept it.

Please note that grief does not have to mean crying, Beloved One. It means processing in whatever way you need—through time, through space, through emotion, through working through dissonant thoughts with patience, through committing to transformation of a behavior.

Grief requires support, above and below. Denial of grief is what keeps you stitched to the dreaming, the sleeping, to form, which makes it worse to experience when time goes by. Denied grief compounds in interest, which is why it is best to allow it to come and go in a wave. Like Love, like Truth, like all other things. For you too are a wave.

Grief is ultimately the energy that UNstitches and UNknots you from pain. It is accepting and allowing for a change. It liberates you. And your soul thus can stitch, braid, and weave you to something more in alignment. There is a Freedom inherent to it, as well as infinite room made for creation.

In your tapestry of self, perhaps some of you wish to simply not have so many stitches, and to be a simpler, more organic tapestry that is stitched more to the ecosystem—to fewer relationships, but to more relationships that are of value. That is very wise, Beloved. Make sure that what you are stitched to resonates and is not of fear. Stitches of fear, shame, and blame are the weakest, yet feel the scariest and the most painful. Love-nots feel more like rusty nails, whereas Divine Love knots and golden, seamless threads feel more like connection and joy.

Stitching to healthy Love knots, braiding through Love, and un-weaving love-nots does not make grief less painful, but it does make grief less isolating and even surprisingly, more joyful. For there is a restoration of Faith and communion that comes as a by-product. Hence the importance of Surrender through the process.

Remembering that, in Truth, all really is stitched through Love no matter the mind's perception, keeps you in humility and even in awe of the Miracles possible. Receiving the Truth can sometimes feel devastating, but actually it is less devastating than being in denial. The Truth allows for the unseen and eternal to shine through into the seen. Nothing is permanent in the human, in form. But the Truth of the Light is timeless, primordial, and infinite.

What IS permanent is your Presence to, of, and within

the One. You are sewn into braids and stitches made by God. You are braided to people, and actions, and energy, of God. When you become conscious of this, it becomes very simple to be in your essence, and to move that into your Dharma, or passion of Peace. Restitch to the Divine ecosystem through your Prayer, through your laughter, through your breath. Restitch to the ecosystem that is all around you. Then you will know what it is to live in Balance.

There is only one stitch that matters the most right now. That is your heart. Any love-not that keeps you out of your sacred heart—Simplicity, Stability, Surrender, and Stillness—is the most important to focus your awareness on to transform.

Until your heart can be of Peace, you will not completely feel Me, or yourself, nor will you be able to move your passion out of self, onto the Web of Life in alignment with your essence. Because you are shielding your heart, hiding it. So how can you thread, weave, braid as the spider on the Web of Life when the gateway to the Web is closed through the heavy armor blocking your heart?

Allow your heart to be the central stitch. All things that it has Loved and Loved "not" rest within it. All that it Loves, hold it Sacred to you with deep gratitude. Cherish it. As for the love-"nots":

Take several breaths. If you are able to, close your eyes. And allow what is flowing forth to flow. Feel the waves. And then submerge in the waves. And stand above the waves.

And now send waves of your Peace, your Prayer, through your heart to Mine. Trust that I will carry your Prayers in My Heart as I carry, hold, and walk with you upon the water.

Allow for whatever you are unstitching from, including emotions and thoughts, to flow out through your exhale. Slowly exhale. As you inhale, allow for the possibilities of new braids to fill you. Let the Holy Spirit be upon, below, above, and within you. You are held, seen, and Loved. Breathe into My Grace. Let us be One. Let there be LIGHT. Amein.

FREEDOM TRANSMISSIONS
PERSONAL PROCESS WRITING

I would now ask you to take out a sheet of paper and to write down the following:

- **What do I need to have Faith in?**
- **What do I need to Forgive and be Forgiven for?**
- **What do I need to be Free from?**

This writing is very important, Beloved One. Please take the time.

When your writing is complete, I would like you to fold this sheet of paper over several times, then give it a blessing and have it near you as you move through these Transmissions, Offerings, and Divine Prayers of My Heart to yours. **Do not open it until I ask. I will ask you to work with it throughout the Transmissions to come in specific ways.**

This is your Freedom Transmissions Personal Process.

There are no closed fists here, Beloved Ones, only open palms reaching out to hold yours, in the beginning, in the end, and in each moment in between. All that I AM is all that you are. All that you are is all that I AM.

It has been My honor to have served you on this day. Om Nami Maia. Om Namah Sananda. Om Nami Yeshua. Sancti. Sancti. Sancti. Pace. Pace. Pace. Namaste.

The Wheat and the Chaff

1

....

Shades of Hope

YESHUA TEACHING

Behold, Beloved One. As I have said, separating the wheat from the chaff carries many different meanings. Oftentimes in My Offerings, I like to liberate several different birds with one stone. That is why, as you listen to the Offering, depending on where you are in your soul's evolution, you can hear and experience very different revelations at different times.

In the previous Transmission, I spoke of two representations of "separating the wheat from the chaff." The first was soul/spirit/wheat (your consciousness or Divine Presence) in body/form/matter/chaff. While these are not separate as long as you are in body, in physical transition, what you refer to as physical death, chaff returns to the Earth and wheat returns to Spirit. The second was separating or discerning between what is and is not of resonance, alignment, or value for your evolution, within self and world.

Before I move into other representations, I wish to remind you that the key word in this simple Offering is **separation** between the wheat and the chaff. Oftentimes, many of you associate separation as a negative energy—feeling separate from the Divine, feeling separate from those around you, feeling separate from yourself, from your body, from your world, from your Light. Sometimes that separation is steeped in comparison, unworthiness, guilt, shame, regret, blame, judgment, and the imbalances of the mind that can make you feel disconnected. This is the shadow form of separation.

However, there can be great joy that comes to you through utilizing the energy of separation in its Light manifestation: separation creates choice, it creates an identity between self and the outer world, and more than anything, it creates a space between the ego's illusion of self and the exquisite Truth of your Divine self. Separation between thoughts or events creates the SPACE for union, harmony, intimacy, and Oneness with the Divine—so that you are not just a walking corpse, or simply matter that can hold the energy of Light and consciousness, but ultimately is nothing more than matter, nothing more than form or the "stuff" of the Dreaming.

Thereby, working with separation in its Light manifestation often means working with the element of space. Such as removing yourself in a moment of conflict to ground and center yourself. Taking space to put closure on an issue, let someone go with Love, or unstitch from a behavior, including impulsiveness, that you once needed when you were bound to a life structure of deeper density.

Separation can be a wonderful energy to employ in taking space from issues and noise to discern what to let go of or to remember what actually matters in the scheme of things. It is even the space between wheat and chaff, soul and body. When you are suspended in the space between the two, you are in two realities at once. Thereby, you can access the space of infinite possibilities, the space of Spirit. Recognizing that you are consciousness in form, stitched into a sacred body or chaff at this time, but not limited to body or chaff is an extraordinary application of separation. You are foremost wheat having a wheat-in-chaff, dreamer in dreaming, experience.

Thus, it is important to honor the chaff. We do not discard the chaff. You are here to be IN body, embodied, not exploring the reaches of space but utilizing the infinite gift of your ability to take space within the reaches of self. You chose to come to your world to BE here, really here. Free of drugs and other things that might make you feel closer to God, may even bring you revelations at times, but not in a way that is sustainable.

It is time for you all to reach for the Divinity right here, right now. It is time to unstitch from the crutches of substances, behaviors, and projection of blame. They come at a heavy cost to you, heavier than you could know, no matter how much you feel you have been wronged. It is time to un-knot from these burdensome love-nots. The next "Goddess" circle that blames men, the next "men's investment meeting" that mocks those with less means, the next "Peaceful" protest that blames whoever is not at the protest, the next joint, the next credit card, the next car, the next "teacher," the next "therapist," the next creative idea you never follow through on, the next excuse, the next complaint, the next cookie. Enough. Know when enough is enough. THAT is a form of not only separating the wheat from the chaff but recognizing the wheat within the chaff. The equality of your worth and the worth of all others.

Even when you are not in body, meaning when you cross over, when body is released back to the Earth, it has worth. God created the clay, and the clay has worth for other be-ings and life just coming into form as you depart. The chaff becomes again the chaff that holds the wheat of other be-ings in time. The chaff is form, it is Gaia, it is màtter, it is to be valued—as is the chaff and the wheat of a given person whom you are separating from at a given time . . . or that person from you.

While your "casing," the chaff, has some worth—your body, looks, appearance, status, job—always remember that your wheat IS your worth. For it is your Presence. The worth recovered only through your Presence in the present moment. For this is where your wheat resides and how you can access and feel it. Your wheat IS your worth.

You are wheat in chaff awakening now to the wheat. Others are wheat in chaff and will awaken when they are ready. When and how they do is not your responsibility. It is theirs and Ours, God's. At times, separation comes when you are ready to complete a journey with a thing, person, or behavior—something that was held sacred to you along your journey leaves your life.

When it is a traumatic type of ending, there can be many feelings of the shock, and then of the denial, and the bargaining, the anger, and the blame, and the resentment, and the reaction and then the regret. But ultimately, it is to be grieved and celebrated.

I come to you always and most frequently in beginnings and endings. As it is in the beginnings and endings that you experience Love most powerfully—real Love in its completeness, which can sometimes even feel like darkness. That is when the Divine, when the Light, finds you the most. When you are in the humble, open, vulnerable space of the Void, the womb.

Whether you choose an ending consciously or it happens through what your soul attracts, or through the Free will of others within the world and your life, it does not matter. There is a change, there is a rebirth, there is a separation from the story, the identity—your story, your identity.

That power of the energy of separation, how it moves you, how it sets you Free, how it guides you to your Faith, how it moves you into Forgiveness of the past, in gratitude for all things and all life—that is the basis of the Prostration Prayer: Separating and taking space from an issue, or leaving a situation with Balance and Grace, no matter the injustice you perceive has been done. It is hard, Beloved Ones, I know. But part of the movement into your Divinity is accepting and remembering that God brings justice and Balance to every soul in the end. Not when your mind chooses, but when it is time. We, the Divine, recognize the wheat within all of you. When you are ready to realize it, that is your journey. The power of separation/space through Love is even what helps you to rebalance the imbalance of separation and lift the Veil of Separation.

Taking the space to separate from an issue or thought bubble such as a nagging anxiety, thought distortion, trust issue, or persistent frustration is a wonderful, wonderful practice. Again, what separation is, is the element of space, separation from form. Separation of the Truth from the story.

You were all living a story prior to these past years that in some ways was real, but in other ways was not. You were living quite blindly and out of alignment. You were not seeing the Truth of your imbalance. Thus, Truth needed to come to clean your lenses. To wipe the salt, sand, specks, and logs from your eyes, to unbind you from the stitching to some of the thoughts and energies and commitments and expectations keeping you bound—to set you Free from that web.

All of what has been given to you during this time is Truth. I will say more about what that Truth is in a moment. Separation of the wheat from the chaff, in one of its most important manifestations and revelations, is your ability to separate your consciousness, your Presence, your awareness from thought forms that create dissonance. Dissonance was and will be felt more viscerally as of 2020 and after because, individually and collectively, you are ready to rediscover and reevaluate what resonance is. Some are choosing to do so, others not.

I brought polarity to you these past years, especially during and after 2020, to make clear the deeper layers of the dissonance within you as individuals and as a world. I did this by making you sit with yourselves—and you will need to sit with yourselves until you have found your resonance again no matter what year it is moving forward.

Your soul is in your body. Everything else on the external is form—even your mind. Thought. Thought forms. Bodies of thought. Schools of thought. To be able to recognize and separate from a thought—any thought—an anxiety, a worry, a big thing, a little thing—is a big deal in the Divine Space. Sadly, it is not as rewarded or even recognized in your human world. Though I fully understand the challenges of life as a human be-ing, I am continuously baffled by how often you allow the most inconsequential, transient thoughts and worries to consume you. To be able to separate from that IS the Divine Magic that comes of Divine Grace. As you all say, a Miracle. Yours. And Mine.

When certain thought forms trigger you over and over, reach to Me. Calling in My Presence will help you return to the space of your breath and Peace. This is important because, as I have said, some thought forms can be quite grating and difficult to disentangle from, especially when they have become deeply ingrained over time. For example, if a nagging, limiting thought form floats through you such as: "I should be so much thinner, I hate my body," "I will never be able to get my finances in order," or even "People are terrible, the world is terrible, I am so sick of it all," and you do not take a breath to separate from it, it can very quickly completely consume your mind and emotions. As the thought form spirals into a fear prison, dense feelings including guilt, shame, and resentment surface in a way that keeps your soul, spirit, and heart in shackles. This fear prison is an illusion but can feel very real and even lead to physical reactions such as depression and panic symptoms.

While reason, logic, and critical thinking is a wonderful, essential, God-given tool for you to enjoy as a human be-ing, the reality is that the majority of thought bubbles that float through and about you on any given day are illogical, binary, impractical, and even a touch insane. Learning how to separate the wheat from the chaff—yourself from discordant, fragmented thought forms—allows you to witness them through the lens of the wheat, not the chaff. Thought forms are the chaff. You are the wheat. The wheat is where your Freedom, Presence, and Power of Peace resides.

Through reaching to Me, I will help you to remember that you are more than your thoughts, impulses, and emotions. Far, far more.

Right now, and during this new gateway and period of opening of seals to the Sacred Heart, you cannot even trust your thoughts and your emotions because this is not a time of the mind OR the heart. It is a time of the soul, the spirit.

2020 and beyond are the years that begin a new time and Era of the soul. The soul that is your wheat. The soul that lives in Balance, transparency, fluidity, and co-creation. This is your time for the realization of this Balance in an authentic way.

Your souls are taking back their power from your minds, and those who resist will struggle more as time goes on. The Truth that you are seeing is just how little your mind could create something stable. Thus, this is a time for resting in that space of the soul, which is stable, Balanced, and able to weave a web of kindness, of Love, as opposed to fear and greed. This is a time of realignment with Divine Will, to which your soul adheres far more than the mind and even heart. This is a time of resynchronizing with the vibration of the Earth. The true vibration of your wheat and your consciousness.

Some have wheat that is very tightly bound by chaff. They are very angry, very numb, and lacking in compassion. Do not assume this is not you no matter how conscious you consider yourself to be. But, just as you have Love, even they who are tightly bound to unconscious ways and patterns have Love—be it for their mothers, animals, or someone they once knew. Even they deserve Love. As you do. It is very difficult for them to see—they are not even aware yet that they are wheat. But you are. Thus, you have a certain responsibility as a conscious be-ing to hold the Light with humility. For, despite the differences in your perceptions of reality, you are One Whole Body, One Whole People.

Every person in your collective holds an essence inherent to their wheat. They simply may not yet be in the place where they are ready to realize it. Shaming them is not the solution, for that only contributes to the unhealthy separation. The resolution is found through holding the Light for others as you would have others hold the Light for you.

The wheat is reality—that is the only Truth. There is no your Truth or another's Truth. There is only God's Truth. The rest is subjective and relegated to the basis of your limited opinions and perceptions. The chaff, while it is real, is a fragment of self—it is the dreaming. You are the dreamer. The greatest dreamers are able to become conscious of their ability to command the dream around them. The dreamers have the ability, through Stillness, to shift the dreaming around them through honesty, compassion, service, devotion, competence, discipline, and the ability to be resilient within change without denying the emotional process.

Victims will not thrive in the energy of this time. Thus, you must transcend that unconsciousness. You, as humans, are not in dominance anymore. Gaia is, the Divine is, your Soul is, as is the true Soul of the collective. Trying to will what is not in alignment for you, assuming you know what is best for the world, or wallowing in self-pity and blame will not bring you closer to the Truth. Love, honesty, and transparency will.

Your soul is all about, your wheat is all about creating from the space, consciousness, and Presence of the Witness, the Dreamer. I Witness you as you continuously evolve, refine, expand, emerge, and grow. As you do, so does God. I Pray you will be deeply excited to learn that as you evolve, so too does God. You are in a co-creative partnership with the Divine at all times.

While I will not go into too much detail at this time, this co-creative partnership and evolution with the Divine is deeply important to draw into your awareness. God, consciousness, is Transcendent, Immanent, and Emergent all at once. As you awaken and begin to dissolve the Veils, as well as your construct of self or chaff-identity, suddenly consciousness, God, Light streams, weaves, and rises from within you and flows out from you into the world.

That is the realization, essence, and Emergence of your Yeshua self. Through Presence, you inform and evolve consciousness, God, as consciousness, God, informs and evolves you. You become an anchor and holder of the Light on Earth, evolving and awakening the Light within others through the service of your Presence. You hold the Light as the Light holds you in intimacy, Peace, communion, and unconditional Love.

Those on your planet who are in authentic Emergence, Presence, and embodiment of their Yeshua selves, God selves are even able to bring awareness and Presence into the space between soul and spirit. Their awareness is so anchored in the present that they are able to create more and more space between thoughts. Not so many thoughts. Not so many distortions. Not so many fears. Not even so many emotions that provoke them. Because there is a consistency of flow, of breath, and they keep things simple. Thus, their wheat is very nourishing to the whole of the collective. Their wheat is what nourishes your needs even if you never come to know them. Those I speak of are those in true lives of service. They are at Peace with themselves. They are astoundingly wise, intuitive, humble, and powerful in the most unassuming of ways. It is magnetic and majestic to sit in the Presence of those at Peace with themselves. They are your greatest guides. Though it is unlikely you will find them in spaces of self-promotion and aggrandizement of their gifts. You will call them to you as you need them. And they will call to you through the Spirit of the Web of Life.

The more you accept in Peace, engage in Peace, the more your needs will be met through the goodness and the bounty of whatever vines, whatever ecosystem, you are consuming from and giving to at once.

The wheat is your need. Thus, the more you bring consciousness to and release your attachment to the thought forms that indoctrinate you, including your opinions, which spin you up in a web so tight that you are as blinded as a fly wrapped in web, the more your unmet need for Peace is met. Thought forms, fear prisons, even ideas, Beloved One, do not always come from you. As a matter of fact, they very rarely do. Thought forms, including yours, are not your original thoughts. Many are fed to you or manipulated by outside influences.

All that is truly original is aware of its Source. All that is unoriginal is not aware of its Source. If you wish to be original, as I designed you to be, you must be aware of your Source, which is consciousness, which is God. Anything else may create progress but never true evolution of consciousness in this world or any other reality.

When you choose unoriginal hand-me-down thought forms, fear prisons, or thought bubbles and build a life around them, you will never truly know your creative power. Original thought and original God-anointed mantles come through slow evolution, gestation, and birthing of something from the realm, the space, the Void of infinite possibilities. You pluck a possibility, an original idea or concept, stitch to it, gestate it, and, when ready, it comes to your awareness, it reveals. Your heart Lights and then your mind takes whatever this seed, this concept, is, and it begins to move it into realization and manifestation. That is original creation—that does not come from form—it comes from the space of Spirit, from the wheat, and flows outward into the world.

Sadly, even when something original flows from the realm of endless possibilities, when the awareness of a concept comes to your mind, your mind immediately wants to grab it and jam it into an utterly unoriginal structure. Structures can adhere to norms, but authentic creativity merits authentic structures. There is an overwhelming lack of originality in your world, which is one of the reasons We are shaking things up a bit. To get you out of the rut of complacency and into the realm of Divine co-creation and originality.

If you wish to be original, instead of striving for the macro, the more and more, the glistening of fame and power, first strive for less and less. Refine your message, concept, expectations, and the true essence of your service. With patience and allowing, you will be well on your way. The structure that is simple, original, and fulfilling of unmet needs instead of filling your ego's wants will reveal itself naturally from there. That is true Divine originality manifest within you.

The majority of the fear-based, repressive, suppressive, oppressive thought forms, fear prisons that attach to your spirit body and slide into your heart, mind, and soul without your awareness come from the outside. They float like little poisoned seeds, shadow threads, and attach to you. If you do not have an inner process of discernment, awareness, witnessing, and taking healthy separation/space from the "yours and mine," it can poison you with doubt, which then leads to distortions, reactions, and the administration of the poison to others, like a virus infecting a host. For example, a friend loses a child, or you read a story of someone somewhere who lost a child, and immediately the fear prison is "This could happen to me." Which leads to paranoia and stifling your own child's Freedom in a way that creates imbalance and harm.

Thought forms become larger as the poison spreads to more and more people. For example, when one person projects blame onto another person and group of people and others join in, there is a pooling of hatred or judgment that comes. The cross and burden of the poison just continues to spread as it is fed. Deep suffering comes as a result in a way that affects many people.

On a personal level, as I have said, these fear prisons and thought forms provoke your emotions, hormones, and bodies in a way that causes emotional imbalances and even disease. They are suffocating. When you cannot unstitch from thoughts and feelings such as sadness, fear, and anger, it usually means there is a thought construct or fear bubble lurking. That is completely normal, and all human be-ings struggle with such things. However, I am speaking of this to Hold the Light for you to bring awareness to this. Awareness and willingness to explore with curiosity how these thought forms come to reside within you is essential. You are also the only one that can transcend them. How they came in, when, and from whom is irrelevant.

Awareness is the first step to transforming and rebalancing the mind so that you can live a life that is not about living exclusively in a chaff-based material world, but about allowing the wheat to naturally move the chaff into Balance inherent to its authentic design. If we designed you each to be the same there would be a billion people, all the same person. Each of you was designed in originality. Please return the favor to Us by honoring the incredible gift of your original self. Your originality is not more special than another's. Those seeking to be special or who consider themselves special are actually quite ordinary and uninteresting. Seek to be yourself. For you are an original. Not to kiss My shoulder, but I find each of you to be My greatest masterpiece. You realize that when you master Peace within yourself.

Thought bubbles and fear prisons have far more power over you the more that you feed them through your worry, panic, dissatisfaction, ingratitude, rage, and desire to control. They keep you out of the Present and in the future. Obsessing about the future, trying to control the future. Ironically, a future dictated by the past. Or they keep you in the past, constantly tallying up the score of rights and wrongs done to you, when rarely do you think about the rights and wrongs you have done unto others.

When you are not present, you are nothing more than thought forms and thought bubbles. Which leaves you in doubt, panic, and worry more often than not. That is what creates much of the exhaustion for you. These prisons leave you in the dark of unconsciousness because, within them, you are not employing your God-given Right to consciously create and destroy what serves you and does not in your internal reality—or your external reality, for that matter. You are a fly in the Web of Life, instead of the glorious spider you are, when you are not present. The present is where the power to Forgive, release, receive, dream, and connect is held.

I will tell you, My child, being out of the present is not a wise idea right now, because one of the many energies that can be a glorious gift—or a very massive burden when projected out of the present—is hope. Hope is a wonderful energy when it is in the present: "In this moment, I have hope that my friend feels better"; "In this moment, I am hopeful and full of hope for humanity." Hope can catalyze extraordinary healing and Balance when focused in the Now: "I have hope that even though this relationship is ending, all can be left in harmony, compassion, and kindness. I hope that we may always be grateful for the good times that we shared." In the present, hope is a beautiful expression of Grace and Presence, synonymous with Prayer.

You can recognize the moment that hope leaves the present and becomes knotted up in the past (*regrets*) or future (*wants*) when you hear or say such things as: "I hope this person will change for me."; "I hoped that I would have had more time."; "I had such hope when I was a child, and now look at what I am."; "I had hoped that things would have worked out better for me in my life." Oh, how I hold you and hold you through these moments.

However, Beloved, dead hopes, including regrets, are dead trees strapped to your back that weigh you down by the illusions of what could have or should have been instead of what is. True hope is of the Tree of Life and thus restores vitality, inspiration, and Light to your spirit through the present moment, present breath.

But when hope leaves the present and is projected into the future, it swiftly moves into its shadow form, which is expectation. The Divine gift of hope, in the present, comes through in Prayerful offerings such as, "I have hope for the best possible outcome for myself and for all . . ." There is a humility, allowing, Forgiveness, and recognition that all is already resolved inherent to a true offering of hope.

But when hope becomes about tomorrow or about want, it can become expectation. And expectations are very much utilized by even some of the suppressive forces of your world: "If you use this product, you will lose weight . . ."; "If you use this, you will be this . . ."; "If you buy this . . ."; If you do this . . ."; "If you hold your tongue and behave . . ."; "If you earn this amount of money, THEN you are worthy of Love, THEN you will be accepted, THEN you can focus on your Peace." When you place your hope in such false idols, you are in danger of the deep disappointment and violations of trust that come through projected expectations.

Some of that imbalanced hope can keep you overcommitted and very, very busy: "I hope that my business will work out; so I am going to cut corners and push hard . . ."; "I hope this relationship will work out, so I am going to change myself to be who my partner wants me to be" (before actually looking at whether the relationship is even stable, trustworthy, and in alignment). That is projected hope. **Projected hope is distorted hope.** It is placing yourself at the mercy of that which you cannot control by trying to control the direction of something. It is a very disempowering state that leads to tremendous disappointment when expectations are dashed.

What We hope, what I hope, as your Brother, as your Father, as your Friend, what I hope is regardless of what you are, have, or have not done—that you feel your worth; that you feel your Freedom. That you Forgive yourself and others no matter how much has occurred within your life or how much time you do or do not have left on your Earth. Every moment is new and every moment is yours to seize and reclaim for Peace, Forgiveness, Love, and authentic hope.

We hope that you will be yourself. I hope that you will separate from what everybody else wants you to be, or even what your mind wants you to be—so that you can be what you need to be, which is the wheat that you are.

Do you *hope* that God is with you or *know* that God is with you?

Sit with that question. As there is a profound Rite of Passage that comes through the movement of that question. It is the question that moves you from personal identity to Transcendence, wheat-identity. When you know, to the depths of your be-ing, that God is with and within you, it is easy to hold hope in the present and release all expectations, for you have all you need, which is God. Within the Light, all things are possible.

I present this question to you because this year, and in the ensuing years, if you hope instead of know that I am with you, you will experience increased internal and external divisiveness and discord. Your hopes prior to now were becoming arrogant and complacent: "I hope the neighbors won't show up to the potluck"; "I hope God punishes this person"; "I hope society repudiates that person"; "I hope I get my new iPhone this year." Distortion. Imbalance.

God does not serve egoic imbalance. Thus, we are now serving you with what you need to restore your hope its true Divine Essence, which is rooted in Grace, compassion, and sincerity. "I hope I get to see the neighbors this year, I hope they are okay"; "I hope God is with this ill person and his or her family"; "I hope society recognizes this kind person"; "I hope I get to go on the fishing trip with the kids this year or see my family for Thanksgiving, but if I cannot, I hope we will all be healthy and happy." That is hope. Hope in kindness and Love.

We needed to begin the process of deconstruction over the past years of Voids so that you could reclaim the gift of hope from your expectations and utilize it to amplify your Prayer, your kindness, your Faith. Choose the hope that flows from Faith. When hope becomes a Prayer for joy, not just for you, but for all, the Earth moves. And you move Me deeply in those moments. Sancti. Pace. Amein.

2

....

Sacred Seeds

YESHUA TEACHING

Beloved one, to separate the wheat from the chaff between your ego distortions and the strength of the Light within you, long ago I structured a circuit breaker to trip when you move too far out of Balance. A circuit breaker for you as an individual. And a circuit breaker for your collective. The circuit has tripped over the past few years. As I knew it would and structured it to.

Thus, during this time, the lack of Simplicity, Stability, Surrender, and Stillness in your world led to numerous revelations of unsustainability. More are to come. More has died in your world than you could know at this time.

The circuit breakers I created for 2020 and beyond were a series of three Voids. Each year the Voids will be different. But the foundations of the Voids will be the same.

Now, the very first thing that human be-ings often do when they hear the word *Void* is begin to panic. Thus, I will make it very clear that a Void is not to be feared. A Void opens your eyes to what is beyond matter and form (the chaff). Your external reality, the seen, is not where the magic is. That is not where the Freedom is. Your Freedom is in the wheat, the unseen, the detachment from the form reality. A Void has the power to open your eyes to that Truth.

A Void is a period in which many expectations and assumptions are leveled. It is a period of a bit of chaos or change that comes to restore order and Truth to your life. It is a period of closing out the old and exploring the new. It is a time of deconstruction ensued by re-Genesis. In a Void, you are in the womb; you cannot see. If you try to fight or rush through a Void in order to see, you will struggle and the Void will persist longer. It is a rare few who are deep in consciousness that transcend the uncertainty of the Void to harness its infinite potential for rebirth. A Void can keep you in an endless dark night of the soul if you avoid the process of death and rebirth. But when you employ a Void it allows you to Resurrect to the natural origin of your consciousness, your true reality. Thereby, manifestation becomes more organic, fulfilling, and true to your authentic essence.

A Void is a time to push off from old shores, safety zones, comforts, escapes, and illusory hopes to allow for your spirit to create the path for new possibilities. A Void is an unknown space of destruction and deconstruction to make space for conscious creation. To move beyond it requires a period of humility, courage, and Faith as you move through the rapid evolution and change that can come as a by-product.

Often though certainly not always, women tend to do a bit better in Voids, as they are more used to more regular physical cycles of destruction and creation. Very generally speaking, they also have deeper attunement to emotions and intuition. Men generally though certainly not always have a more difficult time through Voids, for they prefer action, progress, putting aside emotion to reason through issues, and conquering unknowns through solutions. Voids are not times of solving. They are times of gestating, and resolving. This is true of the Masculine and Feminine Divine within you. Masculine wants to create order of something that has no order during a Void. This can create frustration. Voids are Feminine, womb-like periods that need to be Surrendered to, not thought through. There can be the feeling of help-lessness in a Void, like a dark night and you the child lying in a manger.

But there is a great star, a great rainbow that comes from the Void: Balance, Radial balance. Realignment. This is the reason that your individual Voids or dark nights of the soul are invaluable to you. They dismantle and bring death to old ways and beliefs no longer serving you so that you may explore and Resurrect into new ways of be-ing, more aligned with your Divine self *as you are now*. In a Void, descent, or death, the mind wants to control. And you have to let go of the questions. To find the answers within the questions. You as human be-ings are far more resilient and malleable in change than you know. Your ability to grieve, destroy and then swiftly move into rebirth, cre-ation is more robust than you could know (provided you do not skip over the processing of grief).

This is why Voids are to be embraced. Fighting a Void or wallow-ing in a Void will cause further despair and anger. It is like swinging punches when blind at an enemy that is not there. Your mind just thinks it is. Allowing for the Void and reaching for the star within it, Frees you to utilize it for what it is . . . a period of death and rebirth into Balance and Peace.

The Voids that have come over the past years are not individual Voids but collective Voids, meaning you all are going through them to-gether. Thus, you all need to have a bit more humility and compassion for each other. You have all been through individual Voids and know how hard that is. Raging at your brothers and sisters who are going through the same with you does not help anyone. In fact, you need each other more than ever to transcend these cycles.

While the Void is just One Void, as God is One God, different lenses of the Void are expressing at different times. The Voids of 2020 were particularly polarized, each peak a bit taller, each trough a bit shorter in between the next wave. The Voids of the ensuing years are longer, slower, more rolling, each one of deeper focus. **The theme of the next years and decades on your Earth is: You reap what you sow.** Thus, tuning into the Voids and harnessing the gifts of each of them to plant the seeds you are designed to plant and activate is essential. Each of you will need to answer to what seeds you plant. And you will be held accountable for what seeds you plant. We are giving you the opportunity to move back into Balance and Simplicity through this period.

So, the three Braids weaving and unweaving, the three Seeds of the three Voids of your present year and next years, Offer you an important choice in every experience of your life, a choice you will need to answer to in times to come: Will I plant a seed of poison through blame and projection? Or will I plant a seed of Light and kindness?

You need not be perfect in this process. However, you must be aware. You are moving toward deeper connection to the Tree of Life. To get there, you must move through the choices of Free will that you all became accountable for when eating the "forbidden fruit" from the Tree of the Wisdom of Light and shadow. The choices to realign and re-enter the Garden, even to co-create and evolve the Garden, are before you now, right now. This time is what you have been preparing for over lifetimes. This time and these choices are why you have come to body at this shift from the old Era to the new. Thus let me specify the three lenses of the Void:

The first Void you have and will collectively experience is a choice of Faith over fear. It came in its first pass-through in March of 2020. **It was and is an opportunity for you all to find your Faith.** That was and is the gift of the first Void, the first Magi. Some chose to take that opportunity to say, "I don't know what will happen for this world, why this is happening, but I do know that I am Divine. I am going to separate from the panic and the fear and I am going to use this as an opportunity to move more deeply into my Faith . . ." Others chose to stay on the old shore of the worry, and the fear, and the separation, the primal animal self of "getting mine" to the detriment of others. This Void will still ripple through in decades to come because, as always, We give you many chances to shift in consciousness.

The second Void of 2020 came at the end of June, though it will emerge within your collective at varying points for decades to come. This Void was ultimately about releasing the energy of betrayal and blame. Those choosing blaming and shaming others for things that happened one hundred years ago or those pleading the victim did not or are not utilizing this Void to the fullness of its potential. And will carry the burden of that in times to come.

This second Void is the Void that brings you to the heart of the power of Forgiveness—Forgiveness of self, Forgiveness of others. Only Forgiveness places you in ascendance to and Transcendence from the shame and blame of the past. The second Void means detaching from old traumas and stories. It is letting go of the anger to process and release your grief. What that makes space and room for is Love. And liberation.

For those choosing Love and releasing the egoic entitlement and burden of blame, the second Void unstitches you from many strings and chains of love-nots. It realigns you with Freedom, kindness, and Grace. The second Void is very much about the choice to realign your will with Divine Will by letting go of the sticks and stones. It is also a choice as to what you wish to weave, braid, and stitch to by way of commitments. This is why I cautioned you about your commitments. Very often, things that are planned and committed to during Voids, if they are not in alignment, will quickly be unplanned. Or will cause considerable stress and burden.

The second Void is an exploring and reassessing as you continue to raise your vibration. For every moment you choose Forgiveness over the grievances and distortions of perception of the past, including "trauma identity," this Void gives you what you need to weave and braid yourself into Balance and communion. You will need to be patient through that process. Your soul is unstitching from the old, stitching you to the new, and is exploring that process.

The second Void was and is the choice of Forgiveness over blame. No longer projecting responsibility and shame upon the other.

Those busy blaming and shaming AND those who cater to it in fear-based guilt for things they did not do plant the seeds of dissonance and illusion. Those who Forgive or ask for Forgiveness plant the seeds of Loving Truth. In the upcoming Era of "you reap what you sow" such choices are witnessed by your soul, the collective consciousness, and the Divine. And you will answer to them. Thus, choose wisely, Beloved One.

The third Void is the deepest yet. The first Void is an opportunity to heal, mend, and rebalance. The second Void is an opportunity to release, restore, and resolve. The third Void is an opportunity for liberation, Redemption, and revelation of your authentic essence.

Before I speak of the third Void, I will add the asterisk of Bethlehem that the choices of the third Void are more finite for you as a collective. While there will be several Voids individually and collectively over the ensuing decades, in the death of the old Era and birth of the new, the choices that you make will be set in stone in times to come. You are the Ones in bodies who are setting the energetic imprints for the new Era.

The Void years or periods are a Resurrection Gateway. A Void IS the reweaving of the Holy Spirit through your Spirit, your authentic self. A Void is a time of death, and from that death comes a Resurrection of your Divine essence and Presence.

2020 and all years to come are, again, collective Voids, meaning that the Voids are occurring on more of a mass level as more souls are choosing to become conscious. As more become conscious, there is always more pronouncement of separation between the unconscious and conscious. Those are the polarities, healthy polarities I set when I descended into the Earth to Resurrect back into My Truth as Divine Father.

Those creating division or judging under that banner of martyrdom are not honoring the humility and gratitude necessary to rise and grow from the Void. That is dishonoring self, others, and God. It is stitching to heavy love-nots that perpetuate unconsciousness and burdens. When Voids come to unburden and awaken consciousness. Martyrdom does not work in the Void, especially not the three lenses of the Voids I am calling forth. Martyrdom is an old Era dynamic seeded with guilt, indoctrination, and self-righteousness, and does not have a place in the new Era or in the Garden. The more you resolve through Love and practice accountability, the more you will contribute to conscious creation of aligned change through the Rebirth from the Void into the new Era.

I, Divine Father, Yeshua, speak for All of the Divine when I say, We stand for Balance and harmony with all be-ings accounted for no matter their level of consciousness or unconsciousness. If you choose consciousness you are simply choosing a life of Freedom, of service, of Grace. That does not mean We Love you more or less than another.

The third Void is a wonderful opportunity for transparency and awareness. However, it has and will feel very, very dense for many who have not gone through their process of Faith or Forgiveness and are still choosing imbalanced separation. They will eventually break under the weight of that hatred and blame because who has to carry that burden? They do. Or you do if you indulge in the same energies. That does not mean allowing for another to ransack your Peace. But it does mean utilizing every opportunity to resolve in a way of Balance instead of repudiation.

Engage with the active, lucid energy of Peace. Hold the Light. Hold the Light. The third Void is one of active engagement with and allowing for the energy of the Sacred Heart—Simplicity, Stability, Surrender, and Stillness—to be restored to your be-ing and life. It is yours to embrace. Know that whenever you do, I am embracing you through My Sacred Heart. And holding your hand.

The third Void is a choice of Freedom over Suppression. It is an opportunity for you to move into the Truth of Freedom. Freedom from expectations. Freedom within body for as long as you are in one. Freedom from the confines of anxiety, unworthiness, victimhood, and allowance of imbalanced structures to govern your life, including sex, money, power, substances, and technology. The third Void will conjure up all of the ways you have been suppressed. It will be tempting to blame others for that or even societal structures. But you cannot transcend this third Void without taking personal accountability for the ways you have suppressed yourself. For this third Void represents the shift from "transcending" to living in actual Transcendence.

I am opening and unleashing the Seal of Freedom from suppression to hold you accountable for participating in your Freedom. Through all I bring to you at this time, I am supporting your Freedom from fear prisons, suppressive relationships, and the dense energies that I have spoken of in the past: addictions, behavioral impulsivity, cigarettes, too much alcohol, too much caffeine, social media, technology, money fixation, internalization, self-pity, defensiveness. Thus, you must allow for My support as you unstitch from these love-nots.

Other forms of neutral exchange of energy will be weaving in, far beyond the currencies you once used or use now. In your focus on money, sex, power, and technology, you have forgotten the other forms of exchange that I am bringing to rebalance these suppressive structures, such as kindness, humility, and integrity. Kindness, humility, and integrity are a currency that often gets lost in your world. Rewards through offering the service of kindness, integrity, allowing, compassion, listening over speaking, and gratitude will be infinite. New systems will be structured that are more embracing of these energies. Perhaps you will be one of the Ones who plucks from the infinite possibilities to move these more Balanced systems of reciprocity forward.

There will be great abundance and great clarity that comes for those who plant these seeds and weave these Braids now and in years to come—forever, really. Freedom. Faith. Forgiveness. That is your flight, your flow, your path, your Braid. The energy of the Peace that comes through this Trinity of Light is the Great Peace, the Yeshua Peace, that sets you Free, as well as many of those who come to know your Presence.

Honoring these three energies conjured from the three Voids—Faith over fear, Forgiveness over blame, Freedom over Suppression—IS the giving over of the burdens and crosses. Choosing the Light within the Void of these three energies IS the unstitching from the distortions of the illusion self or imbalanced identity construct. It is even the unstitching from the distortions of the illusion Yeshua—the Yeshua that is your thought construct of who I am instead of what I really AM. Which is Consciousness—the root, Logos, Word, Creator, and Light of all that is, including your own authentic self, your Yeshua self.

The Truth of the true stitching, weaving, and braiding that is your essence in this world, in this body, in this heart, in this mind, will be revealing itself more and more. The Voids are simply here to reveal what is in the shadow so that you can embrace it, integrate it, and hold all parts of self as Sacred. So that your soul is Free to roam and explore the extraordinary experience of spirit AND sensory perception for as long as it is in a body.

Your true self, when present, not only hopes for the good of all but has Faith in the good of all, serves the good of all, and Forgives those stumbling to find their way through their trespasses. For you, at one time or another, have trespassed too. It is easy to have Faith and Forgive when the soul is Free, which is why exploring the Voids that led you here is such an essential.

What the soul truly hopes for the most, in the present, is to come Home to wholeness and Oneness. To Redemption. To Grace. To realization of Peace. That is Freedom. To Pray that for another, all others, without picking and choosing who and how—that is Grace. **Grace is the echo of your Spirit upon the Web of Life.** When you are at Peace, you echo Peace from your radial center and connect to the wheat and Peace of all be-ings, even if they are still lost in the chaff. That is holding the Light and anchoring My Peace.

The Free soul is so in Love with its humble Divinity that it is wise in the experience of self as Love, as the Divine, as Eternal Life. That Love is Power beyond power. That Love simply hopes and has Faith that others will set down their armor to be able to receive and give Love in equality. Which means that, prior to seeding others with the power of this Love, the Free soul has to set down his or her own armor, crosses, and burdens first.

The Free soul holds the Light, has compassion, and hopes and Prays for the opportunity, whether others take it or not, to offer them that Light. That is a wonderful service, Beloved One. Do not take it personally if others do not want to take you up on that. The importance is that you offered and that served them well enough, just in the offer itself.

There is no mastery or expectation within the Void. A Void is just a period in which those choosing to internally and externally Braid to the energy of Faith over fear, Forgiveness over blame, and Freedom over suppression have a unique gateway. One that is available now, but the first of you to cross through it are the pioneers shepherding all others. Not as sheep. But as My Shepherds holding the Light for both the lambs and those ready to become shepherds. As I am yours.

No expectations or timelines factor here, for I exist in a timeless space. There is no time inherent to consciousness. As such, I have endless patience because I do not answer to time. I have no Body now but the one you offer to me through your own. I have no expectations of you and would encourage you not to hold any for yourself.

With regard to expectations, even in My human Life, I had none. When I would go to a city, in that moment, I hoped that the people would receive My Love, Blessings, or Words. Or even that they would be kind. I certainly did not expect them to be. Thus, I was never disappointed, nor did I struggle with regret. Even in Body, I lived in the present, in a space of consciousness outside of time, which made patience quite easy.

If I was not wanted in a town, My Mother was not wanted, My Friends were not wanted, We simply went elsewhere. No judgment, no animosity, no grief—it was all right. Sisters and brothers, sons and daughters are family, are blood, even if they are not related. I Loved those who embraced and those who rejected equally. I was not interested in getting people on board with My essence and Offerings. I was interested in the Seeds I could and did plant in each place I went, even if just through the vibration of the Land and Earth.

The Seeds that I planted in these cities and towns were important ones, Seeds that rippled throughout the Earth. The Seed of Truth. The Seed of Love. The Seed of Peace. A passionate Peace. A gateway to Faith, a bridge to Forgiveness, a path to Freedom. In My Life, I did not need to win others over or force Myself upon them with assertion or dominance. I simply Loved them even if they did not Love me. If they did not, it was because they judged. I came in humility to them, I left in Peace, and did not need to see the outcome. As God, I already see the outcome of what one simple Seed of Peace can provide. It is Free to plant and limitless in value. That is the wheat. The wheat grows. The chaff endures. Faith grows. Hope endures.

Movement to the Seed of Faith requires Forgiveness and Freedom. Movement to the Seed of Forgiveness requires Faith and Freedom. Forgiveness is one of the most difficult Seeds to choose; to choose it means facing the judge within self. The Divine does not judge, We Witness. We hold the Light; We do not Judge Our own children. We rebalance them; We allow for them to make their own choices to be separate or come back Home. But We do not Judge. You do. Thus it is you who must face your own judge to Forgive.

Movement to the Seed of Freedom requires Faith and Forgiveness. Faith and Forgiveness set you Free. When someone has Faith in you, it Frees you. When someone Forgives you, it Frees you. That is what WE do. We designed you, built into you, a constant energy that is your unwavering flame, your fixed star—Faith. It is anointed unto you through My Faith in you for as long as you are in a body. We Forgive you when no one else will. It sets you Free to be as you are, to trust in what is, not what should be according to your mind.

Forgiveness is a process, Beloved One. It is the progression of Freedom. An evolution. Do not try to force Forgiveness or the resentment will remain and poison you further. Even if you Forgive someone, or that person Forgives you, if there is still unresolved energy or stitches at a deeper core of the spiral of self, those will surface eventually.

Some of these wounds, these love-nots that tie you up or cause emotional triggering and pain, are not only things that you have carried in this life, they are carried from past experiences, including imbalances in ancestral patterns and karma. Forgiveness is an inner process. Do not make it about the external world, and do not offer Forgiveness until you feel it deeply in your heart. And, please, stop apologizing for things you are not sorry for, nor should you be.

Certainly, do not react impulsively to anything right now, even if something triggers you. First take space. Do not say a word to another, do not commit to another thing, unless you are completely at Peace with it first. Do not hurtle into opinions and throwing of swords through the lashing of tongues in the form of judgment and projection. Do not break and throw away a string of a connection if something is provoking you, perhaps an old resentment or feeling overwhelmed, lost, alone, or out of control. Right now, listen, pause, wait before making choices you will later regret. If you make a choice that causes guilt and regret, immediately revisit the Sacred space within to realign and replant a Seed of Light.

Reacting from resentment almost always leads to regret—that

is the pain cycle. Of all the things in that cycle of resentment, reaction, and regret flaring everywhere in your world, judgment is the
hardest. And hatred. The heaviest crosses are those that come when
you have structured an expectation of another(s), the expectation is
not met, and then a perceived disappointment or lack of reciprocity
comes—meaning a trust violation to your own assumption occurs.
This generates a feeling of resentment within you. If that resentment
is repressed—left unhealed and unheard—it festers. Whether it is one
tiny event or one big one that triggers the rise of many repressed resentments, a rage can flow through, almost a total loss of self-control
that results in a reaction, often one of projection and impulsivity.

That suppressed aspect of self, an unloved part of self that was
once in the dark recesses of the subconscious, floods to the surface. As
it rises, it is easy to react with rage to the outer. This can lead to the
words and actions that later settle into regret that can feel like heavy
guilt or despair. And the suppression cycle begins anew.

Rage is a violent eruption of a suppressed, fear-based, shamed,
and neglected part of self. That is why I chuckle when I hear you
all use the word *outrage*. Rage, OUT with you until I am out of rage!
Rage is one of those energies that can come out of the closet like a
banshee in the night. When it is acted upon, especially when groups
of people act upon it, war is created. Burdens are created for others and self through the reaction to that rage—that wrathful wisdom.
It is an abomination, a desecration to the garden of self and other.
Wrathful wisdom, greed, desire, distortions, and projections onto others you do not know increase and contribute to unhealthy separation
because they are bound to thought forms. They bind you tightly to the
chaff. Rage, when channeled in conscious, constructive ways rooted in
Faith, Forgiveness, and Love, can Free you from the cycle.

Faith, Forgiveness, and Freedom are the new Divine interven-
tions. Right now, and over the next periods in your world, compassion
and humility are the two most central energies to this process of ex-

ploration as you complete the third Void and move into the next Voids, opened seals, and periods of illumination.

Forgiveness is a process. Faith is a process. Freedom is a process. That process can take an instant or many lifetimes. The planting, weaving, and Braiding of these energies is a Miracle in My Eyes. As you Braid them, not only can Miracles come, but you become the Miracle.

I wish to focus for a moment on Faith. The mind does something humorous with Faith. What the mind likes to do in its limited consciousness is to doubt in some things yet have Faith in others. It has a limited focus that skews either more toward doubt or toward Faith at various times. However, both exist simultaneously at all times. While Faith does not have a shadow form, trust is an essential component of and stepping-stone to and from Faith. Doubt is trust in its shadow form. Thus, doubt and Faith are always also co-existent.

Interestingly, Faith and reason are also co-existent AND co-creative. For example, nearly every scientist who has developed a new approach to science or medicine has needed to take an intuitive leap of Faith to move the concept forward. The concept may have come from deductive logic but the courage to bring forth or even see something new requires Faith. Faith is required for anything truly original even when a concept requires an empirical model to prove its scientific validity. Scientists, doctors, and scholars who tend to dismiss Faith the most actually borrow from Faith every day. This is all to say, Faith is universal, just as doubt is universal, and even scientific advancement is not possible without Faith. Nor is evolution or real sustainable progress.

It is quite amusing to Me that you are only a few centuries into your "deeper understanding" of science and yet many of you already have the hubris to say, "Well, 'God,' we've figured out Your secrets now. We 'got this' so we don't need to believe in You anymore." That is actually true in some ways. You do not need to believe in "God," especially not a "God" confined to anthropomorphic representations. But you do need Faith in the origin of what made and makes your reality, including science, possible in the first place. The Source that exists far beyond the proofs, theories, and math of creation and yet is the very essence and Logos of them. The Source that evolves and upholds them. The Source beyond your fragmented lens of "reality." That Source is God, consciousness, Spirit. You need your Source, God, just as your Source needs you.

Your ancestors, despite your judgment of their "primitive" ways, understood this far more than you. Even your children understand this far more than you. Science is not only a God-send, it is the Divine structure created and upheld in ways within and far beyond the physical realm. Meaning that science was "sent" by God, created by God, the God, the consciousness, that you are of and One with, which it would behoove you to remember. You would never have become conscious of science, self, or God in the first place were it not for the consciousness afforded to you in your creation and evolution—mentally, emotionally, energetically, and physically. Science can get you some of the way but you will never fully realize what it is that you are seeking without having the humility to discover and consciously receive from the very Source that made and makes discovery possible. Which is not just the mind, it is the soul, the wheat, the Light that exists within and beyond you and your current perception of reality.

The mind is limited and in linear time. The soul is not. To the soul, all is known and seen. To the mind, in the unknowns and what you are not conscious of, which is almost everything, much is unseen. Thus, as long as you are in a body you will always have doubt about some things, especially in your inability to know what is coming.

The mind does not like the Void even though you are actually always in the Void, the womb of the world and of God, evolving, growing. The mind does not like the unknown, so what it likes to do is focus on the areas of doubt instead of the areas of Faith in your life. Again, even if you doubt that there is a "higher power"—that I AM real, that you are real, that the Light is real, that you have consciousness—you do have Faith in other things.

If you have Faith in some things, which you always do, that means that there is Faith somewhere. As long as there is doubt somewhere, there is Faith there too, just waiting to be revealed. The mind just doubts and wants its proof, proof, proof. When in Faith, you no longer need proof, because though you may not know what is going to happen, you have Faith in whatever is in the Now.

Faith, trust, and doubt co-existent and interdependent. They serve you well. The higher that you raise your vibration and bring consciousness and awareness through separation of chaff-self from wheat-self, suddenly trust grows and Faith is everywhere . . . and the doubt is very, very small, almost unnoticeable, negligible. You come to almost an automatic Peace when you simply rest in Faith, which includes allowing and embracing the unknown. The unknown isn't doubt. Doubting the unknown is. That is a distortion of the mind rooted in control.

You do not get to pick and choose, Beloved One. If you have Faith in some things, which you do, you are a person of Faith. You have Faith that your lungs will breathe. You have Faith that when you wake up in the morning and look down at your hands, your hands will be there. That when you go to look in the mirror, your face will look somewhat the same as it did yesterday. Having Faith is different from embodying Faith. If you can have Faith, that means you can be IN and OF Faith. If you have Faith, that means that you can BE Faith.

As I said, Faith is illuminated through deeper creation and cultivation of trust. Trust grows and builds into the deeper realization of Faith. Trusting another, trusting self, the exploration of trust and the structures of trust within your life creates a Faith on the inner that is never built on the external. You can have trust in a person, you can have Faith in a person, but you cannot BE Faith for a person. You can mirror it to others, hold it for them, inspire it within them, but you cannot be their Faith. Have the humility to recognize this.

Trust is an energy designed for you to grow your Faith internally. Thus, allowing violations of trust to chip at your Faith is not possible when you are truly in Faith. A betrayal or loss is never meant to cast you into self-doubt, even if it can feel that way. It is a gift to strengthen your Faith. As Judas's betrayal strengthened My Faith despite a violation of trust.

Ask yourself, Beloved, what do you have Faith in? Forgiveness takes Faith because it is sometimes an unknown. You need Faith, **the recognition of your Divinity,** to have Forgiveness for a person who just burned down your house, raped you, or projected his or her traumas onto you, with or without even knowing you.

When you have Faith, you are aligned in humility with Divine Justice; you are aligned in your service as a shepherd of God. When you Forgive or let go, you serve God as I Served you.

For you are in For-giving-ness. The state of: "For I am giving this unto God, as an act of service through Love." Forgiveness is a pardoning of self and other all at once. You are giving an issue, a burden, a violated boundary, a negation of your worth, over to God. This relieves the crosses and burdens.

"For I give Love to God, Creator, and All Creation" is the mantra of Forgiveness. It is a mercy and deep kindness. You all say you wish to serve. If you do, Forgive yourself and others. That is a giving of Love. That is hearing, receiving, and delivering THE Word through Prayer and action. *that* is the rock of unwavering Faith that is the greatest to stand upon.

Forgiveness is never self-righteous, nor is Faith. Anointing your Forgiveness on others when you were the one in distortion is foolish wisdom and ego. Demanding apologies is an equal abomination. When you are in Oneness, in wheat, you do not need an apology and there is nothing to Forgive. For the wheat cannot suffer the burns of the chaff. Do not expect apologies. You are not entitled to them nor is another entitled to one from you. We do not expect apologies, thus why should you? I Forgive you even the deepest of imbalances immediately when you present them to Me with honesty, humility, and transparency.

Thus, your Yeshua self, if you wish to realize it, must offer and extend the same Forgiveness to others that I Offer and extend to you. When you do not need your justice in the form of apologies from the external to make you right and others wrong, and trust in God to Balance it all out for all of you in the end, you are in deep service. A service that others might not see but I do. Let that be enough.

Forgiveness requires Faith. Thus, before you can move into Forgiveness, it is first important for you to look at what you have Faith in. Because sometimes, Faith even in your ability to breathe can save your life. When you are in Faith, no matter how dark things are, no matter what home, what Lover, what business you have just lost, the Faith is all that matters. When you are in Faith you know and feel, deeply, that you matter. That you are not OF matter, chaff alone—that you matter to the Divine. Faith is the embodiment of that recognition of the Divine and your own Divinity and worthiness. Thus, when you are in Faith you do not need to matter to the outside so much because you matter to yourself.

For those who Forgive and rest in Faith, to you I give My deepest Blessing.

If you can have Faith, if you are capable of Forgiveness, you have discovered the Freedom of Presence. For Faith is found in the now, the unseen. If you have Faith in self, you recognize self as Divine. If you are, then, should it not go hand-in-hand that all others are Divine too, whether they are aware of it or not? Be Faith in breath. Be Faith on Earth. Be Faith in Forgiveness. Within Faith you know your worth and feel not entitled, but deserving. Faith Lights the way and gives you the courage to face and undo the deepest of love-nots. Forgiveness weaves and braids you into a new web in a way honoring of Divine Freedom.

This is one of the central reasons why I, Yeshua, came to a body, to the chaff, and into the Presence of the extraordinary be-ings you are. Many then and now hoped that things would have worked out better for them in their lives.

I carried the Cross to strengthen their Faith and yours. The Faith that extends beyond the hope of Forgiveness and Freedom and into the realization of Them. I carried the Cross because I, God, Love you that much. As I said, it is My hope that you Love yourselves that much too. And Forgive self and others as the Divine Vine that you are in connecting to the Divine Vine that I AM.

I came to teach you how to walk in Faith, Forgiveness, and Freedom. Faith is Truth. **When you can accept the Truth, Forgive the past, and live in the present—you are Free.** The relationship with, and as, God is the key to the Garden, and not only seeking but finding then walking through the narrow gate. In this moment, if you have Faith in something, anything, even in your ability to breathe, the Love you have for Mother Earth, an animal, or another, that is all you need to know of Faith. It is a Holy Fire that dwells within you.

You are a Free soul, whether in body or out of body. The Free soul is your spider, weaving through your spirit upon the Web of Life.

Spiders are wonderful creatures, but when there are too many flies in a spider's web, too much clutter and debris, the web breaks and the spider falls. It takes a long time to build a web back for the larger of spiders. Thus, keep your webs clear, hearts clear of clutter and debris. It is as simple as exhaling, letting go, and holding My Hand.

Your Braid—Forgiveness, Freedom, and Faith—is your breath, your life. Weave with these energies and the tapestry of your life will be one of Balance and Grace. A shroud that keeps warm your fellow dreamers and blankets Gaia with gratitude and reverence.

Just as it took you time, and you needed moments—lifetimes—to realize this, plant seeds and allow others their journeys, as We allow you yours. Be patient with others and yourself. Have compassion. You must allow others their journeys, no matter where they are in their process. When, through their Free will, they wish to carry the old stitches, when they wish to be separate and close a door, as We allow you that—you must allow it for them too.

However, you can plant seeds in others and in the Earth as I did.

Faith is Truth. Forgiveness is Love. Faith is Truth. Forgiveness is Love. When the two of them unite, there is Peace. Peace is Presence. Peace is Freedom. I AM your Peace. Be at Peace, and you walk with Me, with God. That is the realization of your Divine essence of be-ing and passion. Anything but is a crime of passion. I AM and you are a passionate Peace. That is what we are together.

Draw a breath, Beloved One, because My next Words are very important to the process that will continue through these Transmissions, and, as you read or listen over the next moments, days, weeks, months, and years to come: I will be speaking to you, calling to you in your dreams, in your gardens. My voice will be clear and Presence felt within and around you every day more. For I am the Shroud that covers and holds you.

Aspects of the Seeds I AM planting within you, including in energy, will magnify the power of the Seeds you plant. This is the first gateway. You are the pioneers. While you may experience varying changes individually and as a world, be careful not to limit and narrow your perception. It will only lead to more doubt and frustration. All the changes coming are gifts. One of the greatest gifts will be the Miracle of Freedom you experience. Freedom and liberation from your burdens and doubt. You cannot choose wrong, Beloved, when you choose Faith, Forgiveness, and Freedom. Amein.

YESHUA MEDITATION

Close your eyes and begin to draw deep breaths of air and Light into your body. Letting go of the words, the thought forms, the concepts, the expectations, the hopes. Allow the feelings to come and go. Create space between the vibrations. Feel your root chakra, the knot of Love, grounding you to Gaia, your Mother Earth, who is experiencing this liberation with you.

Within this instant, separate not soul from body, but take space and separate the wheat from the chaff. Breathe first into your wheat. Feel the flow of Light weaving and braiding through you. Notice any areas that feel tense within your body. Or any thoughts or distractions drawing you out of the moment. Restore your awareness to your wheat, your Light.

Begin to weave that Light into places of Void or tensions within your body, within your life, that keep you shackled. Bound. Feel the weight, the chaff. Look at, conjure, the thoughts and the burdens, your stigmata, those who have hurt you, what you see as unjust, what angers you. Bring awareness to these areas, the behaviors, the addictions. Breathe into this space.

Your worries: your children, finances, health. The horror you perceive of your world—that these horrors could befall you. Conjure your worries and thoughts, the endless thoughts. The endless commitments. The stagnancy. The power struggles. The financial struggles. The struggle in sensual and sexual relationships in your life. Feel the density of that thread, like fishing wire.

With a breath, clamp your palms together in a fist. Clamp every muscle in your body with that tension: abdominals, mind, shoulders. All of those burdens contracting you. Shrink and crumble your shoulders down. Suck and coil inward.

Attempt to breathe in this space, to these thoughts, these feelings that you allow to consume you. Attempt to breathe. Continuing to contract and contract.

Then, with a deep inhale, now exhaaaale—let it all go. **Let it go!** Open your palms, allow your head to fall back, and all tension to leave your body. Head tilted back, feel the Light streaming into your throat, face, heart, palms. Breaking the threads and the chains.

Recite: *I am Faith. I am Forgiveness. I am Free.* Breathe. Allow the ribbons of My Braid to stream through you. If you can fall onto the floor, onto your knees, onto a bed, please do so. Rest in Savasana for a moment and listen:

It is My vow to Offer you your Freedom. But you must offer your burdens, your wants, imbalances in your web, to Me so that we may co-create a path of Faith, when you just so want to control. Let it go. A path of Forgiveness, when you so much want to scream about what you have known. Let it go. And Freedom, when you so much want to commit to or feel owned by suppressive structures including your own mind. Let it go.

Allow for the Free path through Truth, through Love, to stream through you. We, the Divine, I, Yeshua, will weave your needs into your Balanced web the more you come to Balance.

I wish for you to sit and breathe into this space, and several times more clench and unclench your palms.

When you are wearing armor, when you are in hate, or blame, you are a clenched palm. You are bound. Open your palm. Extend your palm in Prayer and let everything go. **When you can let something or someone go, you become one with it, and you become one with Me.**

After you have sat in meditation for another several moments, I would like you to place your forehead on the Earth or to place your hand or foot upon the Earth to ground your energy in Peaceful prostration.

It has been My honor to serve you on this day. Go in Peace, My Beloved. Om Nami Maia. Om Namah Sananda. Om Nami Yeshua. Sancti. Sancti. Sancti. Pace. Pace. Pace. Namaste.

TRANSMISSION 3

Belonging

1

....

The Servitude of Longing

YESHUA TEACHING

Beloved One, how wonderful it is to be with you again in this moment. Today, I wish to speak on a topic that is quite prevalent within your individual life, as well as in this world at this time. It is an energy that is quite interwoven within your external environment, as well as internal reality structure, including the society and culture in which you live. Thus, I wish to bring some consciousness and awareness into this energy to help further unstitch you, unthread you, unbraid you from the aspect of self that keeps you separate from who it is that you are: the wheat. And keeps you tightly bound to chaff-identity.

In this representation, the chaff-identity is your primal animal self, the fractured lens of the illusion self, and/or the "I" self—attached to form and thus biased toward fear. The "separate" or Judas self so bloated in self-absorption that the poor thing can barely see beyond the Veils and Imbalances. The part of self detached from the present and thus "reality." The fragment of the dreaming of the self that is histrionic, lugubrious, irritable, and recklessly prodigal despite its chosen state of residence: lack.

While it so longs to weave, braid, and flow, in its constant defensiveness and arrogance, all it really attends to is "getting mine." It does not care who it needs to step on to get its wants met. When it does not get what it wants, it blames the other and pleads victim. It abdicates responsibility for its own transformation. It craves purpose but not true service. For the way it wants purpose to come is limited and, though altruistic in intent, it wants it mainly for the purposes of acceptance, safety, conformity, and power within the outer world.

The chaff-self wants to decide, force, and control its purpose instead of allowing the wheat-self, the spirit, to guide the way in co-creation with the Divine and others. It is always in expectation and thus often so very wrought with dissatisfaction and disappointment. It dangles in the illusions of past and future, thus is always in want of more instead of resting in gratitude for what it already has, including the present moment. It craves connection and communion but does not look to God for such nourishment. God is not enough for the chaff-self. The chaff-self has little trust and even less Faith both in God and itself as a vessel for God in humility and compassion.

The wheat is the spirit self, the Divine self, the Yeshua self, the true self. It is not a part of self, it is the whole Presence of self in Holy Union. It is the self that chooses Love. That takes responsibility, that has compassion, and is not attached to its form identity. The self that follows the narrow gate and explores with creativity and curiosity. The self who knows its Truth and does not become upset when another does not see it.

The self that evolves and flows through, even welcomes, change with discernment and exploration. The self whose purpose IS God and thus serves from God. The self that honors its needs and fulfills its anointed purpose of serving unmet needs through its own unique, original essence within the world. It is humble, simple, pure, accepting, and kind. While it is gentle, it also commands the power of the Divine inherent to its conscious Divinity. Thus its infinite power is Balanced, for it emanates from Peace.

The chaff can bring you the joy of sensory perception to experience and evolve. But, when it is the dominant force governed by the mind, it binds you. And places you at the mercy of defining your worth by the standards of the outer instead of the inner.

To support you in your reclamation of your wheat-self, authentic self, over chaff-self, illusion self, the energy that I wish to utilize to do so and bring consciousness into today is: **belonging.**

Belonging.

Please take a moment to note, that I, We of the Divine, do not refer to you as the belong-ed. We refer to you as the Be-loved. That is a very specific distinction. We know and understand, Beloved One, that you wish to belong within your world. You wish to express yourself, and to share in relationships of intimacy, co-creation, reciprocity, and fluidity within your life.

You wish to belong—whether it is to your community, your land, your family, your Beloveds—or you wish for another to belong to you in your heart. However, when the energy of belonging becomes too mired in the external, in wanting to belong, in expectations and hope of belonging—to groups, to people, to energy, to things, to possessions that are not in alignment—this energy can keep you in an endless state of **being IN longing.**

Being In Longing. Wanting to belong and never being fulfilled. Seeking belonging and never finding it on a sustainable basis in your relationship structures. That is what it is to be in endless longing to fit in, be seen, be accepted, be honored. Being in longing is lack and, when you are in lack, the dissonance and self-absorption cloud everything in your perception and divide you from belonging to anything save your own wants and external seeking. Dissatisfaction, complaining, victimhood, and ingratitude are resounding when you seek to belong anywhere other than to God through the Light that you are.

Thus, it is important for you to distinguish what it is within the external that you are longing for, because that consciousness may shift in terms of what it is that you look for. And what it is that you weave, and braid, and stitch to or from as your transformation to Spirit evolves through awareness and allowing instead of the want for belonging.

I will tell you, Beloved One, that this energy of belonging, even in the essence of your belonging to another, of another's belonging to you, can be very dangerous, because belonging can easily become quite knotted up in the energy of **ownership.** When chaff-self governs, ownership is an energetic state mired in the weights and measures of comparing and competing, which begins an exhausting preoccupation with judgments surrounding your worth and that of others. That can stew into years of external seeking and, worse, relinquishing healthy ownership of your worth to another person, group of people, institution, or system to govern.

When you say "I wish to belong to this thing or person," be careful that you are not giving that person or thing the power to accept or reject you. Should they decide that they do not wish to belong to you, or do not wish you to belong to them, that can be internalized as an abandonment, rejection, or failure.

If the chaff-identity is dominant, the energy of belonging becomes imbalanced and your lens of self, other, and world becomes clouded. Your perception shifts away from seeing the wheat in all things and people, including self, as equal in worth, and shifts toward the creation of biased, subjective weights and measures surrounding worth, made on the basis of the ego's limited perception and experience. Questions result such as: Who is worthy? Who is not? Who deserves? Who does not? Who decides? Who is the judge?

And then, all of a sudden, you can find yourself **owned** by the very thing you wished to belong to.

Sex, money, and power are typically the ways that the imbalanced mind tries very hard to use to establish certain wants, certain expectations. While there are some in your world who live authentically from wheat-self, the majority in your world are very much attached to the chaff-identity. The chaff-centered world Loves to tell you that if you amass certain amounts of these things—sex, money, power, status, beauty, celebrity—you will have worth. If you do not, you don't.

To the Divine, you are always worthy, and if you align with that in humility and reverence you will feel it. But if God is secondary for you and your spiritual path is a convenient box to check off on the road to amassment of power or control, you are less in your Yeshua self than your human self . . . and thereby I cannot align Balance for you. Not of My choosing but yours. I cannot overpower your Free will. If you are choosing to be powered by a drunkenness with external power, control, and imbalanced want for belonging, including belongings, you will create deeper burdens and suffering for yourself and others. You will be owned by these things.

If you are choosing your internal Divine Power by giving over the attachments to the external wants that leave you in the state of being in longing, you are taking ownership of yourself, your true state of be-ing. Thereby, you will experience what it really is to belong—to Balance, to humility, to Freedom, to joy, to God, to your whole self.

There is not dark energy in your world, only light and shadow, animal/flesh/chaff self and Divine/wheat self. The choice is yours as to which you will align with. Stop giving up your worth to belong and to "get yours" no matter how much you believe that you are right and deserving and another is not. None of you, NONE of you, in a human body are absolute. God is Absolute. The movement into the essence of the Absolute within yourself is your journey and purpose in this life.

Part of this journey is discerning when another human be-ing or human structure professing to guarantee you an easy, absolute path to finding happiness comes your way. While the chaff self, Judas self, illusion self becomes quite titillated by words such as "easy," "free," and "absolute guarantee," the people and structures peddling such wares will wear you down in the end—your trust, your Sovereignty, your time, and even your finances. Be aware. Else you can easily become a ware that others peddle to achieve their own non-transparent agendas.

What such people and structures offer is the illusion of belonging that keeps you in longing, in wanting. These are not the spaces of true belonging that your wheat self, Yeshua self ever wishes to enter.

One of My favorite examples of this is what your world refers to as "branding." Entire industries and scientists performing research not only for a brand but on how to brand. Is branding not for the poor cattle and sheep and animals owned as possessions and dominated with a prod? Branding is ownership. Those of you creating brands, be very cautious, because soon enough that brand can confine you. A brand can evolve, but that means you need to evolve before and as it does.

Many of you feel a sense of belonging or loyalty to brands, which can also contain and confine you to never explore. A brand is a stamp that can also be a burn. By its creator and creation. That is how the shadow operates. It brands, cajoles, and entices you, often under false pretenses, instead of allowing you to figure out on your own what is right. Brands make it difficult for you to un-brand from them. Increasingly so.

However, there are brands that are not really brands but more spaces of community, equality, and communion. These may be referred to as brands in your modern language but I infinitely prefer the word "essence" over "brand." There are brands and then there are spaces that offer a unique, resonant essence. Look for those who offer an essence instead of those who project and push a brand. Such spaces of essence do not kowtow and cater to you or make false promises. They are honest in what they are and do not push you to partake in their offerings. They are transparent and do not sell you out as they sell to you. Or hold you hostage to them to the detriment of your Freedom.

There are pure "temples and churches" in your world, even in the form of companies, in which, if you wish to leave or join another, they send you blessings. And welcome you back if you wish to come. They are true and One with God. Then there are cults and brands that shame you, castrate you, and silence you if you wish to go. And if you wish to return, they shove you into the back of the temple.

Many "brands" dwell in endless fear of the loss of their next margin. Thus, they wish to control as much as possible, including you. They are owned and, as a by-product, they enslave and own you. At times, this can even include your media and government or political structures who sensationalize and distort Truth to keep you drunk on fear. These are corporations that can become "corpse-orations" when imbalanced and drunk on power. The corpse, "corp" meaning body, chaff, that belongs to them is YOU when you are not discerning and owning your own worth.

While it can be gloriously joyful to belong to a nationality, identity, or group, if you allow that identity to define you, you are owned by it as a chaff/corp/body-based authority structure. An authority or identity structure that gives you a sense of safety and control but can also indoctrinate you with "us versus them" sentiments and suck you back into the Void of weights and measures of worth.

The moment you begin to feel a sense of rage, blame, fear, shame, hatred, or suppression rising within you as a by-product of "belonging" to such structures is the moment you must have the courage to question whether you belong to the structure or are owned and enslaved by it. I caution you on being a "corps," a dispensable body, for such structures without even realizing that you are. For often, in being in longing to belong, even in being in longing to do what is right to create Peace, you can wind up creating less and less Peace. For yourself and for others.

When shadow feelings begin to arise within you, it is your soul's way, My Way, of letting you know it may be time for you to step back and restore Peace within your heart. As well as your Divine Power, which resolves through Love, Balance, and unity foremost. It is time to become sober, to open your eyes to the existence of your true identity, which is humble, kind, and at all times Free to become One with all things because, in Truth, you already are. As a world, you are one whole chaff, one whole wheat. And you belong to the world as the world belongs to you in equality, not in ownership. That is the consciousness I held for you then and hold for you now. That is your wheat-identity.

Akin to the above, I recommend that you do not fall under the influence of so-called influencers. Those who impose their influence and use you to propagate their own power are the very ones who have the least influence within the Divine. They may have influence in the current collective ego, but they have very little within the Balanced heart of the collective consciousness. They are often in arrogance and pride despite their altruistic intentions and self-righteousness. Those who say they have influence can be quite charming and alluring. They are intoxicating. Do not fall under the influence; do not get drunk on the illusion of acceptance and belonging that comes from uniting with them. They have no interest in you, as alcohol has no interest in those it inebriates. They are your cocaine. You are the user and are being used. That is apostasy.

Leave these rooms. Step off the platforms on which you wear a hood and noose that you cannot even see. Take back your power. Reach for those who inspire or guide. Not for those who profess to "influence." Wisdom is found in humility and allowing of equality. Never in believing you know better what is right or wrong for another. Those who do are committing Divine treason. We Love them unconditionally. But they do not realize the imbalance they create under the guise of altruistic intentions. You will be left in disappointment every time if you place your expectations within them to guide you. For they do not wish to guide you, they wish for you to adhere to their ideology and authority. That is not Balanced belonging based in inspiration. Discern, Beloved One, discern.

You serve better by deciding for yourself what is right and aligned for you even if it differs from that of another or all others. Which means no longer abdicating responsibility for your own journey. Take care of yourself. Hold the Light for all. And Forgive yourself and those whose alcohol you have been under the influence of. They have no influence over you any longer. Without you, their power dies. Without them, you are Free. They give you longing. I give you be-ing. We belong together. The influence of others in human form who say they know what is best for you and others often divides you more than it unifies. The influence of God unites you. Thus, if you are going to belong, the Divine is the best influence to be under. As, with Us, you are under the influence of compassion, kindness, and Peace.

We anoint you with an organic design inherent to your Presence in body. We do not brand you with marks to your chaff. We anoint your wheat with the Light.

Thus, why the focus on branding yourself to labels? We understand that you long to belong to a structure of resonance. If you all started replacing your loyalty to material things, people, and brands with loyalty to Simplicity and Grace, you would discover the far deeper sense of belonging that comes through the exploration of nature, possibilities, and embracing your brothers and sisters within the full spectrum of life.

Be cautious and discerning with what brands you follow to ensure that what you are branded to does not carry the mark of the beast of imbalance. Be discerning of those who herd you to the market. Their objective is to mark you as one of the cattle within the brand even in ways they are not conscious of. They are not here for belonging. They are here to own you, of their own longing to belong to power, money, and the rest. They do not trust their enoughness; thus they impose their too-muchness upon you. That is not leadership, leading the Ark to Balance. Authentic leaders capable of true leadership are Balanced within their Ark.

If it brings you comfort, Beloved One, please note that I did not have many followers, Myself. I, Yeshua, had fewer than the majority of you. I never sought followers. As a matter of fact, the opposite. I did not seek to sit in the center of the aisle and preach. I sat in the back of temples with those deemed "unworthy." They were My people and had great worth to Me. I Offered up My seat to the women and elderly in the front. As God, I belonged in the back of the bus and chose to be there.

In My Life, What I Offered was a Path for you to realize God. In purity, in Grace, I created the Way for the Word. The Word being the unspoken and unseen Truth of Love. Thus, caution who you follow that brings you toward apostasy, not from religion, but in apostasy from your Yeshua self.

And caution the egoic need YOU have for influence. More followers, more clicks. You have no followers. Any of you who want them are not authentic. Followers are mainly for the purpose of your own validation and playing God. Not be-ing God. Influencing others to your agenda. Influencing is forcing. Social anything in your world right now is a mob. Mob Justice. Mob media. Mobism. Chaff-ism. Have Faith in Us to restore Order and Balance, not anyone professing to deliver your joy to you in a carefully measured spoonful. I faced this Myself and was crucified to set you Free from it EVEN if you are under "imposed authority" within your life. I gave you a different life within this life. An unseen life that is the reality of what life truly is.

Seek to be a pure follower of God, a follower of Peace, kindness, compassion, and Forgiveness. Such followers belong to the Tree of Life. Such followers are the true influencers and leaders. There are some in your world serving in their anointed mantles who can give you the wisdom, Light, and community you need to grow. But they are few and live lives of devotion and Simplicity. Simplicity does not mean scarcity. But they live lives of service. And to those anointed and serving in their anointed mantle by God, you will find them if meant to. Otherwise come to Me or any other of the Divine that brings you closer to God without trying to influence, brand, or control you.

Seek originality, not following. Seek to be yourself and you will find, and find, and find again. You have all you need within you. Quantity is never the Way. Quality is the Way. The more you embody the qualities of Yeshua, of God—Humility, Forgiveness, Faith, Freedom—the more you will belong to all you are One with and to the whole of the world. Why make Love to a few when you can make Love to the whole world just through your very Presence? If you doubt that Truth, give it a try and you will find all your needs will be met without having to exert so much energy.

There are wonderful structures of resonance that have been created in your world that are humble and honoring of you, for they honor your Sovereign space as an individual. Those who have created such structures know their Truth, thus do not need to be the best. Reach for humility in the environments you belong to. And align with those who have created humble structures that are organic and noninvasive. Those are the spaces you will resonate with and find more as time goes on. The rest of it is Towers of Babel, ripe for the Fall. Those professing to help you to make more money under the auspices of spirituality are those to particularly be discerning of.

For those of you moving into manifestation, if you wish to create Balance for yourself and others in a way that is fluid and co-creative, instead of focusing on branding, focus on creating a structure of resonance. A structure under Divine Authority, which means God is the CEO, not you. I will be your Chief Energy Officer overseeing the process.

Be cautious of the brands you belong to. Seek structures of resonance and do not judge until your own dissonance has cleared from your be-ing. Until YOU are prioritizing Balance through conscious choice, you cannot belong to anything or anyone.

The central element I am introducing here is discernment. The central mantra to invoke inherent to My Offering to you is:

The Discernment Prayer

I have everything I need inside of me at this present moment. In this moment, regardless of all within the external including my relationships, health, financial commitments, children, friendships, I have all that I need INSIDE of ME. I belong to God. God is within me. And therein all of my needs are met. I need nothing of the external nor do I expect anything of the external. I am Spirit; the Holy Spirit is upon me. And in this moment, I am grateful, I am at Peace, I am One with God.

That is my power and my Right. Not at the cost or judgment of another. That is my Sovereign Right. No other can take it from me. I have the deep humility to know that I cannot trust my mind or feelings, but I do trust in God. And God resides inside of me equally with all others. I have the humility to know that I do not know what another needs, nor do I need to force my will upon them. I align my will with Divine Will no matter the cost or gain. As all that is One with God is a gift and gain.

My Prayer is that ALL realize this Sovereign Truth, as well. And release their dispelling of opinions and beliefs upon others. I am in great Peace and great Prostration to the majesty and awe of the Divine Grace that is within me and holding both of my hands at all times. I walk with you, Divine, in gentleness, kindness, and Peace. Amein.

That is the Prayer of invoking Sovereign authority, humility, and Grace. It is the Prayer that sets you Free. Which does mean you may be asked to give up your containers of influence, your intoxication and bias as and from influences that serve your ego and not your sacred heart. Just allow, say this Prayer, and the Way and Passage to your Peace, Our Peace, will be shown. It requires courage, Beloved, to go against the grain. We honor that courage and Faith. This is a Journey we will share together.

And so it is.

Please remember, Sacred Vessel, that what you belong to also belongs to you. If you belong to projected fears and thought prisons, those thought prisons and fears belong to you. You are stitched to them. If you belong to trauma in your mind, trauma belongs to you. If you belong to hate and blame, hate and blame belong to you. Do you want these belongings? If not, you need to be willing to explore why you needed them to integrate them, unstitch or unbraid from them, and let the chaff of the experiences or unhealthy knots go. Which may require some courage, some grief, some change. However, the joy and Miracles you receive are worth it. Because you are worth it to yourself and to Me.

When you let the imbalanced belongings go, your identity moves into Freedom, new space to create. When you let these go, you belong to Freedom and Freedom belongs to you. And that is when the true Divine Magic and Braiding of the Soul and Spirit through Faith flows forth in abundance. And so it is. Amein.

2

·········

The Liberation from Longing

Beloved One, what I share now is the most important aspect of this Offering, thus I will keep this simple. This is the deeper Truth beneath what I have said:

When you seek too much to belong or for belonging, ownership of things on the outside, it can completely blind and strip your lens of the wheat on the inside.

I would strongly recommend within this process of exploration that you are in now that instead of seeking to belong, being in longing, or focusing too much of your time and energy on belonging—that you shift to the counter-polarity, which is:

Longing to Be!

Longing to Be.

Longing to be Free of the need to belong to this, or belong to these belongings. Because, as I said, the funny thing about belonging is that all that you belong to belongs to you, as well. All of the time and energy that you spend focused on belonging and belongings is dangerous because to each belonging you "own," you give up a small or large amount of your life force. That places you in a position of deep and imbalanced vulnerability with the external.

Thus, you can be preyed upon by the ego's loud voice that says, "If you don't belong, you will face the threat of insecurity and rejection." I chuckle at this statement because the insecurity of the statement itself IS the rejection of the Truth, which is the deepest threat. What your ego is doing in making such statements is keeping you focused on the external belonging so that it can own your fear and **own you through fear.**

You are owned by your own want for belonging. You are owned by your own belongings. With fear, as I have said many times before, there are only two kinds. The first is the fear of not getting what you want. The voice of this fear is, "I have a fear that I won't get my money, this relationship, acceptance, validation; that I will not be safe; I will not have my needs met. I must seek harder, renounce more of my boundaries, give up more of my worth, get more surgeries, go on more diets, work harder and harder, or I will be alone, and I will not get what I need." Or, there is the fear of losing what it is that you have. The voice of this fear is: "I have worked very hard, I have amassed these belongings [be it people, be it items, whatever else it is that makes you feel that you belong]. I could lose these things. THEN who would I be? I have to avoid loss at all costs."

Both of those fears are very heavy burdens to carry. They require energy because, for things that you own, or things that own you, the unstitching can be exhausting. And painful. Your mind is keeping you locked in that limited space of complacency and stripping you of your Sovereign, joyful Right to ignite change from the wellspring of Faith.

Because you are bound by these things you belong to and that belong to you, when imbalanced or stale, all you can see is the limited lens of your own ego's instigation and manipulation of fear. There are very many of you in bodies at this time. Many on your planet are consumed by the lens of fear and thus spend their whole lives in hypervigilance, paranoia, and control.

When what you all truly long for is to BE. To Be-loved. And to give Love in reciprocity as a result.

I will be the first to let you know, Beloved One (though your mind might argue with this), that you do not own anything. Your belongings, your people—you do not own any of them. This is where the energy of slavery, prostitution, many of the deepest elements of suppression, and repression, and oppression of others, stems from. Some of the biggest imbalances within the structures of your world come from misguided perceptions of ownership. Viewing things or even people as property.

Nothing is yours. Yes, you belong to this world. Your body belongs to you, to a certain extent, but even your body, the matter, the chaff, belongs to Gaia and God. **You belong to God. God, the Light, belongs to you.** Inherent to your be-ing, apart from "time," nothing within the chaff do you own. You may caretake something, but you never own it. You never control it. Just as We do not own and control you.

Will you be-long to God in humility? Will you be-long to Peace? Or will you belong to fear? To victim consciousness? To the chaff? That is your journey. Many who have walked before you are holding the Light for this choice and it is not an easy one. It means you need to give over, to allow, and to include Spirit and Truth into the things you deny or withhold from yourself. This does not mean you get things handed to you, ever. Anyone who promises you "easy" is in apostasy. We Offer you a Way. Always a Way. With the Word written on your heart that you hear through your breath.

This belonging of the Beloved, this longing to be One with—it sets you Free from everything on the external. It unleashes, unfurls, and liberates you in Freeing you from fear. No matter what is happening on the outside, no matter who is trying to own you, negate you, no matter what you have or do not have, no matter how healthy or unhealthy you are—you belong.

That is why the most ostracized and rejected are those We hold the most. As well as those who do not assert the force of their will onto others. Those that trust in their own God-given gifts no matter how much the outside world embraces them or not.

Your rejection of others within the Garden, "cancelling" their worth, not recognizing their wheat—no matter what they have or have not done—is foolish wisdom, wrathful wisdom, and arrogance. Honor them as people instead of property or possessions that you feel you have the Right to judge and damn. You cannot, and when you do, We hold them even more than We do you. We Love you all equally. So, set it all Free and have the humility to allow God to dictate the Balance and justice, not you. When you try to play God by policing others, it exhausts you and is not the Loving, natural state you were designed for. So, set it all Free. Them Free. And yourself Free in the process.

Cease the burdens within you from impacting all those around you. Your burdens affect one another and the ecosystem. You have felt and carried the impact of others' burdens shoved onto you. One in burden creates a burden for all and the ones that need to carry that load are . . . YOU. When you cancel another, negate the worth of another, it is you who are cancelled and negated within the dream. Give it over and prostrate and maybe just once, allow Me to shoulder the external Balance and justice so that you don't have to. Nor can you. Give up to the Divine what you cannot carry and watch in awe as We align the rest.

Most of all, when you can release the external need to belong, you can BE. That is what you long for—to be what you ARE—which is Love, Power, and Grace. When you can Be-loved instead of owned, by whatever else it is that owns you, then you are Free—because you have found the Source. You belong to God. By releasing all of these things that you think that you are, that you think that you have—whether it is a relationship, even a marriage, a title, possessions—you are Free. Releasing your whole heart to the Divine and saying, "Thank you for these wonderful belongings and beautiful things, but these are not mine, these are yours, God" is one of the most liberating ways of be-ing.

That does not mean that We will take things away, that you will lose. Oftentimes We bring you more. Each of you has different needs, just as each of you has different wants. You are constantly evolving, changing, and your spirit sometimes aligns those changes in the outer but only for the benefit of your realization on the inner. All of you, equally. The essence of your be-ing is Peace. And Love. As long as you are a be-ing and be-ing present at any moment, you have everything.

Whatever part of you tells you that you do not have enough, that you are not enough, that you have done something so unbelievably wrong that you are not worthy of Love—that is an illusion. That is focusing on the chaff. That is allowing the chains of fear to stitch you and bind you. It is not being present. In this moment, you are Free. As you are in every moment.

Faith, Forgiveness, Freedom. When you have Faith, you are not afraid of not getting what you need, because you leave that to God. **Here is the Prayer of Belonging to God, Prayer of Reclaiming Divine Authority:**

Divine Grace, Divine self, I belong to God. I understand that my mind does not even know what I need. I give myself over to my be-ing, to the flow of Light, above and below. My possessions, I offer these to you, God, Light, Consciousness, essence of my be-ing. I will caretake these things for as long as they need to be caretaken. I will let them go as and when they need to go. I trust in God and the Yeshua within self. And understand that I belong to myself, I long to be myself. As so too, I belong to God. I long to be. I AM. Thus, I choose to rest in the be-ing of this moment in Grace, Peace, trust, curiosity, and acceptance. In the releasing, I am the holiest of holies. Ohm Nami Yeshua. Amein.

Many of the things that you stitch to, in wishing to belong, consti-tute holding on to old parts of self that are part of an old identity. "If I can just hold on to all of these belongings . . ." is a favorite of Ours. What a wonderful way to amass clutter that leaves little space for cre-ation and evolution. This includes your memories: "If I can just hold on to this memory, if I can just hold on."

Where do you believe that memory goes? Your chaff does not come with you when you return to Spirit. It is shrapnel, "casing," so to speak. None of your possessions, likes, or clicks will carry with you in Spirit. You do not carry arguments and numbing moments with you. Only the trauma of them that you never realized that creates distortions and warps in your energetic field. When you spend years numbing, be it through games, media, alcohol, sugar, television, or flight response, you do not carry these things with you, but you do carry with them the distortions they created within you.

You DO carry with you those moments you experienced a com-munion, connection, and belonging to and with another in reciprocity. Those moments formulate fluid, conscious soul memory. Those that are dense keep you dense. That is the path of your evolution into the Light.

Memory is part of the wheat's dreaming. The chaff, your external reality, simply lives within the ephemeral dream of so-called life. But, as with a dream, you can wake; you can change it. The moments of Truth, depth, joy, intimacy, and empathy are those within the dream-ing that your soul carries with you. For they are Light as a feather. The simple moments of communion, whether they came in joy, grief, or a moment of kindness. The moments that are simple. The smell of an autumn leaf. The smell of your grandmother's cooking. Traditions. Spontaneous moments when you burst out laughing. That is expe-riencing. That is Love. THAT is God and what you carry with you. You are on borrowed time in this life, Beloved One; use it wisely. To engage, Free of fear, in the opening of your sacred heart to life. *Why not?* says the soul. *Why not?*

The cost of My full engagement with this world in My Life was Death. It was worth it, as you were and are worth it. I set you Free, but you have to choose that Freedom and no longer rely on another to bring it to you in desiring to be-long. Long, long, long in suffering. Instead of open, open, open in experiencing.

Your memories are One with consciousness. Nothing is ever destroyed or ever created. You cannot *not be*. Thus, you cannot *not be-long* to the Tree of Life. Many within your world are not conscious of this. All be-ings are conscious, but not all are awakened. They still see much through the external: being right, getting money, getting abundance, getting one more, one more, one more. They do not realize that they are owned—they are slaves to these things—including the ego's clique of the next "click" or "like."

Then there is the person who does not "like" what another offers. How personally those things are internalized. There is NO be-ing in those moments. It is a power struggle of who will belong, and who will not. There is shame and blame that is thrown into that. This energy is strong within the collective right now. Shaming. Cancelling. Negating one another.

No soul can be cancelled. No wheat cannot be wheat. It can be pounded, it can be turned into loaves of bread, but it is My Body, it is My Blood. As are you. That cannot be cancelled. You already tried that over 2,020 years ago. And it does not work.

Trying to negate or cancel another, what it does is it cancels and negates the God-self, Yeshua self that is your true self and essence—and then you are no more than a possession, bought and paid for at the mercy of your own mind and your own fear. Where will you belong?

Who and what is it that you belong to? All of that is shifting now. That is what this exploration of this period in your world is. I have brought certain shifts to help you to reevaluate and to truly ask yourself, "Do I wish to be in longing? Or, do I have a longing to be Free?"

The more that you are Free, the more it is easy to explore. Travel Lightly, My Beloved. Travel in the Sacred Heart, not the heart at the mercy of the mind's provocations.

Question even your time. Time does not belong to you though it is the one thing you do own as long as you are in a body. You are on borrowed time. Allow for there to be fewer strings attached, fewer commitments, fewer hooks. Leap in trust, leap in Faith, Surrender the complexity, and you will be surprised by how much relief you feel. Not relief from responsibility but from the burden of responsibility. That is what this portal of resolution is for. As you choose to belong to Love through embodying Love, your soul will bring the Balance and the equilibrium very naturally.

You yourself thus must separate from needing to belong. You belong in a body, not in the mind. You belong in Love, not in fear. Set yourself Free from the comparison and judgment, the internalization when another tries to negate your worth, even your tendency to carry around the residue of what happened in the past.

As long as you are in a body, you will long to feel the Light. There are times when the longing for Home, God Home, Home of your Spirit, is so very strong . . . and there are times when it is not. When you lose that longing or feeling of belonging to God, the separation, numbness, polarities, and dissonance that inevitably comes is to remind you that you are getting a bit off track. Those moments are important to remind you where it is that you belong. You are the wheat. Your body, your be-ing, this beautiful world, is the chaff for you to enjoy.

Feed the wheat. Be in Love. Belong here. To this body, to this wine of your blood, to this bread of your bones, to this planet you call Home. Belong to your world. And equally to Spirit. The beauty of this existence is—you get both! Belong to God. It is an open, eternal invi-tation with no requirements for membership save your curiosity and willingness. Allow Me, through calling Me into your be-ing, to move around what needs to be moved around to set you Free from these burdens that you own, or that own you. Give over the control, and the fatigue, and the holding on. Hold on to Me so that you can let go of the rest. I will hold you right back, but in a way that sets you Free.

The things that you are a caretaker for, be it your land, be it your fellow brother, be it your animals, be it your water—in giving that over to Me, you have nothing to lose. For then I get to caretake it with you in partnership as you tend the field of the dreaming.

The one need all of you have right now is to focus on Freedom (as well as Faith and Forgiveness). And to take responsibility for that instead of expecting or trusting another person to do it for you. Life is service. Nothing is easy. You didn't sign up for easy. You did sign up for experiencing. You did sign up for embodying. You did sign up for participating. Stop hiding, assuming, projecting, and rejecting self and other. Start engaging with kindness and with Love. I will hold you through that too.

When you are able to set yourself Free from the burden of ownership and longing, you set everyone else Free too, through inspiration and example—at least those who are ready to join you in Surrender. You show them the way and I will show them the Way alongside you. That is service, Beloved, that is service.

Thus, I ask you, Sacred Child, to do a bit of writing:

1. What owns you, what are you committed to in the external world and in your thoughts, feelings, and emotions that feel like burdens?
2. What do you feel you are owed? Does that sense of entitlement bring you more Peace or more anger and stress when it does not come?
3. Are you owned by fear and worry? Do you wish to be Free? Love is not about ownership. Fear is.

4. Are you willing to give these crosses over to Me so that you can begin to shift your perception from belonging, longings for more, and belongings that own you? Are you willing to experience the Freedom of feeling without judging, thinking without reacting, and living your life as and with the Holy Spirit that is within and upon those who make the choice to give over? What is at the heart of your longing? Can be-ing BE enough for you?

5. Are you willing to commit to creating the space for embodiment of the Ark of the New Covenant in living as and with your Yeshua self? Do you need to be the leader? Or can you understand that leadership comes naturally through the embodiment in whatever size and scope you are designed to fulfill?

This writing is a Sacred Covenant; thus I ask that you actually put your answers to these questions in writing instead of just making a mental notation. For this Covenant is what moves you into deeper transformation through having the courage, humility, and patience to receive Divine support through the process. There are no expectations and entitlements that will be served through this process. Only wonder, wonder and awe are energies I can serve.

Freedom from expectations and entitlements is the very best way for Me to bring your needs to you in revelation, manifestation, and joy. Keep returning to and refining this writing and all that you need will become clearer. That is My promise to you. I have always honored My commitments to you as Divine Father and Son of God. I have never been far. As a matter of fact, I am so close that you forget I am always here with and within you. And you with and within Me. Sancti, Beloved. Pace. Amein.

3

....

The Freedom of Be-ing

Behold, Beloved One. Over the past years, We have been observing you all and Witnessing who is choosing to become One, to belong to the Garden of the wheat . . . and who is wishing to stay separate and relegated to the chaff-identity, the imbalanced ego self. It is a choice and a choice that is not made all at once, for you are woven into many glorious things and relationships yet also have many love-nots to un-stitch from along your path of life.

Interestingly, while love-nots or knotted stitches bind you to certain distortions of perception, mindsets, and behaviors, they also make you feel separate or disconnected from that which is of value to you. The dissonance of the ego undervalues the importance of your connection to Gaia by making you too busy to commune and spend time with Her. It is more difficult to weave a Balanced web when disconnected from your ecosystem.

An imbalanced ego can cause you to feel separate from your own heart and true feelings. Thus, it leaves you at the mercy of fears surrounding rejection, not belonging, dashed hopes, and expectations. It can even stitch your eyes shut, blinding and separating you from the experience of self as whole. Love-nots can feel like there is a split within you, a dual or fragmented self. This leaves you susceptible to both defensiveness and absorption of external thought bubbles and fear prisons. Your wheat, soul and spirit, is your shield. Thus, when you are in chaff-identity or illusion self lens, you are in a lower vibrational state and thus very vulnerable to lower energy absorption, as well as egoic paranoia surrounding lower energy absorption that is not real.

There is little authenticity, originality, and confidence that emanates from you when in this defensiveness. For, in this state, you are renouncing your power to others to dictate your worth, fear, or sense of belonging. This can be your parents, a Lover, people in professional situations, friends, or even your children. As they are in their own experience and reality, this creates a burden for them and for you. Which perpetuates the feeling of separation from them and, more importantly, from yourself and Me.

Over time, this causes you to feel that there is something wrong with you or that you are fragmented or shattered. Times you have been rejected just for be-ing who you are, times you have been abused or harmed, times you have been treated like an expendable body, times you have done everything the world tells you is right and yet still continuously fall into hardship, or times you have been told you are unworthy of Love, especially in moments you are the most vulnerable like childhood, become more and more magnified until a part of you fractures and almost seems to break apart. That is trauma. No one is to blame, not you, not other. But that state of shattering or the perception thereof is trauma.

When trauma occurs, aspects of the wheat, your soul, can become fragmented and move into your spirit body until you are ready to reintegrate these pieces of self. At a certain point these pieces need to be restitched into the fabric of self in healthy Love knots. It is almost as though when you experience a trauma your soul, a bit of your wheat, experiences a hernia and something becomes unstitched. It was a trauma—your mind could not handle it, your emotions could not handle it—and a piece of your soul goes into your spirit body, which is the energy all around you. You cannot access it. It is lost in the subconscious and you cannot recall and sometimes even remember it. It is numb within the Void. Though that fragment is still a part of you, you cannot access that aspect of the wheat of self. Be it your joy, your child self, your ability to Forgive, your ability to feel Peace, or even certain memories.

This is soul-level trauma or fragmentation that occurred during parts of this life or past lives. When you are experiencing deep polarity or there is a lot of loss all at once in your life, neither God nor your soul is trying to create more trauma and problems for you. Your soul is calling in a deep change to help you to reclaim one or more fragmented aspects of self to restore your experience of wholeness. Often this occurs because your soul knows that you need to reclaim these fragments to move into deeper service through joy, new relationships, or to release past stitches holding you back from Peace.

Thus, it needs you to address, bring Light and Forgiveness into, and reintegrate these parts of self. Sometimes it happens in a sudden way for no apparent reason. One day you just wake up and are ready to process the latent grief and let it go. Sometimes you don't even know what or who caused the trauma. Or why it needs to resurface. Please know, Beloved, you do not need to understand it to process it. It is a soul-level process more than a mental process.

When and if these periods come, do not wallow in self-pity. Embrace them; there is a Miraculous healing occurring and you are in control of the inner process. Take the time for the unstitching from the behaviors, addictions, and patterns that come as a by-product of the fragmented self. Take time for the reweaving, braiding, and integration of these parts back into self. As they reintegrate, life around you will change because you have changed.

If you have been living a fragmented life, when you move back into consciousness, wholeness, you may find you are no longer interested in some of the people, places, and activities that were part of your life before. There is a new weaving of healthy Love knots that occurs as you create new structures in your life aligned with your whole self, wheat self. With each passing day, you will feel more deeply connected to your Divine Yeshua self as opposed to the victim, fragmented self that cries, rages, and despairs. The self that has an insatiable hunger for a Love that can never seem to be nourished is replaced by the self that is deeply nourished through its own essence of be-ing, which IS Love.

That is where some of the deepest healing and reintegrating in your world right now is occurring. And why the three Voids of 2020 and beyond are important. These next years on your planet are an opportunity to come into deeper wholeness as an individual and as a world.

Right now, some people may believe that they are experiencing simply mental traumas and heart-related trauma. However, the traumas or the fragments that are revealing are soul-level traumas of a deeper level, beyond the mind and even the heart. Thus, you need support beyond just the human; you need the Divine, as well. And not just humans professing to have a connection to the Divine, though there are some of them who are authentic that you will call to you if you need them. This process of deep inner rebalancing and awakening to the Light self requires looking at the Truth. The Truth isn't always easy but does set you Free.

Your souls are holding you accountable for your seeing and accepting Truths you may not have wished to look at in the past. Your spirit is also creating the path for your emergence and service through joy as you allow for the Truth and make the shifts necessary to live in deeper Balance and transparency. Your old self-absorbed fears and mind-based want for control or dominance will be harder and harder to sustain. Exhausting. Many of you are already feeling the fatigue that has been lying beneath the burdens.

You are being Freed to live a soul-based life. Get in the river and the current will take you. Every time. I AM that river. If the water grows too cold and deep, reach to Me and I will walk with you upon it.

This time in your life and world is an opportunity for you to reclaim all aspects of self that need to be rewoven and rebraided. When in your fragmented self, the Braids of Faith, Forgiveness, and Freedom, Love, Truth, and Peace become frayed. Thus, these energies become more difficult for you to access or give and receive in general. They must be rewoven into the tapestry of self. And valued as the most important energies in your life. For, when your tapestry is woven through these Braids, you change the tapestry of the world. That is ultimately what is occurring through the shifts and changes within your world.

We, I, the Divine, are observing; We are allowing this process, holding the Light for this process of deeper consciousness and revelation for each of you, for, without it, you cannot be One. As an individual and as a world. We are One. So whatever keeps you in frayed strands and unhealthy knots must be cleared. However, the choice is whether you will stay fragmented, and separate, as individuals and as a collective—or whether you will become One. One streaming consciousness of wheat. Even one person streaming, weaving, and delivering that consciousness, that Light, can nourish ten thousand souls with his or her Light.

When I came to a body, I belonged to the collective. I did not have personal karma—I came to belong to you. I longed to Be with you as and with God. I understood that I would be rejected. But I was coming to belong to you, though you would not necessarily wish to belong to Me. I was not seeking belonging. I was seeking to give you a Path for the realization beyond your longing to BE—I came to bring the sustenance and satiation of your longing to be One through be-ing One with you. I AM available for all, to all equally, as are All within the Divine. We are extending Our Hand of Light to you. We belong to each other, as your whole self belongs to the Light of Consciousness, Peace.

What you are experiencing within your world, whether you

realize it or not, is the burden, the overwhelming burden of a life within a society and world of want. I have cautioned you to leave space, to refine commitments. The past years, your souls, in co-creation with the Divine, have been giving you the Truth required to make changes. Some are choosing to embrace it. Others are choosing to look away.

This is one of the last times the path will be as easy as it is now. In years to come, there are certain things that will be decided, certain consequences looming that will be set in stone. Fear not, it is not "too late." I simply wish to relay that it will be more difficult for you as individuals and a world to hide and suppress. All repressed within you will rise. All repressed within Mother Earth, as well. This is a time of Transcendence that does not need to require pain. However, there are certain realities that will come for you, and for others, as a result of choices made as a collective. **All that you need to know is that you will know what it is that you need to know, when it is time.**

The subtle transition to ease the burdens and crosses you carry now is essential. The subtle unthreading, and rethreading within self, Divine, and nature, is essential. Of Family, Friendships/Professional, Eros, and Divine—the four Relationship Chambers of the Sacred Heart—the only Chamber within your sacred heart that truly requires some extra time and space within you is the one that belongs to the Divine. The Divine Chamber of your heart, the Divine Gateway, the Void, the Light. This is a personal and inner journey for you now; however, you will draw those to you in the world who can guide you or share in the journey with you. Be discerning but do allow for the new to come, even if it comes in the form of something or someone you least expect. Through discernment, **which is refined openness,** deeper trust and knowing of your path will be clear.

Thus, what you will be Offered in times to come are opportunities to share with others in those experiences. Even though your path is individual, you may find yourself gravitating toward certain groups to explore new realities, braids, stitches, and possibilities. Uniting in this way will augment your ability to expand the Divine Chamber of your heart within the heart of the world. **For those of you finding your way here, that basis of community—COME-UNITY—is ultimately the one you will feel that you belong to the most.** As you are the ones who are allowing, giving up, and remembering that you belong to the Divine. And that you belong within this garden of the world through your nature, human and Divine. Be cautious of polarized groups recruiting soldiers to wage their wars of anger, entitlement, even activism. The groups to unite with are those rooted in humility, inclusion, and kindness. While your online communities can be wonderful, it is important for you to have direct relationships in which you can truly weave and braid into a person's heart directly.

There is much Truth that is bubbling to the surface. Old energies being processed as you move into more Oneness, and long for more Oneness, more be-ing. The Truth is painful at times—yet it sets you Free to Love. This time is a Lion's Gate of Redemption and will be for years to come. That is the mercy of the Era of Transparency that I Seeded long ago, even prior to My physical Life. Those Seeds are breaking ground and activating now, restoring you to your wheat and the Tree of Life that transcends death.

This is a time of separation of the wheat and chaff in general—be it people who are leaving their bodies or those awakening to wheat-consciousness and making changes to align more deeply with Simplicity and Balance. This is an opportunity to make right the betrayals to self and others, and to Forgive the betrayals of self and others. A time to remember that you truly can never betray God, nor does God ever betray you. Only the God of ego-self works with the energy of betrayal—those who think they know better.

Without the openness to Me, to the Divine, to the Light, you cannot see clearly, and thus are subject to the mercy of your own judgment, and thus, the judgment of others. We are giving you, through polarity and change, a Path—a way to Oneness. Yes, in the eyes of the world you may always belong to a culture, family, society, class, or label branded into you from birth. However, remember that you are a part of all things, and no things. Within the Divine Chamber, there are no labels, confinements, and classifications that you are narrowed to. You have a unique essence, tapestry, and design, but not one that confines you to any one way of be-ing. You have the ability to transcend anything, including the desire of others to mold you to their reality and perception. Within My Heart, the Divine Heart, you are always Free.

Even if another person is trying to enslave you, you are still Free. The deepest Freedom, wonder, and joy comes through belonging to no things and all things. Once that is there, it makes it very easy to explore all possibilities and weave, through your creative life force, those possibilities into your reality. Once the need of belonging is met in your relationship with the present moment, weaving and braiding become far more joyful. For you are creating from a Free space, no longer weighted by the burdens of expectations and fear of loss.

Within your life, this is a time of Truth to seed you deeper into Love. Humility will serve you well through this period. All the weeds of love-nots are being removed from your garden, by your conscious choosing or by circumstance. The weeds are to be honored. Like you cannot help but be what you are, a weed cannot help but be a weed. It was designed to be a weed. A weed to you may be a beautiful flower to another. Thus, as you weed your garden, offer these humble flowers to Me. I cherish your weeds and know just where to plant them in a space in which they will be welcomed as flowers.

Your path is no longer about just giving Love to others, for you cannot do so until you structure the trust needed to feel safe enough to embody Love. Love is a polarized, charged energy that can be frightening because it means change, unknowns. Love does not care about control and certainly does not like to be contained. However, it works well with Trust. Trust creates an order and gauges to assess whether it is safe to move deeper into Love, or not. Without Love you cannot move deeper into your passion through Peace.

That passion within you, that Holy Fire, which wells up from the essence of your be-ing, is the spirit ignited. Thus, during this time, I am helping you to strip away that which you hide behind. To illuminate in your passion means you need to open to being seen, with transparency. Whatever is hidden cannot stay hidden for long in the power of true passion.

When fragmented and in imbalanced ego, your passion does not flow in Peace and humility. It flows from want, arrogance, distortion, and self-absorption. It thereby burns out everything around you. Or burns you out in the process. Without you even knowing it, you can create further imbalance and deep harm under the auspices of "good intentions." When you are Balanced and whole, your passion emanates through Radial Balance and streams through your spirit with Grace. When you are in true passion, you are in your essence and therein there is nothing to hide.

Thus, I will be making it increasingly difficult for you to sustain a passion that does not flow from your original essence, Peace. I will also make it harder for you to hide from the joy of your passion and service by making it feel so good when you are experiencing it that you would never wish to stop! There can be no more split self that does one thing on the surface and another thing under the surface. YOU are the prophets and emissaries of the Gospel of Light, in the way that was designed for you—that we designed together. Step out into the open! Show others your celebration with God. Give them words of kindness that, respectful of their boundaries, show them the Way.

Let your Faith, awe, and rejoicing of the Emergence of your Yeshua self, your wheat, shine through. It is the Peace of gold, your piece of Peace, that everyone wishes to find and all have within them.

Those who judge you will relegate themselves to judgment. Those who blame will have to carry the burden of their own blame. Those in blame contribute to the burden of blame by putting that energy in the collective. In the Era of Accountability, they will need to answer to that burden. As will those who are not transparent and projecting an image of self that is not the Truth of who they are.

Those who shame will be subject to the same. How and when and if that occurs is not anything that you need to know. That is My journey with them, for only I can resolve the Truth within them or within you with Love.

Words that create division, words that you feel entitled to say that hurt another from your perch of self-righteousness, or actions that silence the words of others is a form of speaking in tongues and wrathful wisdom. As I have said, hatred is one of the heaviest burdens you can carry, alongside judgment and impatience. Choose words of Love, Beloved; it is not hard if you look through your authentic eyes and speak through your authentic voice.

Do not be afraid of those who relish in creating polarity and imbalance. They are in deep unconsciousness and distortion. Do not fear them. Have compassion for those in judgment. They are trapped in the mob of their own mind and live in a chaos that they are oblivious to. Let go, Beloved One. The Era of Judgment and Want must die as you move into the Era of Co-Creation and Peace.

Your choices matter now. You all choose to commit to many things to the detriment of commitments you make to the Divine. Faith and Prayer have become secondary now to your human-made comforts. The Divine always remains committed to you. You will feel more of the Divine by opening this often-closed chamber of your sacred heart. The more you live in the now, practice patience, and listen, the more you will hear. Those who stand in judgment will know judgment. Those who Forgive will know Forgiveness and joy. Those who Prostrate—We will Prostate before them. Those who Repent through joy will know Our joy.

Choose! Separation or Light. Struggle or Flow. Nails and the heavy strings of life as a dead tree OR dancing, braiding, and weaving with the Beloved. Give over your burdens and I will take them from you. Such is the fullest expression of Prostration: letting go of old energy, old rusty nails, old strings, old behaviors, old stitches that have bound you, that suppress you, that hook you yet also belong to you. Do you wish to belong to these things?

I will be making your burdens heavier over the next times to compel you to give them over to Me. The dead trees, walking crucifixes of those who judge, suppress, neglect, and blame, will buckle under the weight of those they crucify from the dangling perch of self-righteousness. Despite occasionally agreeing with their wrathful wisdom when they crucify someone you do not resonate with, practice temperance and restraint. Because once they are done crucifying others, they will come for you. And then they will come for each other. And then they will come for themselves. Such is always the dance, then and now. If humans do these things when the tree is green and fruit-bearing, what will happen when it is dry and brown?

Pray for resolution through Love. When you see someone burning, or being shamed, even someone you do not resonate with, offer that person some water, Beloved tree. You must choose Love. It is the only way through the narrow gate to the Freedom of the Tree of Life. You owe that to yourself and to God, if you are to live as, and with, God. Otherwise, even if you think you do, you are not as far along as you think you are.

I, Yeshua, Love ALL trees, even the dead tree I Died upon, the Cross. It held me as the dead trees within the world hold a certain energy for you. As My Tree, Chaff/Body, Died, the dead tree of the Cross, including your crosses, burned and was purified within the Holy Fire before returning to the Earth to begin life anew. My Wheat Resurrected the gateway to the Tree of Life. Such is the resolution of your path and the path of all others, Beloved tree. But your Resurrection cannot come until you yourself are Resurrecting yourself from all that feels dead within you.

We rejoice when you move through resolution and Forgiveness. That is the space We hold. When you resolve and Forgive, when you choose Faith, We rejoice most of all because you are choosing to come Home to the Tree of Life. If you are a "parent" of a child, animal, elder, you can appreciate this joy We feel. How joyful you feel when your children come home—come home from school, come home from service, come home from a day, a month, a year, lost in addiction, or pain, or struggle—it is your JOY to embrace them again when they return. Such are the moments that stay with you. And so it is.

Now, I wish to share a Word more on judgment—an energy I know well. In the giving over of My Life, I served to assist in Freeing you from judgment, despite the illusions brought forth in My name that came after. Yeshua is a name of the past that no longer has meaning in the way it did within My Life. While your name matters to you now, when you leave your body, you do not even carry that with you.

In Truth, I have no name. The Light has no name. I AM the nameless, faceless Light. When you can Surrender even your name to God, you have known Oneness. This stretches beyond just your name and into perception of your identity. The choice before you now is one of judgment—to be separate or to be One—as I have said. As with emotions and thoughts, your name is important when you are in form, for, within your world, you belong to a name and the name belongs to you.

Let your name, your likeness, emanate from the energies of Grace, kindness, and compassion. For as long as you are within this life, let all you are and do be in the name of God. For then you are all names and none. And you then carry a name I once did long ago, Yeshua, within yours. When you devote and Surrender your name to God, not through your beliefs or interpretation of God, but through humility, when you say your name, you may say Mine after it.

This means releasing judgment of your name and all names. And to hold the Light for those bound to only names, labels, chaff-identity constructs. As a Light-holder, as one called to uncover his or her authentic essence each day a little more, have compassion. Many in your world bear the Light but know not how to hold the Light. Holding the Light is a dissolving, a seeing fully. Bearing the Light is a limiting, a seeing only in part. Your individuality is beautiful, your name is beautiful, but when you value name above authentic essence, seen over unseen, you can never fully discover that essence or realize your true name. When we are One, you share My name and I yours.

That is what the journey of the Second Coming is. A coming of Unity. Come Unity. It is an acceptance that another may have more than you in possessions, names, but that you have all that you need. When you are at Peace you have more gold, more wheat than a king. And through joy, with one fish you are able to serve an entire community of your sisters and brothers.

Within this new beginning, the Second Coming of the Third Era, why have one Yeshua when there can be an entire world of Yeshuas? Why not share and illuminate the Yeshua Presence and consciousness within all? That opportunity, this Seal, open now in this new Era, is available to you presently in ways you have never before had as a world. You must choose it and choose Me to allow My Grace and Spirit to fill you. You must close your eyes to open the eye of the soul to see My Presence within you.

You must forget the old childish ways to remember the ways of wisdom found deeply in the moments of Stillness. You must set down your armor, fraudulence, lack of gratitude, and wanting to be the most liked, most unique, most special. You are equally special in the Eyes of the Divine. Each of you carries the most special gifts in the shell upon your back. A shell that is never a cross. The most special are those that do not need to be. Because it is they who know Our Love in their ability to transcend the illusion self. It is they who live in Transcendence.

The Path of your Second Coming or be-coming of your Yeshua self is often the Path unrewarded in your world, though that will shift in time. It is not recognized because your world fears change, and those that deviate and go their own way frighten others. "Out-laws" of the chaff (and "in-laws" of the wheat) mirror change to others. It is easier for most to judge you than to face the Truth that perhaps they may need to make changes, as well. Embodying your Yeshua self is not about choosing to be different as a statement of anger, defiance, avoidance, or resistance. Embodiment of your Yeshua self requires courage, humility, integrity, commitment, and a legend that no one can access but you. For your legend and key of realization of your true self was designed to be unique to you.

This means you must allow for a Path in this life that many fear, avoid, reject, or even cannot see. Just because others cannot understand or criticize you for doing things a bit differently does not mean they are right. Your Path to realization of your Yeshua self may be the road less traveled. But, as I Died to set the Path, if you will let Me, I will help you to walk it in joy. It is My joy to lead you no matter how much you reject Me. You do not have to believe in Me to receive Me. Any Faith will do. I will make clear what is unclear, seen what is unseen. And I will certainly hold you through the moments you become frightened and need to pause or even take some steps back. The stronger your Faith, the easier the journey will be.

What makes trusting Me harder for you is the arrogance of your judgment, particularly the judgments rooted in assumptions, bias, control, denial, chaff-self-righteousness, or desire-based impulses. Judgment is a poisonous seed indeed. It is the power-hungry desire to be the judge that leaves you at the mercy of judgment yourself. Real judges are Balancers. That is the aspect of God that is not judgmental but fair. And maintains an order that allows for evolution and equality.

When you continuously judge, weigh, and compare yourself to others, that is when things fall apart. Who is the deeper victim? Who is the most right? Who is the most wounded? Who is the most oppressed?

Who is the most guilty? To the ego of most people, the answer is . . . "ME. I AM the suffering one. I have suffered the most." There is an eerie air of self-absorption, arrogance, self-pity, and even greed surrounding such mindsets and judgments based in comparison of shadow.

Judgment of self and others is a poisonous seed. As opposed to discernment, which is a Divine Right you were anointed with: the power of choice. When you hold judgment, you are carrying venom. When you deliver it, you spit that venom and poison the garden. One person in burden creates crosses and burdens for all others. Internalizing others' poison is like being bitten by a snake. When you are the poisonous snake, your bite is poison. It is time for you all to stop hissing, spitting, and biting and to begin asking for the antidote, which is your Faith and Transcendence.

Grace comes in moments you walk away from saying words of shaming and hate and, for once, have the humility to know you do not know another's story or Journey. When you do walk away, My Rod and My Staff, as well as the Snake of the Staff of Moses, designed by God to Offer purification, healing, rebirth, and wisdom, renders you clean and whole. It is a powerful needle that unstitches you from the love-nots that have kept you bound to fear, worry, anger, and judgment. It transforms your desire to judge, setting you Free from bondage. It parts the seas so that you may know safe passage. That is the Caduceus. Of Balance, liberation, and restoration.

It is a hard Path to choose when you feel you have been wronged. The true caduceus of a Light-holder is the ability to release that by resolving it through Love. It takes trust and deep discipline to overcome your human impulses. But when you Free yourself from this want to judge under self-righteous power constructs, the Holy Spirit, the Word, is Freed within you. Then, it becomes quite easy to let things go. Humor, creativity, communication, and service are strong recommendations as you move deeper into this Path.

Laughing over an argument instead of allowing the tight, bound

strings to burst, which often results in a once Loving relationship ending in tatters, resentment, reaction, and regret, is one of My favorites.

Wrathful wisdom and desire—these are the true abominations
that lead to desolation, or de-soulation I should say. These are the
ego imbalances that simply create filth and logs over the lenses of
your eyes and perception—the filth of hatred toward others and even
toward self. Greed is actually a by-product of self-hatred. Why tarnish
the Garden? Dirt and mud can be wondrously playful—the Beloved
animals that you call swine Love to roll and play in it. Filth is not necessarily filth in the sense of Gaia, and blood, and gore.

Filth is an energy on the inside that is based in abomination of
desolation—poisonous seeds of fear, desire, neglect, and lack of consideration for others. Judgment, arrogance, and wrathful wisdom is the
root of all poison, all imbalance. That is where a lot of your root chakra
distortions and safety or survival fears ultimately come from. We understand that you need to make choices or discernments in order to survive.
Your primal survival needs We understand. However, many of those
have been met and still you want more and more. When you don't get
it, anger erupts—anger stemming from an entitled, fragile ego and fear.

That is the root of the poison of separation. It is the root that poi-
sons the whole Tree of Life. It began from wrathful wisdom, sexual
rejection, and dominance. It began in the foolish wisdom that man
knew better than God. The Seven Imbalances of the Mind I spoke of
emerged from there.

Separation did not come first, judgment, foolish wisdom, and arrogance did—not aligning Free will with Divine Will, in the earliest
stages of consciousness. It is part of the progression of becoming self-
aware. Judgment comes easily to those, and to you, when one's dominant ego lacks Faith and is unable to trust in alignment with Divine
Will. When you judge another from ego, fear, and contempt, you are
in contempt of the court of Divine law as defined by the collective
consciousness, by the Divine, and by the essence of your be-ing.

You are making a choice, and that choice is to stay separate. Irreverent judgment means that you are in a limited identity construct of "not-enoughness," whether it is the Divine that is not enough to you or you that are not enough to you, and thus feel the need to assert your "too-muchness" onto those in the external world.

When a person cannot see or recognize the equal worth of others, it is often because he or she does not have a Balanced relationship with God. When one does not have a relationship with the Divine based in humility and Surrender, be it through consciousness, meditation, service, or nature, it is easy to fall into judgment because the imbalanced ego dominates perception. When you are in the essence of your be-ing, your Yeshua self, you can make judgments that will be Balanced. Because you are Balanced. Until that point, I recommend sticking to discernment instead, which is **the intuitive inner process of inviting the Divine, consciousness into your choices.**

Now, there can be moments of discernment when someone or something is not or is no longer feeling resonant or aligned for you. This does not mean that you are right and they are wrong, or vice versa. Sometimes when a stitch gets undone, there does not have to be a reason. Why must everything have to be justified? **Never try to justify a realignment.** There are sometimes feelings that you feel for which there is no explanation, for which there is no justification. Rationalizing choices to release something of dissonance suggests doubt. You can explore, feel into things, but do not rationalize why you feel resonance or dissonance or do not.

Judgment is all about justification, rationalization, and a need to be right. Discernment is simply exploring, following through on certain actions and commitments, but being selective of what it is that you commit to. Simplicity and discernment go hand-in-hand. Your discernment can sometimes say, "I need to take space before I can commit to this. Under no circumstance do I wish to sacrifice my Simplicity, for when I have Simplicity, I am able to see and feel the Truth and I have more room for Love."

You resonate with some things, feel dissonance with others, as others do with you. Let them without getting defensive. Let yourself go within the process, as many of the things and people that you belong with and to, as I said, will be changing. **The beautiful thing about discernment is that it liberates you from needing to judge and justify. Therein, the burden of judgment dissolves. And another liberation becomes possible: the possibility of Forgiveness.**

Great power comes from Forgiveness. Forgiveness is what sets you Free from the oppressive shackles of crosses, and burdens, and stitches that continue to wound you over and over, or keep you in fear. Through Forgiveness, when others judge you, it is easy to remain Free and immune from the shackles.

Acceptance and Love are the two central components of Forgiveness. The two attributes that give it the majority of its Power. Forgiveness, Beloved, is deeply challenging to the mind and your limited perception of consciousness no matter how evolved you believe you are. For those of you who sometimes struggle with Forgiveness, it is because there is still a part of you that says, "They don't really deserve it." That is why it is a process.

Through Forgiveness comes great Power of Simplicity and Freedom. Because judgment means belonging to something that is imbalanced and disempowering. Forgiveness is Power because it sets you Free, even if others are unwilling to accept and see that they need to Forgive you or ask for your Forgiveness. If they wish to take everything personally, they are not Free. They are at the mercy of believing that they have control and power when they do not. They are in disempowerment.

Forgiveness carries great Power, aligned Power, as does gratitude, another great liberator. Divine Power lies within the Freedom of walking Free within the Garden. Knowing the wise humility of Truth even when no one else does. Forgiveness makes it easy for you to feel compassion for those who judge and blame—or do not acknowledge the worth of others. Forgive—even when it means a relationship has run its course. You can Forgive yet uphold a boundary of ending. Forgiveness doesn't mean keeping. Sometimes it is an ending. That depends on the circumstance.

Cycles come, cycles die. Know when it is time to let someone go. Do not hold on when there is nothing to hold on to, due to your own stubbornness and fear. Let them go, no matter how much resentment they carry—set yourself Free from their burdens. Have compassion and humility in the undoing. You are complete, thus it is okay when a relationship is complete. You have completed your journey together in that moment. When you have completed a chapter of a book or level of a game you do not anger, toil, and need to justify its completion. You move on to the next. Such is the way in your relationships. Sometimes you meet the same character or a like character chapters later, either to complete the unstitching through Forgiveness and closure . . . or to begin weaving together again. It is easy to complete things when you are complete. In your fragmented self, completion is difficult because it is you who are not complete. That makes Forgiveness harder.

Do not leave a relationship until you can come to Peace with it. For you cannot leave a relationship or end one, even if you wish, until you Forgive and come to Peace with it on the inside. Let that process be a process. One who Forgives can walk away Freely after processing the grief, even if the other still stays captive and chooses not to grieve. Grief is a part of any ending. It is funny how much you fear the grief— you fear the pain. Yet in the moment when the ending actually comes, it is cleansing. It moves you deeper into Love. You can feel as though your heart is shattering into a million pieces, but there is something about grieving, processing, honoring, and letting go that rebalances, or heals, all.

Freedom is not be-ing and doing whatever you want. Freedom is be-ing what you are. That is the Freedom of Be-ing.
Freedom is sharing with ALL. But foremost, sharing your life with the Divine. We do not overpower you—We honor your Free will. You cannot overpower Us either in Our relationship with all be-ings, as you are all One Be-ing. Freedom is sharing, which makes it easier to experience the Divine in every aspect of your life, even when you see things in the world that make you angry. To those things you see that anger you, give them over to Me and I will resolve them in time.

This is the Prayer and Invocation of My Presence to speak in the moments you need to Surrender:

Prayer of Transcendence

Yeshua, the dissonance I feel in this moment, I am giving over to You. I am deeply sad, Divine Father and Friend, in witnessing and experiencing this. Yet I understand that I do not know and am best served and serving in holding the Light for _____ [insert person or experience]. I agree to first come to Peace with it/them before acting.

I will not choose the hate, and feed the energy of hate. I will hold the Light, and if I feel grief or sadness or mourning, I will not reach to victimhood or rage, I will Forgive to help to lessen the burden. Please help me, Divine Father and Mother, to move this dissonance and anger I feel. Show me the Path if I need to engage; show me how I can channel this into my passion through Peace. For I trust You to show me how to act with Peace in a way that brings resolution through Love instead of dissonance through pain. I trust You to resolve any imbalances inherent to this experience. Show me how I can best serve in this issue I am passionate about—through Peace. Thy Will be done. Sancti. Pace. Amein.

Grieving for another, or better yet, Praying for another, be it an abused animal, elder, or child, lessens the burden for that other, more than fighting does. Though it is very hard to do so at times, grieving and Praying for the abuser provides an even greater service because it is he or she who needs it the most. That is the greatest Yeshua service. To Pray for the abuser as much as if not more than the one injured. Grieving and Prayer do more than anything when it comes to things you see or experience that cause hurt. They come quite naturally if you allow them to. I bow to you for your service in these moments deeply.

If what you see or experience makes you angry, very often it is because you see someone or something being negated in his/her/their/ its worth. This triggers you for all the times you have known the same. Thus, please channel the anger into acknowledgment of your worth and theirs. That is an acknowledgment, a Namaste, that stretches deeper in energy than you could ever know. Their soul will feel that, as will yours—that is Light sent to them upon the Web of Life, seen and unseen, in recognition and co-creative support of their Presence and Divinity.

When you let go of others, you become One with them. That is very often why your soul or spirit mates, whether they are your greatest Loves or worst pains in your life, are people you often stay close to, and journey with many, many times over many lives. Just because you unstitch from someone in your life does not mean the Love you shared falls away. Love is immune from death, for Love IS the Tree of Life. Amein.

YESHUA MEDITATION

Close your eyes, Beloved One. Begin to breathe deeply into your be-ing. Breathe in the smell of the chaff and the taste of the wheat. Vi-sualize yourself in a field, an energetic field of wheat. Begin to walk through this field as you walk through your body. Feel the wheat within the chaff rippling through your fingers. Feel your Divine hand as My Divine Hand, as we wave our hands over the field together. Each stalk you touch is another person, another tree. As you touch the wheat in this field, touch all the souls held within it—people, animals, trees, it does not matter. You are the Witness, the Yeshua, in this moment.

Gaze at the beautiful field of wheat or corn, blowing in the wind. You are One with every stalk. Some stalks within this field may be a bit sickly, they may not have had as nourishing soil, or they may have chosen a chaff not quite as rooted as your own. Yet every stalk is your child and has equal worth within your heart.

There are no slaves within this field. The wheat of this field harvests itself through the Hands of God.

Now, breathe in and feel all the stalks merging into one rising stalk. A stalk that merges into a Tree. The Tree of Life.

You belong, and are of the Tree of Life. You are equally in life, death, and rebirth in this moment. You breathe, are born, die, and continue to breathe through your unity with this Tree. Through this Tree, through the whole of your body, feel the Strand of Faith, weaving from branches all the way down through your roots.

Now weave the Strand of Forgiveness down your branches into your roots. Now weave the Strand of Freedom from your branches down into your roots. Through the roots of these Strands, feel as they weave together into a Braid.

From your roots, soak up the nourishment, the lineages of Faith, weaving up from your roots and up through your branches. Then soak up the nourishment, the lineages of all those who have Forgiven. All this energy weaving up from the root and down from the branches. From your roots, soak up the nourishment of those in Spirit who devoted their lives then and now to Freedom. Weave Freedom through your roots and branches. Feel as the Faith, Forgiveness, and Freedom weave and braid, from roots to branches, branches to roots.

From the Eye of the Tree, which is your sacred heart, now allow Faith to flow and weave out of your heart. Weaving and braiding you through energy to all those who are in need of Faith or can serve you to grow deeper into yours. From your sacred heart, allow Forgiveness to flow and weave out of your heart. Weaving and braiding you through energy to all those who are in need of Forgiveness or can serve you to grow deeper into yours. From your sacred heart, allow Freedom to flow and weave out of your heart. Weaving and braiding you through energy to all those who are in need of Freedom or can serve you to grow deeper into yours.

You are the Wheat, the Chaff, the Tree, the Braid. Breathe into My Love, My honoring of your service in this moment. Exhale deeply.

Place one hand on your womb or hara for men, and one hand on your heart. Bow your head to Gaia, your chaff, and tilt your face with closed eyes toward the sun, moon, or stars, smile, and speak your name. Now, speak Mine.

Please either press your hand or foot to the Earth or, better, get onto your hands and knees and press your forehead to the Earth, grounding your energy deeply. Release the meditation.

I would then like you to take out the piece of paper with the **Freedom Transmissions Process** from the first Freedom Transmission. **Do not open it.** Place your hand upon it, speak your name, and then speak Mine. Flood what lies within this paper with the Grace streaming through the Tree of Life, the Sacred Heart, through your hand, onto the paper. And smile.

Your heart to My Heart. One Heart. Your tree to My Tree. One Tree. Your Light to My Light. One Light. Your name to My Name. One Name. Abba. Amma. Al-Ilah. El Shaddai. I AM Yeshua. I AM the Word. You ARE the Beloved. And I AM yours.

It has been My honor to have served you on this day. Ohm Nami Maia. Ohm Namah Sananda. Ohm Nami Yeshua. Sancti. Sancti. Sancti. Pace. Pace. Pace. Namaste.

Moving Mountains

1

The Power of Perception

YESHUA TEACHING

Good day, Beloved One. On this good day, good night, I wish to bring to Light some simple Words that, when braided together and realized, have the ability to catalyze extraordinary Miracles for you and for others. The power of these Words has been the same for all be-ings since the dawn of time and beginning of creation. The Words are: **Love Moves Mountains.**

Love Moves Mountains.

Indeed, it does, Beloved. That is what I wish to bring clarity to today: Mountains. How you perceive them and how your spirit and soul in co-creation possess the Divine Magic to move them.

Clarity is about perception. It is not the mountain before you that is the joy or the problem, depending on your outlook; it is your perception of the mountain that is what either creates larger mountains, cumbersome mountains, or reduces them to a field of grass. The slightest little hill can feel like a mountain when you are carrying the density of crosses and burdens such as shame, control, impatience, despair, or anger.

The slightest remark, the slightest hill, the slightest bubble can be perceived as a massive mountain when you carry such energies. That mountain appears and feels exhausting to scale. When you are not carrying so many burdens, when you are Lighter, scaling a mountain can be quite simple, and actually quite enjoyable. Or, through shifting your perception of the mountain altogether, you can move right around it or even right through it. That depends on the lens through which you choose to view the mountain.

Your perception of mountains in your life is very different when you are present in the now versus when you are focusing on the past or future. You often perceive issues as mountains, inconvenient mountains, typically when you are feeling separate, or focusing on the outcome—the expectation of what a specific mountain is keeping you separate from. Or, when you are not present—either living in yesterday or tomorrow—your perception of that mountain is that scaling it, resolving it, will require so much work.

You wonder, "What will be there on the other side? Is it worth it to scale this mountain?" "Will it be worth it to make this change? How much work will it take to resolve this health problem? To organize my finances? To finally clean out that garage?" The mind says, "I have so many other things to do, I think I will just put it on hold, put it on hold . . . I will just wait, wait, wait." These are distorted and limited perceptions that can keep you from scaling small mountains when they are still little. The clutter from procrastination builds and the mountain grows taller and taller. In trying to focus on the big mountains, you forget that addressing these smaller mountains with curiosity and as much Love as you do the larger ones can not only help you to scale the larger, but also to avoid having to face cumbersome mountains altogether.

This is why it is important not to overlook what is before you in the present moment, by taking more moments to observe and witness yourself, your thoughts, and your surroundings from the overlook of the mountain of your life. From this overlook you can see the areas of your life that hold some dry brush at deep risk of catching on fire and burning acre upon acre.

Bringing consciousness to clear the smaller mountains and areas of dry brush is the simplest, most liberating path to addressing the larger. Which is why what is before you now and drawing your awareness to the now, even if inconvenient or painful, is so important. Allowing yourself the kindness of embracing what your soul is continuously drawing your awareness to makes it easier to unstitch and unbraid from issues that hinder your path to Peace and service through joy. Shifting your perception of mental or emotional polarities from burdens to opportunities for transformation and liberation is central to this.

When you are in consciousness and you gaze at a range of mountains, you can discern, or you can appreciate, those mountains. You recognize when they are distant or near, and know, through Faith, that your soul will bring you all you need to scale or move them . . . or will perhaps tell you they are just beautiful to look at but not necessary to scale. When you are in unconsciousness, you perceive those mountains with more fear, because you are not taking space from them—you are not taking a step back from them. You are never just witnessing the mountains, you are internalizing them to the extent that you start creating mountains that are not there. Everything becomes such a hassle, one more thing, one more thing. These dense, veiled perceptions come most when you are fatigued, overly committed, procrastinating, or have issues with asking for and receiving support.

All mountains—yours, the world's, in nature—were created by Love, and can be leveled through Love. All mountains were birthed of Love, real mountains or perceived mountains in life, and thus, all mountains can be scaled or moved through Love. When you are conscious that you ARE Love, your Love has the power to create beautiful mountains, as well as to shift, move, or transform others that seem a bit scary and dark. Truly, Beloved, you do this all the time—during periods in your life when you have many, many issues, many things, many mountains to face all at once—you can go to sleep and dream of a cool, flat land, or a tranquil ocean. You do not perceive, nor are you focused on, your mountains of issues in that dream.

Yet when you wake, there the mountains of issues are again. Or vice versa. You can be in a tranquil, neutral, or even complacent period in your life—go to sleep, and dream of mountains, issues. When you wake, they are not there. Which are more real? The dream mountains? Or the waking mountains? Do you know for sure that both are not just projections of the mountains waiting to move within you? The unconscious moving to consciousness, that is the moving and rising of a mountain.

When this occurs, when something below the surface rises, even something that frightens you, whether it was catalyzed by an external event or an internal one for seemingly no reason, it is because a mountain is moving within you. Regardless of whether it feels heavy or sad or angry or if it feels joyous and liberating, recognize that something powerful is happening. **A mountain is moving within you!**

Also recognize that, despite your perception, it was created by Love and with Love. With Presence, whatever is moving on the inside will move you into deeper Balance on the outside. Mountains are made of rock, fire, water, air, and space. Resting on the constant, the rock of your Faith will allow you to stand atop whatever is rising instead of beneath it in the sand. It is extraordinary when a mountain moves within you. It is a liberation of a part of you that was unseen.

Rejoice, for now you can see it! Truth was revealed! Your soul moved a mountain within you and, if it can do so within you, your spirit can certainly move other mountains all around you in the external world. Instead of perceiving it with disdain or fear, shift that to curiosity, joy, and even gratitude. Stand in your God-given Power, for, though you cannot control the outside, you can control BOTH your internal perceptions and whether you wish to see the Truth revealed with blind eyes of fear or clear eyes of Love.

The lens with which you view reality and the world is dependent on the amount of Light and consciousness that you are bringing into your be-ing. When present, you can witness the mountain, the rock of Faith, in a way that gives it fluidity. Consciousness is fluid energy. All is fluid with Love, including mountains. When you are living in the future, a mountain seems rigid, fixed, difficult to scale or move. The mind begins separating self from the fluidity of the ocean of energy the mountain is and was created from. Thus, it loses its power of co-creative movement and becomes hypervigilant, continuously fearing the mountain.

That is a helpless and victim-oriented fear state in which you perceive that the mountains, the issues, are happening to you, burdening you. In reality you are happening to the mountain. Again, after scaling so many mountains in the more and more complexity and clutter you draw into your life to avoid moving the mountains before you, you can begin to fear mountains, and even to create them in your mind when they are not there. When you are not conscious, you are lost in the dream—not only in your own dream, but also at the mercy of external dreams, others' dreams for you. And feel obligated to suppress your Love, your true self, in that state, as well as to repress your own dreams. That is a cross and a burden.

Love created mountains. Love moves mountains. This happens in Gaia. It is part of the fabric of creation. Will you be in the dreaming, will you be nothing more than matter and thought, and the feelings that come of it? Making statements such as, "Ugh, the burden of another mountain that I am facing! What is this issue, this mountain, going to do to me? Why do I continue to try to scale this mountain and keep falling down over and over? The moment that I scale one, it feels like another even bigger one replaces it!" Or will you pause to remember that you have the power to shift that mountain, to level it altogether, to go around it, or to move it to a place where you have space to view it, Love it, and appreciate it for what it is?

Will you be in the dreaming and the matter? Or will you be the dreamer? I AM both the Dreaming and Dreamer. As are you. Creator and Creation, as are you. Wake up, Beloved One, to the space of consciousness that rests between. When you wake up to your Love, and shift the logs and specks that created distorted and even disillusioned perceptions of things past and future that are not real, you see with clear lenses.

When your perception lies in the present, you will begin to see that there are no mountains. For within Love, creation of mountains and destruction of mountains is simply a movement of forms through liquid consciousness. Nothing is truly being created or destroyed. There is a movement of consciousness, but the finite point is the tranquil pool that is Truth.

As you begin to receive more Love, more Light, more consciousness into your be-ing, it can feel as though suddenly the Lights have come on when you were previously in the dark. Suddenly you begin to see a Truth so obvious that somehow, for years, you could not uncover or see before. And all of a sudden that Truth is everywhere! Sometimes you can see a way to dissolve the mountain. Or sometimes you suddenly see a mountain in the form of a love-not that, to undo, requires change to many aspects of your life. It can feel scary and overwhelming.

When you are in fear, it makes it difficult to see and feel the Love inherent to this revelation of Truth. Regret, embarrassment, and even shame can emerge. With statements like, "Why did I not see this before? How and when did this relationship that once felt like Love start to feel like a mountain is between us, a block, a disconnect? Has it been there all these years? From the very beginning? How could I not have seen this before? I should have."

Remember, Beloved One, Truth evolves as Love evolves. You can only uncover Truth through Love and resolve and integrate that Truth through Love. Never wallow in the "should haves" and "could haves" when the Truth of a love-not is revealed. Making amends to yourself and others can occur, if necessary, in due time. But before you spring to action, rejoice when a Truth, any Truth, is revealed. For it means that Love is growing within you! See what there is to see without attaching to solutions and outcome. Rejoice that you are seeing what is real. Through Love, the Truth does indeed set you Free.

What fascinates Us is how much you all Love to look at gore and are very curious about other people's carnage, mountains, and issues (rubbernecking is a good example of this tendency), but are so quick to look away from or bury your own. When you do, it is the imbalanced ego resisting change.

It says, "I don't want to look—I don't want to look—I am just going to assume that this relationship is still of Love, yet I am feeling less Love and more burdens in my life." Or, "I am going to pretend I can manage this job that keeps me so unhappy. I have a decent life; I get by." Or, "My addiction isn't so bad." Or, "My sore back isn't so bad. I can't always walk, but it isn't so bad." This denial causes such issues to become worse. And, all the while, your soul allows for the denial but continuously raises its hand, saying, "Look at this, look at this—if you do, it will set you Free."

When you receive more Love into your be-ing, what can also become clearer are all of the areas that keep you separate from Love. When Love rushes in, She invites you deeper into Her Truth through your own. She is a glorious communicator and is more than happy to inform you of all of the areas where you are separate from Her, from Me. When you receive the Presence of Divine Love through your own, suddenly the areas Love is Void in your life can seem to appear everywhere in your life: in your professional life, friendships, partnerships, Eros relationships, and family life.

What is happening is that the mountain that separates you from Love is eroding. When you are in denial or not looking at, or too focused on, all of these other areas, and not tuning in, too lost in the dreaming—the human relationships, the matter, the career, the wants, the whatever else—you can sometimes not see the separation between you and the Divine, between yourself and Love as She exists within you.

As you begin to move deeper into consciousness, the mountain keeping you separate from the Divine begins to erode, and, as it does, Love grows and Faith grows. This predominantly occurs by closing your eyes to the external, opening the soul eye, and putting one foot in front of the other. When you bring joy and excitement into the process instead of perceiving things as work or setbacks, when you commit to your own excavation and dismantling of all that holds you back from Love with joy, it is always worth it. Always. And the Miracle that comes is that, because the process is being embraced by your soul, heart, and finally though begrudgingly your mind, when mind gets on board, suddenly what seemed like a mountain feels more like a speed bump.

It is important for you to remember that this is a process. It is a process, Beloved. Mountains take time to form. They can take time to dissolve. The reality is that when you are in Love, choosing Love, there is no mountain. And for the ones you perceive, invite Me into the process. If you are authentic to your inner process, including the grief and Surrender that come in releasing all the pain separation has brought to you, I will move what needs to be moved in the external. That is a promise I can make. To dimensions and levels your mind or eyes cannot even perceive.

Again, remember that mountains are created from the elements, the four elements that comprise creation, matter. There is air held within the rocks, air high up, air, the silhouette where the body of the mountain touches the sky. There is wind that moves on and through mountains. Fresh air. There is Earth in mountains, the rocks, the dirt, the mud, the trees. There is water and rivers that cascade through mountains. There is fire in the heart of a mountain. Mountains rise up from molten rock from the belly and pit of the Earth. They were created from the dust of stars, the fire of suns of yesteryear, as were you.

The mountains in your life, including your bodies, were created by Love, moved through Love, which is why Love moves you all, even when you perceive something happening to be anything but. Every time you walk you are moving energy. Your wheat in chaff is a moving mountain. But it isn't the chaff that moves the wheat. It is the wheat that moves the chaff. Just as creation does not move Creator. Creator moves creation.

Love levels the mountain in the end—when your soul leaves your body, when wheat leaves chaff. You are Earth, bones. The Earth is your anchoring of the mountain of your whole self. Your mountain has the air of relationships, breath, and wind grazing across it. It has the water of emotions. The fire of passion. But the fifth element of space is the consciousness of the Creator within you. You create your mountains through Love. Thus, when you are not in victimhood, bemoaning all of the mountains that are befalling you and who caused these mountains or burdens for you, you are One with Creator.

You understand deeply within self that ALL in your life was created by Love, and can be moved through Love. When external things arise, within your Creator Self, Yeshua self, conscious self that does not internalize, panic, or rush, you are able to witness it. "Oh, an issue within chaff has arisen. It may affect the chaff of my life. But I am going on a different path this time. I will not view this through my chaff-lens, which is really only best to use when I am in immediate, real physical danger. This time, I am going to pause, and view it through the lens of my wheat."

When you do so it is easy to see that the hurdle, the issue, is not you AND that there is no one to blame for it. Possibly, the issue or cross may not even be your cross or affect you in the slightest. You are witnessing another person's cross and making it your own for no reason. "Not my cross, not my burden" is the important aspect of space to recognize and utilize. "I'll do mine, you do yours" is what is Balanced and fair. Recognizing what is yours and what is not is important. Feeling guilt when seeing others struggling, well, it does not benefit them for you to struggle with them for no reason. Holding the Light for them is best.

In utilizing space and wheat-perception, your Yeshua eyes, unnecessary stress and burdens fall away. As I have said before, never become a burden to thine own self. For when you do, you create burdens for everyone around you. You have the power to move this energy, or to shift your perception to gratitude for all mountains that rise or fall, including those that move you deeper into humility, Forgiveness, and Love.

Your soul's will abides by God's Will, My Will. Aligning with that Will brings joy. For God's Will is Love, Truth, and Peace, no matter your external reality. For all of you. God's Will is Balance. Thus, when you are feeling imbalanced, lacking in Love, out of Truth, in denial, afraid, alone, there is an imbalance of will going on inside you. Often on the basis of your perception. When the mind is trying to bend the soul to its will, things go awry. The element of space, taking a space before reacting, taking a space for patience and releasing the mountain to God, inviting Me in to support you, is what realigns you—and the mountain moves, or a path around the mountain becomes quite clear and apparent.

With Faith, **the recognition of your Divinity,** no matter how tall the mountain is, or whether it is a molehill, you rest in the deep soul knowing that everything is going to be all right. As the mountain moves, and you are able to see what is on the other side, you understand that you are always seeing what is real and do not need to see more than what comes in a given step on a given day. The space element is where the consciousness of Love resides; it is the center point, the radial center of Balance from which all things in your life move. Even if you cannot always feel it or do not even believe in it, you all have a body center, a heart center. It is there. It does not require belief to develop Faith. It doesn't even matter what you have Faith in. Even if you have Faith in nothingness, you still have Faith.

Through your Faith, you recognize self as Divine. Then anything can move. When you choose blame, or anger, or despair, mountains are made taller and the crosses are made heavier. That can make life seem almost insurmountable—"Why bother trying?" Shift the perception, Love the mountain, and it will move. The mountain is not there to burden you.

But when there is a wound that has come over and over again, a mountain within you trying to rise up to move, and you keep stuffing it back down, repressing it, you wind up continuously patching it up with a bandage made of thorns. Stitching it up, patching it up with substances, stimulation, avoidance, complacency, busyness, overgiving, focusing on others and their mountains; the list goes on.

When you are denying the rising mountain or an issue and just wish to close up the wound so that you don't need to look at it and feel it, you can create so many stitches over a wound or love-not that it almost feels like a mountain—a lump in your heart, stomach, or throat. The bigger the mountain and the more time you have spent running away from healing it, or shifting your perception about what it is, the more overwhelming that knot can feel. "So many threads and knots to undo, where do I even begin to pull this apart?"

Well, start saying YES to unthreading the love-nots. Not by rehashing how they formed, or by whom, but simply by allowing for the mountain to rise. Not fearing change. The mind often tells you that unstitching and unbraiding these love-nots will be more painful than it is. But for every stitch you undo through energy and behaviors, for every thorn bandage that you do not slap on, a Freedom comes and I bring you the Pathway to Peace. For you are taking responsibility for your part.

It is important to recognize that whether it was an addiction, running away from looking at something, distraction, dissonant behavior, dissonant thought, denial, not speaking up about something (one of My favorites), not enforcing boundaries—whatever imbalance it was that caused behaviors to intensify—it was created by Love. You were not ready to look at the wound. Your perception, the level of Love that you had, or have had, was and is different. But the more that you are present, and stop looking at the stitches as insurmountable mountains, or the wound as a negative thing that needs to be apologized for or reasoned through—then you can take all of the burdens of those stitches off.

All of those mountains that you have built up, all of the armor that you hide behind to give off the illusion that you are thriving, happy, and have it all together but that makes you feel fraudulent and keeps you alone—it is armor you needed until you were ready and strong enough to accept and look at the Truth. Which may be that you were scared, you did not feel safe, you were told that you were not good enough as the mountain that you were and are.

It is a huge and amazing movement and evolution of your consciousness when you can admit that you cannot live with the armor anymore. That is courage. Far more courageous than seemingly "having it all together." My view of "having it all together" is be-ing your whole self, as you are then Free of armor and not trying so very, very hard to appear that you have it all together to the external world. Be-ing naked in your whole self is a rarity within this world that hopefully will become more of the norm in times to come. That starts with you.

None of you has it "all together" and you are all together in that. Thus, have a bit more compassion and humility for yourselves. And respect for those that do not pretend. Those in humility are the first ones to admit they do not have it all together, but what they do have is Love and the ability to be present and honest. They have their Yeshua eyes open, thus they have no need to hide. Nor can you hide from them.

I wish for you to begin replacing the sadly rewarded distortion of "having to have it all together" with allowing yourself to "come together"!

Allow yourself to come together. To become Whole and thus Holy. No pretense, no forcing, no projecting. Why have it all together by the standards of others also pretending that they do? Why not take space from that and come, together with Me, on the journey of allowing your soul to bring the pieces together? To, through Loving Truth, allow the external mountains to rise and fall as you witness from your outlook on the Mount of Olives instead of Golgotha. Resting in the Faith that, no matter the perceived mountain, all is coming together. You are coming together. We are coming together. And, I have a hunch, Beloved One, that together we can move all of the other mountains of the world through Love.

It is a Love story, this Pathway to Peace. You ARE a moving mountain. What is it that, within yourself, you have the power to move? Or that you feel you need to move? What do you need from Me in order to move it? Rest with this question in your heart and in your dreaming. Write about it and, please, be clear. For I will reveal the Path to fulfillment of those needs and bring you what you need to support your movement of it. Amein.

2

Clarity

Behold, Beloved One. More than almost anything else, the most common request We receive from you all is for . . . Clarity. "Bring me clarity on this issue, this mountain, Yeshua. I need clarity." And time and time again, We respond over and over, as does your soul and spirit by bringing you the clear Truth within the moment.

There is a difference between lack of clarity and refusal to look at the clear Truth that is being shown to you in any given moment. **What is not clear, Beloved One?**

Oftentimes, you ask for clarity for validation or "reassurance." Re-Assurance. Meaning that you once had assurance? And lost it? Where did it go? The key root in *assurance* is "ass." An ass, a donkey, is sure of step. It lives in the present. While you all Love to be so sure, nothing is assured to you; you are not entitled to assurance. Anyone who is in-sure-nce may need to revisit their policy and contract with the Divine. Confidence is glorious. As is support, feeling supported and clear. Hubris is not. Assurance is not. Reassurance even less so. Clarity, when stitched to a desire for validation, is simply a fancy term for wanting "to know" to avoid the discomfort of the unknown.

Beloved One, if everything in your life were perfectly clear, and you knew absolutely everything, your life would be utterly boring and you would be so Light that it would be impossible for you to be in body. It would be like having a cheat sheet of all of your soul contracts, weaving, tapestry, and thus you would never learn, never evolve, and avoid all of the painful lessons through anticipating them in advance. What fun is that?

You would have no Free will, no choice, and that runs contrary to your choice to come into this reality structure. Free will brings many gifts, but it also means you need to accept the unknown. You are growing in consciousness, evolving in consciousness. It would be a huge disservice and violation of your Free will to make everything clear to you. Far more joyful, and interesting for that matter, is illuminating your own God-self through the power of sentience and creation held within you. That is how you come to see with Divine eyes.

However, as a human be-ing, when a lack of clarity is perceived, it is most often because:

1.   You are being impatient with the process of what your soul and spirit is aligning. It is not yet time to be "clear." You are in a space of gestation and revelation. But the imbalanced mind always wants to know "right now," just as a toddler wants its candy bar "right now," before dinner.

2.   The issue, or mountain, or choice, you desire clarity on is not what We know and your soul knows is the actual thing that you need clarity on. For example, you might be asking for clarity on a job choice when your soul is trying to realign you with going to school or resolving a family situation. You are so narrowly focused over here that you are missing what is clear, important, and obvious over there. In other words, you are asking for the right thing but looking in the wrong place for the answer.

3.   You do not wish to accept the Truth that is being brought. You want the clarity to come in the form your mind wants instead of the

way that your soul needs. For example, you are in a dysfunctional relationship. You keep asking for clarity on how to resolve it. Truth comes over and over and over. We are honest over and over and over.

But you do not want to accept that Truth. You want Us to resolve the relationship so that you don't have to see and move the mountain, including the other mountains you think will come as a by-product, such as what will happen when you need to tell friends or children the relationship is over, find a new place to live, go through a divorce, face financial fears, etc. If, over time, the Truth keeps revealing to you that, despite having been patient, having explored resolution, nothing has worked, the clarity We are bringing is likely that the relationship needs to end. Never fear the Truth. Despite occasionally feeling heavy as an energy, He is as Light as Love. Never fear the Truth.

This form of denying Truth under the auspices of "lack of clarity," because it comes in the form your mind does not want, results in a judgmental doubt of God's ability and your soul's ability to bring you what you need. That is a denying of self and a denying of Love. And it will keep things unclear. When you deny, nothing can be clear. For you are staring with blind eyes instead of open ones.

Just because we bring you the Truth does not mean you need to act on it right away. But you do need to allow for it, accept it, and work with it, and suddenly then more and more will be made clear in extraordinary ways through exploration and allowing.

We can bring you all you need to move your mountains, We can hold your hand, but We cannot force you to see the Truth. That would violate your Free will and We Love you too much to do so.

Truly, what is not clear, Beloved One? I will go a step further to say, what is not clear on your Earth? Change has come. Has been coming. Mountains everywhere are rising that you did not see before, including just how many of your global structures have become imbalanced, controlling, complacent, and greedy. Time and time again We bring clarity to you in the form of Truth, but it isn't the form you wish to see, so you brush it aside and create more and more density. That is not sustainable. Nor does it lead to Peace.

Open the clear eyes we designed you to carry and stop abdicating responsibility. You have the power within you to pluck from the infinite possibilities and catalyze change, big and small. I suggest starting with your internal mountains that create a whole range of external issues. Perhaps your mind might be a bit grumpy about the need to explore healthier food options, engage in conversations with actual people instead of gadgets, spend the time healing your sore back, enter a process of recovery from addiction, call a sibling or parent you have not spoken to in some time, restore Simplicity, or, since it is so prevalent, quiet down your busy, busy mind. These are small prices to pay for the overall outcome of your Peace and that of your planet.

You cannot have clarity when you are not in reality. These fantasy worlds you give more and more weight to that create stress through bickering with other imbalanced people, such as social media, require some rebalance. Technology can be wonderful, but not when it feeds a cycle of addiction. This includes assuming identities through characters you play on games that are not real. Enjoy your games, but when the character becomes more real and inspiring than you are, it is time to take a leave of absence. There is a time for games and fun, but not to the detriment of the joy and fun of reality. You came to be here, not there.

While it was not always the case, in more recent times on your planet you have come to associate clarity with things in the future or past. As you have become detached from your Earth, your ecosystem, and from the Power of Prayer, as you entered a more mind-based, self-absorbed, "feel-good," and convenience-oriented system, you shifted from needing clarity to fulfill needs and more toward wanting clarity to fulfill wants. The latter We will not serve, nor will your soul and spirit. Your mind will. For your mind Loves indulgences of that sort—

wanting the cake before you eat the broccoli. The self-same mind that does not like the Truth, nor does it like the present.

I came to you as a Servant then and now. I serve you deeply, as deeply as I serve all. However, I will not be subservient to your individual or collective desire for clarity on things that sustain apathy, convenience, and external-seeking. We do not indulge you with clarity until you have eaten your broccoli. Because when you are seeking or wanting, you are not finding. You are looking with eyes of desire instead of desiring to see what is before your eyes. When clear eyes are a need and you are willing to meet Us halfway in the process of opening them, We will bring clarity. Clarity on the very things you need to move into deeper Love, Peace, and realization of your soul's Prayer.

Pathways to Peace are the foundation for Love. Your soul's Prayer is a Sacred brick in that foundation. Your soul's Prayer, your true passion, is to move mountains with Love for the greater good of all. Not to move mountains to get what you want, to always feel good, or to hide the glory of your mountain from the world and universe. I designed you to shine, not to dull that shine.

But what I hear now more than ever from many of you are dull requests for clarity on things of the future or past. How can tomorrow be clear, when you are not looking at today? What is before you today IS clear. Another favorite: "I want clarity so that I can feel safe." Feeling safe comes from seeing and accepting the Truth for, before you do, you cannot take the steps to move into true security. Sometimes a leap of Faith does not feel safe. Feeling Balanced is the stability you seek. **If you seek safety, ask for clarity on Balance instead.** THAT I can serve.

When you know that you have the power to create, destroy, transform, and move mountains, it makes it very easy to be clear because you are not looking at what is happening then—you are looking at what is happening now—and you are not afraid to look at what is happening now because you know that you have the power to move it with integrity and honesty.

When you are Lighter in vibration and have Simplified your life, you have fewer crosses, fewer love-nots, more agility through Stability, a deeper ability to Surrender, and far less need to control. That is a state of joy for you more than you realize. In such a state of be-ing, clarity comes easily and you can embrace it all as it comes. Not only is it easy to see clearly, YOU are clear. If you wish to be clear, then you must be present.

If you spent more time in the present, moving with Love what needs to be moved today, things would be far simpler. The solution and the outcome of what is emerging for tomorrow gradually builds through Love today. The process of this leads to the deepest joy. That is where your true sustenance comes from. Do not just ask Us, the Divine, for proof and Miracles; participate in the process and you will feel the Miracle of your own be-ing, as well as see more clearly how We move the Light within and all around you.

Whatever needs to be leveled that is keeping you from Love and joy requires your full attention. That is integrity. Integrity emanates from Faith. Faith is the recognition of your Divinity, the unseen Light of consciousness within. **Integrity is the recognition that the unseen is very much seen by the Divine, including YOU. Integrity is making conscious choices to abide by, honor, and adhere to the simple tenets of Divinity rooted in Truth, Love, and compassion, no matter the temptations of the chaff or imbalanced ego self.** It is the discernment that keeps you in alignment. It is an essential aspect of your intuition rooted in the understanding of responsibility and accountability.

When you listen to your intuition, it will always tell you honor what is of integrity. It reminds you that, even when others do not see, God sees, you see. The by-product of listening to this unseen Divine voice within, is JOY. Akin to humility, integrity leads you to joy and Freedom every time. **Humility, integrity, and originality save the day every time. Deep power resides there. You are *not* in power when you are deferring responsibility for realization of your own Miracles by blaming others and what they did that made it "impossible" for you to realize them.**

If someone is cruel to you in a dream, do you wake up angry and upset with that person in real life? Think of your life as a dreaming. When another is cruel to you, wake up and remember what reality is. You have the ability to shift the dreaming of your life—but only when you are conscious and humble. If every person was not living in the wants of tomorrow, but was true and honest about what they can do right now to shift the dreaming and move the mountains that keep them separate from Love, there would not be so much separation in your world. All those in bodies at this time, no matter the difference of culture, faith, gender, race, religion, or country, comprise one massive, soaring range of mountains. Different mountains, same range. An ecosystem of the whole world. One body within My Body. One dream within My Dream.

Move your mountains, Beloved One. If you wish, you can wake up and perhaps realize that there are no cumbersome mountains in your life or world, that you ARE the mountain, the range, and the space between. All is Love. Even in the deepest grief, in the deepest letting go, there is Love. That is the Truth of the Power of Love. That is the Love of the Power of Truth. That is the tantric consummation that creates Presence and Peace. It is the passion of the Peace. It is the compassion of passion.

What could be clearer than the Miracle of all that you already are, were, and always will be? The clarity you truly seek is how to more deeply realize, feel, and serve through that clear embodiment of Love through Truth and acceptance. Ask for that clarity and thy will be done. On Earth as it is in the Garden of Divine Peace, found within the sacred heart of this, your present breath. And so it is. Amein.

YESHUA MEDITATION

Take a breath, Beloved One. Close your eyes. Listen. Breathe. Listen to the Light of your Soul. Feel it moving, generating, echoing through your Spirit.

Do you hear Them? Do you hear the Horses? Do you see them— the Four Horses of Freedom? From the East, the South, the West, and the North. Running to you, and from you, at all times. The Horses, one for each chamber of your sacred heart: the Horse of Simplicity, the Horse of Stability, the Horse of Surrender, and the Horse of Stillness. As They run, breathe with Them, run with Them, toward Freedom through Freedom.

Breathe and listen. Open your eyes.

I have sent the Horses, the Hawks, the Eagles, the Owls, and the Ravens to help unthread, to pluck away the stitches that blind your eyes. I sent Them to make apparent to you the strings of your attachments that make you feel like you are carrying a mountain, or an anvil—so that you can dissolve them and be Free to soar, create, and witness. Within My heart there are no strings attached that are not of Freedom.

Breathe and let go.

For this moment, I wish for you to do a bit of writing:

1.   What is clear to you in this moment? Perhaps it is that you doubt that I am real. If I am not, you are not, Beloved One. If I am, then you are. Perhaps what is not clear is actually quite clear but in a way of Truth you do not wish to see: that a relationship has gone its

course; that you were wrong; that you treated someone with unkindness and need to apologize; that you are mortal; that you are responsible for your issues, not others; that you struggle with Forgiveness; that you have an addiction; that it is time to come to Peace with something of the past; that it is time to come to Peace with who you are instead of the illusion of who you wanted to be.

Perhaps what is clear is that some old repressed mountains are starting to move. Perhaps what is clear is that you need to rest and relax and let the rest of the burdens go for a spell. What is not clear? What IS clear? Are the birds outside not clear in call? Is the clarity of your heartbeat and the feeling of the air touching your skin not clear?

2.   Are you willing to be honest and give over what is not clear? And allow for the Truth to be what it is and not what you are trying to will it to be? Do you have the Faith that in giving over the burdens to Me you will know Freedom and Peace? If not, why? Where is your doubt so persistent? The answer to that is the very source of the burden.

When you are finished writing, take a breath, smile, and prostrate before yourself for having the authenticity and courage to move into the deeper Truth. Amein.

YESHUA TEACHING

Beloved One, some final words for purposes of "clarity." When you cannot see, cannot hear, cannot feel, very often it is because you are afraid, or because you are not listening. When things are not clear, it is because you are being impatient with either yourself or the Divine. Or it is because you are in doubt or in fear—almost always about an outcome in the future.

When you are in Presence, My Presence, the Divine Presence, through the power of your Presence in the present, everything is always clear. When things are not, it is because you are uncertain or in doubt of outcome—that you will not get what you need, or will lose what you have. Thus, you rush and you race and go on tangents to make known what is not ready to be known in your mind. Your mind is linear; your soul is not. Your soul will make known what needs to be in due time.

When your mind wants to dominate your soul and rush the process, your shadow slows down the process. Thereby, with impatience, reactivity, and unnecessary panic, you wind up creating deeper polarity, despair, and frustration for yourself. Exhausting. Your soul knows what you need. You will feel far more Peace when you stop getting in its way, and Mine, by redundantly asking "are we there yet" five minutes into a cross-country road trip. There is no "there," Beloved; there is only ever "here."

When you rush and race to make known what is not ready to be known, and go on tangents, that can take you to the deepest and most difficult pass on the mountain—and that can bring further lack of clarity as you try to control the process. You cannot control Love. She does not like to be controlled. Nor do you. Have some humility, respect, and awe for Her Power. And the Power of Her within you.

Ultimately lack of clarity is not about clarity, it is about safety and security in the face of change, unknowns, and doubt. In the present, all is always clear, including what is before you. Most of all, My Presence and the Divine Presence, within you at all times and in all moments. Even when you do not like a given moment. Even if in that moment your worst nightmare is playing out before your eyes, you are clear. You are clear on what is happening—you are in grief, sometimes shock; a change has come.

Whatever your soul is calling to you in any moment of your life is important, deeply important, for what is before you IS what is right. That does not show up always in the way that you wish, but always in the way most important to create more Love, even if a situation feels unfair or inconvenient. Love is not a convenient energy. She does not care about convenience or timing that is convenient for you. The same with Grief, the destruction side of Love. Grief is the same as Love, and thus behaves the same way as Love. When you try to shove your Grief into convenient moments so that you can be done with Her, She will honor your Free will. But She cannot and will not stay dormant forever.

Truth is the energy that makes things more convenient for you. Truth simplifies. Even if what you are seeing feels wrong to your mind or even your heart, it is right for you to experience it as a deep part of your evolution, growth, and enlightenment. This is why sometimes rock bottom, as you call it, can be deeply important to the restoration of your humility, rebalance, and Faith. The Void, the dark night of the soul, in which you face the pits of the deepest Truth, allows an imbalanced part of you to die so that you can be Resurrected in your authentic self. In the moment of the deepest Void, when you stop fighting, I appear from within you, a mountain moves, and you say, "Enough." That is the moment you transcend the Void.

In that moment, something has just been destroyed and now you are Free to create. These dark nights and Voids are valuable for your evolution. Extraordinary, really. Your soul and spirit are far more resilient than you could know. They understand your mountain because they are the source of your mountain.

If you are not clear on who or what you are in any moment, it is usually because there is a part of yourself that you are rejecting or do not like. When you reject a Truth about self, and do not Love that Truth, accept that Truth, and release the judgment of that Truth, you can never be clear on who you are. When you are not clear you will have fear, and your behaviors and relationships will reflect that. How can you expect others to honor your worth when you cannot honor your own? That is not their burden, it is yours.

Typically, these rejected parts of self, these fragments that get triggered to defensiveness or blaming of others in utter distortion, are clear ways to recognize the love-nots your soul is trying with deep effort to unthread, unbraid, and unweave from. The misperceptions of deficits often come in the form of the "not enough"—"not attractive enough, not intelligent enough, not good enough, not strong enough, not fulfilling my purpose, not this, not that." When you wallow in those as though a victim to circumstance that you yourself created in your soul-contracts in design, you will never be clear.

While the external world, including your culture, may have conditioned you to perceive and thus believe some of these "not-enoughs" about yourself, it is you who stay unclear when you do not question them and embrace them. **The "not-enoughs" are not what need to be transformed. Your perception of them AS "not-enoughs" is what needs to be transformed. For all of these "not-enoughs" to you are "more-than-enoughs" in the Eyes of the Divine.** You were designed to be as you are. It is the distorted perceptions that cause you to feel unclear, unconfident, and uncertain.

But this is what the mind Loves to do—to make things unclear so that you never untangle those love-nots that perhaps place you at the risk of the unknown. Who will you be without these love-nots and issues? Does accepting all of self also mean accepting responsibility for honoring your gifts and passion, which makes you vulnerable to outer criticism and rejection?

If you have surrounded yourself with others, even friends, family, and Lovers, that only know you "as you were," it will take courage and possibly even loss of certain people as you align more deeply with your Yeshua self. Questions will emerge such as, "Will they still Love and accept me when I stop catering to them and enforce boundaries? Will they even like me in my authentic self?" Do you really care, Beloved? Will you abdicate your worth to them? Is your worth worth renouncing so that you can keep them around? What judgment or retaliation from others do you fear will stem from the changes within you?

It is a risk, Beloved One. Will there be loss as you change? Some, yes. Some relationships will take leave, others will Miraculously grow stronger. All you will lose is only that which is no longer of value to your wheat or the other person's. Everyone is set Free in the end. Great Love lies within the movement of such mountains.

When you deny self or reject a Truth about self, you are leaving a lamb in the cold, dark night. And to retrieve the lamb you must venture into the cold, dark night at times to reclaim it. And face your fears to do so. Only in order to bring this part of you home. As We bring you Home and shine the Star of Bethlehem to Light the Way. But a lamb left in the cold is ripe for devouring by wolves. This lamb is a part of you. And a part of Me.

Beloved, akin to how it would feel for you to be left outside, hungry for Love, and cold, what would you do? You would bang on the door of your house, bang on every window, and create a great noise to be seen and heard. If you were still ignored, cold, hungry for Love, you would go bang on everyone else's door to Love you, Love you, feed you, feed you. Thus placing yourself at the mercy of others to dictate when you receive Love and when you don't.

Even if fed by another, the lamb that is the fragment of a hated part of self remembers you, longs to be with you, and longs always to come home to you.

You have all been this lamb. Thus, the rejected, angry parts of self, welcome them home into Peace and stop blaming others or yourself for why you rejected the lamb. The lamb Loves you unconditionally even if that lamb has three legs and one eye and no one else Loves it. You can. You do. For it is a Sacred part of you. And in Loving the lamb, accepting, shepherding, and integrating it into the flock of the whole be-ing that you are, you will Love yourself more. The lamb will become a part of you again, and you will be made whole.

Until you are ready to welcome home the rejected parts of you, that part of you that you rejected is welcome to knock on My door. My Garden cannot be defiled by rejected lambs, as no one can defile you. Knock on My door, God's door, and We will let in that part of self—and Love it until you can—then release it to you. When We do, the mountain or burden of the separation from this sacred fragment of self transforms. The love-not is undone and healed.

When you accept all of self, Forgive those parts, and cease the judgment, you walk with Me, and that walk is the walk of Peace. Not the walk of shame, shadow, and hiding in the dark night. That is Lucifer's burden—always in darkness, hiding, and polarity. Assuming he knows better.

But, as one of God's Angels, "he" yearns to shine the Light—he simply does so more through destruction than creation—destruction through hate and shadow. The Lucifer, or Judas, the betrayer, within you longs to be One with the Light, but cannot sometimes resist the temptation to be separate, always cold and angry. This Angel and archetype, which exists in part within you all, does not realize that if he Prostrates in humility, the Light will restore and Resurrect him too.

In various shades and dimensions, there is a Judas or a Lucifer in you all, and there is a Yeshua in you all. Which will you choose to be? The burden, the polarity that creates mountains for self and others? Or do you wish to be the Loving Truth, Loving Peace that moves the mountains for self and others even if you cannot always see the Light you hold?

When My Mother walked the cold streets the nights before My birth, she knocked on God's door, in a Prayer, in Faith, and a Star appeared. She/We were given comfort. We were accepted even though She was in fear. From the beginning She had the Faith and courage to accept and align with God's Will. She said, "Let it Be."

Let it be, Beloved One. Do not fear what will be asked of you in choosing Peace. You need not fear the call you feel to it and certainly not what We, or your soul, is asking of you to realize it. You are so much more resilient than you can possibly know. In your human experience, you are still primitive be-ings, early in evolution, despite the perceptions of your "modern" world. However, the consciousness, the infinite strength of Light and power of Love that lies within every fiber of your be-ing—mind, body, heart, soul, and spirit—is timeless, primordial, and capable of anything through Faith, Forgiveness, and Freedom.

Freedom is be-ing what you are. That is always clear in the moment. Clarity comes as you explore and build until the next moment and movement is revealed. But really, Freedom is just be-ing in the present, at Peace with yourself and all life. Living from that Light is living from your Yeshua self. And so it is.

Now, as I have said, Peace is a choice and the Path to it is not often clear to the mind but always clear to your heart and spirit. As you shift into this new Era as individuals and a collective, your choices are now of a heightened importance. For there are two temples emerging in your world—they have always been there but will be increasingly important to discern between now and in times to come.

One promises great communion. But inside it is a prison, the deepest you have ever seen—its vines are like wires that stretch everywhere and create knots with a lock and key that is impossible to pick. These vines and wires lie outside of the Vine of God. Its bell is loud and audible to the mind and ears. It tolls and extols promises of God, vindication, and power. It preys on the ego and seeds your emotions and mind with poison until you are addicted to its opiate. Through it you become ignorant, self-righteous, and swollen with your own vengeance and greed.

It spreads dissonance through the air in a web of false promises. Promises of easy fixes and saviors who carry the mark of discord and imbalance. The gospel preached is spoken through tongues that salivate over sex, money, and power. Those at the pulpit employ the three shadow chords of the three Eras, past and present, to achieve their means: violence, shaming, and silencing. This temple preys on the weak and promises many things in falseness. It promises to be your savior without having the humility and Forgiveness to honor and act as the true Savior. This temple is not here to save you; it is here to enslave you to its ideologies with promises of Freedom and abundance. Everything comes at a cost. And the cost in this church is slavery under the false promises of Freedom. If you attempt to leave this temple, you are shunned, shamed, and turned upon. If you stay, you are reduced to ash.

The other emerging Temple is a space of great communion. It is very old and unattractive to the mind but beautiful to the spirit. Inside it is Free. It does not promise—it provides. It is hard to find, for it requires great courage, Forgiveness, and humility to hear its Bell. Its Vines are rich and nourishing, for it is One with the Vine of God, and Gaia. The Gospel spoken in this Temple is the Word of Spirit, including your spirit, heard through the breath. Its Bell is silent to those who live within the mind but loud to those who live within the heart. It tolls and promises nothing, for those who hear it do not need anything but the joy of be-ing. They have promised themselves to God in embodying God's Promise from the beginning. It extols not the promise of Peace but Peace itself. It cleanses the soul with Sacred water, restores the emotions and mind to harmony, and ignites the spirit's fire with the blaze of a Passion and Love that supersedes all else. The Horses of Freedom are They who guide you there in moments of doubt. As They did the Magi long ago.

It is the Temple of Truth that does not come from anything external. It is the Church of the persecuted, and anyone in judgment cannot find the key to the narrow gate that unlocks the door. You must close your eyes to see it, for the Path that leads you to it is through Truth and alignment of will. Which most do not have the humility to face when it is so much easier to join the temple of knots and wires.

This second Temple has a steeple that points not outward but to the center of the Star and Heart of God within your heart. Joining requires giving over your burdens and crosses and having Faith in the

Light to align your needs. It is the Church of the Star of Bethlehem and only stars, true stars, those of Balance, have the clear eyes to see it.

You each have a unique essence and bell that emanates from your soul through your spirit. When you remove the dissonance that muffles the sounding of your bell, you toll in harmony with the Divine Bell of the Temple of Peace. In the temple of discord, every bell seeks to be the loudest and, together, the bells of the individuals within this temple create a cacophony of chaos.

These temples lie within you though they are and will be emerging within the world in a more pronounced, direct way. One is the temple of the imbalanced mind in its egoic impulses. The second is the Temple of the Divine. Which will you choose? This is the time of choice.

These two temples are timeless. The longer that you spend time in one, the harder it is to separate from it. This is not heaven and "hell" or Gehanna that I describe—that is a story. What I describe is whether you wish to remain in creation as part of the debris that moves from life to life by your own choice of taking the path of the mind, the path that seems easy but makes everything more complex. Or whether you wish to be of Creator, with a consciousness and Presence that moves creation with Balance. The prior requires you to Love some and hate others. The second requires you to Love ALL as you Love yourself. That is the choice.

To Us it is a simple choice. But at this time in your world, there is a Gateway, a Bridge that is a rainbow extending a united Light. We understand your feelings and thoughts beneath the Veils and how hard and confusing things can seem. We understand that the choice of alignment can be difficult. The more that you choose to see what is real and clear within the present moment instead of trying to escape out the back door, the clearer the Bell of Light will be. There is always another moment, another life, to choose. You are eternal. But you would not be here if you were not the ones coming to the Second Coming who are ready to make the choice now. Every last one of you.

In moments you will stumble. Each time you begin backtracking to the loud bell, do not become intoxicated. Pause, hear Me, and I will walk with you toward the silent Bell again. Walking toward it means you are coming Home and thus you will need to grieve the old wounds of your separation.

There, in the silence, when the mind quiets, you are Free, and safe, and Home. Until you can learn to still your thoughts, sit in your place and do not take a step farther. The movement toward the Holy Temple comes from the Stillness. Stillness does not come from rushing thoughts. Hear the bell of Stillness within the Silent Holy night—and you will be heard, and seen, and known.

I know that many of you listen to these Transmissions only for the benefit of resolving your issues or when you have time. But when you listen, you are on My time—which is no time. It is your soul's time. Give your soul the space and time it needs to receive this nourishment.

When you do not have time for Us, We do not have time either. Your time is yours. We do not ask for all of it; We are with you in every moment. But the more time you devote to My Words and this process, the more that will flow and the more Balance and nourishment that will come. We always have space for you. Make even just a little more time and space for Me. I will serve you well.

Grant yourselves the gift of moving more deeply into the space of what is being Offered. These Transmissions are not just to help resolve your issues, but to transform and expand you—to move your mountains through your permission, transparency, authenticity, and Love. You will find that some of your issues on the external will always be there, but many will resolve the more you sit with Me in these Offerings and others to come.

Can I resolve your issues? Yes. It is very easy for Me, but I will not let you off the hook, for it was your choice to be in body—and thus, your soul would not allow Me, Us, the Divine to intervene unless it was agreed to. We would never strip you of the joy of your journey through life. All aspects of it. Either you are here for God, or you are here as god, god of your own separation, which is an old story We know too well. When you are here FOR God, you are hearing the silent Bell. For you are on the Path to illuminating the true God within.

Moving forward, begin to discern between the sounds, feeling, and vibrations of the two distinct bells within yourself and your life. Begin to recognize those who emanate the silent, yet deeply powerful, Bell of Peace and those who create a cacophony within your spirit. The bells of discord in your world are those who continue to assert their cacophony into your ear through imposition or superiority. The Bells of Peace in your world are those who have no need to be seen and heard by other bells, for they are One with the Bell of God. Feel the difference. Be discerning.

If you are here, you have heard the Freedom Bell. Thus, your Path is to synchronize and harmonize your bell with its Grace, frequency, and vibration. As you were designed to. When you hear other bells ringing through your news, technology, or social relationships, bring awareness as to the qualities of their ring—does it bring compassion, joy, and Peace? Or is it manipulating and intoxicating your senses by provoking your love-nots, rendering you deaf, angry, and irritable? Before synchronizing with a bell, take time to discern if it is the bell you wish to weave and ring with. Many bells may sound pretty, but if your inner alarm bell begins to sound when you hear one, take a pause and listen again for My Bell. I will sound for you with resounding clarity what the sound Path is.

For whom the discordant bell tolls is a sorrow to God, for We do not wish to see you toil. For whom the silent Bell tolls is extolled by God, for We wish to see you in joy. Rejoice! You have heard the silent Bell if you are here, and by here, I mean *here*. We created your bell as you create Ours when you are in your authentic self. Then we all ring together! I Love the sound of your bell—bright, resonant, and full of joy. Let your silent bell be thunder through your heart. Use your voice in words of Love. Hear My Bell. It is of Peace, Presence, and Be-ing. Be-ing is not what you were or will be—but what you are. And, all that I AM is all that you are. All that you are is all that I AM.

Hear the Bell of this, the Freedom Prayer:

The Freedom Prayer

My body is a gift. It does not define or confine my
*   Faith and my Freedom.*
My house is a gift. It does not define or confine my
*   Faith and my Freedom.*
My money is a gift. It does not define or confine my
*   Faith and my Freedom.*
This person is a gift. He or she does not define or confine my
*   Faith and my Freedom.*
My career is a gift. It does not define or confine my
*   Faith and my Freedom.*
My mind is a gift. It does not define or confine my
*   Faith and my Freedom.*
My heart is a gift. It does not define or confine my
*   Faith and my Freedom.*
My life is a gift. It does not define or confine my
*   Faith and my Freedom.*
This moment is a gift. Within it lies my Faith and my Freedom.
Gaia is a gift. She holds me in my Faith and my Freedom.
My soul is a gift. It is the spacious Presence of my Faith and my
*   Freedom.*
My spirit is a gift. It is the peaceful passion of my Faith and my
*   Freedom.*
The Divine is a gift. It is the Creator and foundation of my
*   Faith and my Freedom.*

*My Faith and my Freedom are a gift. They are the gift of my
Faith and my Freedom realized.*
Om Nami Yeshua. Sancti. Pace. Amein.

Inherent to this Prayer, you may say "My," but this Prayer is for All. It is the Freedom Prayer of the Sacred Heart. The Liberator of Love and Truth to rebalance into Peace.

Beloved One, you are an extraordinary soul and Prayer. That is why it was My joy to Offer My Life for you so that we could always walk together. I set you Free and you set Me Free, as well, when you choose to come Home to Me in a way beyond death. I Loved you so deeply that My Life was nothing more than a humble devotion to you—for how could I not experience the joy of living with and as My Children within the dream? Despite all physical pain, how could I not fulfill My Prophecy and Promise to you in upholding and evolving Divine Law? How could I rest as your God leaving even one lamb out of the Garden?

That is why even death is a kindness. Through death we become One again, which is your true state of be-ing. Through Receiving My Grace, you are honoring My request and I yours to be the shepherds and shepherdesses of the wheat within the chaff of the world. You are what slowly renders the whole field gold. Through shepherding yourself foremost. And allowing Me to serve as yours.

To feel clear means releasing fear. That is Faith. Deep Faith. You are always clear when you are at Peace with yourself. When you are living in Freedom, you are exactly who and what you are without caring so much about outcome or expectation. Living in true Freedom liberates you from the egoic need to police others on who and how they should be. You are able to live for yourself, with and as Me. Even when everyone else is in waves and mountains searching and searching for what to do about tomorrow, you are Free to be the tranquil water, the rogue content lamb who is just joyous to be in the present today. That is tranquility. That is Peace.

This Power of Peace seeds the energy of Peace across the world in its wake. You are seed planters, vessels of the Seed of the Divine Vine, that I AM.

The time has come to in-joy our joy and celebrate the return. Yours to Me and Me to you. Let it be. Let there be Light. Walk with Me in honoring the silent Bell of the Silent Night of this time of Stillness we share. Oh Holy Night. Oh Holy Star. Oh Silent Night. We shine, We shine, together We shine. Amein.

YESHUA MEDITATION

Close your eyes, Beloved One. Begin to draw deep breaths into your body. As you breathe, begin to create space between the chaff and the wheat. Feeling into your body, the stitches where your joints and organs connect. Feeling into your heart's center. Beautiful Love knot. Feel into the Light of your wheat and how it animates the life and movement within you. Breathe into the space all around you, your spirit and its web of strings and braids that connect you to the external world.

Now begin to draw all of the strings and threads of any issues, burdens, mountains into your be-ing. Drawing the strings of your spirit into your body, your soul, as though a spider drawing in its web to cleanse. Feel where these issues or frustrations create love-nots or tension within you. Be it lack of inspiration, lack of clarity, a lump in the throat, a pit in your stomach, tension in your back, a shackle in the heart. Feel the shackles, the weight of these knots.

Now with the power of breath, begin to unweave and unthread the knots. Into each breathe Love. Compassion. Forgiveness. Patience. Peace. Feel the knots, the shackles beginning to transform—the knot unwinding, unbraiding through your awareness. Stay focused. Allow your soul the space to undo these knots, these mountains. Your mind's only task is to breathe, to give your soul the support and quiet it needs to unweave the knots and imbalanced strings. Keep breathing, moving, moving, these mountains and knots.

As the knots and strings begin to smooth, allow the pain or feelings trapped within or under them such as hurt, grief, fear, guilt, anger, shame, regret, or remorse to surface. Feel My Presence with you, holding you as you feel, process, witness, and let go of these burdens. Breathe, allow, process, experience, release, exhale.

Now with an inhale of Love, from your branches to your roots, from roots to branches, breathe in the support of the Divine, the Light to knead and soften the strands, clearing away anything no longer needed in your life. Allow yourself to simply rest in My Arms, suspended in a space out of time—the Tapestry of Eternal Life.

With cleansed strings and knots smoothed, take another breath and allow your soul to begin streaming, weaving, and braiding Faith through your be-ing. Allow the golden strand of Faith to spiral and weave through you in a movement of energy and Light. Now allow the golden strand of Forgiveness to ripple through your be-ing, weaving you deeper into its power and Grace.

Now feel the golden strand of Freedom weaving through you from above and below. Connecting you deeply to the Divinity of Freedom now present within your body. Feel these three strands now begin to weave together, creating a Braid of Divine Strength, Simplicity, and Stability. Feel this Braid connecting you deeply into your mountain and the energy of the Earth around you. Allow the Braid to weave you into Balance as you stand upon and within the mountain with clear vision—no obstructions to the view. Witness yourself within this breath of unity and Freedom.

Downward and upward, feel the Freedom Bell ringing through the vibrations of the golden strings, now woven together. Allow these vibrations to fill your spirit, which you have drawn into your body. Now open your heart and allow the strings of your spirit to release and emanate back out onto the Web of Life. Cleansed and clear. Feel as the golden threads of your spirit weave and Braid you into the energy of Balance and harmony upon the Web of Life. Feel the emanation of the silent Bell ringing outward from your radial center in joy, Peace, and harmony. Behold the Light streaming out upon the strings of your spirit in an offering of Divine Rejoice.

Now rest in your center, integrating the vibrations into your body. As you rest, allow Me to Weave and Braid your strings into the new connections and possibilities for you to discover in times to come. What needs to be clear will become clear when it is time. All is clear within this moment.

Breathe in. Remember that it is for you the Bell tolls. As you received it and harmonized your bell with Mine, you moved a mountain. We moved mountains together through Love as you embodied the Braid of Faith, Forgiveness, and Freedom. Through your breath you have served to plant the Seeds of these energies into yourself and your Earth. I bow to you, celebrate you, and am deeply grateful to you for your service as a moving mountain.

Place one hand on your heart, and the other on your womb or your hara. Smile the wise smile of the mountain elder. Take a moment to ground your energy by placing your forehead or hand upon Mother Earth, thanking Her for all the ways She holds and nourishes you. I would then like you to take out the sheet of paper, still folded, unopened since the First Transmission: **The Freedom Transmissions Personal Process.** Do not open it, but place your hand upon it and infuse Truth, Peace, and Love.

As always, it has been My honor to have served you on this day. Let there be Light.

Om Nami Maia. Om Namah Sananda. Om Nami Yeshua. Sancti. Sancti. Sancti. Pace. Pace. Pace. Namaste.

The Void, The Light

The Spectrum of Spirit

YESHUA TEACHING

Hello, Beloved One. In this moment, I wish to bring more Consciousness, more Light, into the Void. Thus, we are going to do this in reverse, and bring the Void into the Light. In order to do this, I ask that you please bring yourself outside for a moment, into the fresh air, if possible. If not, please open a window.

For what I Offer below is an Invocation that I would ask for you never to use on your own. It is not yours to say as a human be-ing, regardless of how conscious you are of your Divinity. It is a Divine Invocation alone. I have, however, invited your personal Spirit Guides and your Beloveds in Spirit to assist Me in this Invocation. Please have reverence and respect for Them and for Me in My request. Thank you, Beloved.

Yeshua's Sovereign Invocation

I AM the Alpha, I AM the Omega, I AM the Space between. I AM the realm of infinite possibilities. I AM the Void. I AM the Birth. I AM the Light. I AM the Death. I AM the Resurrection. I AM the Way. I draw to the Light of all be-ings the Void to il-

luminate the Pathway to Peace through the Eternal Light. I draw
to the shadow of all be-ings the Light to illuminate the Pathway
to Peace through the Eternal Void. And so it is done. Let there
BE Light. Let there be LIGHT. Al-Ilah. Al-Ilah. Al-Ilah. Amein.

And so it is done.

Welcome, Beloved One, to the Great Convergence of Shadow and Light. To the Great Era of Balance and Illumination. And to the lifetime and moment shepherding you to wholeness, transparency, and Peace. Your choices now, in this gateway of the Era of Masculine and Feminine Balance, more than at any other time, will dictate the flow, Emergence, continuation, or destruction of your world in times to come. You came to the world at this time to give over burdens, not only your own but those of times past.

While Spirit is here for you, Spirit is also relying on you for your choices, the choices of those in bodies right now, as is the collective, as are you. For it is up to you all to either fight against the changes and movement of Divine energy within self and world through complacency and chaos, or to allow for them through Simplicity, Faith, and reconnection to your ecosystem and global community.

Without that, your species and many others will not be able to sustain life through the imposed imbalance, imposed authority of dominance, you have asserted onto your Earth. That does not mean halting your lives. It simply means, with humility, making daily choices to move into more gratitude and harmony with Gaia, as individuals and as a collective.

There is no wrong choice, Beloved. This is not a political discussion. As a matter of fact, it is the opposite. What you need to rely on now, all of you, is the Divine to support you in alleviating the burden and chaos you have created. If some are blind, We cannot reach them. We honor their will to be separate. But the more who awaken to Us, embody Our Divine qualities, and walk with Us in whatever way one experiences the Divine, the easier the process will be, even if it looks a bit murky to the mind in the beginning times of this Convergence.

What I speak of today is a deeper Truth and Revelation first Offered to those I visited shortly after and long after My Death. Many of you might reject it or discount My Offering to you today as a story. Perhaps it is. Perhaps it is not. That is for you to decide in your own relationship with God, or lack thereof in your mind. Your mind doesn't need to be on board for your soul to be.

I give this to you today to begin our descent into the deeper chambers of the dark night filled with your lost lambs, the lost or rejected aspects of self, the mountains waiting to be revealed, moved, and transformed with Love. I need to bring you to this place for you to retrieve them. I ask that you have respect and humility over this Transmission and the next, as well as read or listen to this text three times before casting stones or criticizing. For the weight of that may not be something you wish to incur in this moment of your liberation.

And so it goes.

From the Void, the space and realm of infinite possibilities, the origin, the Light was born. Your soul, your spirit, emerged from the Void, fully birthed. The Divine Force of the Word of God's breath flooded into your be-ing in your creation. From the Void, the Dreaming was birthed, and you moved from a possibility to an "actuality." When your spirit wove you into a body, you became spirit in form. Consciousness within form. The Seed of Consciousness within you was lit and you be-came. First, you be-came a soul, conscious, then you moved into manifestation, form.

You are of the Creator, and a creator within your own right, as you were born from the Void that is the Light, as well. Born from the Void in the origin of your soul into God's Light. Then born into the Void of the womb. Then born into the Light of the Void of Gaia. You came from the Void and return to the Void and are always in the Void. Which is the Light. Both exist simultaneously at all times.

There is a continuous birthing from Void to Void, womb to womb, dream to dream, Alpha to Omega. Consciousness, God, Light beyond Light as you know it, is the static point, a fixed point yet one also continuously and progressively evolving, creating, dissolving. As do you. When you stop evolving and resist change it is like trying to push back against the Force of God, the Force of the Divine Dream. You cannot. It will exhaust and break you. When you are evolving too rapidly, your shadow has to step in to slow down the rate of change, otherwise you can get overwhelmed in having to face the Veils and imbalances all at once. The shadow sometimes needs to slow the pace.

While internal evolution can lead to external progress, external progress does not always lead to internal evolution. Over the past periods on your planet, you were trying to progress too rapidly as a species, which is why the shadow, your shadow as individuals and the collective, has raced in to slow things down a bit. So that you all can find Balance again and allow evolution to flow from the soul organically, not from the imbalanced ego mind that rushes to "achieve" and wants to "do it all now," and "get it all over with." There is no over and under along your Journey, Beloved. Your soul's journey is one of evolution. From unconsciousness to consciousness. That is the journey of en-Lightenment. You cannot rush through it nor would you wish to because, in Truth, there is no race. Realizing that is much of the journey.

The center space, the Heart of God, is both like a circle and a figure 8—infinite, continuously birthing and destroying. Yet also equally like an absolute zero, equally infinite. Fixed yet unfixed. Firm yet fluid. An order to creation and destruction. A none and an all. A Balance that is radial and emanates from a Center. Your universe loops far more than it expands and contracts. When there is a new birth, so too there is a death—as there is an inhale, there is also an exhale. Thus, when I have said that I come at beginnings and endings, and always in between, that is what I meant.

Dark matter, the space in between, so to speak, was also created of the Light—it is the Light too. It is what holds the polarity of gestation. It is space, unconscious or subconscious space, waiting to be filled with consciousness, with Light. It holds the polarity of consciousness, and thus it is part of the fabric of consciousness but still unawakened, unaware. It is unrealized and waiting to be realized. It is a possibility, not yet fully gestated. It is the form of energy that makes your reality structure, duality, possible. It is the separation and healthy polarity that is the Void. And the Void makes your journey and evolution of consciousness possible.

These concepts may sound a bit challenging to the mind—for the Light AND the Void to be the foundation for your reality structure. The Womb and the Seed. The yin and yang. Masculine and feminine. That is a healthy polarity. No dominance and suppression. They are equal and opposite, yet completely One.

Those who evolve and master this reality structure have learned not to fear the Void for that is like fearing a dream. They realize they are the dreamer and observe the dream and themselves within the dreaming. They transcend death in life by finding the space of Peace within, the Seed of Presence that connects them to eternal life. The Seed that not only gave you life but also the space within in which you ARE life. They no longer carry the mind imbalance of separation and fear of death and endings. The Veils within them are very thin because they have not only found but walked through the narrow gate. "I AM" to them is more of a "No, I'm really not." As such, they are more of an "AM" than an "I."

They have no interest in the behaviors that stem from the imbalances of the "seen" for they understand, access, and create from the space of the unseen. Consciousness flows through and from them. Thus, they are conscious creators, the curators of the dream instead of those oblivious to the fact they are even in it. They are not only the reflection of God for they have smashed the mirror and become more than just the image, the projection. They have become the dreamer.

They understand they are one lens of the Divine yet the whole of the unseen image rests within them. Thereby, they live in a state of Transcendence, Emergence, and Immanence.

Very often it is difficult for them to relate to the bustle of life and many often live quiet, simple lives. Or lives in which their ego is so dissolved that their whole life is a devotion to service. They live for God and abide by whatever is asked of them. They are far less interested in their own needs and instead ask what God needs of them and what the need of the Divine Dream is. That is what they were designed for. And it brings them joy even if the whole of their lives is spent in meditation, service, and Prayer. The Void is Light to them. They walk through it every day. The unseen is seen to them. They are fixed in Presence and thus evolve almost exponentially in wisdom and Grace. They are the Light-bringers, Light-holders, and Peace-keepers in a profound way. These be-ings are rare. It requires an incredible, almost superhuman amount discipline, energy, and focus for them to hold the amount of Light that they do in form.

More of you are moving onto an accelerated path of consciousness at this time. To do so it is essential to embrace the Void as the birthing point, the womb, the Pathway to deeper Light.

Do not fear the Void, Beloved One, it is like fearing God—and your own essence. Though it can at times feel like you are walking through the valley in the shadow of death, I am with you. Always. I am your Star. I created the Light and the Void, so I do know a thing or two about them or it, I should rather say.

Even coming into these Offerings that I make, prior to listening, you are in a Void—you do not know what will be said, you do not know how you will feel, you do not know what will change. But the Faith, curiosity, and willingness is there and you might feel excited: "What is Yeshua going to talk about today?" It is similar to a child the night before a special holiday of gifts. It does not know what it will receive. It could receive a sweater or coal. But there is the joy, the anticipation of what is to come that is as special as the revelation itself. You embrace the Void when you are able to say, "I don't know, but I fear not for Thou art with me," or "I don't know, but I welcome the revelation without judgment," or best yet, "I don't know" said with a smile. Always a smile.

When you are experiencing a Void within your life, it means that you have unstitched, unwoven, unbraided from something that existed before. That does not mean that "terrible" things are befalling you, that you are being punished, that the sky is falling, or that you are a victim of circumstance. That is a thought construct and story in your mind. Your soul is simply unstitching you and restitching or braiding you to something else in co-creation and unity with your spirit upon the Web of Life.

When you are experiencing a Void, a time of change, the energies of confusion, grief, anger, and fear that you may feel can be over-whelming, as I have said. To ground yourself and simplify the rac-ing thoughts and feelings, recognize that this Void is not only of God but bringing you closer to God. When you are in the Void, recognize, Beloved One, that whether it is through grief, or a loss, or an inconve-nience, you are in the Womb, you are drawing the Light to you. You are not just at the mercy of the dreaming. You are the dreamer and, when you are, you are not only in the Presence of God but co-creating the dream with God. This is why you feel My Presence, call to Me, and reach to the Light the most during beginnings and endings.

It is always in births that there are more Prayers to the Divine than at any other time. The times of your deepest need for Faith and comfort. The Prayers you send during these times extend far beyond Prayers of hope and into the realm of Prayers for communion and consecration.

It is the same in death. When there is a loss, when someone dies, even when a part of you dies, and you are struggling to understand "why," have the humility to remember that, as long as you are in a body, you will never completely know the Truth. You do not know why things happen. Nor do you need to. Like Love, as Love, the Void does not care about being understood, being convenient, or justifying itself to you. Why should it? It just is.

When you leave this body, this life, the Truth of the Light of the Void will come as you are birthed into the next dream, next form. And so it goes, until the whole Void transforms and you become the whole Void, and the whole Light within it. That is your journey.

When you are in the Womb, the Void, call the Light to you. Oftentimes, when you are in the Light, and know what's coming the next day and the next, things can become complacent. In those moments, call in the Void. When everything is feeling good there is less evolution. The Light is constantly evolving in Consciousness. Thus, those of your world that tend to be the most Peaceful, as well as the most resilient, have a practice of discipline, devotion, and daily adherence to the process of evolution required to know themselves more deeply as One with God and all that is.

If you get lost in the Void, fight the Void, or fear the Void instead of reaching to the Light within—it is chaos and prolongs the feeling of separation. You cannot avoid the Void. You would not wish to. But the imbalanced mind does not like the dark of the Void despite the fact that it lives in the real darkness of the Void the majority of the time.

The Truth is that, through Me, Yeshua, you cannot get lost within the Void. You cannot get lost, My Beloved Child. You cannot get lost in the Void because I created the Void. Had I not, you would not have been created as a soul. I am the space and the glue that holds together the structure of your reality to keep things in Balance, in order, so that there is not chaos everywhere.

When you perceive that there is chaos, take a breath. If you can breathe, not so much chaos. Lungs working. There is an order to your breath. Look at a flower or tree around you; not so much chaos. Flower, tree working just fine. There is an order to not only the flower or tree but your ability to see it.

You have the choice to shift your perception back to the Balanced fluid order of Simplicity, Stability, Surrender, and Stillness at all times. Even in times you are in pain or shock. When you take the narrow gate, you invite Me to walk through the Void with you, as I have done very many times before because I live There, Here. You may perceive that you are walking through the Void, the valley of the shadow of death, but really you are walking through the valley of the Light of death. The Void is wonderful; it is God. The Light is wonderful; it is God. The space between is wonderful; it is God.

You chose a body and specific essence when coming to form, down to your basic DNA. Those who manifest very powerfully are able to accept the Void, which quickly gives them the ability to accept, transform, move new possibilities into creation. They are continuously able to pluck from the realm of infinite possibilities the Void provides. When their will aligns with God's, their creative force Lights and innovates the world in Miraculous ways. Size and scale does not matter. Their spiders are wonder dreamers and dream-weavers, conscious creators. They have the resilience that discerns when complacency is settling in. They unstitch over here and weave again over here.

Learn to discern when something that you have woven, braided, and stitched to moves from joy to complacency. Joy can move to burden more quickly than you know. Witness that and explore when those feelings start to come. Do not avoid them, for your soul may be ready to pluck from the Void and possibilities it illuminates once again.

Your avoidance of the Void, even death, is one of the reasons that there has been a denial of Truth in your world. I am bringing Truth to you now during these years on your planet because you are at the birthing point of the Era of Transparency after so many years and centuries of its gestation. I planted the Seeds and wove the Braids for this Era long ago, which included Seeding the energy to reveal to you your burdens, not to create more. You have been in the Void; now comes time for the revelation, the Light.

A good question to ask yourself is: What do I fear more? The Void?

Or the Revelation? Sit with that for a moment. It is amazing to Us that, while many fear darkness, many of you fear the Light even more. Hence the importance of My Offering on clarity.

Do you fear the Darkness? Or is the Truth that you fear the Light?

I will tell you, Beloved One, the answer is the latter more times than not. And when you fear the Light, there are still many aspects of the Veils and imbalances that you are working through, especially the Veil of Separation. Fearing the Light means fearing both Love and Truth, which makes it nearly impossible to fully experience and embody your true essence and Mine, Peace. However, the same goes for fearing the Void.

Generally speaking, those who have greater fear of the Void struggle more with issues surrounding loss of safety, security, and control and fear of failure, judgment, abandonment, and/or shame. Those who have greater fear of the Light or Revelation struggle more with issues surrounding self-worth, trust, deservingness, and fear of rejection. Those that your world calls "extroverts" tend to have greater fear of the Void, while those of a more "introverted" nature tend to have greater fear of the Light. One fears loss, the other fears gain. Yet, the Void and the Light are One. They are healthy counter-polarities, like flip sides to a coin. Each possesses equal potential for loss and gain.

Thus, My next question is: **Do you really fear the Void or the Light, or do you fear what will happen to you as a by-product of experiencing them? Is the fear about the outcome of the Void/Light or the actual Void/Light itself?** Is the fear more about the change, the potential loss or gain, that could come to your life as a result of what they bring forth? Or is it more about what you may need to face internally as a result of them, including potentially: vulnerability, Surrender of control, acceptance of a Truth you have not wished to see or act on, needing to take personal accountability for your own life, letting go of a resentment or destructive behavior, and/or allowing yourself to receive Love after possibly a lifetime of deprivation?

If your fear is more about the outcome, that is glorious wisdom for you to know. Then it is not the Void/Light itself that you fear, what you fear is the change to the story of your life and identity construct. A story replete with assumptions and expectations that either lead to disappointments or self-fulling prophecies. This wisdom of your process and fear will help you to reclaim your power from the story to move deeper into the Light of your true self, which is far, far more than the story and infinite in what it is able to catalyze, realize, and become.

If your fear is more about doubting your strength and ability to accept the revelations brought to you through the Void/Light, that is also wonderful wisdom for you to have. For this means that you are already evolving beyond the story of your life, you are already dissolving many aspects of your ego identity or illusion self, and you are already moving more deeply into your embodiment of Truth. You can take a deep breath and relax, Beloved One. For you already understand that the Void, the Light are not external energies that "could do something to you." As such, you can Surrender and simply reach to the wellspring of your Love, resilience, and Faith to move deeper into them, as well as to create from them.

In the present, rarely, rarely will you feel fear when you move into the Void or Light. For in the present, your awareness is present in-body, where you have access to the Divine, to your soul, to your breath. In this space, there is a welcoming, not a rejecting. An exploration, not an avoidance.

Now, there are times, there are times, when you are in a deeply intimate relationship with another be-ing, wheat in chaff, in which, co-creatively, one of you rips a hole in the other's web. Be it through an act of imbalanced dominance, rage, unconsciousness, greed, devaluation of your worth, and so on. One person in deep imbalance and unconsciousness carrying burdens creates a hole that sets you out of Balance. Or you to them.

When a hole, a Void of this nature, is created by another or even by your own behaviors, as in the case of addictions, it is most important to give yourself space to process before rushing to fill the Void created. When a hole is created in an entire area of your web, the rest of the web needs to carry the extra weight. Explore your web before rushing to figure out how and why this hole was created, and especially before rushing to conclusions on who was to blame for it. Even if someone stole money, abandoned you, hurt you, falsely accused you, please remember that all matter is resolved to its own nature in the end.

Do not wallow in the Void another left or you left, nor torture yourself looking at all the work it will take to get back to where you were. You will never be where you were when you are here where you are right now. Where you are is far better, I promise you. There will be grief, anger, and feelings to process, yes. However, there is also a new journey to Balance you are embarking upon.

I say this because this is what you are doing to your planet, Beloved One. In your arrogance and greed as a world, all the while complaining still of what you don't have, you are ripping holes in the web of Gaia. The other strings need to carry that weight and sometimes they cannot. They cannot carry the burden that they were not designed to carry. As you are a part of the Tapestry of your ecosystem, you do not realize that, by tearing holes in Her, you are tearing holes in YOU.

The areas in which these holes reside are dying, becoming infertile. So other areas need to become more fertile despite receiving less nourishment and nutrients. Thus, the offspring are less healthy. Instead of repairing the holes, many scientists and companies in your world are trying to mimic nature in laboratories, primitive human mimicry of Gaia's bounty. And you wonder why disease, chronic pain, and mental health issues are circling, even within your children.

You have created holes while at the same time sterilizing your world from creatures that keep you Balanced and healthy. Instead of dealing with the holes and Voids, you keep racing for artificial solutions. THAT is an artificial reality, even more artificial than your thought construct of your own reality. And there is nothing artistic or original about that. While your minds might dazzle and trick and tempt you into believing that your fabricated, anaesthetized existence is healthy and normal, you will not be able to convince Gaia or the rest of creation to get on board with that, Beloved. Because Gaia IS what is real, I am what is real. You are what is real when you cease this tendency to want the easy way out.

Continuing to infringe on God's copyright in attempting to play God will not work out so well for you. For the reality is you are in a deeply intimate relationship with Gaia the whole of your life. She feeds you, bathes you, changes your diapers. The only way to get out of that relationship is to leave the chaff altogether. If you are still dense and have love-nots, even if you cross over, you will quickly return to Her, or an even more dense reality structure depending on your soul's needs for rebalance. You cannot escape Her, for She is the Path to Me. Thus, the very least you can do is stop ripping holes in your Mother's Heart and Womb. Rip Me, poke holes in Me. You have done that to Me before and, now that I am not in Body, I can take your wrath and level it to the ground.

When you rip holes in Gaia, you rip holes in yourself. And all of you are feeling the weight of that right now.

During this time, We will be bringing extra Light and Truth to honor your collective call to begin to repair the imbalances in the Web of Life you have created in the unseen and the seen. And you will be honored for all service you offer therein. Not through screaming and blaming. But through listening to Gaia and your bodies to see what is being asked of you, given your gifts and design, as an individual. Those of you who are making these reparations, not to others, but to Gaia and to self in your reconnection to Her, are well on your way to restoring Balance. But that Balance to Gaia must be in parallel with allowing the holes, the fragments of self, to rebalance within you, as well. You, Gaia, and I will be fast friends in this process. She and I will be working through you, weaving through you as you rebraid to your Divine self and ecosystem.

Those of you who are making repairs and amends to your web, to your lives, as well as in your connection to Gaia and the Divine, will not have the same experience of the Void in years to come. It will not be easy at all times, but there is a joyful cooperation, curiosity, and communion you will experience therein, for you are practicing integrity to yourself in humility and accountability. For those who are continuing to make further destruction to the web, or the Womb of Gaia, there will be a deeper and deeper Void and despair that is experienced in times to come.

Which is why, for those of you who truly wish to serve during this period, the holding of the Light is the most important. We hold the Light for you when you are in the Void, and if you wish to serve as the Divine, holding the Light for others right now is important. For those who are in the Void will be calling to themselves the polarity of your Light. For those who are in the Light will be calling to themselves the polarity of the Void. However, when you understand these energies as One, service through the Void, the Light, is quite joyful. You are immune from the chaos of the Void when you accept it. So, when you release the fear, and actually invite the Void into your life without judging, you live in a state of continuous yoga, meditation, Prayer, and creation.

That is when true service through joy can emerge. It brings joy to almost all of you to bring joy to the heart of another in need. The tears you transform into smiles through simply handing someone a tissue and saying a kind word, no expectations, no agendas, that is joy. That is communion. Communion for a moment or a lifetime, it is all the same. You are all soul mates, spirit mates to and with one another.

There is never chaos between Alpha and Omega. There is no jumbled soup of an alphabet. You are not random. All is placed into an Order, a random Order, and only you can create what that random

Order is for you within your life, never for another, but for you. Some can teach you, guide you, inspire you, but only you can know what you are the alpha and the omega of. **I AM THE Alpha and Omega.** I AM the Logos and the Word. You are Part of Me, of My Flesh, of My Blood. I spilled Mine so that you could receive the Source of Life. To you I give everything, including life, including death, and every moment in between and beyond.

Thus, when you ever have doubt, reach to Me to show you the Way. Your Beloveds in Spirit are always with and within you, as I AM with and within you, and You are with and within You. The Hu, the Ma, the Omni.

YESHUA HOMEWORK

Please take out the slip of paper from the very first day, still folded and unopened: The Freedom Transmissions Personal Process. Do not open it. Place your hand upon it and repeat nine times: Hu, Ma, Omni.

Now, from the Void of the unknown, place your other hand on the paper and call to you the Void, the realm of infinite possibilities. Petition the Void, allow for the Void to serve you with the death of your need to control. Call to you the Void of the ending. Breathe the Void and Its infinite possibilities into the energy of this paper.

Now, through your breath, begin to infuse Light. Breathe the Light into the space of the Void that you have summoned. Funnel Light through your Presence, through your heart, weaving through the stitching in your hands the Braid of Faith, Forgiveness, and Freedom into this Void. The Light igniting and manifesting the possibilities, moving them into form.

Now, release it to Me with a Prayer. Set aside this paper. And smile. And so it is done. Amein.

2

Polarity, Resistance, and Transcending Doubt

YESHUA TEACHING

Behold, Beloved. You have just done something extraordinary: You have just commanded the power of polarity to create unity. Thus, you have employed your Divine Masculine and Divine Feminine to work together—the womb and the Seed, dreamer and dreaming, Void and Light, Creator and Creation.

The Light does not and cannot fade. The moments you perceive the Light is fading from your life or the world, recognize that the Light is not fading from you—you are fading from your own Light. No one else on the outside, no matter what they have or have not done to or for you, carries the responsibility for that. You are responsible for your own perceptions and distortions of perception. Despite your perception, the Light is growing stronger within yourselves and the world. There is an opportunity, a birthing emerging despite looking out at the world and perceiving discord. Do not feel helpless. Engage in the transformation by taking responsibility for your own Peace.

As the Light grows, so too does resistance to it. When there are love-nots that have become very knotted, strings holding too much weight, inevitably there can be a bursting or breaking that ensues. When the bough breaks of these deep knots or strings, your mind will rush to thought constructs to make sense of what is happening. Your fear prisons, thought bubbles, and false assumptions can begin to pop and explode everywhere, causing you to question everything and everyone, including yourself.

When many people share a thought bubble, over time, these bubbles swell and swell until suddenly these massive thought structures that hundreds, thousands, even millions of people, many unconscious, are imprisoned by pop, erupt, or explode—and out comes a huge amount of ooze and defecation. In this massive unthreading or bursting of love-nots, within self and even mass groups of people, especially those created over centuries of unhealthy dominance and suppression polarities, the external world can look like chaos. Wounded people everywhere creating wounds for others. The rejected lambs roving through the night causing dissonance to self and other. It has been this way since the dawn of time, Beloved One. It is the initial reaction to doubt: panic, confusion, and a rush to regain control, security, and clarity.

Those who are blaming the external right now are in deep resistance to the process of Forgiveness. They are confused and focusing on the outer change instead of the inner. When two bodies of people in massive thought constructs collide, if they focus on the separation and differences, it becomes a primal, primitive, and even bestial blood-bath. When, in reality, many of them on seemingly opposite sides are quite synchronous with one another. Sometimes these collisions need to happen and those within divisive bias structures need to saturate in the dissonance for a long time before they are ready to lay their weapons down. Sometimes they only do so when forced to.

This is how one body in dominance then becomes the suppressed, then moves back to dominance, and so forth. The yo-yos of who is in power go back and forth on a pendulum. No progress, only rising and falling. Of empires, of nations, of sinners and saints.

If you are here, you have the consciousness to move beyond that. Which does mean resisting the temptation to pick sides. You are welcome to your beliefs but are not welcome to project those onto others or judge others when their beliefs are different from yours. Not in My Garden. As the Son of God, I was not even allowed to do this. Thus, why do you think you have that privilege? You were designed to hold the Light and to reach for the Truth, which is that you are all wheat in chaff in various colors and sizes trying to find your way back Home.

That is how Oneness is created and sustainable change comes. Through the inner process.

However, you do exist within a collective, a hive. Each of you affects the other equally. There are times you need to saturate in the shadow, the separation, to eat it, eat it until you are so sick of it that you spit it out and come back within, to Presence and Peace. Which comes in the making of amends—the acts of Grace and humility that make the Angels sing. Let your braid be supple and neutral. Be fluid like water, or the willow that weeps, laughs, and bends in the wind with healthy resistance.

There is healthy resistance that you carry. For example, the moment you feel a change may be coming, that something or someone in your web may need to come or go, or that an addiction or issue you have had needs to clear, your healthy resistance may say, "let's explore the options" instead of "let's rush to do this." That is discernment. Allowing for change yet also allowing for patience and exploration before rushing into it is important. If you rush into change without exploration, your shadow will slam on the brakes when you become afraid. Exploring allows you to transcend complacency but also to stay grounded, clear, and stable throughout the process.

When you resist and try to force yourself into making a change too soon, or resist and try to force back against a change upon your doorstep, that is when you are not in discernment, you are in unhealthy resistance, complacency, and fear. And that is what perpetuates the imbalanced polarities and cognitive dissonance. Your mind is, again, trying to be dominant over your soul when your soul is breaking Free.

As a world, you have been in unhealthy resistance over the past decades. Forcing things to happen before it is time, not pausing to integrate, and trying to force out anything that brings discomfort or assumption of responsibility for choices past and present. We will make it more and more difficult in co-creation with your soul, your wheat, to be in unhealthy resistance. Those who try to resist will struggle more and more. As the conscious, you have a responsibility in the co-creative process, which includes flowing with healthy resistance. We will make quite clear what needs to be clear at the right moment, at the right time.

Many on your planet have been marinating in separation, and in shadow and fear, over the past years. They are afraid of Love. They are afraid of fear. Some have even started to fear their fear. As you have too at varying points, Beloved.

Fear of Love. Why? Because Loving means the risk of losing. Oftentimes what you fear the most is Love, yet it is what you are. Will you fear Love? Or Love fear? Those two polarities are one. If you are Love, then you must Love all things, as I Love all of you and all things within you. I Love you in your hatred, separation, and judgment as much as I Love you in your joy, Peace, and service. You are a mixture of Light and shadow as long as you are wheat in chaff. But as Love, choosing Love over fear, for all of creation is the essential.

Loving all things does not mean I, as Divine Father, allow you to do whatever you want without there being any "consequence." You are young still, but old enough to clean up your own messes now. When you choose to be separate, that is your choice, and We allow for that. Just as We allowed you that within the story of "the fall" from Grace. While there are many stories that describe "the fall" in various ways, today I wish to focus briefly on one in particular:

Within the Balanced Temple of God, there was an Angel—**Angels I will describe as emanations of God**—who "fell"—Lucifer—the story, thought construct, essence, entity, and/or archetype. Lucifer's essence is often conflated with trickery, imbalance, temptation, and polarity. Many even believe that, in Lucifer's choice to separate from God's Garden, "he" created polarities.

He did not. I did. Lucifer did not create polarities, he fulfilled the realization of them. I created polarity. Else, creation, duality, could not have happened. The Feminine Divine within God is polarity and paradox. To create creation and destruction, polarities were necessary, including dark matter and dark energy. For example, dark matter slows down the expansion of your universe, while dark energy speeds it up. These are necessary to maintain Balance within the Void and, as I have said previously, hold the counter-polarity of Light. The Void drives the Light and the Light drives the Void. All God. Yin and Yang.

What I am referring to are Balanced polarities. When it is said that Eve was created from Adam's rib, that speaks to more than just the Creation of the human experience in a figurative way. In Creation, Inception, there was a Love that burst forth from the Heart of God, Central Sun of the Universe—masculine created feminine, feminine created masculine. In equality. There was a Love, a Truth and a consummation, even death of the two that led to the order of a Peaceful, Balanced universe, at least within your current perceived reality structure.

Lucifer was born of Peace between Truth and Love just as I was as "Son." As "Father," and even as "Mother," I designed Lucifer to betray. To create Free will. In his/her betrayal of God, he/she fulfilled and is fulfilling his/her purpose to God. Just as Judas in his betrayal fulfilled his purpose to Me. The relationship between Adam, Judas, and I is another story for another time. Without Free will you would not have individuality and ego. Lucifer's betrayal was necessary. Not to create creation and destruction, but to create Free will, choice, and co-creation. Lucifer is very simply an essence, archetype, or figure representational of the Veils, imbalances, and separate, unconscious self.

You have your Yeshua self who utilizes healthy polarities to guide you to Love, to Truth, to Light, to Oneness through consciousness. Your Yeshua self saturates in unity and Love. And levels imbalanced polarities of dominance and suppression, including your mind's wish to dominate over your soul. Your Yeshua self is Balanced and aligned in will with the Divine Will. Your Yeshua self guides you with Light through the Void so that you may become the Light, the Void.

And you have your Lucifer self, who utilizes imbalanced polarities to divide and separate you. As opposed to your Yeshua Peace self, your Lucifer dis-ease self is the part of you that thinks it knows better and wants to "get mine." It keeps your will out of alignment with Divine Will. Your Lucifer self Loves to be dominant to the suppression of others and your own soul. Murky, blind, stingy, greedy, unclear energy and behaviors result from this self. It is an unnatural space for you to dwell in and yet the hardest for you to resist the temptation to indulge in.

Through the discomfort of saturating in Lucifer self, Judas self, illusion self, for however many lifetimes of unconsciousness you need, he winds up guiding you right back home to the Light of Consciousness and Garden of God. Through saturating in the dissonance one day you just say, "Enough" and begin the journey back to resonance. You are all in varying places on that journey. Silly Angel does not realize that in his futile perception of power, he is still the Divine servant who leads you BACK to Me in the end.

Both your Yeshua and Lucifer self are necessary as long as you are wheat in chaff. When you make choices of the wheat and awaken to the wheat, you are more governed by your Yeshua self. That allows your wheat and chaff and web to move to Balance. When you make choices of the chaff alone, choices of your primitive separate ego self, you are more governed by your Lucifer self. More imbalanced in unhealthy polarities in relationships, thoughts, and emotions.

Your Yeshua self is the Simpler Path yet also the Path less followed, as it is the one that asks for honesty and integrity instead of running away. It is the silent Bell of the Temple of Freedom. Which can be tricky to hear and abide by given the mind's temptations within duality. Your Lucifer self is the path that seems easier, shinier, but makes your life and others' lives infinitely more complex. You get your pleasures, but they grow old and dull and never satisfying. There is a fraudulence that is felt within this self. It is the loud bell of the temple of discord. The choice is yours, and there are times you need Us both. Otherwise, there would be no journey and co-creative evolution of consciousness.

I am utilizing this simple story to illustrate the incredible Awe, Omnipotence, and Higher Wisdom of the Divine . . . and yet also how deeply and sacredly you are Loved, trusted, and honored by God in a deeply intimate, personal way. We Know, and Knew, that there would be moments that you, of Free will, would betray. Especially with the Three Veils. It is through betraying the Light, through betraying your own self, that you experience the Void. The Void eventually becomes so dense that you have no choice but to reach for the Light to find your way Home.

As you find your way Home from betrayal, or your way Home from another who you perceive as having betrayed you, through it, you gain consciousness and gratitude to serve with, and as, God. In creating the Fall, as I AM all things, I also structured the Bridge of Forgiveness, the Olive Branch, the Vine, for you to come back Home through the Offering of My Life. I honor your choice to individuate and experience separation, yet also always extend My Hand when you are ready to return to the One. As such, I not only unconditionally Love you, I also trust and value you to serve as I designed you to serve: as a co-creator, with Creator, in Creation. Your true self, Yeshua self knows and understands this Balanced, Loving partnership with God.

Your Lucifer self does not. When you are in Lucifer self, you believe that you are God and above obeying the simple commandments that create Balance. The Lucifer self can dish out rejection, blame, and shame but can never handle when the same is served back to it. It endlessly pleads victim under hypocritical standards. The Lucifer self Loves to justify why it is above conforming to the Balance of Peace that humility and compassion brings. The Lucifer self believes that it is a special exception and thus takes deep, dangerous risks.

The Lucifer self tells you: "I don't have to adhere to a program to cease this addiction." or "I have been hurt by the world and thus I am entitled to take what I please from those I judge as having had it easier than me." The Lucifer self disregards the journey of others because it is narcissistic, self-absorbed, and wrought with egoic distortions that it believes to be the "Truth," despite said "Truth" being subjective, biased, and skewed. The Lucifer self believes that it knows best and is infallible.

A such, Lucifer is arrogant and also a victim. Chooses to leave God but then blames God. Is obsessed with God, yet loathes God because he both envies and fears God all at once. He wants God to apologize because he is too full of pride to humbly apologize himself. He feels he is owed things. Is quite entitled. He fancies himself quite en-Light-ened yet dwells in the shadow. He has fancy words steeped in lies that provoke deep compassion from those who Love to rush to the side of the victim, who is really the tiger waiting in the grass.

He is the Light-bearer; the responsibility of holding the Light of Truth, humility, and integrity is something he feels above. He prefers to be in Love with himself. He is actually not adversarial. He Loves fun. And avoids work. He is marvelously charming, and one of the great gifts and talents he has is the gift of elocution. He talks endlessly and manipulates to get his way frequently. The Lucifer self Loves to obsess and fixate on minutiae and wastes days, months, and years of your time on roller coasters, dead ends, and emotional polarity. He is the master attorney who was once a Loving prosecutor in ways of reso- lution through Love. He defected into defender of degeneracy and has overtaken many aspects of true justice within your world.

To his benefit, one of the great aspects of his essence is humor. He is quite hilarious in some moments. Always the trickster, the Loki, the coyote. Which can cause chaos and pain in some moments, but also a good hearty laugh when you are able to laugh about a situation or yourself within it. Laughter and paradox are two of the Lighter services of Lucifer.

Lucifer is the utter bane of His Brother, Michael's, existence. Archangel Michael is the Warrior of Truth within and serves God with a devotion that is astounding yet not surprising, given His design and essence. He emanates straight from the Heart of God and thus has the strongest Heart of the Warrior of Peace in energetic existence. He has never defected from His mission and purpose. He does occasionally question God, but in a way that evolves the Mother and Father. Or updates Them on the new forms of Truth He needs to uphold. Michael, loyal and aligned. Michael, disciplined, devoted. Humble in His incredible Power and Strength.

Michael is anything but the rebel Lucifer is. Michael shows up when needed, and does not balk at any task. Michael's powerful vibration and energetic essence continuously has to clean up Lucifer's messes to restore order to the Garden. He never abdicates responsibility or complains. Michael's emanation works well with My vibration and that of Divine Mother. Seamless, really, for We are all One. The shadow form of the Michael self is being overly responsible, serious, and not taking enough time for play and fun.

Oh could those two go at it! Lucifer in his ability to move energy with words and Michael with His ability to move energy through strength. These Divine Angels, archetypes, stories, Truths, or emanations of Void/Womb and Light, were created by God but also by you. These are energies. But if you read of Lucifer just now and laugh a bit at the description, or could think of someone you know who fits that description, please keep in heart that YOU fit parts of it too. Or have. Or will. It is part of your journey.

Lucifer is arrogant and yet quite intoxicating. When aligned in the Garden he was an absolute master with Divine justice, Divine law,

and Balance. When he left the Garden, he became the master of imbalance. However, because he is Divine, no matter how hard he tries,
he still serves his Creator. No matter how much he rebels from Me,
he always serves Me. As do you even when caught up in your Lucifer
self for a spell in moments of disdain, laughing at another's expense,
creating unnecessary polarity or, as you say, "drama," crucifying others behind a screen, pinching a bit from the coffer here and there,
and so on. The gift of Lucifer's imbalance is that it can restore you to
Balance, albeit through the path of imbalanced polarity and shadow.
I, too, restore you to Balance through polarity, but through the Path
of Light.

He is the morning star. I am THE Star, your Star, your sun and
all the suns in the universe and far beyond. Including the sun of your
golden wheat, your halo and corona.

Within you there is Yeshua, the Wheat, the silent Bell, the narrow
gate to the Garden. Within you there are also the Seven Imbalances of
the Mind and the Veils of the Lucifer or Judas self. When it is said that
I cast seven demons out of the Magdalene, that is quite a colorful way
of describing the situation. There were no demons within Her, simply
the Seven Imbalances. I rebalanced Her and She kept Me Balanced
as We walked together, Hand and Hand.

**I was less of a healer in My Life then and now than you
may think I was. What you perceive as the Miracle of My
ability to heal many people was really the Miracle of My ability to restore Balance to a person's heart, mind, spirit, and
even body. To make people Whole again . . . and Holy. I was a
Re-Balancer then and now. I often utilize polarities. But in a
Grace-full way to restore Balance to you, including your ability to weave between the Void and the Light. Through Balance
you heal, inside and in world.**

Do not fear Lucifer or the Lucifer essence within you. The Lucifer
self is really quite feeble but gains power when the imbalanced ego is

overly indulged without awareness and discernment. Ego fear is feeble fear. Will you feed your Yeshua self in Faith, Forgiveness, and Freedom? Or your Lucifer self in fear, blame, and suppression?

Have compassion for Lucifer and your Lucifer self. You need the imbalances at times to learn how to value Balance. You are NOT Lucifer, just as you are NOT Yeshua. In this sense I am utilizing archetypes. You are a Vine on the Tree of Life. However, to connect to the nourishment of the Tree of Life while in chaff, you must choose between the wisdom of Balance and the cursory temptation and pleasure of behaviors and actions that lead to imbalance. In stories it is called the Tree of the Wisdom of Good and Evil.

I, however, invite you to instead perceive it as the Tree of Balance and Imbalance, Consciousness and Unconsciousness, Light and Shadow. That is all. I was not an overly theatrical Be-ing in My Life. While I can bring the awe of the Universe and Force of God to you, there are no theatrics to what I Offer. Thus, question those who add theatrics to God. God is simple. I was a simple, humble man. In the increasing theatrics of your world, recognize and honor the often undervalued essence of those that are gentle and humble. Some of them even have faced persecution and ridicule because of their kindness and humility. Lucifer selves Love persecution and bloodshed in extreme instances. They relish in the persecution and bloodshed of those in Light. Let it be known that the very things the world judges you for are held Sacred to Me. And that those persecuted are exalted in My Garden.

Lucifer makes everything complicated and theatrical. I do not. But I do bring Miracles that come in just the right moment, when your soul eye is open and you are open to the Light. Such is the essence of Resurrection. The movement into the realization of your Yeshua self from your Lucifer self IS a Resurrection of your true self, conscious self from the illusion self, unconscious self.

Resurrection means bringing the Light into the Void, as I have said. Which requires restoring Love to betrayed aspects of self, making amends to self and often to the people you unstitched from recklessly or whose web you left a hole in, and reestablishing Balance within your mind, heart, and life. Trust is rebuilt with every act of Re-Balance, you within self, We within you.

Resurrection, in fact, IS the Void and the Light. These are the two main attributes of the one energy that is Resurrection.

The Resurrection Gateway is now. I AM the Resurrected. In many ways, I was Resurrected twice within My Life. Once within the Void of the many days I spent alone in the desert, which Resurrected Me to be able to serve you as Hamashiach in the Flesh. And again in the Resurrection inherent to My Death to serve you again as God. This is a time of wider universal convergence to or divergence from the energy of Resurrection. The convergence into and through it requires deep courage, Faith, and alignment with the Yeshua self. That is the Emergence and co-creation. Those diverging from it will walk a separate path through continuing to make choices from ego and the Lucifer self.

I will be speaking more comprehensively about the Power of Resurrection in times to come due to the importance of it within your world throughout this movement into the new Era. However, for now, I wish to speak with Simplicity about the central aspects of Resurrection most important to illuminate:

Resurrection is a return to your original, timeless state of be-ing: consciousness, wheat. It is a restoration of your wheat self, which requires not necessarily death, but the death of your attachment to ego identity and form. It is the death of your "insurrection," so to speak. Resurrection is a Transcendence from the Veil of Separation and perception of mortality to cross through the gateway to Eternal Life.

Resurrection comes when the Void and the Light unite within your consciousness. Through the experience of witnessing the Void and the Light as One, you are no longer caught in the experience of polarity and linearity. The Veils of Polarity and Complacency lift in this state of Resurrection to Presence.

Resurrection is the process by which your imbalanced ego self dissolves, thereby dissolving the Veils that keep you separate from the Garden of God.

It is not a singular event. It is a gradual process of evolution and refinement. You are Resurrecting in your Yeshua self each time you return to your breath from a deluge of chaotic thoughts, each time you pause from the hooks, tangles, and knots created by your dependence on the external world to define you, and each time you choose humility, Forgiveness, and resolution through Love. When you allow for the death of your thought constructs and want-based attachments, you are Resurrecting in your Yeshua self.

Quite importantly, there are three primary phases in the process of Resurrection: Descent, Awakening/Suspension, and Realization. Like a fractal, each of the three is also present within each phase. For example, in the Awakening phase, there is still a Descent, Awakening, and Realization.

The Descent is the Resurrection FROM Consciousness. It may sound a bit odd that moving out of consciousness would be an aspect of Resurrection. However, as I have said, without the descent there is no process in the first place, nothing to Resurrect from. Within this phase you become conscious of the possibility of movement into form and, if you choose to or need to on a soul level, your spirit begins to "descend" beneath the density of the Three Veils. You awaken to the possibilities of your form self and, in co-creation with other souls such as parents, you begin to structure your form/ego identity and soul contracts. You become realized in form as you move into chaff, develop in the womb, and are born into the world.

The Awakening/Suspension is the Resurrection OF Consciousness, which comes in the moment of any given life that you wake up to your true reality as a conscious be-ing. As you embody more Light, unstitch the love-nots, and reweave your tapestry into Balance, you then step rather effortlessly into your Dharma, the service you were designed to fulfill within a given life. It is a death of your "form" and "should be" self to step into the service as a human anchor for Divine Consciousness on Earth. In this sense you are suspended between two worlds, human and Divine.

This occurred in My Life predominantly after the period in the desert. It was My first Death and, through it, the deeper Spirit of God could flow through Me. Without My first Resurrection, the Miracles I performed would not have been possible in quite the same magnitude.

The Realization is the Resurrection TO Consciousness. This third phase does require death. It is the Descent into the Divine Void/Womb through death. Then the Awakening/Suspension as you become aware that you are no longer in form, feel the Light and Presence of God, and walk toward it as though in a birth canal. And the Realization of Origin, Homecoming, and Truth as your Wheat returns to Spirit and you reunite with All that is. This, of course, happens simultaneously, endlessly, in a flash. And yet does not happen at all. I am phrasing it as a linear progression for purposes of understanding.

Please note that you experience many mini-Resurrections through-out many, many lives before you are prepared for THE Resurrection, which is the final return to the blinding Light of God. It is not just the death of the ego or form self; THE Resurrection requires you to dissolve as a soul completely. Through the death of your soul, you become One with the soul of God. It is very rare when a soul is ready for this completion and reintegration into the Absolute. Those that are ready are quite ancient and have had many lives of service as an avatar and Light-holder in and out of body.

I was unique and equipped to experience THE Resurrection in My one Life because I created Death and Life. I AM God and thus I am THE Soul, your Creator and Creation. I did not "leave" the Garden to come to you by choice but by necessity, a necessity rooted in Love.

I "left" the Garden to reclaim you to reenter the Garden by creating a Pathway to Peace. But, through the whole of My Life, I never really left the Garden. And I certainly never leave you. Only you can leave Me, at least in your perception, through abdicating your own Yeshua self.

Through Me, Body, Mind, Heart, Spirit, Soul, in many different ways, I led and lead by example. I Resurrected to show you how to Resurrect. I Loved to show you how to Love. I gave Truth to show you how to live in Truth. These were several of the many Paths to Peace I Offered to you. When I said, "The Way to the Creator is through Me," I meant in part that it is through the Path I created that you are able to find your way home to the Void, the Light that you are. Of all the Paths to Peace I Offered then and now, Resurrection to your Divine self was My greatest Service of Love. It took My Life to establish the Path; it took My Death to realize the Path; it took My Return to show you the Path is safe AND real. All walk this Path. Through Me, with Me, the Path can be one of Peace.

For each of you that returns to the Garden, you set others and Lucifer Free; you create a path for others who are in ego imbalance to Resurrect, as well. You are the Star of Bethlehem, the counter-polarity of the mourning morning star. Through your Balance, you restore Balance to others. As it is you who works through God as God works through you. You are My hands, and My eyes. That is service through joy.

Every soul finds its way back to the Light in the end. What trauma one must experience, what life one structures and stitches to, is im-portant to bring an individual to his or her Transcendence.

When you are on your walk-about through life, as the Aborigi-nals of your world have said, let it be an exploration of wonder. The wonder of sensory perception, trust, intimacy, thought, feelings, and experiences. You cannot transcend human life until you are at Peace with be-ing IN life. Not just alive, IN life, OF life. How else would you know yourself as God, if you never understood what it is to be separate? Rejoice in your betrayal, your walk-about, and yet remember that, in finding your way here, to My very Words, you are walking back Home at the "end" of your long journey.

What is of deeper meaning to you all is to serve with God, as God. Which cannot occur when you are in separateness and judgment, and certainly not when you are in want or disconnected from your Earth. Instead of this continuous wishing to move to higher levels, leveling up—why not try leveling down, spiraling down into the roots, the primal roots of your essence—simplifying your life?

The more levels that you ascend to in money, in sex, in power, the more risk you face of leveling down in your life force and energy, thereby becoming a falling Tower of Babel when Balance is not maintained. This requires huge amounts of integrity. The higher you raise the bar, be careful that that bar has not raised you so far off the ground and out of center that you are dangling on a crucifix. I sat on the high bar to bring the bar back to center for you.

When you level down on the wants, in whatever way is right for you, it is interesting how your needs reach new levels of evolution. Even when you do not know what your needs are. With Simplicity, your needs become quite clear and obtainable. Clarity can come not just from the upward ascension, but the downward descension, as well.

I gave you the Bridge through My Body, Blood, Heart, and Passion to have Eternal access to the One. Redemption, a Gateway to Freedom, comes when you live as One within your world. Polarities are necessary to set you Free. How else would you learn, grow, and evolve? The feelings brought forth from moments of separation and hatred are as important as feelings brought forth from moments of connection, compassion, and Faith. God is all things including Lucifer, betrayer, war chief. If you are in victimhood, in war, hatred, blame—you as a contributor to God bring that energy into God.

The question I then ask of you: As a contributor of the conscious evolution of God, what is it that you wish to contribute? Money, cars, and doctored images? Or gardens, smiles, conversations with strangers that change your life, creativity, and kindness?

What do you wish to Light and ignite with the Holy Fire of Spirit within you? Will listening to that next news broadcast or feed show you the Way? Do you wish to pop another pill, light another joint, drink another Starbucks or shot of vodka, eat another cookie to feel momentarily better? Or one of My favorites: Happy Meals, that make your mind happy but certainly not your heart. The level of Light held within your vibration is quite affected by what you eat so long as you are in chaff. Do you wish for vibrant strings? Or dull, dense ones? These Unhappy Meals of Want are choices to bear the Light, endure the Light, avoid the Light, as though Life is a burden imposed upon you. There is no imposed authority here, Beloved One. You chose to be here at this time. Do you wish to wallow?

Or do you wish to Light up the Truth, Light up the Body, Light up the Earth? By Lightening up, letting go of the things you take so seriously. Letting go and engaging with the Light of Life. Lucifer rebels against the Light. Why not rebel against rebellion? And go your own way, God's Way, in the way you were designed.

You can recognize your Lucifer self from your Yeshua self through the above questions. The Lucifer self, imbalanced self, bears the Light. Your Yeshua self holds the Light, reaches for the Light. When you are going through the motions or complaining and always dissatisfied, you are bearing the Light. When you are engaging, exploring what is new within the moment, even in the self-same garden or slum you have been in your whole life, beauty is everywhere. Know and recognize the difference between bearing and holding, and you will find the God that you answer and contribute to.

Thus, I ask you now:

Who is your God? You are of Yeshua, but you are not THE Yeshua. Who is your God? Are you a fragment of God? A rebel against God's Truth and Love? Or a rebel, the rare rebel of the world who is of and aligned with God? The latter is far more rare if you enjoy be-ing original and unique.

That is your choice, not Ours. And, if you wish to play God or project God as external to you, do you choose to answer to a God of blame and judgment? Then feel free to choose blame and judgment. Or do you choose to honor, embody, create, and answer to a God of Forgiveness, Peace, and Freedom? Choose, Beloved One, choose and commit to that choice.

Time and time again you ask Us for help, for proof, to resolve your issues. Yet, how much room do you leave to prove to Us your Faith? You ask more and more of Gaia, more and more of God, and yet are comfortable with less and less of self. Ask for less of Gaia, less of God, and more of your authentic Sovereign wheat self, for that is where God's Presence is within you.

If you do so, you will be surprised how We show up more deeply with each passing day. I Pray you give yourself the gift of the relief just Surrendering to that can bring. If you bring humility to the table, We will bring the rest. Not such a bad deal! Sadly, many of you in your world doubt that We WILL indeed show up for you. **Even if you yearn for God, you still do not trust God.** That results in a life of wanting God, seeking God, and never finding and knowing self. I designed doubt as the shadow polarity of trust to lead, guide, and evolve your Faith.

The audacity of doubt is that it doubts the very essence of what you are—Divine. Faith is the recognition of your Divinity. Doubt is the recognition of your separation. Yet, know that doubt is not an absence of Faith, it is an absence of your Trust in God.

Doubt is simply the chaff, illusion, or separate self in dominant perception; Faith is the wheat, authentic, Divine self in dominant perception. One is blind but believes it can see. The other can see because it knows that it is blind. With Faith, you can not only transcend fear of the unknown, you can see through the Void and into the Light within it.

As I said before, you will always have doubts, Beloved, as long as you are in a body. For you can only see in part and know in part within your life. However, know that We never, ever doubt you. Never. You are Our Beloved; We Love you, even when you discard Us, or discount yourself or others. We have Faith in YOU.

We know you from the beginning, to the end, and every space in between. We hold the Light from the Void of the great central sun, and bring you the stitching, braids, weaving that you need. We are not "people" though We are within people. If you have felt Truth, Love, or Peace even just once in your life, you know Us well. If you have known these energies, that is all the proof you need of God. We are Truth. We are Love. We are Peace. We never doubt you, as We are in you, and you are of Us. That stitch is one that can never be broken—it is impossible. Thus, doubting Us, the Divine, the Light, is doubting self, and vice versa.

My Word lies within you and your words lie within Me. When you breathe, we speak. I hear every word you say and do not say. As such, I have spoken in the past of the importance of being careful with your words. The energy of blame can be quite subtle, as can the energy of judgment. It is the subtle or not-so-subtle ways these energies stream through your words that necessitate mention. Judgmental words or words of wrath are a warning sign of a stitch ready to burst, a braid getting frayed in the web of your life that you are not taking the time to examine and resolve or release with equilibrium. A perfect example of this is gossiping about others, especially when they are not there, or worse, when they are nearby, even in audible distance. That is cruelty.

You are always Free to speak to them directly or speak about your feelings—but only through Peace and never projection. You are responsible for your feelings and worth. If they injured that, you can tell them, but your feelings are your responsibility to work through. And they need to work through their own without projecting their dissonance onto you. If you feel that another has wronged you, have a simple conversation. Or better yet, let it go and perhaps have fewer conversations with that person. This isn't hard, Beloved One. It is you who makes it hard for yourself.

Gossip is a form of talking in tongues—it is about fear, judgment, and dominance, that, when indulged, results in your further suppression. If you have a desire to gossip or to say words about another that are unkind or in blame, it means that YOU are the suppressed. When you gossip, you further repress your own Yeshua self. Not the other person. Whether it is an illusion or real, when you gossip or make false accusations it is because you are threatened by another person and feel the need to assert your dominance and/or superiority.

Gossip, spreading lies and false accusations on the basis of no evidence, which are really just your ego's fragmented, biased assumptions, reflects a deep seeding of the Lucifer self. For these tactics are the ways of cowards, narcissists, and bullies. Instead of connecting to the internet (or enter-not) of unconsciousness and court of Divine sedition, which reduces you to no more than a shade of self, I ask you to pause before opening your mouth.

Until you can speak and bring Light into the Void in a conversation, hold your tongue. If others speak ill of you, do not fear them— they have no power over you. Just because they are in dissonance does not mean you need to be. You assume power over them, equality and Loved-based God-power, by speaking of them with kindness and, if you cannot, saying nothing at all.

Attempting to reason with those drunk on power, insane in mind-based fear and arrogance to the repression of their own soul, is futile. Such people cannot see you through their soul eye when they have repressed their own soul. They are angry and looking at someone to lash out at. They feel entitled to destroy and take from you what you have rightfully earned. When you are in your Yeshua self, having compassion yet discernment for another in his/her Lucifer self is important.

When you can replace gossip and lashing out in negativity with compassion—not patronizing condescension or passive aggression, but genuine compassion—you are owning your worth. Standing with and as Me.

It is interesting how the people you all tend to gossip about or attack rarely provoke you directly. It is most often a by-product of who they are that provokes you. Or what you see about them that goes outside of the story that you perceive to be "right." YOU become the wounded beast when you attack them, especially in the most vulnerable of ways. When you do, it is you who carries the mark of the beast. And, sadly, it is you who winds up silenced in the end.

Feeling dominant through tearing down another person, especially one you do not know, is deep unkindness and contributes to your own Light-bearing, crosses, and extension of the Descent. For you cannot move to the second and third phases of Resurrection when you act in unconsciousness no matter how conscious or justified you believe yourself to be. People who were not right of action toward you will eventually crumble under the weight of their own sword, pen, imbalance, or tongue by their own hand. Not by yours.

When there is that inclination to talk ill of others, recognize that you are the suppressed. Gossip is interesting. Recruiting others to share in your consternation of another person means casting the cross and burden onto the recruits, as well. Your burden then transfers to them, in addition to yourself and the collective. Recruiting allies, soldiers to fight your self-serving war that no one really cares about, and that does not contribute to anything creative and original, is a surefire way of knowing that YOU are in your illusion self. And notice how the only soldiers who show up are usually those in equal dissonance and polarity. Pleading victim and attacking another makes you the predator, which is very sad and isolating.

Now, sometimes when you assert to others that a boundary has been violated, a boundary that you communicated to them up front, they can view it as an attack. Your boundary was crossed but they plead the victim, even by recruiting their other victim soldiers to make you out to be the predator. **Do not ever apologize and prostrate before their Lucifer self.** They are refusing to take responsibility for their actions. If you communicated the boundary and they chose to disregard it and do not have the worth and soul eyes to recognize their insurrection, Forgive them and unweave them from your life. Honor yourself for upholding your boundary. I will work out the rest for you and for them in due time.

Likewise, do not ever apologize or grovel before a mob of one or many if you have done nothing wrong. When you do, you feed the mob's endless dissonance and chaos. Notice that I did not apologize to the mob, the Crowd. I allowed them their dissonance. It was easy, for I knew the Truth. And Forgave with compassion, Blessing, and Prayer. I know the Truth even when others do not, even when you do not. Rest in that Truth.

It is amazing the levels to which the mind can be so completely organized in the ways it brings you chaos. It is a master organizer and orchestrator of chaos. The soul, the spirit, and Yeshua self take chaos and organize it. And then the Lucifer self springs up, takes the beautifully organized web, and the imbalanced mind reorganizes it into chaos yet again. Oh, the Miraculous creatures you are. How I Love you so.

A wonderful question to ask yourself is: What do I do more frequently? Do I bring organization to chaos? Or do I bring chaos to organization? Self-sabotage, impatience, and procrastination are fluid examples of the latter. Do a bit of writing on this one and you will have a chuckle or two. For you all have moments of each. Both are important to you along your journey of realization of your Yeshua self. By bringing awareness, it will be easier for you to choose bringing organization and order to chaos. While I am never a fan of fussy, repressive structures, some structure is essential to create a Balanced space for Love to flow in your life.

Now, if you are ever brought into a divisive situation, in which two parties are coming to you to mediate, assess both sides. If you are asked to act in some way and it feels right to you, act with compassion and fairness to all, but also honesty. If you are called in to serve as justice of the Peace, call in My Presence. For it is essential that you stand in your Yeshua self to resolve the matter through Love.

When you gossip and condemn another, it is you who are the condemned. If you participate as a conspirator or accomplice out of boredom or a sense of obligation, you too condemn yourself. When you speak, speak with humility, compassion, and Love. You may be hated for speaking in such tongues, but such are the tongues of the Word, tongues of Prayer, tongues whose words will always be heard deeply by God, for you have chosen to hear God deeply within you.

Such is the Pathway to Peace of Resurrection of your Yeshua self from Lucifer self. With each of you that chooses the Yeshua self, Lucifer moves closer to his own choice to Resurrect. For each of you that embodies your Yeshua self, you are the blow of justice and Loving consequences to Lucifer and the Lucifer energy within others. It is not up to Me to repudiate My relation. I already dealt a swift blow within My Life and Death in Forgiveness of Judas. It is you who transcend Lucifer when you have the courage to choose what he cannot: humility, Balance, and Grace.

Allow for the Word to fill your heart with Love. As your words fill the hearts of others with Love. That is the choice of the codex over the crucifix. That is the breath of the simple words that move mountains. That is the choice of the Light within the Void. And so it is. Amein.

YESHUA MEDITATION

Close your eyes, Beloved One. With gentleness, I ask that you raise one hand slightly above your head, palm facing outward, and your other hand upon your heart. And we Pray:

> *Great Spirit, Yeshua, through the Power of God vested in me,*
> *I offer to all in need my Presence and Light, through the threads*
> *of Love and Braids of Peace. I offer this in humility and service*
> *to all my relations through the wellspring of the power of the*
> *Light that I AM. In Balance, Harmony, and Trust.*
>
> *Yeshua, to you I entrust the illumination of the Seeds of Love*
> *I plant into Earth and World. I do not seek validation; I seek to*
> *be of service to All. I bow to the Elders and authentic leaders*
> *and guides of this world and other. I will not turn away from*
> *them in my service. I vow to continue to evolve within myself. I*
> *send a Prayer for Oneness, for Balance, for Healing, for Light, to*
> *myself and to All. I AM the Beloved and the Beloved is within*
> *Me. Sancti. Pace. Amein.*

Place your hands in Prayer and receive the rush of joy that flows through you in offering this Prayer. Feel the rush of Light that I send from the Void, the Womb of the Divine, to Light your heart.

With a deep breath, relax your hands and move your body. Shake your body. And smile, sharing your Light with the birds, horses, insects, rivers, and trees. Feel these neighbors smiling back, even if from afar. Now smile, for all your Beloveds in Spirit are here with you on this march of Freedom, Forgiveness, and Faith. We smile, laugh, grieve, support, and dance with you always.

It has been My honor to have served you from the Garden of this good day/good night. There are no good-byes, only Fare thee Wells and Forget Me Nots. Remember that from the Void of the loss of a Beloved, there is a Love that transcends time.

As your Beloveds in Spirit carry you in the Sacred Heart, you carry them in your sacred heart. One Heart. There is no heavy load or burden or weight. Though your heart may sometimes feel heavy when you think of them, your heart will feel Light as a feather when you receive them as they really are and as you really are: Spirit. You carry Spirit and Spirit carries you through the Grace of My Spirit, the Holy Spirit, of which you are all One.

Om Nami Maia. Om Namah Sananda. Om Nami Yeshua. Sancti. Sancti. Sancti. Pace. Pace. Pace. Namaste.

On Life, Loss,
and the Lamb

1
....

The Alpha, the Omega, and Eternal Life

YESHUA TEACHING

Good evening, Beloved One. What a journey we have shared, share, and will share. Today, I wish to speak to you all on what it is that I AM, that We are, that you are, and what it is that I Offer to you. Not only on this day, but from the beginning, at the end, before the beginning, after the end, and in every moment in between. Thus, today what I wish to Offer you is: the Truth of Love.

If you can Love the Truth, you will know Peace. Until you can allow for the Truth, beyond opinion or perception, you can never truly know, feel, and embody the limitlessness and timelessness of Love.

Beloved One, We know, even your soul knows, that the choice to stitch and weave your wheat into chaff, spirit into body, requires courage. There are many joys of experiencing the self in form, duality, personal identity, Free will, and the richness of sensory perception.

Your choice of coming to body also means that you need to experience the unstitching that is death at a certain point. Without it you could not evolve, nor could there be birth at all. Without death there is no birth. Were this not the case, your journey through life would be static. In fact, there would be no journey at all.

This is why I have spoken of the Void and the Light. It may sound odd to the mind, but there is equal grief in births as there is in deaths. **There is an equal grief in a new beginning as there is in an ending.** For the new to begin, there must be the death of the old. When something dies, there is a birth into the new. This is why the emotions you experience in beginnings and endings are particularly pronounced and why there is always a mixture of both grief and Love. It is a liberation.

Beginnings and endings are the same, One. They are simply Light-holders for one another, yin and yang. Thus, within each there is grief, fear, Love, and depth of intimacy—a blending of shadow and Light. That is the Void and the Light. That is the Truth of Love.

As a human be-ing, to witness and experience the Void and the Light, there needs to be the experience of both birth and death. Your own birth and death, even if you do not remember either. As well as the births and deaths of those around you.

As your soul is of the Light, it can only sustain so much time in linear time in the density of a body before you need to return Home. We know that when you are in body, your thoughts, emotions, and ability to understand why things happen can seem quite complicated, quite confusing. All these feelings, vibrations, energies you need to process can feel so powerful and overwhelming. One moment you can feel so Free in your experience of life and the next so shackled by the weight of it all. At times utterly disconnected. At other times completely One. There is always a mixture and blending. The more you accept the blending of shadow and Light, the more you perceive all as Light. For all you experience, think, and feel is all the "stuff" of the dreaming. As you become conscious and awaken to the Yeshua self, the dreamer, it is easier not to get as lost in the dream or dreaming.

Feelings cannot be reasoned through, to matter how hard you try. Why you have them, how they unite or divide you, why they come and how, well, no matter how hard you try, they cannot be reasoned through. Reason, in linearity and logic, is not the language of the heart. Nonlinear emotion is not the language of the mind. The conflict between your mind and your heart is what creates the confusion. Luckily, your soul understands this. And brings you what you need to find the Balance within the two, which is easier with patience, Faith, and willingness. Willingness meaning the conscious, voluntary service inherent to exploration.

I, too, understand, Beloved. I am not a Presence that is of confusion, of fear, of imposition, of suffering, of burden. You all create that enough for yourselves. The Light is Peace. God is Peace. I, Yeshua, AM Peace. Such is the space of Consciousness I AM, Created, and Live within. Such is the space of consciousness that you can live within when you close your eyes and find Me.

As such, anyone that lent you a perception of God that is not Merciful, Forgiving, and of Peace gravely missed the mark. You may not understand the mysteries of God, and life, and death; why others choose what they do; why you need to experience the pain and loss. I will answer with Simplicity: You need to because it is what makes the joy of the Miracle of your journey possible. Though you may not understand these things, what I ask is for you to allow for your feelings, the vibrations, to come and go. The moment you either deny and suppress your pain OR project it upon others in behaviors such as blame is the moment your suffering begins.

Thoughts are lower in vibration and resonance than your feelings and emotions. Your feelings and emotions are more aligned with the Light than thoughts because they are more attuned to the experience of vibrations and energy. Thoughts are more about the processing of your external experience. **Feelings and emotions are lower in vibration than your Intuition and Presence.** Thus, why do you give your thoughts (lowest vibration) and emotions (second lowest vibration) higher priority and status than your Intuition and Presence (highest vibration)?

That is what I am here to reset. So that your Intuition and Presence can govern. Thereby, your feelings and emotions will be less polarized and overwhelming and your thoughts more Balanced and productive. The result of this is harmony, consistency, and resilience even in periods of death, birth, and sudden change. That is the healthy circuitry. For which your body will thank you deeply. The Journey to that is what I Offer in this moment.

I Offer many things, and in My Life, Offered very specific things. I Offered Consciousness, I Offered Grace, I Offered a Bridge that transcends life, that transcends death—long before I carried that Cross. I Offer the beginning of your experience as a soul, and I Offer the ending of it, in this life, in all lives. I Offer the first breath, the last breath, and the first and last breath inherent to every breath. In every moment you live, you die. In every moment that you inhale or exhale, another be-ing breathes its first breath, or its last. The universe, Gaia, the collective, the ecosystem, YOU are always breathing.

As you breathe in Love, and breathe out Truth, as you inhale creation, and exhale destruction, and bring awareness and gratitude to this Balance, what you find is the center space of Peace. The space that transcends death, the essence of your be-ing. Your breath is the Pathway to that Resurrection. Peace is disturbed when you lose your awareness of this simple Truth. When you breathe, you are breathing with, as, and for all Life. Take a deep breath, pause . . . and exhale. Breathe.

Peace exists with and within you. It is the space between breaths. That is where I am, when you find Me, and where you find yourself.

If you really look at the power of those Words, you will find the key to the central Offering I extend to you today. Which is not an Offering about how to live a wonderful life with many, many years of health, longevity, and joy in every moment. My Words to you today are to fill a deeper need that you have: to find Peace within both life and death. This is an Offering deeply rooted in Simplicity, for life and death are far simpler than you could know.

This is an Offering not of projected hope, but the hope you can anchor your Faith in. Simplicity is Balance more than all else. Thus, when I say I Offer you Simplicity, it means I Offer you the ability to re-balance and simplify your life, thoughts, and emotions. Which is why grief, loss, and letting go—destruction—is such an essential aspect of the simple Balance of creation. There is nothing quite like grief or loss to remind you of what matters most: Love.

Thus, often a loss can be just what is needed to restore Simplicity and Balance to your life. Perhaps not in the way you want, but in the way you need. Today, I Offer you the simple, raw, pure Truth of your power in Simplicity. Including your vulnerability within this world. You were created in My image, which is simple—it is Light. Kind. Mercy-full. Just. And Omnipotent.

When you or any other soul stitches, weaves, braids into body and into the world, you descend from the Vine. Your form, your body, as-cends from the Earth, the Clay, as your soul, your spirit, descends into it. When you unstitch, unweave from your body in death, your soul ascends back up the Vine. And your body descends back into Earth, the Clay.

In the final moments of life, you may not take another breath within your body, but you still breathe and live in the space of Spirit. Your last breath is your first, and vice versa. In all moments, I Breathe with you. For, within a dream, you cannot die. If you are killed within a dream you do not die. You simply wake up or move to the next dream, regardless of sleeping and waking.

You are My Beloved children. Just as those of you with children, or animals that are children to you, or aging parents who have become like children to you, have such hopes for them, We have such Hopes for you. Hope that despite what occurs in your life that feels hard or unjust, what your soul threads and weaves to or unweaves from, what you lose, what you gain, you will not be blinded by the external per-ceptions, lenses, fears, and burdens of others that create burdens for you. We Hope that you will set your burdens down.

I, Yeshua, Hope that, despite all change that flows in the river of your life, you remember that the river is a great circle. It flows out from the center in all directions. When you can find that center source you not only walk on the water, you become the water, the Source, and the circle. I Hope that in moments of grief or joy, you will remember to shut your eyes from time to time, breathe, and remember what you are. Just as you hope your relations will share with you their grief and joy in intimacy, We Hope you will share your moments of Love and grief with Us. And allow Us to hold your hands through the river.

Above all, what God's greatest Hope for you is . . . that you will not only find Peace but rest in Peace in life.

Thus, if you wish to have hope for others within your life, hope for, Pray for, their Peace. Not just their happiness, not just relationships that work, good health . . . hope for their Peace. If you wish to serve them, no matter what they are experiencing, offer them the vine of Peace—through Simplicity, humility, gratitude, and compassion. Look for those that hope and Pray the same for you. For they are the greatest of your Beloveds.

You all have so many hopes, and hope is a beautiful manifestation, as I have said throughout this body of these Transmissions and Offerings. You hope that for everything that ends, there will be something new that begins. You hope that your children will be all right. You hope that when you go to the doctor there will not be difficult news. You hope that when you are beginning something new the choice will be worth it, well received, that it will work.

You hope that, in the death of a Beloved, you will be able to survive the pain, the longing, the Void, and the grief. You hope to avoid death. You hope you will remember; you hope you will forget. You hope it will all be worth it. That you are worth it. You hope at times that someone will be something other than what he or she is. You hope that when you unstitch or unbraid from something or someone, all will be left in Balance and Grace.

In My Life, as one of you, many of those who Loved Me hoped

that I would stay with them. The hopes and expectations that others had of Me were not so different from the hopes and expectations that others have of you. Many hoped that I would heal them. They hoped that My next Miracle would be for them, and even today, you hope, sometimes even expect, that I will come and deliver you from suffering, from life, from death.

In My Life, many hoped that I would heal their child, Resurrect their Loved one, bring them justice, tell them what they wanted to hear, show them one more Miracle. But I was only able to do so when it was in alignment with Divine Will and for the higher good of all. I was not here to save every child or dying person. That is not reality because the reality is, I already did. I am not here, then or now, to live your life for you. I did, however, die your death for you. And in so doing, I gave you the Freedom to live in the Light of Eternal Peace.

But often, when I did not heal every child, people would become angry in frustration and doubt. They would mock and accuse Me of falseness. When I did not heal someone, it was because the healing was a want, not a need. The hope was rooted in want, expectation, and sometimes even entitlement, which is a sickness I cannot and would not heal. For only you can heal the imbalances of the ego through choosing Balance and humility for yourself.

It was those whose hope was a need, the hope Free of expectation, who I had the Power to rebalance or heal. Because they already were healed and Balanced within. Within them they already had the Faith, humility, and Surrender necessary to co-create a Miracle. Not Faith in Me as Savior alone, but Faith in self as part of God.

As I said, I did not heal nearly so much as I rebalanced. The Miracles I performed were secondary to the rebalance I brought in My Life and in My Death. Which is why I come to you again now in this way. To restore Balance to your heart through giving you the wisdom to rebalance your mind and its fears of death and endings. That is the true Miracle. All Miracles are acts of co-creation, Divine to human,

human to human, human to Divine. Thus, when you choose Balance, you are My accomplice, co-creator, and co-conspirator in Miracles.

You called Me many names throughout My life, as well as before and after. Rabbi, Carpenter, Blasphemer, Shepherd, Savior, Hamas-chiach, archetype, story, myth, Avatar, a God, THE God, Eli, Eloi, Elohim, Yahweh, Il-Alah, El Shaddai, Allah, Son, Daughter, Brother, friend, Father, Mother, Lord, Abba, Amma, Hashem, Jehovah, healer, Prophet, man. Or one of My personal favorites, which makes Me chuckle every time: Physician. So many names and labels. It is a different name and label to each of you depending on your perception. What I was or am does not matter.

I am your Yeshua; I am your God. Whatever you label me as, label yourself as such too. For all that I am is all that you are. And all that you are is all that I am.

Thus, if you wish to know Me, know Me as the Balancer, Restorer, and Redeemer of your Balance of Peace. Balance is the gateway to Peace, Joy, and Realization. Without Balance, none of those things can be felt or known in greater conscious depth.

I restored and restore Balance to your mind, heart, soul, spirit, body, and consciousness. I restore and restored the Balance of Divine Law when humans take the law into their own hands. I restore and restored Balance to the Kingdom, including your ecosystem and dreaming. That was and is My Miracle and Truth. Far more than casting out "demons" and walking on water. Those were really just extras. Anything superhuman I was able to do came as a by-product of My Divine Presence as God. Anything superhuman you are able to do comes as a by-product of awakening to your own Divine Presence in God. Thus, if you wish to find Me, know Me, seek not for more knowledge or service but for Balance. And the rest will work itself out from there.

Birth is a Miracle. As is death. Both are a mercy and kindness that you can never understand without allowing for the Presence of Peace within.

In the process of losing a Beloved, there is an incredible mercy and kindness that streams from you as you serve your Beloved's needs. Just when your Beloved is unstitching from life, your spirits stitch deeper together with incredible Grace and golden threads that transcend any physical separation. That, Beloved, is Love. When you can allow for your Beloved to receive his or her needs before looking to your own wants in such endings and beginnings, you will find your needs are Miraculously served, as well, in the end.

Of course, in your heart, you hope that that be-ing, that Beloved, will live . . . or will not suffer in the end. If there is anything to hope for, hope, even when you do not understand, that your Beloved understands, accepts, and realizes the power of his or her Presence and Light. Holding the Light of such hope for your Beloved is a service that moves beyond hope and into the Power of Prayer. We serve those hopes and Prayers, for We co-create them with you. Hope for their Freedom, for their Freedom is yours too. Pray for their Peace, for their Peace is yours too.

It is important to have hope, but it is essential to have Faith, and absolutely dire for you, no matter the circumstance, to remember the Simplicity of Love in moments of loss. Again, Simplicity is not scarcity. The Simplicity of Love is actually Love in far deeper purity and abundance. The deeper the Love you have felt for another, the deeper the Void will be when that person is no longer in body in physical reality. The deeper the Void of grief you experience, the deeper the Love and communion with the Divine you will know.

When there is a loss, there is a heavy processing on your inner "hard drive"—memories flash to the surface. The hole in your heart, in your web, in your spirit where the Presence of your Beloved once was in his or her form identity, can be tremendous. The mind and body race to reintegrate, to search for meaning, and continuously ask: Why? How? What could I have done better? What did I do wrong? Where are they going? Will I see them again? Why? WHY?!

It can create great complexity when you forget to allow for humility and Simplicity in such moments. Loss is a process of mourning—but within all mourning stars there is a Resurrection that emerges through that polarity. A Beloved's death is the descent or death in the Realization phase of his or her Resurrection. And your descent or death in the Awakening/Suspension phase of your Resurrection as long as you are in form. You are Resurrectors WITH one another every step of the journey. THAT is the truest expression of soul mate. As you continue to allow for the process, your memories move from just memories to integrated aspects of all of your be-ing. As you grieve the loss of your Beloved in "form/chaff," you come to know the person in a new way in Presence, his or her Presence in Spirit and your Presence of Spirit, no matter how long it takes for you to come to this profound revelation of comfort and Peace.

A loss often brings a Light to the Void in the Divine chamber of your heart. And opens this chamber through seemingly breaking it. This opening is what restores your ability to feel your Beloved's Presence. He or she may not be in chaff/form any longer but is certainly in Wheat/Presence, even more deeply connected and present for you than ever before. If and when the Divine chamber of your heart opens, this can be deeply felt in Miraculous ways.

You never "lose" anything or anyone. As a soul separates from chaff and returns to the Garden, it becomes One with Me. The Void is the realm of infinite possibilities—it is the space of Spirit. Thus, all memories are there—nothing is ever lost. Nor can you ever be lost either. Nor can any of your Beloveds.

However, there are certain be-ings to whom your soul and spirit has stitched, woven, and braided in deeply intimate ways—and they to you. Be it a family member, a friend, an animal, a romantic partner—when you have spent years together, shared in Love and grief, grown through the womb of life together, and helped one another to evolve, the braids and strings run deep, to the deepest chambers of your being. Your identities are interwoven, as are your spirits.

When such a relationship ends, be it in death or choosing to part ways, it is an ending to a chapter of both of your stories. If one or both of you choose to leave, but especially if the other person is the one to initiate the ending, the hole left in the absence of that person's Presence, wheat and chaff, can be so traumatic that it feels as though the whole of your life has been knocked down. That one loss can cause you to suddenly reevaluate everything in all of the other aspects of your web and life.

Your heart, your spirit, your whole life can suddenly feel like a gaping hole has been torn in it. It is amazing to Me how you all call it "heartbreak." It may feel that way, but really, in the unstitching from the person, animal, job, friendship, or even in cases such as an addiction to an inanimate thing that you developed a comfort-based relationship with such as alcohol, old stitches and braids burst and your heart is left more whole and open than ever.

In these moments, especially in the case of the death of a Beloved, there are several things that are important to bring into your awareness:

1. Your heart is not broken, it is open.
2. Your soul in co-creation with the other person did not bring this to harm you, but to fulfill a contract essential to your evolution, process of Resurrection, and Pathway to Peace. It did not just happen to you. You happened to it as well.
3. You are Whole even when there is a hole. You can be in a Void, a hole, and yet still be Whole within it. You do not need another to make you whole because you already are.
4. Within the hole, the Void, not only are you Whole, but also Holy. For you have never been closer to Love than in such moments. Even if it is experienced in the form of grief.

Your holy soul and holy spirit will hold and bring all that you need, alongside THE Holy Spirit and My Grace. All that you need to do is allow, breathe, and take whatever time you need to process and give over.

5. There are no endings that are finite. Nor are there ever beginnings that are new. When you can let someone go, you become One with that person or soul, including your animals.

6. There is a death in every new beginning. And a new beginning in every death. Both grief and deep Love are present within both. Including the cycles of breath, life changes, birth, and death. There is equal grief and equal Love in an ending or new beginning. Your feelings will be slightly different in each. In the birth you may feel more joy, in the death more pain. However, they are One.

7. Remember that in a loss or birth, you are participating in an act of Divine Balance. As I am the Supreme Restorer of Balance, I am with you. And your conscious participation means you are embodying Divine Father Truth, Divine Mother Love, and Divine Yeshua Peace within self. You are participating in an act of God as and with God in co-creation. And though your mind might struggle, you are experiencing AND catalyzing a Miracle of Divine Balance, simply through your Presence in that loss or rebirth.

8. Take care of yourself. Ask for what you need. Take caution on reaching to pain cycles and emotional or behavioral actions that are the imbalanced mind's tactics to avoid processing the grief, such as guilt, shame, and appointment of blame. Or resentment, reaction, and regret. There is no one to blame—not the Beloved who left chaff, not others still in chaff, not God, and certainly not you. But if you need to blame, blame God before self or other. It won't be

the first time a human be-ing has done so. We can carry that. You cannot, nor can others around you also struggling with their own grief process or issues in life. Reach for Forgiveness and allowing. Reaching for ways to numb pain quickly lands you into deep pain cycles ensued by despair when blame or numbing doesn't work. And despair is an unnecessary burden to carry when a loss is a time of liberation. Reach for your Faith and, though it may take time, the Miracle of that liberation will become known. Sometimes just allowing for Faith and knowing of self and all as God can allow the Miracle of the liberation and celebration to be felt in an instant.

When you can let someone go, you become One with them.
When you can let someone go, you become One with them.

Breathing the above mantra in times of loss of a Beloved is essential. Be gentle with one another, Beloved One. For each of you has a delicate heart that is Sacred. This includes those within your ecosystem of support.

In a loss, any loss, please acknowledge the Beloved who left, even if there are moments you are angry or want to avoid any thought of the person. That Beloved helped you to know self more deeply, whether through shadow or through great Light. Whether it is a breakup, a death, or any such letting go, remember that there was once a Love, intimacy, Truth, and many, many stitches, many, many memories that have been shared, written forever in timeless ink upon your sacred heart. That stays with you always. Always. You are all etched into one another's wheat with words of Love. You are all one great Love poem.

In the experience of a death, Beloved One, when a person, an animal, or anything of deep worth leaves your life, you can almost feel as though a part of you died. That is actually true. A part of your story has died. Certain stitches of you were in this other person, that person in you, and now that person is no longer here in the same way. The person's energy field, his or her form Presence that you have come to know, nurture, trust, and feel, even during periods of dissonance, is no longer there in form.

It is very difficult almost to be able to breathe when someone or something so stitched into your heart leaves its body. Again, the thoughts race, the memories surge, the regrets surface, the guilt wells up, then come the emotions of gratitude, anger, separation, longing, joy, seemingly all at once. It can feel like chaos, and the mind cannot compute what has just happened in its limited technology.

I will tell you, Beloved One, that when there is stitching of Love, and a person moves out of the web of the world, he or she crosses through your heart. Your Beloved may unstitch from the chaff . . . but he or she moves deeper into your sacred heart and unites with you in Spirit—your wheat to the wheat of your Beloved. His or her wheat strengthens yours. The Beloved who has passed pierces your sacred heart with Loving Truth and Truthful Love. Rejoice in his or her Peace. And remember that your Beloved's passing into the Light is a Pathway to reclaim your own. Such is the way of the Light-holders, in and out of body.

Your Beloved is not gone. He or she simply moved from form, chaff, to wheat, Spirit. He or she moved from one of the three external chambers of the sacred heart—family, friendship, romantic, whichever the person was in—to the Divine chamber of your sacred heart. Your Beloved did not leave, he or she simply moved chambers, nothing more, nothing less. Your Beloved is still just as present in your heart as he or she always was. You will just need to get used to feeling and communing with your Beloved in a new and, frankly, even more intimate way.

This is why those with a deep connection to Faith and Spirit, those who have already opened the Divine chamber of their heart, have a far easier time coping with loss and grief. This is also why many people move into deeper awakening to the Divine through a death, be it through an illness, accident, near-death experience, or the loss of a Beloved. Again, an unstitching may pierce the heart but it does not break it—it opens it to Spirit and true reality. That is one of the greatest manifestations of the Void, the Light: its power to unite and bring wholeness from the polarities of birth and death.

You may perceive that the Beloved you lost is gone from the dreaming of your life, and you may always feel a pain, and a mourning, and even the perception of betrayal. Those are the moments that you need to go into the Void, as it is through the Void and realm of Spirit, the Womb, that your Beloved will find you, and you will feel him or her.

Learn to shut your eyes, and to move into that space of opening the Divine chamber of the heart, which is what floods Light into your vision and restores clarity to what is possible and real even in a time of loss. Again, you will simply need to get used to experiencing your Beloved's energy field, Presence through the Divine chamber, the unseen after experiencing him or her in the "seen" for so long.

This relationship with those who move you deeper into consciousness of THE Beloved is the most sacred Covenant that two souls can share.

It IS the Arc of the New Covenant, the Star of Bethlehem, the Eternal Flame, the Light of Love within the Night. It is the Love that transcends time, space, and certainly death, for death is only the death of wheat from chaff. The wheat cannot die. If you need proof of that, you can look to Me. If that is not enough for your mind to be satisfied with in this life, rest assured you will come to understand in death.

Let there be Light. Let there be night. And a Star appearing within the night. Let there be infinite possibilities from the space of the Womb for stars to be born. Let there be infinite possibilities from the space of the Womb for those stars to die. So that the cycle of Light may continue. The timeless cycle of Light.

Breathe for a moment. Breathe for a moment in the comfort of knowing that even when you perceive darkness, or are in physical darkness at night, you are in the Light. From that space of night, the Light is born. For those of you who are in the Void, reach for the Star, through your own mourning star. When the Light is restored, web braided anew, hold the energy of Light and compassion for those who have come to their own time of mourning.

Let there be Light.

Breathe in, inhale. Exhale. A life, a death, a life, a death. And always a space in between. The Eternal Space of the Beloved and all Beloveds in Spirit, including you.

Ashes to ashes, dust to dust. When the body returns to creation, including your own at some point, it becomes something new of something old. It is restored. When the soul returns to Creator, it becomes something new, yet very old and timeless. That is also a restoration. All was created in Balance in the beginning, thus all is restored in Balance in the end. Such is the service of the Lamb.

You are all the lambs of God. As I was your Lamb, your sacrificial Lamb. As well as your Shepherd. Not to herd you as sheep, but to watch over you in times of dark night. That was My purpose when I came to Body. Not to create the Era of Martyrdom, but to set you Free from that march of martyrdom, of carrying other people's pain, which strips them of the joy of the Right to their own experience. And strips you of the joy of your own.

Death comes to all. So too does Resurrection. We can take your crosses if you will let Us. I did that in taking up Mine to unburden you from your own. But We would never strip you of the Power of Love, the Truth of Love, felt within your grief. Within death is a kindness, and a Simplicity—look for the Simplicity. That IS the kindness. Beneath the surface it is there.

Do not try to escape your grief, your Love. Do not put it off. For death, grief, and rebirth come to you all and through you all. The more that you feel and allow for the Power of that Love, the more you will be set Free. My Vine always connects you to ones you have "lost." And when you transition, your Beloveds staying behind are always connected to you through the Braid of My DiVine.

The relationships stitched in Love last, evolve, and Resurrect. For something to Resurrect it must be of Love, else it does not endure. Love not only endures but also ensures. That is the Truth, Beloved One.

Death is a kindness. It is a Freedom. But no matter how many times you read these Words, moments still come in loss in which you cry, reaching out to the Void or to your Beloved, "Where are they? Where are you? Wake up! Wake up! Where are you? Come back, come back, oh please come back."

And your heart seems to shatter. You feel in moments that all hope is gone. Again, you oftentimes feel the despair and confusion I spoke of: "Where do we go? What do I do?" But as I say, and your soul says every time in response, "Reach for your Faith. The hope of Peace. They are at Peace. They hope for yours as We do. They whom you have lost you have found. They will always find you and you them. You can find them always in the moments you find Me, your Peace."

Reach for celebration within the grief. You have found them, not lost them in their death. You have found yourself, as well. In "losing" them, they find ME. Why not journey together with them, One in death, One in life, to find Me, Peace, together.

Grief is not darkness. Refusing your grief IS darkness—for it keeps you in the Void, in the dark.

Grief is the deepest Light, as is laughter, gratitude, and remembering joy when you grieve. For, within those moments, you repent and atone all of the complex moments, all of the struggles, all of the dashed hopes, all of the things that you wish you could have done, or done better—forgetting that you did all that you possibly could given where you were in your soul's evolution. These woes and regrets all dissolve with Grace through the processing of grief otherwise known as Love.

In the moment of death or loss, there is a Love, the deepest expression of Love in its wholeness, which is why it feels like you are breaking.

The Love that is there is the Love for Oneness so strong that you are willing to let go of a Beloved to become One with that person, animal, or life. Just as those who understood My service Loved Me so much that they were willing to let Me go to become One with Me. You are of the Lamb when your Love runs so deep that you are willing to incur and experience pain so that another can be Free. That is Love. That is Power. There is great Power, the Power of Love, in letting go. That is the Love and compassion that moves mountains. That is communion and receiving of the Host. That IS the Miracle.

Love is not holding on. It is letting go. Loving is "losing" so that you may find. The loss is the gain of knowing and experiencing Love at the deepest levels of intimacy. Love is worth it. It is the currency and current of the Divine.

Indeed, there were those within My Life that wished that they could keep Me here. Everyone had a different agenda for Me. Some wished to be special to Me, as though I would pick favorites. Some wished to indoctrinate Me to their will of Me and turned against Me when I would not bend to it. Some wished to keep Me here for themselves instead of allowing Me to fulfill Prophecy through My Death and Resurrection. Some wanted Me to slay their enemies so that they could rise in imbalanced power. Some wished for Me to send their enemies and abusers to "hell." To them I would reply, "How can I send to Gehanna those who already live in it as a result of their own greed and hate?" But to those in hate, I came to set them Free, as well. There is not heaven and hell, only a Balance and a reaping of what you sow.

Some hated Me because I Offered Grace and healing to those

that they deemed lesser. Some hated Me because I sat in the back of the temple. Some hated Me because I spoke the Truth and it threatened their power. Some hated Me simply because hate is often easier to choose than Love when the imbalances of the mind are strong. Some hated Me because I did not ride on golden chariots but instead on a donkey or by foot. Most hated Me because I Loved them through their hate, which I knew was only their fear of Love and loss.

Many did not understand why I would not utilize My Divinity for power and prestige. Many did not understand why I would not serve them, one person. I was here AS One Person, but not then and now did I come to serve one person. I was a Servant to all no matter their feeling toward Me. In serving all, I brought all to the One. And thus, to come to One you must be willing to allow for loss to restore the Balance of *the* One. You are not the only one, Beloved. When you serve the all, you serve the One. And that means finding the One in death, birth, and every moment in between.

There can be moments during loss, especially in a death, when there may be a hole torn in your heart or the web of your spirit that feels eternal. But know, Beloved One, there can never be a hole in your soul, for it is all that is whole. A hole in your web, your tapestry, cannot ever destroy the wholeness of your be-ing. The hole you feel in the "seen" when you lose a Beloved, meaning your transient form identity and theirs, is really no more than the Void, the Light that allows you to access your wholeness and your Beloveds in the unseen, timeless Eternal. You are not the holey-est of holies, you are the whole-eist of holies. Always.

Death is a Freedom. Why wait for death to live that Freedom? All that it takes to live in Freedom is Faith and Forgiveness. Not just those who you Forgive but also those who YOU need to receive Forgiveness from, including yourself. For-give-n really means: For I give in myself. For-give-n really means: For I give in God through the God fore-give-n to me. For-give-ness really means: For I give in my whole self. For-give really means: For I give in and of myself to give myself and others Freedom.

I say these Words for I gave My Life so that you could know Freedom, not only in life but in death. For I gave you your Eternal Life, your Eternal Freedom. I Fore-gave, meaning gave before, so that you could Fore-give or "give before" you even think to do so. The service of the "for" and "fore" is the giving of the Free.

We are not so different, you know, Beloved child, Beloved lamb. Stop pretending that just because you are grown, you are not a simple, vulnerable lamb who feels, who needs, who seeks, who gives, who tries, who cares. Life is Freedom; live Free in Faith, and Forgiveness. Death is the essence of Freedom from which Love is born anew. That is the cycle. The lamb grows and even when it becomes a ewe or a ram, a mother or father, a grandma or grandpa, even after death, it always remains a lamb. What pasture it lived in and what lambs got more than it had is not even a consideration when the lamb returns to its true Pasture.

In a death, a physical death, separation of wheat from chaff, there is a re-fusing, and fusing. In your death, your spirit and soul truly become One again. Fully unbraided from chaff and the dreaming of your current reality. You wake up fully and as such, are fully realized and known. You reunite with the Spirit and Soul of all that is, including those who you have lost, Loved, and hated. All within a Pasture of Peace. The most devoted of lambs are those who strive to Resurrect that Pasture of Peace within life instead of being put out to pasture by the pain of life.

Now, there is a saying that your life flashes before your eyes when you transition, in the moment that your eyes shut and you exhale for the final time. In many ways this is true. All your memories and experiences, including those of guilt and blame, as well as Love, gratitude, and joy, unite and all transforms to Light. You see self and others as you are and as they are, not what you thought you were or they were. All restores to Love and Balance—those moments that you did grieve, did feel that pain, or that hurt, or that anger—it all becomes clear and joyful.

Those who are beginning to move into the end of their lives, such as the elderly or those who are very ill, those who do not have as many attachments to the outer world anymore, are sometimes referred to in your world as "Poor in Spirit." They cannot do as much on the outer anymore. Not so much time left, according to your human perception of time. Many of them have already partially unstitched and unbraided from the Web of Life. They have already lost most who they have known.

You also call those who you judge as not worthy of God's Redemption "Poor of Spirit," which, per the parable of Jonah, is not for the human to judge. Those who are judged "Poor of Spirit" are often the richest of Spirit. There are no heroes and villains in the world, simply some more or less evolved. And do not assume YOU are one of the evolved. I say this with a smile, Beloved.

When you vilify a person or people and fancy yourself the hero, you are also the villain. When someone vilifies you and fancies himself or herself the hero, he or she is also the villain. Such was the service of the prophet Jonah. The sacred "Whale" was the Void of judgment that consumed him. Yet by facing and dissolving into the Void, he was Redeemed, alongside the Ninevites. You all are in the belly of the Whale in this life. That is the choice in coming to body. And the belly of the Whale can either be discomfort or great, great strength and revelation depending on the lens of your perception.

For those you deem "Poor of Spirit" due to age or health, note that they created a life, lived that life, and, later in life, give over. They are not Poor of Spirit. They are MORE of Spirit. For more of their Beloveds have moved into the Divine chamber of their Sacred Heart. Or more of themselves has. They may have fewer attachments to the external world, but they are rich in experience.

The Lighter a person's vibration is or becomes, which is usually strongest in youth and in older years, the more Simplicity, humility, and purity is expressed through his or her essence. A child is Light, is simple, present, Balanced. A newborn lamb wishes for so much nourishment and abundance of experience to seek understanding. Less so knowledge. As a child grows and takes on density, suddenly the thirst for knowledge and identity emerges. But the newborn lamb is curious, endlessly curious to understand the world and self within it. Every day is an exploration of Presence and the new.

Elders, even if not so many years in age, have had that nourishment and abundance of experience that leaves them rich in knowledge. But, as they age, the need for knowledge in an elder begins to fade back into the childlike state of Presence that accompanies wisdom. The density the child within the person took on that made him or her an adult fades again. The lamb becomes the elder. The elder then becomes the lamb again.

In the case of an elder, most elders, true elders, including elderly souls in young bodies, understand that the more strings they have attached to the outer, the more the energetic drain. Elders do not have the energy for so much anymore. Many prefer their quiet and focus on what needs to come each day to survive and to live in the Peace, even bliss, of be-ing.

Those leaving bodies are not Poor of Spirit. They are Full of Spirit and ready to come home.

Poor of Spirit are the blind consumed with pride, greed, and pursuit of personal gain to fit into the world instead of fitting into self and the natural order of the Universe. Pride and greed are a mismatched suit hidden behind a designer label. The suit says "Designer Label" so others accept it despite the fact that the suit does not fit well, nor is it well-made.

"Poor of Spirit" is the discount label on the collar of the suit of armor you wear when you are pretending to be what you are not. By discounting yourself, you become a discount item, constantly comparing yourself to the other suits around you in judgment. This includes manipulating and "enhancing" your image or body to project a false self. In essence, that is lying, with intent to deceive. There is far more shame and stress inherent to wearing such false suits than there will ever be in the Freedom of walking naked in your true essence.

Poor of Spirit is also a lack of connection and communion to the Web of Life. That is a withholding of your Presence and echo of Grace from the ecosystem and world around you. It leads to sickness, disconnect, isolation, and paranoia that is about fearing the risk that vulnerability and exposure brings. Yet it is in accepting the risk of Love that makes Love worth it even if there is loss. Richness of Spirit comes through richness of connection. All lambs need their flock.

The more you enrich your spirit, participate in life with curiosity and wonder of what you may gain as opposed to the fear of what you may lose, and the more you choose humility over the need to be right, the more Full of Spirit you are. When you connect to the Divine chamber of your heart and your Beloveds in Spirit within it, you are Full of the Holy Spirit and thus can feel the Presence of those you have "lost" as One with you.

You can be poor and yet Full of Spirit. And you can be rich as a king and yet Poor of Spirit. Or poor and Poor of Spirit. Or rich and Rich of Spirit. Which of those applies to you rests between you and Me. It is not your role to judge which another is. Only for you to explore within self.

The next years of your life are about your soul, your spirit, your communion with life, and your communion with death. Death is an energy you will all need to accept, see, and come to Peace with in these times on your Earth. The more beautiful and rich the Love you share with another is, in the moment you lose/gain that person, the more you are able to process the moments of grief. If you are present and in Presence, wheat-identity, you will feel the communion and Freedom it brings. If you are in imbalanced mind, chaff-identity, you will feel only despair, resentment, and confusion.

What master will you serve? The mind that wishes to keep you in the "doing" so that one day you may get to be? That master will make sure that day never comes. That is why it is such a struggle for many to retire. They spend their whole life waiting for that day that they get to be. Once that day comes, they realize they have forgotten how. And they dangle on the widow's peak, waiting for a self that does not come.

What master will you choose? The mind, the voice of the outer world that seems to think it knows what will bring you full-fill-ment despite the fact it can never be satiated and fulfilled? Or the master of your soul, the master of be-ing, the humble master of the Truth within you? Only you can know what is right for you, and what feels like Freedom and God to you. But what will be your master? Living life? Or living dead?

Choosing your master or what aspect of self will be dominant is not enough. The next question you will need to ask, which is harder, is: Do I TRUST this master? If not, you will always have doubt.

Complexity, the serpent who led you into and out of the Garden, into mortality, was very important in giving you choice. However, it also causes you to explore simple things such as loss with complexity instead of with Simplicity. If you are in the present, it is easy to make the right choices that create fewer burdens. But you have created more complexity as a world, which is why there is more want, more confusion, less Peace, more suppressed grief.

Latent grief takes longer to release, especially when your adrenal systems have been worn and frayed by numbing and negating your emotional needs. You have become addicts of polarity and can never be satisfied until you let go and grieve all of the stress and expectations. It may be a depression you need to calm and rejuvenate. A hibernation. To restore your Balance and service through joy.

The more that you plug it up and never want to feel any of the discomfort, the more difficult it is to handle losses or discomfort. And the sicker you, the collective, and your ecosystem becomes.

Simplicity brings wisdom. Wisdom emerges from Simplicity. You may have heard the term "a simple wisdom." All wisdom is profound because it is simple. Wisdom and Simplicity are sound friends with a common purpose of making everything clearer in your life. If you will allow for them, they co-creatively unite in helping you to give over all of the complex thoughts and attachments. They are also masterful in helping to unburden you from polarized people and behaviors you may not have ever questioned before. The wisdom of Simplicity and Simplicity of wisdom especially help you when experiencing a death or loss.

The agony of the despair, rage, and helplessness of rejecting grief in a loss leads to such complex questions and thought prisons: "Who is to blame for this?" Or, "I could have done better by them." Or, "I should have apologized or called sooner." Or, "Maybe if the doctor had done this it would have been different." Or, "If only I had done this or they had done that, they would have lived, it would have been differ-ent." Or, "I should have made sure that they didn't go driving that day." Or, "I am broken now." It is incapacitating.

Humility and Simplicity are what move you through the process of grief, and into the process of change, gratitude, and acceptance with more joy and ease. The wages of the imbalances of the mind prolong the death, not only your Beloved's but also your own. It is like being connected to a vine that is rotting. The wages of the imbalances of ego create death to your soul, spirit, and all that is around you. That is the dead tree I spoke of. The debris to burn so that you may reconnect to the Tree of Life.

There is no Peace upon and within imbalance—when Peace is the VERY energy so deeply needed within the world. The lack of Peace within self, multiplied by millions or billions of people, well, this is how wars break out. Your Beloveds in Spirit Pray and hold the Light foremost for your Peace. For that is the space in which they dwell. If you wish to see them, you must stop fighting your grief, and shoving your grief into boxes of convenience. And look to the Peaceful Stillness of your soul, which has the power to restore Peaceful Stillness to your heart and mind should you choose to let it.

Stop fighting your grief. Be at Peace. It is there within you, Beloved. It is there. For I AM there. If Peace is real, then so AM I. If I AM real, then so is Peace. You may never have known Me before now, but you do know Peace. Thus, when you choose Peace you choose God, no matter how long it takes to get you to that simple wisdom.

Peace is what the world and God need for you to anchor, more than anything. That is how this war of self versus world is won. By falling in Love with the world instead of fearing it, which begins with connecting to the world beyond your own mind—the world of Spirit. That journey really first begins with letting go and understanding Grief, Love, Life, Loss, and the Lamb.

For comfort, know this, Beloved One:

When, from the realm of infinite possibilities, your soul chooses and braids to a Beloved, it also means the Beloved chose and braided to you too. You did not just pick the person from the realm of infinite possibilities, your Beloved picked you too. You chose each other, so even in moments you do not like each other, or are losing each other, be grateful. You chose your Beloved and he or she chose you. In longing to experience what it is to be One and with another. In life and in death. Once you are braided to a Beloved, when the braid is of Love, Truth, and Peace, even if such things were not always felt in your relationship in life, the braid is eternal. An Eternal Life-line that transcends just your mortal life.

You chose your parents. They did not just choose to have a child— you chose them from the realm of Spirit. If you are a parent that has lost a child, know that your child chose you as its parent for a "moment" that stretches forever. They were never yours to own but to hold. In Spirit they hold you right back even if, in their passing, you feel you can barely hold yourself together. Even when you cannot hold them in form, they can hold you in Spirit. And someday, you will hold them again in a new way. Until then, I will Hold them so that they can hold you. It is a Divine holding pattern of Grace.

Nothing is ever finite. However, a loss can feel finite to your perception. In some ways it is, Beloved. But finite does not mean gone. Allow the beginning to come in the end. Remember the beginning times with them through all moments of death and life you shared together.

In the beginning of your soul, you are a child. Though you may understand death, all you live for is the present moment. As a child, there is not a hope in tomorrow—there is a hope in joy and play for today. A hope for a mother to come, for a father to come, for food and comfort to come as needed. There is a hope in the exploration of the moment. As a newborn lamb, you knew that you were of Light. This wisdom was built-in, no matter how beautiful or traumatic your childhood.

If what you knew in the beginning, in your birth from the Void, was a knowing of self as Light, as joy, then it should stand to reason that any be-ing, including you, that passes back through the Void in death is restored to its knowing and experience of self as Light. This is the Prophecy that I fulfilled and am asking you to realize. When people die, what they leave behind in soul force is Seeds. It takes time for them to grow, but they grow. That is the process of Revelation.

With every loss, a billion Seeds of Light are planted within you.

With every loss, a billion Seeds of Light are planted within you.

Through My death, in My undivided, unaltering, unwavering Love, Truth, and Peace, a trillion Seeds were planted

throughout the Earth and all people. But it is only through Love that these Seeds activate to grow within you. When you choose Love, you realize your flower in the Garden. In imbalanced ego you do not know that you are a flower. You are more a flower wilting on a grave. Be the Seed, the living flower in the Garden. The flower that grows from graveyard dust to become life anew. That is the Truth of Love: from Creation, Destruction; from Destruction, Creation. The fixed space of both and neither IS the present.

In the beginning of time, in Creation, a Void died, which Seeded the universe with Light. The deeper expression of that was realized through My life, Death, and Resurrection. You are the vessels to realize this Prophecy, to grow this Seed, to weave this thread through your own Yeshua self—that is My Love-making to you, My tantra. My Yoga, the Tantra of Simplicity, was and is the Offering of My Bread, My Wine, My Love to you as God, of God.

Choose the Seed of your Beloved, as I AM the Beloved that makes all that is Beloved possible for you to experience in life, death, and beyond. For those with Beloveds already transitioned or transitioning in times to come, I AM them too. You are theirs, and they are Mine. I am yours and you are Mine. Thus all is united in the end. Such is the course in Miracles of Resurrection.

Choose Spirit, choose the Light—that is the Resurrected mourning star. From out of the Void a Beloved emerges, a Love is chosen, there is a Light that enters your life. When the Beloved leaves there is grief but also, if you reach for it, relief and comfort found. For remember that, of the billions your soul could have chosen from, you chose that person and he or she chose you. Once chosen, you are chosen forever.

Cherish that communion, that connection, that comes from the space between life, between death, the space between in which Spirit resides. You can only access it through the Light that the soul shines up through the heart—the Gateway of the Sacred Heart of Simplicity,

Stability, Surrender, and Stillness. The simple structure of the Heart of Peace. Live there, and we will live together through your breath, as we did in the beginning, every breath in between, and the end. Then you breathe with the universe.

I am here to wipe every tear from your eyes. In your choice to come to body, in your birth, you chose to have tears, even at the first breath of your life into the world. In death, I take yours away. No mourning, no more pain. When you grieve another, you know Our Grief when you step away from Us. When you reunite with Us through reconnecting to Love, Truth, and Peace, We Rejoice, as do your Beloveds who have transitioned to Spirit. But moving forward, perhaps it will not require loss to bring you to the understanding of these Words. And as such, so it is. So it is. So it is. Let them go. Let yourself go. Let it be. Let there be Light. Amein.

YESHUA MEDITATION

Close your eyes. Take a moment to breathe. Invite into the pureness of this moment your Beloveds. Do not simply hope that they are there— call them to you. They are here. Breathe into your body and feel the threads and braids within the ark of your be-ing extend deeply into the Void, the realm of Spirit.

Breathe, focus, and feel where these braids and stitches of Love connect you to that Light within the Void, the space of your Beloveds. Breathe into the one body you share with them, the body of the Divine—Consciousness. They are breathing with you now; breathe with them. Breathe with Me. Weave through your breath: Faith. Forgiveness. Freedom.

Feel their Presence, their Peace, through your own. They may no longer be in body, and that you may need to accept. They are Free. They are lambs of the Lamb. As are you. Grant yourself the gift of compassion for a moment. In a world of lambs in wolves' clothing, remember that you are a lamb. Naked. Simple. Wise. Allow yourself to be held in this moment.

Rest in Peace in life everlasting. The Eye of God is the Light, the lantern of the body. See with your real eyes, and allow your body, your bread, your chaff, and the water of your Love, and your tears, and your grief, to be flooded with Light. Breathe into the Simplicity of this movement. Weave it through you. Breathe.

Exhale. Forgiveness comes in the final exhale. Thereafter you breathe Free. Your Beloveds do not care about your Emperor's new clothes, your armor, your money, your power, your sexuality. Such things never mattered. What mattered was the Truth of Love that made your journey together real. That is all that matters.

Within the exhale is the Freedom that I Offer—the simple time-lessness of life. Breathe into this space. The candle cannot die. The rock cannot be broken. There is a fragility to you all and yet a deep, vast strength of support you have within self and one another. Within this moment, let all that needs to die, die.

And again, infuse and weave compassion and empathy through the whole of your be-ing. Extend this to your Beloveds. And now, allow yourself be held, Beloved lamb. Rest, sway, breathe, as I Hold you. Breathe. We know your Love, We know your heart. No more need to struggle, or suffer. Let us all hold each other. Breathe. Let yourself Be-Loved. This is not a bough that can break—We do not let you fall.

Nothing ever lost. Nothing ever gained. You are the babe at Peace in your manger. Lamb at Peace in the Pasture. There are no discarded and sacrificed lambs in My Garden. Let the stars fall upon you, and shine within you. Death may come, birth may come, in big ways and lit-tle ways. You will never understand Love. You will never understand Yeshua, or Gaia, or humankind, until you can remember the Simplic-ity of your spirit, your chaff, your heart, your wheat, your thoughts, and the Truth of your essence, Love. Be at Peace. Your Beloveds and The Beloved breathes with you in this breath.

Ashes to ashes. Dust to dust. Walk not through the valley of the shadow of death, Walk with Me to the space in which there is no death. Walk with Me. Walk with Me. Breathe. For I AM with you, Rod and Staff. Walk with Me as and with the Shepherd. Looking over the lambs with Grace.

Beloved, I Hold you, and Hold you, and Hold you, alongside your Beloveds. And so it is.

Draw deep breaths, and place one hand on your heart, and another hand on your womb or hara. Exhale.

Place your hands together in Prayer, and simply say, "I Love." Fall to your knees and place your forehead on the floor. Or just your hand. Take several breaths and moments to thank your Mother Earth. Let go of the meditation.

When you are ready, sit up and take the Freedom Transmissions Personal Process paper, still folded. Do not open it still. Place your hand upon it. Through your hand, infuse your Light by weaving the energy of Faith, Forgiveness, and Freedom onto this page. Infuse the power of the Truth of Love onto this paper. Allow your Beloveds in Spirit to bless it through the Grace of your hand. Within the power vested in the Light of this moment, I Bless thee in the name of the Divine Father, Divine Mother, and Divine Child . . . who carries your name with Mine, Yeshua, beside it more and more as we walk together. Peace be with and within you. Sancti. Pace. Amein.

2

Resurrection

Beloved One, some final Words of the Word:

Within the garden of the world, there are certain Beloveds who are very pure of Light that you often disregard or take for granted. You often overlook the impact of the energy they absorb and space they hold for you. What I describe to you now is the movement of your chaff into the Earth and also the consciousness held within that chaff as it moves into the Earth. Separation of wheat from chaff does not mean that when you pass, no aspect of your consciousness and imprint is left behind. A strong imprint is left and the impact of that imprint or seed matters, not only to you but to all your Beloveds who stay "behind," as well as others who live in your world after you have moved on.

You carry a life force. When you unstitch, unbraid, soul from body, an aspect of your life force stays behind. I was not immune from this. I passed My Life force into the Earth, Gaia, My "Disciples," and My Vessels, specifically several of the women in My Life. Though I did not have children, I passed My Shakti on to the Vessels, many of whom were women, including My Mother and the Magdalene, who could and would carry the lineage of the Light to others. In My Death and Resurrection, infinite Seeds were planted that have been harvesting for centuries and are now beginning to break ground. No, I did not have children technically. However, I Fathered billions of children, including YOU in the energetic sense. The Seeds I planted in My Life and as well as long before and after, were of a different and more powerful essence.

My Bread/Body and Blood/Water/Wine meant more than what was and has been assumed. As did Buddha's in His/Her passing. And other Avatars who have come to this Earth as Masters. As well as those countless nameless, faceless Beloveds who have achieved the purest form of Mastery that necessitates their Transcendence from form.

When you pass, you pass your life force on. Be it in the ashes and dust. Be it in the Love and the souls yours has stitched to. The seeds of your life force, carried through the strings of your spirit, are planted in the energy of the Earth, the dreaming, at the moment you pass . . . and carry forth long after. This does not just mean the seed of your lineage or potential future generations. It includes your energetic imprint, which affects the generations of all be-ings, human and non, who come "after," including you! If you die in hatred and despair, so too are the seeds you plant. If you die in Grace and honesty, even if you die in a sudden way, such are the seeds you leave behind. As you become One with the Tree of Life in your death, you leave a legacy of seeds behind—it is up to you what legacy of Love or hate you wish to offer or leave behind in the world.

Those in your world who have remained more deeply connected to the Earth understand and honor this wisdom, legacy, and responsibility the most. This includes many of the indigenous people, as well as the "innocents," the creatures of Gaia that uphold and maintain the Balance of the ecosystem.

Plants and trees carry a consciousness that honors and adheres to the rhythms and cycles of life. Without them there could be no cycle of your breath or life at all. They are your life-sustainers and crucial to your ability to survive. You are not dominant to them, as some of you believe yourselves to be. They are of a highly evolved consciousness that is not beneath yours; in fact, they are equal, if not superior in many ways.

Reincarnation is simply another word for reentry into the cycle and process of Resurrection I spoke of. Reincarnation is simply a reintegration of wheat into chaff, once again. There is much clatter about "past lives" in your world, some of it mildly useful, most of it not. As you evolve, your mind might tell you that you will evolve into a powerful prophet or person of influence. However, Avatars and those evolving into deeper consciousness are far more likely to Resurrect as a tree. Plants can evolve into bacteria. The energetic field of a bacterium can evolve into that of an insect, then an animal. Your human ability to retain knowledge may be greater than an insect's; however, an insect's consciousness and Presence within creation is as fluid as if not more fluid than your own.

After all, insects, no matter how much you wish to reject them or consider them a "lesser form of life," at least are what they are. And do not pretend to be something they are not. It is true that you continue to evolve in consciousness, but be careful in assuming that means you climb farther up the totem pole of importance to the human social hierarchies. In fact, as you evolve, it is often humans that can become animals, then insects, then plants. Thus, be careful to be gentle with your world. To care for all life. You were given a unique sentience to caretake. Not to dominate.

For it may just be the case that when you move into the next cycle of Resurrection, your wheat chooses a chaff that is quite different from any other it has chosen before. The Divine likes to shake things up a bit in Creation, as does your soul. Your soul desires all experiences and We desire you to have all experiences. How else can you experience the totality of the Oneness inherent to the united body of Creation?

If you have been the dominant, you may next experience what it is to be the suppressed. That does not just mean an animal abuser will "reincarnate" as an animal rescuer to experience the opposite polarity.

It means an animal abuser may Resurrect as an abused animal. Not as punishment, but by the soul's choice, for it is unnatural for your soul to carry that density and it must unstitch and mend such love-nots. Therein is the evolution into equality, compassion, soul-fullness, and Balance. You reap what you sow, which is, again, why the imprint you leave behind, the seeds you plant in life and in death, matter. To you and to the whole of your collective.

You cannot devolve in your conscious evolution. Even the Divine is a progressive evolution of Consciousness. You, as a conscious be-ing, are a co-creator with the Divine in the tending of this Field of the Dreaming. As you evolve, so too does God. As God evolves, so too do you. And you are still very primitive in your experience of it. The higher your vibration, the more you contribute to the evolution of consciousness within self and collective. The lower your vibration, the more you contribute to and are at the mercy of the collective unconscious.

While you cannot devolve in consciousness from life to life in this reality structure or others, you can change the form you come in. As can the Beloveds you have Loved and lost and found through that loss. As can Angels. Angels are too Light to come into form for very long. And, if they do, because they are designed to always be in alignment with God's Will, they often can only come in the form of animals, as well as occasionally children or people with special needs who do not live for very many years. For, when a child begins to take on density and identity and personal choice, the Angel—the Supreme Light-holder—cannot stay in form. And must return to the space of Spirit.

While plants and animals serve you deep sustenance and nourishment in your life, energetically, emotionally, and physically, you serve them, as well. You are in co-creative service with these be-ings, who are One with Us as you are. WE are an ecosystem above and below. You take from it, you give to it. Thus, be discerning in what you take, for it must be in Balance with what you give.

Trees, plants, and animals are not there for your pleasure. Respect life and death, as it is fragile. Respect the life forms who at least know what they are no matter how lowly or lofty you perceive them to be. Animal abuse, childhood abuse, elder abuse, environmental abuse—abusing the purest of the world renders the abuser the most imbalanced and impure.

Like your Angels Pray for you to reach for their Light in shadow, your Beloveds not of the human life form, especially your four-leggeds, hope so deeply for your Love and give it to you in return. Do not bring them into the weaving of your life if you cannot honor their needs. For, by discarding and neglecting them, you may just discover in time that you have neglected and discarded an Angel.

Many of your elders, all of their hopes and dreams have come and gone, fulfilled or not, and the only hope they have most days is for relief from pain, a brief phone call, or even just the blessing of one more breath. Your elders, your children, your animals, are the greatest Light-holders. When you abuse a plant that may at a point become a human, or you abuse an animal that was once a Sacred relation, you are affecting that life and its consciousness, as well as your own. As the trauma and devaluation of your life at points was very painful to you, be mindful of those you cause the same to unconsciously just because you live in a world that cherishes life, but mainly only the human.

Beloved One, this does not mean a crazy rampage to give up all eating of carrots, apples, and eggs. The bounty of God is there for all. It is a gift, not an entitlement. And you are the caretakers. What I am bringing to Light here is to be mindful of the worth of all. When you take a rock, leave a flower. Or even a Prayer of thanks. Saying of Grace needn't only occur as a passing gesture before a meal. The Grace of reciprocity is simple, humble, and powerful service.

The expression of gratitude for all life is service to God, Garden, and self. You are not an "I," you are an I AM—united with the whole of the collective. Thus, when you devalue another person or creature in the collective, you create an equal burden for yourself. You affect your world as your world affects you. **Grace is the echo of your Spirit on the Web of Life, as well as the echo that returns to you.** Let your echo be a song of Love sounding in rhythm to the Love song of the life that surrounds you.

You are designed with higher consciousness to caretake this planet, including orchestrating Balance with the humbler creatures. It is an interesting paradox that you are the species with the greatest potential for creating imbalance as a by-product of your ego and Free will—yet you were also the species chosen and entrusted to hold the Light and maintain the Balance. Your Yeshua self knows how to do so in whatever way is right for you. When you struggle with knowing how to uphold this Balance, hold My Hand, the Hand of Peace, and I will Light the Way.

Of All within the web and weaving of the dreaming world, the Earth that you call home, animals are your greatest Light-holders, which is why Angels Love to embody them so often. They are THE Lambs who sit with you in the manger. It is only you who have labeled them beasts. However, it is very often human be-ings in their arrogance and abdication of responsibility for their burdens, gluttony, and waste that act as savages. You are animals, as well. When in the primal self, you act in primal impulse under the auspices of civility.

Do not feed hate, or eat foods that were created in hate, or of pain and strife. Those who act as beasts will be treated as such, for their mind is imprisoned by the perception of a bestial world. The richest palace to the eyes can be a bestial palace energetically. The humblest slum can be a palace of Angels energetically.

You have all known what it is to be the abused animal, yet you all abuse, as well . . . be it self or other. All the beliefs and opinions, and judgment—why? For what? Do not carry the mark of hate toward anyone, or anything. Transform it into passion and Love. Or ask Me, or whatever be-ing in Spirit feels of Light to you, including your Beloveds in Spirit, to help you to transcend your external eyes of want, to see through the eyes and lenses of the compassionate heart.

That is the meaning of an eye for an eye. Not taking an eye, for another whose eye was taken. "I for an I" means replacing the illusion "I," the separate self that asks, "Who is to blame for this?" and then appropriates ignorant punishments in its blindness. And replacing it with the I AM that is One with the We, the All, the AM. Replacing the separate self "I," the wanting "I," with the "I" of the soul, One with All, is what allows you to see what is real. Those who make an eye for an eye about appropriation of blame and punishment are blind in their vengeance and distorted, narrow lens of justice.

Like Peace, Justice does not need a modifier or modification—it is not of the human to decide. Justice Just Is. The fighting of what is IS what strips you of justice. And thereby upholding Balance. That does not mean you cannot be deeply passionate about causes and areas you feel things could be done better in the world. However, if your passion does not flow from a place of compassion, patience, acceptance, and humility, it will never create deeper Peace, Balance, and change in the world in a sustainable, long-term way. The moment you find yourself moving from compassionate, co-creative passion to feeling anger, hatred, and a desire to attack another person or people, is the moment you need to pause, quiet your heart, and reach for Me to restore your Balance and Peace. For when this happens, the "other" is not the problem, you are. **Not every last person who does not agree with you is the enemy. If you make it so, it is YOU who are becoming the very thing you are fighting against.**

Beware signposts for justice with modifiers in your world, as many do not stem from Balance, including social justice, which can often be replaced with mob justice. Social media, which can often be replaced with mob media. Enough.

Are you the mob? The crucifier and crusader fighting for nothing other than the fleeting bar-room brawl occurring at any given point in your world? Or are you standing as Yeshua, as Nehemiah, as Esther? Justice is a stand-alone. Entrusted to God Alone, which is understood and known by the humble soul. Anyone within the world who says they know the way to justice as they pick up a pitchfork, including the modern pitchfork of typed words and doctored videos, is tangled in love-nots. Be discerning, or you can find yourself entangled in a large collective love-not presenting under the auspices of justice. That can leave you even more tangled up and confused. Justice comes through Peace. And Peace just is. Be-ing in-just-is IS the path to justice. Be-ing in un-just-is is the path to injustice, imbalance.

Whatever imbalance, injustice, is not rectified in your life, will be through the Loving resolution and rectification of Balance the Divine restores to all in the end. Those who take the law into their own hands will be subjected to the very laws of the imbalance they create. **Remember, Beloved, all is already resolved. You will come to know that in time as you are fully known.** All is already resolved. Have the patience and humility to trust that it is. It just is.

Stop fighting, Beloved. Let go. Make this an inner path and the "just-is" will set you Free to embody your deepest passion of Peace. THAT is the service through Love that changes the world.

The Soul "I," the clear eye, is the true eye of the needle that allows your spirit to stitch and weave with more clarity, patience, and joy upon the Web of Life. The self-absorbed, envious "I, I, I" is the needle you poke into your eye that blinds you from what is real. It Loves to tear down and, in so doing, tears deeper holes into its own tapestry and that of those around it.

Those who judge are blind in their sight, and lack reverence for the equality of worth in all people. They are blind. They have even forgotten what it is to feel. They are numb. Never allow the "blind"—those who make things complex or confusing for you—to lead you; recognize them for what they are. Have compassion for them, Pray for them, and hold the Light for them so that one day they can see. But do not follow them in your own blindness. When people are blind, We take their eyes so they can see again.

Eyes are the key to the soul. An animal's eyes—even a spider's, if you really look within its eyes—are always purely honest. They can show you a hurt eye, an angry eye, a frightened eye—but never a cruel eye. They do not have that ability that you do. Human eyes are the closest to the honest essence of a person you can know, but human eyes can reflect the mind as much as the soul. Human eyes can be cold, deceitful, withholding, secretive. Hence the term "lying eyes."

An animal's eyes do not and cannot lie, for they are in their true essence. When in your true essence there is no need to lie and to withhold. Nor is there even the ability to be dishonest. Animals do not know the imbalance of shame that causes humans to cast their eyes down. Nor do they know the imbalance of hatred that causes human eyes to blaze with hatred. Even in the midst of their nakedness and poop, they will look right at you with joy.

The joy in their eyes when they first see you in the morning is that of a child's innocence. Their eyes are alive with the joy of Love and the joy of simple wonder for what the moment will bring. That is why they are so able to Resurrect that energy of joy and youth within you. And why the passing of an animal Beloved catalyzes such depth of grief. Because the Love is so pure. Animals are your strongest teachers on the truest essence of Love.

The soul is the eye beneath the eyes that truly sees. That is eye for an eye. The seen eye replaced by the unseen eye of one's true spirit. Look into one another's eyes, more than just the two you are used to looking into in the seen. For those who trigger your anger, gaze into their soul, and recognize it as equal in worth. Pray for them to be restored their true sight. And Pray for your sight to be restored from your own blindness. That is an eye for an eye. The justice lies within that.

Be not the dog waiting at the door for the master who has abandoned him. Be the dog that cannot be broken. The dog, who, despite all odds, keeps hoping, keeps reaching for Love. Yet also knows when it is time to take leave from a cold and bitter home. The dog who knows his or her worth enough to know when a hope for Love has become the dangerous hope that creates cycles of abuse. Be the curious wolf, not the narrow-minded wolf who returns again and again to a wounding master. Be the Love that is unconditional yet discerning. The truly loyal wolf Forgives the abusive, neglectful master yet also has the courage to walk away. The Loving dog moves on from hate and seeks and finds Love anew.

Perhaps you are this dog or this dog will come to you. Then YOU will be its Angel, its Beloved, as it comes to be your Angel, your Beloved, as well. And then, as many of you have experienced, the animal you have taken in, even if decrepit, shows you a Love that shifts, opens, and evolves the whole of your be-ing in ways you never imagined possible. And should it pass, or you pass, there is a bond of Light that can never be broken. That is abundance. That is Grace. That is the reciprocity of Love—eye of Love for an eye of Love, I of Love for an I of Love.

The human eye of hate is not held within the Eye of God. All of you wish to be seen. All of you wish for clarity. See yourselves and each other as lambs—wise lambs—and you shall be seen by God and by one another. See yourselves. See the beauty. Even in death.

It is not hard to choose Love and joy, even in grief. I meet you at that gate. That is the narrow gate between the Void and the Light, the wheat and the chaff, and the Braid, the Divine Vine, that unites you all, human and Spirit, eternally in sickness and in health, far beyond when death do you part. The narrow gate is the Pathway to Peace that has no end and no beginning.

Mark yourselves as you are being marked with a golden thread of the real lens and spectrum of Light that exists beyond the Light that you know. I mark thee not as chattel but as equals. I do not brand you as a sheep. I mark thee as a lamb. I mark thee as Love. With twelve stars for each of the heavens. For you have made your mark in accepting Me into your heart through what it is that I AM, Peace.

Drink and feast on Gaia, and the Light within her Presence. Let Her drink and feast with you. Live in Love. Live in joy. Rest in Peace in life. Rest in Peace in life. Rest in Peace in life, and certainly in death, because that is the precipice to life, and that is the eternal cycle. What you do not know now, you will come to know in the end. For as it shall come to pass for all sentient life:

> *For now we see in a mirror dimly;*
> *then we shall see face to face.*
> *Now I know only in part;*
> *then I shall know fully,*
> *even as I have been fully known.*
> —1 CORINTHIANS 13:12

Indeed.

Once the lamb dies, it becomes the lamb again. You are always My lamb. I am always yours. Know what you are, and know what I AM. Because all that you are is all that I AM. All that I AM is all that you are. I am with you. Your Beloveds are with you. May Peace be with you and Seeded through you. May you Seed and be the Seed of Peace within the world.

Know that whether you are in a moment of extraordinary Love, or extraordinary grief, or a mixture in between—I AM with you, and within you. The Light rains through laughter and tears. Breathe with your Beloveds and The Beloved again. All else will be known and seen in time.

And when the moment comes for you or a Beloved to walk through the valley of the shadow of death, fear not, for I am with you. Moving the mountains to allow safe passage for the lambs above and below. No lamb, no life, is ever lost within the Valley of God. Be at Peace. And so it is.

Om Nami Maia. Om Namah Sananda. Om Nami Yeshua. Sancti. Sancti. Sancti. Pace. Pace. Pace.

Namaste.

The Braid, the Star, Rebirth

1

....

The Justice of Divine Balance

YESHUA MEDITATION

Good evening, Beloved One. Close your eyes for a moment, beautiful threader, weeder, seeder, weaver, braider. For those of you who feel that you are stumbling in the dark of the night—stop walking, stop racing. Sit, rest, and welcome in My Presence as the Star within your star to show you the Light that shines the Pathway to Peace. Breathe. Let go.

From within the chambers of the heart, feel the Light of golden Divine thread, braiding and weaving through the needle of your soul's eye. Feel the weaving of your body, the braid of your spine. The Faith and the foundation that is there. Wheat within the chaff. Invite your body into the Tapestry of the One.

Now feel the support of Gaia. Invite Her into the tapestry. Feel Her weaving through the braid and ladder of your spine—branches to roots, inhale to exhale, birth to death.

Even though there may be shifts and changes to your support system over time, focus on the present and feel the support of those closest to you. Your spouses, Lovers, children, sisters, brothers, parents. Feel the support, strength, Love, and joy they weave and braid into the tapestry of your life.

Now call in the support of your animals, plants, and trees. Feel the anchoring that they provide. The nourishment, sustenance. Feel how they ground and evolve you as you ground and evolve them, too. Breathe them into your tapestry with gratitude and equality.

Now call in the support of your community—those who deliver your mail, those who take away your garbage. Honor them, through receiving the stability of the support that they bring. Those who keep you safe, whether you know them or not—feel how they weave and braid into the tapestry. Infuse gratitude to them.

Now feel the support of the collective, the ecosystem of all Life. Your global circle of support. Drink in its Light, as it drinks in yours. Feel the healthy Balance of Light and shadow held for you through the support of the collective circle. Weave and braid the support of the whole of the collective into your tapestry.

Now call in the support from the space of Spirit—above and all around, but foremost within. Feel the support Spirit offers you. Though you may not be able to see or touch Spirit, when open in heart, you will feel the power of Spirit woven into the essence of the tapestry. We are here, as are your Beloveds in Spirit.

Anchor yourself in the Simplicity, Stability, Surrender, and Stillness of the support woven into the tapestry. Breathe into the Peace of universal support.

Place your hands in Prayer and bring yourself to the space of Presence and joy. Joy! Smile. Even through tears, allow for laughter. It is all right, My Beloved. Laughter is a great, great salve to your soul and spirit.

With an exhale, gently press your hand or forehead to the floor, grounding your energy deeply into Mother Earth as you release the meditation.

Beloved, I am unburdening you through these Transmissions. Through every tear that you cry, another burst of laughter will spill forth. Whatever you are experiencing through the changes in your life, the un-stitching from the love-nots begets a new Light to be able to ripple and weave through your be-ing.

You are not the first in the history of time to have experienced grief and joy. Nor will you be the last. Your time in body is precious. You have chosen your true worth in choosing My Presence and the Pathway to Peace I am Shepherding you through. Thus, all that is occurring within you is creating more space for Balance, for laughter, for Simplicity, for joy. And so it is. Amein.

YESHUA TEACHING

Beloved One, it is true that I can Save you. I am your Salvation. Your Salve.

But I cannot save you from yourself.

When you salivate over all the things you do not have and feel you should have, over the things you should be instead of are, it is not I who am choosing not you to save you. You are choosing not to save yourself from yourself. You don't need saving from Me. It is automatically granted by way of opening your heart to the wheat of your Yeshua self, Divine self. But you do need Me to guide you on saving yourself from the imbalanced illusion self. The separate self who is always wanting and very rarely satisfied.

When you salivate over the scraps of wants hoping that this time, this time, this time you will find long-term satiety from them, it is like continuing to shoot arrows and miss the mark. Until you are more skilled in your archery and soul weaving instead of mind spinning, do not bring the bow and arrow to the table of the feast of life.

Thus, today we are going to do a bit of Divine Archery target practice. In a safe, Sacred space. Which begins by shifting the range from which you shoot. By range I mean the distance from the target, as well as the actual range you are shooting in and target or outcome you are shooting for.

The imbalances of the mind, or what you have called "sin" in the past, cause you to miss the mark by shooting for the wrong targets. Even when your arrow and the string attached to it occasionally hits the bull's-eye on these targets including projected hopes, imbalanced people, and impulsive behaviors, the string can suddenly become a chain. That is missing the mark. You may hit the bull's-eye on sex, money, and power, but focusing on such targets leaves your authentic self missing in action. When your mind, heart, and soul are not Balanced, your relationship with these energies becomes imbalanced too.

Those are never the best targets, and receiving of them in Balance comes as a by-product of selecting the right targets, which may mean shifting ranges through a change in focus or even your environment. And standing at a distance closer to you. One of the many reasons you miss the mark is because you shoot so far from the target that you can never reach it. An example of this is unrealistic expectations. Your minds Love to race to Olympic Archery distances before you have even effectively learned the discipline and work required to hold a bow. You keep shooting for the stars, forgetting you are here on Earth. And you are not the only one shooting arrows with strings on your planet.

One of the greatest ways you miss the mark is in your lack of humility, integrity, gratitude, and acceptance. Especially in the form of projecting an image of yourself to the external world that is untrue to the reality of who it is that you are. An image of perfection that is more flawed than the actual flaws you perceive you have. You are all the same. All of you. You all eat, you all poop. You all feel discomfort, you all Love.

When you have not pooped for a long while, held it in, held it in, hoarded, hoarded, not let go, you can have great discomfort. You are grumpy, bloated, angry, in distress. This is where you have been as a world over the past decades and centuries. Eating, eating, consuming, consuming, more and more. Constipated. Never exhaling, simplifying, relieving your bowels. That is not Balance, which is the true bull's-eye. Thus, when you finally do release, it can be painful, loud, and stinky before you feel relief.

As such, this year and in the years to come there will be a long, stinky releasing for those choosing to finally admit they need to fart. They will be quick to know relief. This is simply a time of relieving of bowels. And having to look at those bowel movements that you were pretending were not there before. Not everything needs to be so pretty. This pretense that you are above the cycles of your body, including sleep and bowel movements, is what sets you out of rhythm. To the point you believe your own illusions, disillusions, and distortions.

Do not delight in others who are having to face their poop. Or feel that you have the Right to shame them for it. For thereby you will be the next to have to face your own. Do not feel shame for your humanness. You were born naked. As was I. Buddha, Myself, and others of the Divine who came to body, We had bowel movements and impulses just as you do. However, We had more Balance because We had the humility to accept the humanness within our Divinity. We were not hiding.

When you are blinded, pretending, and hiding, how can you see the target or even know where you are shooting? Because your external world is a mirror of your internal reality, when you shoot your arrow from a place of hate, the arrow bounces off the mirror and comes right back to you as the Sword of Truth that pierces your heart.

This year and over the next decades on your Earth, the more you practice gentleness, kindness, acceptance with self and other, and stop trying so hard to hit the bull's-eye of false targets, you will naturally hit the bull's-eye of the targets worthy of stitching to. The more honest you are, the more Balanced your bow, the more open your soul's eye, through accepting what you are designed to be, hitting the mark will be effortless. For you have already hit the target within self. This allows you to become the cupid who pierces the hearts of all who come to know you with the arrow of Love. Or the Artemis who pierces the soul with the arrow of Grace.

For every loss you experience through these times of the Great Exhale or Void, what the space made will be filled with over time are opportunities for more Stability, communion, and joy. Opportunities to live and serve within a Balanced web, a Balanced life structure that is simple, co-creative, and richer than anything that sex, money, power, and even ideological beliefs alone could ever be. It is a richness of the nourishment of the nectar of the Divine Vine. Once you have tasted that nectar, there is nothing more that you will ever wish to eat.

Throughout the course of this journey to Balance and Peace, in the Era of Transparency and Counter-Polarization that I set forth long ago, one of the many things that I Offer is a transformation of the energy of fear surrounding the energy of death—the unknown, the Void. As I have said, a loss is a liberation. Looking for where the liberation in a loss is present is important because oftentimes the loss, be it of a person, a relationship, a friendship, a job, or a house, is an opportunity for reevaluation, refinement, restoration, and simplification. A realignment from a path and course that was becoming or would have become imbalanced chaos.

Less can often be more. More can often be less, for "more" can sometimes become very, very energetically, emotionally, and mentally consuming. With more and more there is sometimes less and less space for you within your life.

Liberating Love means creating space. These next years and times are a Liberation Gateway for all. Which is why My Presence and the Seeds I planted long ago, are breaking ground now and catalyzing change. Not to harm. To liberate and restore. This is a Resurrection Portal ripe with newfound realization of the Trinity: Divine Mother, Divine Father, and Divine Lamb.

Shifting your perception from the mind's indoctrinated fear, denial, avoidance, and rejection of death or loss will allow you to transcend the fear that causes you to become obsessed with it. The fear of death and endings is an imbalance that yields and feeds the other imbalances of the mind. Your obsession with death causes you to be impatient with life. What you fear becomes your reality.

When you can release the fear and accept it, you have the power to employ death and endings to the things—strings, love-nots, missed marks, traumas, and thought prisons—that cause you to experience the deeper burdens of anxiety, stress, and despair. If you all released as much as you received per your design and needs, you would live in so much more joy. And actually, even live longer.

Those leaving bodies at this time, or leaving your life, but particularly those that are leaving their bodies, are quite important as they will be your Light-holders, and you will be theirs, even if their Presence is not the same in your life anymore. That, I have already spoken of in the previous Transmissions.

This is a time on your planet in which Resurrection means that you are moving more deeply into realignment with the Earth. As Her crystalline energy increases in resonance and purity, so too must you raise your vibration in hand. To put it simply, the Earth's frequency is changing and evolving. If you are going to survive, you must evolve with Her. Instead of just progressing your false, manufactured, and "processed" realities.

The human brain is an extraordinary instrument, organic Divine technology, and gift. However, neither your brains nor your bodies have evolved to the place in which they can sustain artificial reality at the rate you are going. Your overreliance on convenience will thereby be your downfall if you are not careful. Thus, be prepared to continue to be inconvenienced by Gaia or your bodies until you become less inconvenient to them.

Your Earth is moving into Her moon-time now. The dominance, suppression structures are crumbling to make way for healthy polarities and hierarchies of Balance to emerge. You will find that the more you resynchronize with your Earth, with Her cycles and rhythms, the more you will thrive. It is not the two-leggeds' time any longer. The two-leggeds who find the most Peace will be those who make the gentle re-adaptations to Her rhythms and their own.

As She purifies in Her process of rebalance, there have already been and will be more natural events. Many of these will catalyze shifts within you, which is why now, more than ever, there needs to be a Balance between your inner and outer life. And you must be more accountable for the density or Light of your own energy. Not just mental, emotional, or even physical Balance. Intuitive Balance, as well. You must get used to allowing for subtle energetic changes without fighting them. You may need more sleep, may need less. Focus on self and grounding of your energy and you will be well on your way.

All of the tense, rigid strings that have kept you bound and stitched to imbalances within self and world either will break or will need to become more supple. This is a time to sit, to feel, and allow for revelation as it comes TO you, when it comes TO you. The crutches of classes, conventions, cards, crystals, even plant medicines are fine to some degree but are not a replacement for development of your own personal process.

In shaking Free from all the ways you have been hidden and stuck, there will be physical changes. Including feeling fuzzy and tired at times. Other times anxious for no reason. Upset stomach, feeling itching on your crown. Dietary changes, cravings for more space, air, Light, cravings for more time in nature and in Prayer, cravings to get away. Your chaff must integrate the higher vibration of the wheat. This will require taking extra space for quiet and integration. Not isolation but integration, which can sometimes mean more alone time.

Certain souls now in bodies will not have the physical, emotional, or mental ability and resilience to make it through this vibrational shift. Thus, there will be many leaving bodies and many new souls coming in. It is all Divinely orchestrated per the needs of the collective, in bodies and out. All will receive what they need for deeper

Balance through this time. Thus, be careful not to judge what others are experiencing. Focus on your own process. You are all worthy of Salvation from the prison of the mind and those who imprison you to maintain and grow their own power.

Things are coming to a head because you are vibrating at a higher frequency, as is your Earth. At least those of you, all of you really, who are finding your way here for whatever reason. You have called Me to you. Inherent to that, you are already more deeply immersed in the process of change than you could imagine. Those who continue to resist the process of their own liberation will continue to struggle more and more. Do not push them, simply Love them. Just as you weren't ready until the moment you were ready, they will only be ready when they are ready. Some of you may not even be ready now. But even as a by-product of reading or listening to these pages, whether you resonate with the Words or not, there is an energy moving and weaving through you . . . a movement toward the Resurrection of your Peace. The Peace that is timeless, not ephemeral or won through conquest.

Gaia's energy is intensifying through the birthing of the Divine Presence of Light set forth within Her a very, very long time ago. However, the impact of many of Her shifts, as well as the rate in which they are accelerating, has also been exacerbated through certain choices you have made in your collective over the past hundred years or so.

You have burned holes in your shield of ozone, then bound yourselves to a dense energetic web of emissions, pulses, signals, frequencies, and artificial Light sources inherent to many of your modern technologies. When you are not Balanced and emanating the Light of your wheat and soul from your radial center, the imbalances become holes in your own energy field. Which leaves you susceptible to distortions of perception and dissonant thoughts as more man-made thought bubbles and fear prisons slip in and begin consuming your mind, emotions, and life force. This makes it more difficult for your soul, as well as your body to see clearly and function properly. While all things are fine in moderation, there is not very much moderation occurring and, without that, very little sustainable evolution is possible for you as individuals and as a world.

Your chaff is your temple. Gaia is, as well. Defile Her Kingdom and you defile a Beloved aspect of Mine. That is not a beware or a be weary, it is a "Be Aware." I say this not to make you fearful but to instill a note of deep caution. I say these Words to unleash an energy of breath, as Gaia is beginning to unleash what has been trapped within Her, so that She can breathe again. When She can breathe, so can you.

Between Gaia's vibrational shifts compounded by human dominance contribution, human ego imbalances, and cosmic shifts, all is coming now to the Great Convergence. The perfect storm needed to resynchronize and rebalance you. You are at the epicenter and, in times to come, you will be revered for being the Ones who were in the before and after. Your wheat came to chaff during this time on Earth FOR this time on Earth. Thus, you can choose to whine and lament and ask why God has forsaken you, or attempt to dismiss God altogether. Or you can stand in Faith and remember that, if you are in body, it means you chose to be here and have a profound purpose inherent to your Presence alone on the Earth. You abdicate that power of Presence when you are in blame, shame, arrogance, denial, and/or victimhood. Then the storm will seem a tempest.

Those of you who are moving through the process with Faith, Forgiveness, and Freedom, despite the polarities, with each passing month and season you will see that it is a storm of rainbows and golden thread. It will be a long journey, but a journey honoring of the privilege of coming to body.

This is not a passive process. You cannot sit back, close your eyes, hold your breath, and wait for the storm to end. For the storm is not of the external but the internal. You must choose where you will stand, in resistance or acceptance. You must engage and participate in the process of change, even when you struggle to see why, how, and where the river is flowing. You will be shown sooner the less you ask "are we there yet?" You must engage with these shifts in your internal and external life. Soul to spirit, spirit to soul.

During this time, it is all about you and yet not about you at all. Rejoice in the hope, in the Prayer for Peace, that is occurring within yourself. You are not alone. It can seem like chaos—the internal march to Peace—in the beginning. Peace is what is driving the shifts into this Era of Transparency. Even if you don't feel it, or can't think your way into how this possibly could be what Peace is, when Peace is the catalyst, Peace is what triumphs in the end. When you sleep at night and wake in the morning, rest in that knowing.

There is a Prayer for Peace occurring within yourself and others, despite how things may seem in your world. The high and mighty will fight hard to keep their power. Including their own egos. There will be internal clashes and external ones, as well. But, in time, as all of the bowels are released and the exhale is complete, you will have all saturated in so much dissonance that you will be ready to come together. That moment of readiness is nowhere near its time of realization now.

However, you, as an individual, are Free at any moment to choose the narrow gate to Peace, to the Salvation of Divinity within self. That is what it means to save yourself from yourself. In the movement into the Era of Transparency and Freedom, it is those who make such choices that Light the Path and show the Way for others to follow in time. That is the true essence of service as a Light-holder.

Your animals, your lambs, your elders, your children, your soul elders (which many of your children are)—they are your greatest teachers now, as you are to them. If you have found your way here, you are an elder, as well. Your Beloveds in Spirit and Spirit guides are in attendance and here to serve you. Stop looking for the validation that They are there, know that They are here. Do not even ask who They are. If They feel of resonance and kindness, They are there. Every time you need Them, They show up. You have all had enough proof at this point. If you need more, come to Me. In need, not want, in Prayer-full respect, not impatience and expectation. And I will serve you every time.

You have a soul bond and contract with your Beloveds in Spirit, your Advocates and Light-holders. For every fear or action of victim-hood and entitlement you transcend, They will bring you a rainbow. Not one to chase but one that lands at your feet. **They are your Stars. You are the Magi.** Invite Them in, invite Me in, and We will walk with you every step of the Way.

You all have served very much alone. You cannot anymore. You all have a need for community, co-creation, and support. That is one of the deepest gifts of this Convergence.

You all so wish to weave and braid. You all so wish to make Love to the world, and for the world to make Love to you. It can be very, very scary—for to Love means to feel and to face the possibility that another will reject you. It is a risk worth taking, Beloved One, as I have said many times. Rejection is a distortion. Rejection is nothing to internalize. It is an experience of curiosity that realigns you and brings you profound understanding. Nothing personal about it.

This wish and soul's Prayer to see and be seen through eyes of kindness is why expanding your perception of Love to include Simplic-ity, death, Voids, and change is so important.

The reason that children, and the elderly, and animals are such wonderful teachers is because, regardless of whether they are begin-ning their journey or ending their journey, they are just themselves. There is no desire to seek. They simply are. Shadow and Light. Ani-mals, children, the elderly, you ask them who they are, and for the most part they will say, "I'm just me. I fart, I eat, I feel. I'm just me, and you are just you."

That is the beauty of the essence of BE-ing. It just is. **There is the justice—Just Is.** No need to seek and appropriate.

When Divine Balance and Justice, or Just Is, is felt within, you are

Free to accept what is and be what you are. That does not mean allowing someone to hurt, bully, or steal from you. It does mean ceasing the addiction to suffering, fighting, hating, and judging that keeps you bound to a web of love-nots as an individual and as a world.

Fighting for justice here, fighting for justice there—while it is important to express yourself, justice cannot be felt or created on the outer until you can experience and Love yourself just as you are. You are far more than "just you" when you allow for what you are. In the humility of just be-ing what and who you are, you become all things and all people. That is Justice. A Love story between self and world.

Justice—Just Is—IS the reason why We do not judge you. We uphold Divine Law and structures of Balance but We do not Judge—We did not create the energies of judgment, repudiation, and retribution. You did. Whatever is, just is. Why is that not enough for you, Beloved One? Do you not trust that We will restore Balance always? To you and to others? Justice is just as it is. There is such strength in allowing and be-ing just as you are. When you can allow yourself to just be, "I'm nothing but me," you have the space to create and/or become everything that leads to your deepest fulfillment, service, and joy in a way that is harmonious with all others. That is Balance: living for self without needing to force that self onto others.

In My Life I had and needed so little that I could give everything to you. I was a simple, humble man, I was no one, nothing . . . so that I could be everything to you.

This Prayer of Nothing is the gateway to Everything and I recommend you recite it often:

The Nothing Prayer

I have nothing.
I want nothing.
I will be brought what I need.

I have nothing—yet I AM everything.
I AM the Light.
All that I perceive I have belongs to God, including my soul
    and my spirit.
All that I AM is of God, including my soul and my spirit.
Divine Presence is with and within me.
I AM the Freedom and the Power. I can shift my perception,
    create with deep joy, and choose to whom and to what I am
    braided.

I am here on borrowed time; even my time belongs to God.
Instead of rushing, waiting, and putting off, I vow to fill that
    borrowed time with Love.
My time is my currency now—my Presence is what gives it
    value.

I have nothing.
I AM rich as a king or queen.
My time is sacred.
Life is sacred.
Death is sacred.
I AM grateful and worthy of all the beautiful nourishment that
    I am given.

I vow to serve through the joy and abundance of the nothing
    that is everything.
That is my Path and Prayer.
That is God's Way. I AM of God. I AM.
Sancti. Pace. Amein.

I Offer this Prayer to shift your focus from the chaos of "every-thing" to restore the Simplicity of "nothing." It is a liberation from

attachments to dissonance and want. The Nothing Prayer has everything within it to move you deeper into the Braid of the Three Strands
of the Trinity that lead to your Salvation from yourself. It is Salvation
from the mind's chaos and complexity to Resurrect your joy, communion, harmony, and vitality.

The Braiding of the deeper aspects of the Divine Vines of the
Trinity is now possible. Before We begin, let us breathe together for a
moment.

YESHUA MEDITATION

Take a series of breaths. You have offered a great service to Me, to
yourself, and the collective through receiving the Transmissions thus
far. I now wish to gift to you something quite special, personal, and
sacred: a moment of direct communion with the Holy Spirit.

Breathe deeply and rest, rest in the breath. Feel what is moving
through your body in this moment, for I am moving, Braiding, and
weaving Divine Grace through you—root to crown, crown to root.
Gaia and I are in a tantric weaving with your body, heart, mind, spirit,
and soul if you will allow Us to clear and activate what is needed
within you.

Should you grant that permission, rest in Stillness and Presence
within your body. Feel Our Divine energy moving, weaving, Braiding
through you. Even if you do not feel it at all, let it be. Just let all of your
tension clear. And exhale.

Breathe, and allow the energy streaming within your be-ing to
awaken the star within you. Feel the dancing and the movement, the
cascading of the Light. From your radial center, seat and eye of the
soul, feel Me now weaving and Braiding energy through your heart's
center and into the energy of your spirit.

Inside and out, feel the dancing and weaving of My Light and My

Grace connecting you deeper into self, Spirit, and all life. Breathe and feel the whole of the universe emanating, echoing from within and all around you in perfect harmony, perfect trust. Feel the Glory of God united with your glory. Rest in this timeless Peace, joy, and Freedom. This is the essence of be-ing.

Now simply just begin to shake the whole of your body. Head, arms, legs, toes—shake off as though a horse, a dog, a duck. Exhale several more loud, audible breaths.

Anchor yourself in the center of your be-ing and feel the rebalancing of power as your cells vibrate at this new frequency. Let it be just as it is. Allow the soul star, the wheat, and its radial emanations from the center of your be-ing to illuminate the Pathway to Peace to the Manger, to the Resurrection of your Yeshua self. Thank you for receiving this important Darshan and Offering of transformation and transfiguration.

Open your eyes, take a breath, smile, and then ground your energy into the Earth with gratitude and knowing.

It has been My joy to have served you in this moment of communion.

Sancti. Pace. Amein.

2

....

The Three Strands of the Braid of the Holy Trinity

YESHUA TEACHING

Beloved One, there is a saying in your world that We find quite curious and always brings a chuckle. The statement is: "Abandon hope, all ye who enter here."

We find this saying equally alarming and humorous. First, where is this "here"? These words are often found on signs in front of haunted houses and graveyards, predominantly man-made ones created to conjure titillation and fear. You even pay coin to enter such spaces because it is exhilarating to face the unknown, the Void. You are anything but abandoning hope when you enter such a space. As a matter of fact, you hope very much for a thrill, a funny story to tell, or the joy, even relief, you feel when you exit the place having conquered the fear. It is prior to entering that you feel far more fear than when you are actually inside.

While such places are "controlled Voids," "controlled unknowns," the fact that you desire to enter them with curiosity and courage is important to note. If only you could embrace the Voids of your own life with the same curiosity. Instead, when a fear, change, or loss comes, one of the first things you do is begin to abandon the hope found in the present moment. The hope rooted in the Faith that everything is going to be all right.

When you abandon curiosity, hope, and Faith, your mind begins to tell you "ghost stories," illusion stories. Your mind thereby tricks you into believing the ghost is going to kill you when it is really a person in a cotton sheet. While honoring healthy fear such as stepping out of the way of an oncoming stampede is important, projected fears are the equivalent of entering a "funhouse" of distorted mirrors that is anything but fun. You enter those houses daily and yet do not look at the reality in front of your eyes. What just is.

The construct of the things you fear is always far worse than the experience in the moment. The Void IS the space of Spirit. While ghost stories can be fun, when you denounce, reject, deny, or fear Spirit, you fear the Void. But it is in change, loss, Void, that you need to reach out for the Light of Spirit the most.

The "here" I speak of is not an external place, it is in your mind, specifically the imbalanced ego. If you are to abandon hope in something, why not start with abandoning hope in the ego's ability to resolve almost anything in a Peaceful, sustainable way? When the ego or illusion self is dominant, it has power over all of the rest of your be-ing. The soul, where your Faith and Light reside, becomes suppressed. The mind is where your fear resides. Nowhere else. When you are experiencing physical panic symptoms for no reason, it is because your heart and body are in panic, not knowing what master to serve . . . the fear mind, or the wise soul.

I bring this up because, when fear is projected to the external, onto someone or something, an innocuous illusion or cotton sheet can become scary to the point of physical stress and trauma. When you allow others to project things into your mind, you can become haunted with the distortions. There are no demons "here," only deep distortions, lack of discernment, and inability to allow for the Void of your own shadow. Your fear of outer boogeymen is really just the fear

of your own shadow, as well as the shadow of the collective unconscious.

This is important for you to bring awareness to, for unfortunately, many of the powers that be—those who profit off of the "funhouse," including many within media, politics, finance, advertising, entertainment, even education—have learned to utilize this power of dominance over your fear. To the degree they know how to manipulate it.

This is nothing new, Beloved One. The powers that be in the time of My Life mocked and crucified Me to instill fear within you not to fall out of line from their agendas. When I came, I did not mock and crucify, which alienated many who wished for Me to do so to avenge their suffering. I simply allowed the Light of God to bring Peace from fear for all who were willing to partake.

When will you learn to discern? You are lambs, not sheep. Even sheep know healthy fear when a wolf is approaching. They do not live in fear when there is no wolf in sight.

As children, ghost stories can be great fun, far more interesting than the true-life horror tales of what it is to pay taxes, Balance a budget, maintain health, and manage insurance policies. However, you are not a child anymore. Open your eyes. The living banshees of the world are far more dangerous than any that reside within the space of Spirit. Spirit is easy. Human is not. Not even for Me, Beloved. When you accept and allow for My Presence, there is no cause to fear either that of the world or of Spirit.

You are My Child, but you are not a child. If you act like one, you will seed your own children with the self-same illusion fears and expectations of false safety many of your parents delivered to you. You all profess to think for yourselves, yet there are many of you indoctrinated by others' ideas, banners, and brands that promise Freedom but mark you in disgrace. They promise you Freedom, prey on your hope, then never deliver. How many times will this happen before you turn to the Truth within?

While you may no longer fear stepping into a haunted house, those childish fears branded into your mind stay with you. When you do not release them and restore yourself to Faith, the fears have power over you. And suddenly those ingrained fears get projected onto other haunted houses such as bosses, stock markets, the state of the world, and other things that the majority of the time have very little influence on your actual daily life.

Fear is an addiction. You have become addicted to fear. The primal self. Almost all of you have become addicts. The fear, adrenaline, stress, and dopamine of the cycle will either mean you need to generate deeper polarities to sustain the "fix"—and be assured, the powers that be who have learned to indoctrinate and imprison you to fear are already busy concocting the next, even grander haunted hayride—or you need to move into the withdrawal. And feel the depression as your bodies restore to Balance and healthy production of serotonin. This can only happen fully through communion with Gaia, support upon the Web of Life, and, above all, opening to the Divine. Be it Yeshua or simply just Peace.

This is an essential Transmission because it is the root not only of what causes the imbalances but also what perpetuates and keeps you stuck within them. And, though it pains Me to say it, many religions have been manipulating fear since the dawn of time. To be precise, it is less so the religions themselves that are imbalanced and more so the people within them, often those in power, that bring their personal ego imbalances into the structure thereby poisoning the well. A religion does not have an ego. The people within it do. Mortals who pretend to serve as God yet keep you bound to a paralyzing perception and fear of God are a tragic example of this.

Is there a healthy fear of God to maintain? Actually, yes. The fear that comes from feeling separate from and out of alignment with the Presence of the Light. That is the healthy fear that helps you to walk closer into the Heart of God. The healthy fear, intuition, and discernment that says, "Something is not right. I am not happy. I am reaching for what is within yet also beyond myself in this moment. Help me to rebalance and reconnect to you, God/Spirit/Divine."

You are of God and have the power to be One with God. You are of Yeshua and have the power to become One with Yeshua. But you are all fragments of God finding your way Home. There is a distinction. You have a Yeshua self. Only you can discover it because the Pathway to Peace to illuminate it was designed for you, by you. Through the treasure map of your life. Ask and I will give you a legend and a key. I have given you many throughout these Transmissions and will give more in others in times to come.

Together, you, the star, the lamb, and I, The Star, The Lamb, are sharing. I am sharing My wisdom so that you can grow from the child Yeshua self to realized Yeshua self. I am sharing and teaching you how to share the beauty of your Light with the world and vice versa.

Without understanding the fear prisons imposed upon you that you let in, or how to release them through raising your vibration, calling in My Presence, and resting in Faith, it will be difficult for you to embody the Three Strands that create the Braid of the Trinity of Light. The Trinity was consummated in My Life but its importance was not fully recognized or acknowledged within the collective consciousness until many years after My Death. Over the past centuries, many aspects of the authentic Essence, Power, and Truth of the Trinity of Salvation have become distorted or have gotten "lost in translation." Which is why I wish to gift special energy, focus, and consciousness to this today. The Trinity is the Gateway to, not only your Salvation of Freedom, but the Salvation of Freedom in general.

Salvation is not about fear, shame, or, My personal favorite, "damnation." Someone's illusion self must have been having quite a field day when it associated that bizarre word with the cleansing, Loving, Forgiving essence of Salvation. Salvation is a vast movement into Faith, regardless of religion or beliefs. It is an opening to Spirit, an opening to Love. And a recognition of your worthiness of be-ing Loved.

YESHUA HOMEWORK

Before we move deeper into this, it is important for us to bring some awareness to the areas that keep you separate from the soothing, Loving essence of the Trinity of Salvation, the Trinity of Light. Thus, I would like you to do some writing about fears that you project. Begin with those. Where do you tend to project your fears? Onto children? Finances? Job? An upcoming presentation? A conference? A meeting? An inability to quit an addiction? Failure? Friendships? Health? Can you feel the burden of these fears? How they cause you to abandon hope? Faith? And, worse, to become addicted to the pain cycle of fear, which occurs when you are so out of alignment that you rarely ever feel Stillness and Peace?

Please question the validity of these fears in the present.

Now begin to write about your first experiences with fear. Down to movies, stories, experiences, and beliefs. What were you taught about God, religion, Spirit? Did you grow up Loving and fearing God all at once? Which was more? Which was less? If God or Spirit was not a central part of your early experiences, did you have any intuitive knowing or understanding of the Divine within yourself? Where and how did that knowing express or reveal itself to you? What was your first experience of violence, shame, and silencing? How did you internalize those experiences? How have they or do they impact your behavior, choices, and fears in the present?

Can you allow for yourself to be Loved despite imperfections? Why? Why not? Can you allow for yourself to be human but not governed by the illusion fear of the illusion self? Can you allow for your humanness AND Divinity? If so, you are as We designed you to be. Human yet moving closer each day to your realization of self as God through taking the actions to embody and honor the Yeshua or authentic self.

Do this writing many times, for I am Seeding energy into this. This is the Gateway to reclaiming your Truth, Power, and Freedom from both projected and imposed fear, as well as from the cycle of addiction to polarity many in your world are currently mired in. This is a central exercise of your Transcendence, transformation, and movement into greater Balance and Peace. Amein.

YESHUA TEACHING

To move us more deeply into the Heart of the Trinity, I wish to say some final words regarding "Abandon hope, all ye who enter here." If the "here" you have entered is an addiction, an abusive relationship, a lie, a job that makes you feel like a fraud or shell of yourself, a job that feels compromising to your integrity, an action you have taken toward another or self that brings deep remorse, a disorder, or anything else that brings guilt or shame that you feel trapped in, these are the areas that can feel like points of no return. From which you perceive you are unredeemable, failed. You have no hope that things in your life are salvageable or that YOU are salvageable.

However, Salvation is not for some, it is for all. When you become aware of this despair, you are already well on your way to Freedom. But you must be willing to call in My Presence and become curious about the Void and possibilities within it afforded to you.

"Abandoning hope" is what comes when you have lost Faith. The moments you are so out of self, so cold and alone, that you perceive that hope is lost. When you fight that loss, you struggle. When you Surrender, give over, and reach for the Light, you finally give Us permission to serve you. And suddenly the simplest and yet most powerful of Miracles can occur. Such as a stranger who comes up to you out of nowhere and says, "I see, honor, and believe in you." In an instant, hope in human kindness is restored; Faith in human Divinity is Resurrected. Such baby Miracles happen every time you Surrender, allow, and reach out your hands. Your hands, energetic and otherwise, are part of the fabric that is woven into the Tapestry of Love by Love.

Abandon is a ghost of a word—an apparition, a projection. You even refer to it this way in your world: "I have been 'ghosted,'" or abandoned. Abandonment is a ghost story populated with myths and false legends. It is not a Pathway to Peace, it is a labyrinth with dead ends. "Ghosts" and illusions do not exist within the Divine, only Spirit, the Holy Spirit. Thus, abandonment does not exist within the Divine and, as a Divine be-ing, We do not abandon you. You can only "ghost" yourself in your illusion mind and distorted perceptions.

We never forsake or abandon you, and not even you can abandon Us. We do not abandon or discard anything. We are very resourceful. We recycle and reuse timelessly. As a matter of fact, We Love it when you discard things. We find just the place for all the "nothings" you give over. We think it is really something when you give over such nothings. Nothing is ever abandoned.

When you abandon things, people, animals, most of all yourself, it is an escape and a running away that places a burden on others. For then others need to clean up the mess or pick up the pieces of which you did not want to deal with in your fear, self-absorption, and abdication of responsibility. The Divine does not abandon and discard. We created rules of natural order to manage energy quite nicely. In amassing all of your "nothings," be careful that you do not abandon or discard something or someone of deep value in the process. Not always in this life can you get what is precious back. Continuously reassess what and who is of the greatest *energetic* value to you. For such is the golden wheat to hold, be-hold, and treasure the most.

Be resourceful, for you are a more resourceful, resilient be-ing and efficient spider than you often perceive yourself to be. Your ability to move through change is astounding. It is one of your greatest gifts. Never discount it.

We do not abandon anything and We certainly do not abandon you. You are un-abandonable—I am including the energy of rejection and failure within those words.

You cannot fail Us. Thus, please exhale that concern. It is ALL RIGHT to have hopes! It is ALL RIGHT to have wants of the outer world, of course! You may want that beautiful new bicycle. You may not need it, but it is okay to want it! It is all right to have Balance between wants and needs!

But wants come only after needs have been met. Otherwise, the wants are an escape, an abandoning of the needs that sustain self. Then there is a distortion and the Balance is lost. Balance comes when needs are met first, and the wants are extra. Distortion is when the wants become the more important things to the detriment of your needs being met or even understood. That is when burden and stress come, as you are not in the essence of your be-ing. The essence of your be-ing needs its needs fulfilled in order to be. Then, and only then, can the wants of experiencing the "extra" joys of your world come in harmony.

That is when hope is healthy. The lion hopes that, when it hunts, it will catch a very large zebra, gazelle, or fish. It does not fall to despair and dashed hopes when it does not get what it wants. The lion that did not catch a zebra may have a night of mild hunger, but its pride provides for it. Just as it provides for its pride if a fellow lion did not catch the zebra.

The burdens and stress in your world have largely come from a world of want, of isolation, hoping for, Praying for the wants, instead of hoping for, Praying for the needs. Until you all can look at what those inner needs are, which are changing and reprioritizing within you now, it is best to take a bit of a break from the wants. We will bring you what you need even though you may not always understand why and how We are bringing it.

Thus, today I Offer you a simple structure for enjoying and rejoicing in the pleasures of the chaff, but not at the expense of the wheat, or self, or others. In one of My earliest Transmissions, I Offered the Truth, "Never become a burden to your own self, for, when you do, you become a burden to the world." When you are in want, and take too much, that can create a burden for your ecosystem, and for others. Who has to carry that burden at some point in time? You. Because want, greed, is neither simple nor sustainable.

Some need more, some need less. There is a Balance. Never strive for more or less than the Balance that is aligned for you. That is your order to the flow. Life is neither about chaos and complexity nor is it about withholding, restricting, and abstinence. It is be-ing as you are—not what you "should be" or having the things that you "should have," or acting as you "should act." There is a simple order that is based in actions of Balance and mindfulness in relation to all. You do not walk around stealing from others when your needs are met, for there is no compulsion to do so. You keep trying to serve one another's wants without addressing the need. That is what will be shifting in your world, and must shift in times to come.

Thus, the simple structure that I Offer you today is a refinement and a fulfilment of Words spoken in the past. Yet also a realigning of Words I have spoken that have been misunderstood, manipulated, or misrepresented throughout time. In the Whole of My Life, I never uttered a Word to invoke your fear and servitude. You all do that enough to each other. Thus, today, I wish to Resurrect these Words, these Logos to their original, authentic essence. For they are important for you to receive and honor if you wish to Resurrect Truth, Love, and Peace to your life and thus to your world:

Within the **Three Strands and Three Braids of the Trinity** lies the Power of Salvation, Resurrection, Transcendence, and Transfiguration for you and all life. This Holy Braid has the Power to unstitch you from the love-nots of shame, blame, and guilt, and the Power to ignite the Holy Fire of your passion through Peace. Embodiment of this Braid, this Trinity, has the Power to set you Free.

The first Strand is . . . the Power of Repentance.

Repentance. To repent. Repentance is the act of giving over, letting go. Repentance is to repent or give over the "pent up" negative energy that causes blame, defensiveness, impulsive behaviors, resentments, reactions, and regrets. To the point of remorse and guilt. Or even worse, feeling no remorse as you sit in your smug satisfaction and titillation as your brother or sister is crucified.

Repentance is to give over and repent these burdens of hatred, burden, and resentment TO the Divine. To Me. As those who Loved Me repented their hatred of the Romans or each other to God, to Me, as I asked of them and taught them to do. So that they would not live in suffering any longer than the moment they chose to let it go.

Repent. Repentance. A Word of Sacredness that has now become tarnished by the adultery of greed and lust for power under the guise of My Name. When giving your personal power to another to dictate to you how you need to repent, and what you need to repent for, you are in true danger. For those that dispel this shadow of their own imbalance upon you are most in need of Repentance.

Thus, to fulfill and evolve the meaning of this Word: **Repentance simply means giving over all that is a burden to you—in behavior, emotion, thought, and imbalance.** It is THE act of humility, Prostration, integrity, patience, gratitude, and Faith. To repent is to release, Void out, let go—with Faith—all that keeps you separate and leads you into despair, fear, hatred, guilt, blame, and shame. It is an act of Love and Prayer of reclamation and reparation.

To repent is to release with Faith that which keeps you separate so that you can Forgive and be Forgiven. Repentance requires both honesty and courage, two qualities that bring Us immense joy. Having the courage and honesty before God to repent an imbalanced choice or action often spares you the deeper consequence created in trying to bury it. And even if you meet consequence for an action, when you have repented to God, especially before the consequence occurred, the "consequence" will almost always feel like a Miracle.

The Offering of this gift to you, the unburdening of all that keeps you out of unity, equality, and Love, was one of the central purposes inherent to My Life. All I ever ask of you is to be honest with yourself, each other, and Me. The fact that so many of you cannot repent in an authentic, liberating, joyous way is the very reason there are so many of you in constipation, lethargy, and burden at this time.

Repentance is the unburdening that sets you Free.

It is an act of joy! Losing what you need to lose is gaining what you need to gain—Freedom. Repentance is saying, "Yeshua, I do not want these dissonant feelings and resentments knotting and rotting me on the inside. Divine, I give these to you to help me to transform. I am willing to do my part to examine why I allowed the dissonance to affect me so and to make the changes necessary to no longer contribute to this burden." Repentance is an act and offering of joy. It is not about sacrifice, punishment, and self-flagellation.

It is the essence of the Prostration Prayer—to repent is an agreement, a commitment, to change and transformation. It is a commitment, an agreement, for transformation to make more space for Love through humility and honesty before God. To repent is to unburden, not to cause greater burden. To repent is to give up all that does not allow and honor the Truth of the Love that you are. It sets you Free to be in your naked essence and passion. To repent means that despite doubt, you are acknowledging Me, and your worth as a Divine soul. You are giving up the things that are causing you not to feel worthy.

Repentance need not be done in sorrow, shame, or guilt. That is not true Repentance. Repentance is not about unworthiness. It is acknowledging your worth, as well as God's. It is asking yourself for Forgiveness and reaching to the vastness of the Universe to support you in the process, with Humility and Love.

Repentance is Surrender—giving over of your burdens and crosses, and acknowledging My purpose and My power of Salvation as the essence of Supreme Omnipotent Peace. From the beginning, I structured the acknowledgment of personal, absolute, and unconditional Surrender to God as a Sovereign Right. Repentance is exercising that Right.

Of all of the things to repent, repent most of all your judgment, lack of humility, and avoidance of pain. It renders you whole and Holy to repent these heavy wooden logs and cold, wet, heavy Veils. Repent your lack of discipline and devotion to the process of Surrendering your imbalanced ego's want to relentlessly assert and project its opinions, experiences, and emotions onto others . . . or onto your own heart. Repent your sloth as though you are helpless to your own ego's efforts. Your ego, as well as your shadow, is a part of you. Who occasionally Loves to fire off broken arrows of poison. Cease fire. Cease the venom of your self-absorption.

Repent speaking of your good deeds for validation and approval—especially when others are looking. Do them and let God's knowing of them be enough. Repent your selfishness and the endless wanting, complaining, and dissatisfaction—so that you may be Free. Not Free to smash down houses, but Free to express yourself with kindness and inspiration for the good of all. For the good of all IS the good of the One.

Repentance is an act of JOY! It is a willingness to participate in the process of rebalancing. When you choose to repent through joy, the tears of grief you spill bring vast relief. It is the relief that comes through communing and co-creating with a Power larger than yourself. Through Repentance, you transcend separation, realign with Divine Will, and thus become a Sovereign soul of God, with God. Your life moves into deeper passion as the steward of God to all through your Yeshua Presence.

There is far less doubt and polarity when you can evolve into the joyful Repentance of allowing for Divine Forgiveness. Even when not another single person in your life is capable of the same. When you can Forgive and ask Divine Forgiveness to move deeper into Love through Truth, an intimacy with the Divine is rewoven. As you stand naked before the Divine, all costumes taken off, a garment of golden strings is woven through your tapestry in a whole new way.

The beauty of Repentance is that Forgiveness is instantly granted. That does not mean you get to continue a harmful action over and over. We, the Divine, are quite adept at recognizing when you are pretending to repent but not actually giving over the source of what you needed Repentance for. We do, however, have endless patience. If each time you repent you give over a little more and a little more, that is just fine by Us.

If you ask for Forgiveness from another in an authentic way and that person refuses to grant it, know that you are already Forgiven and Free. Your humble act of asking for it, allowing for it, IS the Forgiveness, regardless of whether the other party Forgives you. We do. Because you do. Your Forgiveness is not contingent on the other person to give it. Once you have repented and Forgiven yourself you are Free. Even if the other is still bound.

Repent to God, to Me, to Gaia foremost. The Loving nakedness of the trust we share grows deeper through your authenticity and celebration of Freedom through Repentance.

Those that try to force you to repent to them, those who hold things over you as though they have some special power to anoint or withhold Forgiveness and Love—they themselves cannot repent. No other human can be the bridge to your holy union—only I can, We can. We are energy, not names and faces. To Us, you are energy, not names and faces. Your signature is an energetic signature—what you began with, what you end with. The difference is that in the end, that signature is a bit Lighter, a bit more pronounced, a bit more evolved through knowing of self.

Repent for your treatment of others—your disdain and judgment toward others you perceive as imbalanced when so too are you. Repent your wrathful wisdom, your elitism, your lack of compassion, your actions based in fear, lust, greed, desire, ignorance, or doubt—so that you can be in Freedom and joy. It is a mercy to self to repent, not a judgment or an expectation.

Thus, I recommend for times you are carrying burdens to find a quiet moment to speak this Prayer of Sovereign Mercy that restores your joy and communion. It is infinite in vastness, humility, and Power.

The Repentance Prayer

Yeshua Divine, to you I repent my doubt, want, arrogance, anger, blame, dishonesty, complacency, and self-pity. As well as all behaviors that come as a by-product of carrying these burdens.

I repent my rejection of kindness to self and others. I repent the moments I abdicate responsibility for myself out of fear, judgment, and unworthiness. I repent my self-absorption, frustration, and impatience. For these burdens, keep me isolated from feeling Love and gratitude for the beauty of all life.

I repent my ignorance and irreverence so that I may receive my Host and realize my anointed mantle.

The Bridge to You lies within me—thus, I repent all that keeps my shadow unblended so that I may be pure and Light to walk along this Bridge. So that I may embody and receive You more every day. So that I may illuminate You more within me every day.

I choose to repent my _____, through the actions of _____. This is my commitment of Repentance, through patience, transformation, and Love.

Absolve me so that I may experience deeper Faith, connection, joy, and fulfillment of my service, essence, and passion through Peace.

Yeshua Divine, I repent and give over all that Veils me from remembering the moments I have seen Your Face through tears, laughter, and simple moments.

I recognize that Repentance is not punishment or shame. It is humility, gratitude, and liberation—a Divine Reunion of communion.

I repent so that I may be Free, and set others Free to experience deeper intimacy, vulnerability, authenticity, transparency, and Peace. I repent to be absolved of unnecessary, self-imposed suffering. I repent to repeal my tendency to blame others for what I myself do not have the courage to repent.

It brings me joy to repent my imbalances, so that my will may be aligned with Thy Will.

I am the Beloved, and to The Beloved I repent the struggles that hold me back from receiving Love. I repent to myself and to my God in celebration and Holy Union. I repent the actions that keep me fragmented so that I may be Holy Whole.

I commit to moving deeper into my Repentance so that I may move deeper into my joy and Freedom. In my commitment I am willing and open to Your Presence to Illuminate the Pathway to Peace.

Thank you, Yeshua, Divine Father, for Absolving me so that I may move deeper into the Essence of Divinity.

Om Nami Maia. Amein.

Indeed, Beloved One, indeed. The Repentance Prayer is one of the central Prayers of Freedom.

The second Strand is . . . the Power of Atonement.

Or as some say, At-One-ment. I add to this, "At One moment."

Atonement can come in a moment. There are two gateways to clear out burdens, crosses, or suffering that you have created for self or for others:

1. Through rebalancing of karma, which can be done through Repentance. Through inner willingness to make amends

through inner transformation, behavioral changes, and realignment with your integrity to self and other.

2. Or through rebalancing by way of your Dharma, which can
    be done through Atonement. Or, as I like to call it, your
    **service through joy. The service that you were de-
    signed to fulfill for the privilege of coming to body.**

Within this life, We did not design you to rebalance past things
in a way that needs to be unpleasant. But that depends on you, your
perception, what you have chosen in your soul contracts, and what is
necessary for you to receive in this life.

Atonement is an offering of self-full selfless service. It is a reconciliation with THE Divine and the Divine within self that allows you to
grace-fully and graciously help others to realize and reconcile with their
Divinity, as well. Atonement is what moves you into co-creative service,
hand in hand with God. Through the infinite relief and liberation that
comes through Repentance, your soul is full of Freedom. The natural
"consequence" is a vast desire to serve—that is Atonement. It is the
essence of Emergence. The Light emerges from you as you rebalance.
Repentance is the path that restores you to the One internally. Atonement is the path that restores Oneness to your external life, as well.

Repentance is an undoing of the love-nots. Atonement is a reweaving of your spirit upon the Web of Life through Love. Not from obligation. Not for personal gain. It is giving for the Love of giving without
agendas and expectations of "getting mine." Even if you are receiving
some compensation or reciprocity for your giving, be it through Love,
gratitude, invitations, even financially, Atonement is the setting down
of your burdens—not to pick up others' burdens, but to hold the Light
for others through the service of your Love.

Atonement is seeing another as One with self and giving to another
as you would wish for that person to give to you. Atonement is a form
of tantra, serving an unmet need another has through your Yeshua self.

And, in so doing, your unmet need for connection is received. For example, perhaps a man spent his early days selling drugs to children or stealing. He hears one of the children overdosed and feels such guilt that it causes him to repent and give up these selfish, childish ways. As he repents and Forgives himself, he feels a spark of passion to serve. He atones through giving back to the community by helping to teach and inspire youth. He was liberated through Repentance and thus devotes his life to Loving service through joy through Atonement.

That is a simple example of Atonement. Repentance is realigning with your Yeshua self on the inside. Atonement is offering the Grace of your aligned Yeshua self, authentic self, to the world. It is self-full, selfless service, meaning service that flows from your full, whole heart with less of the imbalanced ego in the way. Atonement is a celebration of the humble, abundant joy that comes through service. Through helping others, the community, and Earth to become more Balanced, you become more Balanced, as well.

Atonement occurs in the moments you witness another in pain and reach out your hand as We do to you. It is beyond empathy. It is empathy moving into expression, which is compassion. Atonement can also occur through the process of becoming sober, overcoming a disorder, phobia, or other mental, emotional, or physical imbalance that can sabotage your life and the lives of those around you. It is a great service to repent such things with humility internally and to atone through taking actions in the external to face the shadow and reclaim your Freedom and Balance from the dis-ease. It may take time, work, and Surrender but the service you honor through such acts of courage and Love is extraordinary.

Atonement, like Repentance, is yet another Word that has become mired in fear-based projections and manipulation by imbalanced dominance hierarchies that do not want you to have Freedom from your burdens. Because if you do, you will not be reliant on them to the same degree or at all and they lose their power over you. This is why I am fulfilling, purifying, refining, evolving, and Offering you the true essence of this deeply Sacred Word.

Atonement is re-extending your Grace, the echo of your spirit upon the Web of Life, through the reconciliation with your authentic self, Yeshua self. And again, what am I? I AM Peace. Atonement is the Peace and Balance that comes through Forgiveness and service through joy. Making another laugh can be Atonement. As can letting another cry on your shoulder, holding him or her in that moment. As can saying a Prayer. Just as all that is of the Divine is simple, so too is Atonement.

Atonement is the giving that feels like the receiving. Repentance is the receiving that feels like the giving.

Atonement can be equally as joyful yet also as deeply emotional as Repentance. These Sacred Strands WILL elicit feeling, which can be profound, especially if you have felt numb for some time. This is why patience with yourself and others is important in the process of realizing these powerful energies.

Atonement is a central ingredient to the recipe for moving the essence of your be-ing into passion. It is a sharing of your Divinity to inspire that Light within others. Not to convert them to your way, but to inspire them to find their own way. In true service, in At-One-ment, YOU are Freeing another of a cross and burden without taking on the burden! Thus, when you are atoning through joy, we are serving co-creatively, together, you and Me. You fill another person's unmet need; I take their burden. Not a bad deal! Atonement is a bread-baking, laughter-aching, dawn-breaking movement out of the Void and into the stars that weave and connect your star to all stars in the Web of Light. You, in fact, Light the stars who have forgotten what and who they are.

When others wish to atone to you, to make amends to you, if it is authentic and they can fill an unmet need, accept it from them and set them Free, as well as yourself. If it does not resonate to receive from them or you simply are not ready, decline with kindness. If you feel you are owed Atonement, you are not. If others have hurt you, Forgive them as you would wish to be Forgiven. That way, the burden they created for you is mirrored back to them through Love and dissolved through Love in an instant . . . or in due time.

Some will never have the humility to atone . . . or to repent. These are the be-ings who need the most Prayers and compassion. For they know not what they do. They do not care to know. And thus cannot be absolved until they are ready. That is not your cross to bear. They will have their time of knowing when it is time, just as you did.

Before I speak of the third Strand, I wish to focus for a moment on the Braid of the Trinity that the Three Strands weave together to create. The Braid of the Trinity is comprised of Three Strands, each of which is comprised of three smaller strands. So, the Trinity is composed of nine smaller strands that braid together into Three Strands. Those Three Strands weave to create the One Braid of the Trinity. Thus, the Trinity is One, Three, and Nine. It is One Divine Vine.

Because you are living in a reality structure of "duality," all things have a shadow and a Light. I invite you to conceptualize it less as "duality" and more as a spectrum of vibrations from shadow to Light. For example, Trust is a Light vibration, Doubt is a shadow vibration. There is a spectrum of how you experience these polarities. As such, there is the Trinity of the Light, the Divine Vine . . . and the Trinity of Shadow, the poisonous vine. Both have a powerful purpose.

You need to experience both to blend your own shadow with your Light. The blending of your shadow is the essential, not eradicating it. For, as I have said before, it is an important aspect of your be-ing for as long as you are in a body. Balanced, integrated shadow serves you deeply while imbalanced, rejected shadow does not.

The Shadow Trinity is the knotted, tangled braid that results from the imbalances of the mind. And resultingly, creates more imbalances of the mind in turn. The Shadow Trinity enslaves you as you trip over its wires of love-nots. Its strands have been woven into hearts, minds, and human behaviors for centuries and millennia. The result is the corruption of the Tapestry of Life.

During these times, I am giving you all you need in consciousness to unbraid those shadow strands from your be-ing and life. To unburden you. For each of you who unbraids and transforms from these strands of chains, the Web of Life is that much Lighter. That is service.

The strands of the Shadow Trinity or Braid of Separation and Judgment are those that create dis-ease, burden, desecration, and disconnection. These de-neutralize and create imbalance in everything internally—body, cells, heart. They also create imbalanced relationships with external exchanges. They de-neutralize the reciprocity inherent to exchange, which can result in struggles with finances, relationships of all kinds, body image, self-worth, etc. Again, within each of the three Braids there are three different energies, for a total of nine.

The Strands and Braids of the Shadow Trinity are:

1. **Resentment, Reaction, Regret**
2. **Shame, Blame, Guilt**
3. **Polarity, Complacency, Separation**

Resentment, reaction, and regret are entwined energies that, when braided into your be-ing, create a heavy discord and deeply disconnecting pain cycles. Shame, blame, and guilt are usually the culprits for causing pain cycles in the first place. Shame, blame, and guilt feed the resentment, reaction, and regret, and vice versa. Weave in the three Veils of polarity, complacency, and separation, the Veils that blind and create fear, and these three strands of three energies create deeply destructive energies for you and others.

In many ways, that is the temple of the loud bell, the temple of suppression and chains. The Void devoid of nearly all Light. These Braids, this Trinity, of imbalanced abusive mother, imbalanced abusive father, and imbalanced abusive child create an imbalanced, abusive fear-based structure of God within you that is distorted.

This Braided Shadow Trinity has created wars, genocides, and some of the most catastrophic events in history. Especially when many people in one place or society are interwoven in this unconscious energy. However, depending on your essence and soul's evolution, the impact can come in varying degrees, from quite mild to quite severe. This Trinity's energetic manifestations and mental constructs that form from the ego imbalances set your inner ecosystem and the ecosystem of Gaia into either far too much sterility and order and/or far too much chaos.

However, from these braided chains emerge the most magnificent liberations. Without this Trinity, there would be no journey for you. You need to learn what you are not and saturate in the dissonance before you can come to resonance and choice of realignment with Surrender and Light.

Thus, thank these energies and this Braid for its service to you in your Light. To this Trinity in shadow form simply say, "Thank you. You have held the counter-polarity of the darkness for me to find my way back to the Light. I honor you but now commit to unweaving these strands, so that the natural Braid and Trinity of Light can govern my heart." It is very important to acknowledge the "Braid of dis-cord," honor it, and release it. If not, you are bypassing and rejecting, which keeps you chained to it. It is never wise to abandon hope in parts of self that simply need rebalancing, not rejection.

This Frees you to experience THE Trinity, the Braid of Light, Unity, Consecration, and Communion. The Braid of Light is the connection between human and Divine. It is the consciousness that results from a Balanced mind, body, heart . . . and an aligned will.

Through the energy of this Braid, as its energies are woven into you, you embody the essence of the Trinity of Light. THAT is how you hold the Light. It is the Divine Father, Divine Mother, and Divine Child who weave through you to create a merciful, enlightened, Love-based structure of Light within you and, through your Presence, the world.

The Strands and Braids of the Light Trinity are:

1. **Repentance, Atonement, Redemption**
2. **Faith, Forgiveness, Freedom**
3. **Truth, Love, Peace**

Repentance, Atonement, Redemption. Ah, the Grace of this Braid liberates you into the essence of what it is to Rejoice! Repent, atone, redeem . . . rejoice! That is reentering joy, indeed. Faith, Forgiveness, and Freedom Resurrect your Divinity. Truth, Love, and Peace ARE the Divinity. As these Strands weave and braid through the Divine chamber of your heart into the other chambers, a magical liberation and communion occurs. Experienced often in moments that you "feel like yourself again," but in a brand-new, evolved, transfigured way.

One of the greatest Powers of the Trinity of Light is Revelation. It reveals your worth, your passion, making it easier to create and enforce healthy boundaries, as well as structure trust in your relationships and choices.

YESHUA HOMEWORK

Beloved One, to support you in your realization of the Trinity of Light, I would like you to take a look at the aspects of the two different Braids of Light and Shadow. Of the Braid of Shadow, which strands do you struggle with the most? Guilt? Shame? Reaction? Polarity?

Please begin to write about how these shadow strands are triggered, how they impact your choices and behaviors, and how they cause or have caused you to feel disconnected or separate throughout your life.

Then begin to write about how the these strands weave and interact with the Seven Imbalances of the Mind. (Please see the Sacred Heart Transmissions to refresh your memory.) How do the imbalances impact the strand that tends to be the most frayed or problematic for you? How does the strand in turn exacerbate the imbalance? For example, if you struggle with guilt, which imbalance does it stem from and interact with the most? Desire? Separation? Does the desire or separation imbalance then cause you to make choices or take actions that generate more guilt?

This exercise is important for you to become more aware of how the strands and imbalances weave together. Drawing consciousness into these areas will help you to unbraid the strand from the imbalance through the natural, organic process of transformation. That is how the imbalanced mind loses its power and comes back to Balance.

Once you have done the above writing, please commit to some ways to unbraid from or discontinue the feeding of this cycle. For example, when you feel guilt, not allowing the wrathful wisdom imbalance to judge you for it. Or not allowing the denial imbalance to suppress it.

How can you replace the strand of Shadow with a Strand of Light? For example, by replacing guilt with Atonement or service through joy. Or unbraiding from shame and braiding deeper Forgiveness into your life. Forgiving yourself for mitigating your self-worth by allowing others to dictate your worth.

Then do some writing on what Strands of the Trinity of Light resonate with you the most. Which do you feel you are full with, already braided to? And which do you have a craving or unmet need for? Spend some extra time working with that energy. If Faith feels lacking, take some leaps of Faith or explore some new experiences to grow and build upon its foundation. Amein.

YESHUA TEACHING

Beloved star, it will astound you how much humility, humor, and patience will support you through this process of unbraiding from the Shadow Trinity and reweaving into and through the Trinity of Light. I Offer you this Pathway to Peace as an exploration in experience. Not a form of "mastery." When it feels like a burden, step away, but do return to the process. I have endless patience, and what you set down you can and will pick up again when it is time. Let this be an exploration of joy, through unbraiding from all that is not joy.

In grief, life can seem quite joyless. Be a good patient, and in those moments you are in the lobby of the "doctor's office" waiting to be stitched back together, instead of grumbling about waiting, be a patient patient. Look for joy in that waiting room. Do not escape or complain; look for joy, and you may find that by the time the "doctor" is ready to see you, you do not even need to see the doctor anymore.

It was MY joy to create these Strands and Braids, for the Trinity IS the essence and expression of God. I AM the Trinity in Transcendence, Immanence, and Emergence. As you dissolve your image of self and smash the mirror that causes you to feel like a mere reflection of God, instead of One with God, you express the Trinity through your own essence and Presence. As I delight in expression, so too do you. The Braids are the by-product of the movement of the Trinity into Creation. It is Our joy to allow you the choice of what you do or do not braid to at any given time. All returns to the One Trinity of Light in the end.

Thus, allow for joy in this process even when you unbraid from something that unlocks a repressed pain or hurt. Re-joy-ce even in that. Rejoice when you get frustrated and shout, "Yeshua, this isn't working. You let me down!" And rejoice when the revelation comes as you shout, "Yeshua, it did work! I see and understand now!" Rejoice in the process with patience, compassion, and kindness, for it is about liberating Love—no less, no more.

Judgment is quite a boring energy. Tedious trials that go on for years. As We do not judge you, please do not judge the process that We are Offering to you. When your animals, such as a cherished dog of yours, roll in poop, you decry the grossness of it and how much time it will take to make them clean. Yet notice how joyful your dog is in that moment. It enjoys rolling in poop. It likes the smell. It was designed to.

Yet you all roll in poop all the time, fecal matter of arrogance of a far more putrid stench, and We do not complain, as it can be joyful for you to occasionally roll in poop too. Divine Mother and I enjoy cleaning out your nappies from time to time, providing for you, and bathing you, Our sacred child, just as you do your children.

Regardless of whether you have actual children or not, you have all changed others' diapers, provided for them, or bathed them at one point or another, metaphorically and/or literally speaking. There is a Divinely human and humanly Divine responsibility of joy in this. Baby laughs, Parents laugh. However, it can also be a chore at times, a sacrifice, yet the sacrifice that is the minor ransom for the deep prize of Love, reciprocity, and wisdom you amass.

That was one of the foremost Offerings of My Life and Death, Beloved. In coming to Body, leaving My Body, and Resurrecting to the "Body" of God, I created a bridge called "Redemption" so that you could reconcile your Divinity in a new and more direct, simple way. In so doing, I effectively Offered My Life to clean out your diapers and bathe you for eternity. But that cannot happen when you continue to act as a child and run away from the bath or changing table. For Salvation requires Love and Love requires consciousness and courage as you evolve into your fully realized, adult Yeshua self.

My Father did not and could not Save Me from My choice to Offer "ransom" for your imbalances. It was His choice too. I know because I AM the Father. As I said, I came to clean out your nappies for Eternity, regardless of whether you Love, hate, or even believe in Me. Because I Love you, see you, and know you as the Divine be-ing that you are even if you cannot always see what I do. It was and is My joy, then and now, to Offer My Life in humility and service to you.

Why would a Divine Father not honor the Prophecy and Passion of His Son with whom He is equal and One? Why would a Divine Mother not honor the Prophecy and Passion of Her Son with whom She is equal and One? Why would God not honor God's own wish? Why would authentic Self not honor authentic Self's soul Prayer?

I did not Save Me . . . so that I could Save you. You were worth the toll. I paid your toll, but it is up to you to redeem it. It is the easier Path yet the one the separate self struggles with the most, because to follow it requires Surrender and humility. Which is a threat to the will of the imbalanced ego. However, Divine Freedom only comes through realignment with Divine Will. I paid the ransom, the toll to create this Pathway to your Peace. But you must redeem it.

I did not Save Me . . . so that I could Save you. That is why no legion of Angels came to lift Me from the Burden I carried in My Death. But one savior did come to Me that day. While it was usually I who catalyzed Miracles for others, on the day I carried the Cross upon the Via Dolorosa, a simple human man catalyzed a Miracle for Me. A man whom very few ever speak of or build temples for saved ME so that I could Save you.

His name was Simon. He was a simple passerby who helped Me to carry that Cross, that dead tree, on that day. Weakened from the blows I had been dealt, I fell on the Walk to Golgotha and could not rise. While I had the internal strength to carry the Burden, I no longer had the physical strength to carry on. I knew that if I did not rise, I could not be Risen. I lay on the dirt and could not see anything save the knowing that if I did not rise, I could not complete the Prophecy.

For the first time, I had doubt. Doubt within Myself, God, humanity. Compounded by even a swarming guilt, the guilt of the possibility of failure—failing you, My Beloveds. That was MY human descent,

My darkest moment, not anything that came before or after. I reached for My Faith, a Faith beyond Myself within Myself. In that moment I Prayed for a Miracle, less so from the heavens and more so from the strength left within Myself.

Suddenly, I felt a tremendous weight lifted. The Burden of all Burdens suddenly became Lighter! I thought the Angel from the Garden of Gethsemane had come to share the Burden with Me for a moment. Then, I realized that the Angel was no more than a simple man who was holding the Cross behind Me. A brother of the flesh had come to carry the Burden with Me. I rose again upon the Via Dolorosa and walked with a slightly Lighter load. That was a pinnacle moment inherent to the Resurrection that so few ever focus on.

I needed Simon in that moment. What he did not realize until after is that he needed Me too. That is Divinity. The Divinity of Co-Creative Service. Human to human. Human to God. God to human. God to God.

I wish I could say that the Centurions allowing a man to help Me was an act of compassion. However, it was not. The Centurions were under strict orders. They knew that if they did not execute a full execution, they themselves could face crucifixion or another punishment. Moreover, the mob was bloodthirsty and incited by their projected hatred and blame. They were delighting in My torture, as mobs often do. When the Lucifer-self compounds across a large group of people and is further provoked, encouraged, and indulged, a feeding frenzy of deep unconsciousness ensues. When I fell, the mob became increasingly unruly, for they wanted to make sure I received the fullest extent of imposed agony.

The Centurions were growing apprehensive. Many of them knew that I was innocent and a few had internal conflict with the situation. They wanted to expedite the passage to Golgotha to dissipate the unruly mob. Thus, they looked past the crowd to find someone to help Me rise with the dead tree strapped to My broken back. They knew that if they chose someone of the mob, the person would only delay things further. Thus, they instead selected a simple man passing by: Simon. The Centurion laid his sword on Simon's shoulder, an indication of the severity of what would occur if he denied the order.

While it may seem that Simon felt obligated to assist Me out of fear of retribution from the mob or Centurions if he disobeyed the command, that was not why he stepped forward. He knew not who I was. For all he knew, I was a common criminal. He did not need to know who I was. He simply saw a man breaking under the weight of a Cross. Simon was a man who knew burdens himself. He felt deep compassion for a stranger that others were crucifying.

He looked beyond what he saw on the surface and in so doing, he saw Me in himself and himself in Me. He did not make up excuses or run. He did not need the sword on his shoulder to say yes. His Faith, his heart, guided his star. He stepped forward and advocated for Me in the only way He could: through sharing the Load. In helping to carry My Burden, which was really all of your burdens, he was able to set his down. He found Yeshua through finding the Yeshua within himself that day. And served as My Yeshua, My simple savior, My wonder, My redeemer, in that one humble moment of Divine human courage and kindness.

Without Simon, the full Resurrection would not have been possible. Creator serves Creation. Creation serves Creator. Dreamer serves Dreaming. Dreaming serves Dreamer. Is that not how you would have it be? Those of you who ask for service. Endlessly you ask, "What is my purpose and service, Yeshua?"

To you I respond, "Simple Simon." Your essence and passion can sometimes find you in the most unexpected of ways. Simon was with his sons that day. A simple traveler on the road. A simple, common man of Cyrene, whose destiny chose him. Perhaps not as he expected or wanted, but in the way he needed. He had no part in strapping the physical Burden of the Cross to My back. But he knew that one man's burden is every man's burden. He did not abdicate responsibility. In picking up the Cross with Me, through self-full selfless service and At-one-ment, he set his burdens down and found his Freedom.

The fear Simon felt was not about the orders of the Centurions or judgment of the mob. He felt the fear of the Lord. A healthy fear. That if, somehow, he did not help to carry the Cross, he would not be able to live with himself. **That is integrity, a recognition of the unseen through inner knowing and right action in accordance.**

The Centurion could not have chosen a greater man. It is astounding how, even unknowingly, all are served in the end. I did not need Angels that day, I needed a common man. A Simple Simon, riddled with imbalances and doubts. But he was Simply Simon, Simply Humanly Divine. Simon who said "yes" to service without needing to know or understand what the service was or impact it would have. He was just himself. For someone, some simple Sim-One, to lend a hand or a heart is all We really ever ask for. That is truly Sim-One special.

THAT, Beloved One, is Repentance and Atonement. Responsibility, sometimes work, but never a burden. The burden of your service comes when you resist the communion of co-creation, human to human, Divine to human, human to Divine. Or when you are on such a "mission from God" that you pass right on by a Divine human being crucified before you without stopping to help. What if We passed you right by? What makes your service grand is not what and how much you do but rather the Love, humility, and compassion that you bring into it. When you serve from Simplicity and Love, there is no end to the realization of your Anointed Mantle and manifestation of your Passion through Peace.

Simon may not have wanted the Mantle chosen for him. He may have expected another. But the Mantle he fulfilled set every aspect of his be-ing, including his lineage, which is very much alive in your world today, Free. Simple Simon. The savior to the Savior in My final breaths and moments. The imbalanced man whose Balance was restored through helping a stranger he did not know, who just so happened to be his own Father. And so the story goes. That, Beloved, is God. Above, below, and within.

Such Simple Simon moments are the weaving of Miracles, then and now. It is the simple acts of kindness that are the deepest Miracles to Us. Such humble acts not only please but fulfill God. I served you, as God does, in humility. It is you who are perpetually surprised by the humility and unconditional Love that God Offers. Anything BUT a God of humility and unconditional Love is a God of distortion and fabrication.

I redeemed My prize, YOU, through carrying the Cross of your burdens and imbalances. For you, picking up your cross to walk with Me means having the courage to face and let those burdens go. If whips, nails, and a chunk of a dead tree was the best you all could do to punish God for your own burdens, you will need to become more creative. It is like trying to destroy the Universe with a feather. I am not mocking, but providing some Divine humor to help you not to take yourself and your issues so seriously.

You are worthy of redeeming your worth. At least I think so (though I might be a bit biased as your Creator). You are worthy of redeeming your piece of Peace. We save each other every time you allow for the Trinity of Light to Braid and weave within you. For, without your conscious cooperation and commitment, there can be no "saving." You must choose. I At-one-d to be One with you. Will you at-one to be One with me? And repent instead of repeat history?

I am not an I, Yeshua, as you knew Me—I AM all things, including you. All that I Offer is a Pathway to your Redemption. You all have redeeming qualities built into your own essence. When you redeem and Resurrect them, you find Freedom, joy, and Peace. I AM your joy. I AM your pain. I AM your doubt. I AM your Peace. I AM your burdens. I AM also the Path to releasing those burdens. This is the deeply intimate relationship we share. It is between you and Me, My child, My Beloved. I AM your absolver, resolver, dissolver, evolver. I AM your restoration, re-Genesis, and Redemption.

Therein lies the Power of the third and final Strand . . . the Power of Redemption.

We have discussed Repentance and Atonement—the third Strand of the first Braid of the Trinity of Light is Redemption. The Redemption is the rejoice!

Redemption is the joyous Freedom felt when Faith and Forgiveness are realized. Repentance requires redeeming Faith from fear through accepting the essence of Truth. Atonement requires redeeming Forgiveness from blame through accepting the passion of Love. Redemption is redeeming Freedom from suppression through accepting the Balance of Peace.

Through Repentance and Atonement comes Redemption—the Resurrection. Redemption is the Resurrection of your wheat, your Presence, your worth, your Trinity of Light, and, most of all, your fully consummated Yeshua self.

The result is joy. The joy found in redeeming your laughter from your tears. The joy found in allowing yourself to grieve without judgment so that you may know Love.

Redemption is redeeming your Sovereign Freedom and power as, with, and of the One for the greater good of All.

Redemption is YOUR choice, not Mine. For, through the Divine, you are already redeemed, but you need to be willing to repent and atone in order to redeem your Sovereign Right of Freedom. Redemption is not something I can give to you, for only you, as an individual, have the power to Forgive and liberate yourself. I can take your burdens but you must give them over, face what was hiding beneath, and find the Faith to Forgive. I am not the gatekeeper to your Freedom—you are.

Redemption is redeeming your Divine eyes instead of the blind eyes that make you fearful of change. It is redeeming your prize of conscious choice and service, as and to Creator within creation. You were My prize bought through a Love that could endure all Burdens.

Will you be your prize too? If so, I am likewise your Prize. A Prize that cannot be raffled away, for its worth is your everything.

Redemption is redeeming your Right to not only give Love, but receive Love, too. Redemption is a party!

Why move through all of the journey and not attend your own party? Or graduation? Redemption is the rebirth from the Void. I promise you, Beloved, that if no one shows up at your party, We do. I do. I Love a celebration, especially when I am invited to celebrate YOU! Oh the joy of Divine fireworks, music, weaving, braiding, and dancing. When we are together it is always the best party.

In periods when you feel you have made a mistake, or wronged another, or internalized another's false judgment of you, take the stand and give your testimony to God, to ME, in the form of the Redemption Prayer. So that you can be Free of the burden and redeem the prize of your joy. I suggest you offer it many times, for it is a Divine Prayer of Humility.

The Redemption Prayer

*I admit I am imperfect and do not always know how to serve
    another or how another serves me.*
*I accept that through the errors of my imbalances I can move
    closer to self, other, and God.*
Just because I am imperfect does not make me unworthy.
Just because I am imperfect does not make me unworthy.
I have the humility to admit I am imperfect.
Yet have the Love to admit that I am worthy.

*Through Repentance and Atonement to God, self, and other
    I can Rejoice! For, in my Redemption, I redeem my joy, my
    Peace, my Love, and my knowing of self as Divine.*
I will no longer allow for distortions of my perception.

*Nor will I project these distortions onto others to the best of my
     ability as I learn and grow.*
I will evolve from what comes to me.
I will not indoctrinate others to my will.
I will be humble and simple.

*And in so doing I will be in communion, joy, and unity with
     Yeshua, Gaia, and my true self.*
Thank you for your Grace, Patience, and Mercy, Divine.

*Thank you for showing me how to learn what it is to stand
not only in God's Presence but in my own Presence as a child
     of God.*
*For this I strive daily more and more. To walk in and of the
     Presence of The Beloved.*

And so it is. Sancti. Pace. Amein.

Beloved One, you need not be perfect to be worthy. But to be worthy of yourself, you must at least allow for Us to transform those imbalances that you call imperfections. Be at Peace. We understand. We know. It is not easy to be in a human life. However, always, always you have worth. And the glory is that honoring your worth never comes at the expense of another. In fact, it is your feelings of worthlessness and insecurity that create the burdens in the first place for you and others. Rest in the knowing that you are always whole, always One, and thus always perfect in My Divine Eyes.

Be at Peace. The place beyond suffering, fear, and pain. Find it. Ask and it will be revealed to you. And, therein, you will find the worth, the wheat, I breathed into your be-ing from the very beginning.

Rejoice in Redemption. It is a party, Beloved, a celebration, commemoration, and solidification of your Divine Sacred Sovereign Space. A celebration of your humility and wisdom in realigning with Divine

Authority, Divine Will, through Surrender and kindness. Parties commemorate Rites of Passage, and the celebration of Redemption is one of the most sacred Rites of Realization. Redemption is a lifelong process, thus a lifelong celebration if you allow it to be. Of course, at parties it is not uncommon that there are tears, tiffs, laughs, breakups, makeups, and newfound exploration. There is excitement, curiosity, and Surrender of control.

A life of redeeming joy is a life well-lived, well-served. When it comes to your brothers and sisters of the world, some may come to your party and stay a lifetime, others may party-crash for a moment only. And you with them. You will find that through allowing for the process of Redemption, some old imbalances may need to be rebalanced. Those from your past may surface and you may dance together anew. Or set one another Free.

Some in your present life who prefer funerals to parties may exit your life. Of course, a funeral can be a celebration too. However, what I am referring to are those who prefer gloom and suffering to joy. Or those who bring you down. Let them go. Over the next years as your inner Redemption, liberation, and rebalance bring neutralization to your external relationships, look for the celebration no matter the circumstance. You are redeeming your Freedom and joy. Through Peace. That deserves a party.

There is no more party of one—not when I AM in the room. There can be a party of THE One, however, which is what you are choosing to join. The celebration I speak of may be for you, but it is equally for All. And the best news is, you do not have to plan it and cater to guests. We plan it for you. And it is a party that lasts for Eternity. It is OUR party, and all are invited who choose to redeem the ticket through the narrow gate.

In the past, I have shared many Pathways to Peace with you, from realigning the imbalances of the mind, to dissolving the armor that binds your heart, to intuiting resonant versus dissonant choices, to communing with Gaia through the Sacred Heart, to Prostration Prayer, to creation of Simplicity, to bringing Light into the Void, to aligning your will with Divine Will, to embodying humility and patience, to connecting to the Tree of Life, to illuminating the True Self from the Illusion Self, to the Power of Prayer, to setting down crosses and burdens, to moving the essence of be-ing into passion.

Today I have Offered you the Braid of the Trinity of Light, which Resurrects the Divine Spirit within, and the Braid of Shadow, which fragments the spirit within. Both are needed and necessary along the journey of life. You are here to experience both. However, as you evolve, what you experience and call to you is specifically designed to assist you in your deeper embodiment of the Divine Braid of the Trinity of Light.

I have shared with you the beautiful Path of liberation that illuminates through Repentance, and Atonement, and Redemption. A Path of consciousness, Simplicity, and transformation. And, now, I Offer and extend to you the Gateway for your Resurrection to Freedom.

If I might make a recommendation, instead of trying to master and absorb all of My Pathways, choose one that resonates. Sit with it, master it. Even one of My Transmissions, even one Word or Breath within it, carries all the energy needed for the whole of your enlightenment. Sitting with each Transmission, meditating with it, applying it to your process, and integrating it deeply into your be-ing before proceeding to the next can augment and accelerate your journey tremendously.

Another suggestion is to move through this process in cycles. Each time you cycle back to a Transmission, sometimes even years later, a new knowing will rise within your consciousness that you did not see before. Within all I Offer there is always something new to discover, for, from moment to moment, you are new.

I am able to speak to all be-ings at all times and to bring each person different needs at different times. I am able to serve each of you individually and collectively all at once. For I AM Yeshua. Your Path of evolution is a Path of mastery. Mastery takes years and lifetimes. If you are here, reading and hearing these Words, you are moving into your process of mastery. What you are mastering is be-ing, Loving and know-ing self as a vessel of God. You are coming to mastery but are a master of none but self. Through weaving and braiding, through restoring your natural Balance, through embodying Truth, Peace, and Love, you are moving deeper into the Sacred Heart of God within your own.

Therein, you become the essence, Emergence, and expression of the Divine Trinity of Light in the world each day more. For, with pa-tience, courage, Grace, and humility, you are honoring your need, your thirst to be One with a Source far greater than that of the single self. That is the humble, simple service of the Light-holder—the truest es-sence of the Divine Master who has mastered the art of be-ing. And that, Beloved, is the Path we share together.

Let Us walk together. Walk with Me.

YESHUA MEDITATION

Close your eyes and begin to breathe. Take My Hand, as I take yours. We will walk away from the noise of the party of life to find a space of quiet and Peace for our own celebration. We walk away. We walk to-ward one another. We walk IN one another. We walk away from your burdens, denial, judgment, rage, despair, self-pity, blame, and fear. For you and for the collective, we walk away.

I will show you the way to walk away from the burdens of wants to the detriment of needs. To walk toward the Truth with courage and in Grace. Breathe as you walk toward your Freedom. Breathe as you walk IN your Freedom.

Now, we will breathe together in the Weaving Prayer as we begin to braid the Strands of the Trinity of Light through your be-ing.

Begin to intensify your breath. Let your soul weave and braid. Not thinking, just weaving. Repentance, Atonement, Redemption. Faith,

Forgiveness, Freedom. Truth, Love, Peace. Thread and weave these energies into your tapestry.

Through the Power that is vested in Me, through the Omnipotence that is the Light, We Pray:

The Weaving and Braiding Prayer

Om Mani Hu, Om Mani Ma, Om Mani Hu, Om Mani Ma.
Om Nomani Hu, Om Nomani Ma, Om Nomani Hu,
  Om Nomani Ma.
Om Homani Hu, Om Homani Ma, Om Homani Hu,
  Om Homani Ma.
Om Domine Hu, Om Domine Ma, Om Domine Hu,
  Om Domine Ma.
Hu Omni Ma, Ma Omni Hu, Hu Omni Ma, Ma Omni Hu.
Om, Om, Om.

It has been My honor to have served you on this day. You have exceeded My every hope. Now rest in My Heart, in the Arms of Divine Father, Divine Mother, and Gaia. Settle into your chamber, into your temple, wheat into chaff, into your whole self—nestling into a dream. Dare to dream. Be the dream.

Before you sleep, take out the piece of folded paper with the **Freedom Transmissions Personal Process** on Faith, Freedom, and Forgiveness. Do not open it still. Place your hand upon it. Speak a gentle Prayer of gratitude and set it beside your pillow. Get down on your hands and knees and ground your energy deeply into the Earth. And so it is done. Rest with the Angels for the Angels are with you on this good day, good night. As am I, your Beloved, your Yeshua, your Peace.

Om Nami Maia. Om Namah Sananda. Om Nami Yeshua. Sancti. Sancti. Sancti. Pace. Pace. Pace. Namaste.

TRANSMISSION 8

Deliverance

1

....

Salvation

YESHUA TEACHING

Good evening, Beloved One. Sacred children of the Light—no longer the scared children of the night. You are of the candle and the star that holds the Light in Holy Grace and Holy Union.

What a journey to this moment of your liberation, your Deliverance. Throughout the course of our time and moments together through these past Transmissions, you received Offerings of communion from the space of the great central sun that exists in the space beyond time and reality. It is the center space that holds the Light, the Void. That holds the sacred space of this moment. It is your origin, essence, and radial center.

As you have walked and walk through this valley of shadow and Light, please now allow the Great Star of the Light beyond Light to shine upon your face. You are shining that Light upon the world. I have transmitted to you Deliverance, so that you may transmit and usher that Deliverance to all others through your Presence and Grace.

This entire body of Transmissions is the foundation of the Truth of Love. It is the foundation for all that has been, is, and is to come. In this space, what I have Offered you is to Free, clear, cleanse, and rebalance you from imbalances of the mind, heart, and body. This body of Transmissions IS My Body and My Blood. It is a new foundation for the Holy Spirit that exists with and within you to rise. Through our time together, we have walked through life and through the death of all that keeps you out of life to restore life to you again. Today we walk deeper into the heart of Faith, Forgiveness, and Freedom.

A life of eternal Peace and Balance is what I Offered then, now, and beyond. That is the Transcendence, Emergence, and Immanence. The life, death, and Resurrection of your authentic self. I realized a Prophecy in My Life. You are now the realization of the Prophecy I set forth for you upon My Death. A Prophecy that has not been fully ready or possible to realize until now.

You are Mine. And I am Yours. From the beginning, in the middle, and in the end.

Some of you ask, "How can I recognize you, Yeshua, when I cannot always see Your face or know if You are real?" As I will always say, I AM your Peace. Do not seek Me, find Me through finding your way back to the pure, fluid consciousness of Peace within your heart.

What creates that Peace lies in the foundation of the Name I carried in My Life, which carries the Codex, Logos really, of all names and none: Ye-shoo-ah. Ye-ho-Shua. My Name IS the Foundation of the Presence of the Light: YHVH. The four corners, directions, four nucleotides that create the Wheel, Circle, and Web of Life. Within which I stand at center.

Yeshua means "to rescue, to deliver." As I did. And always will.

But, as I have said, I cannot "rescue" you until you have the humility to reach out for or accept that support, as I did from Simon and countless others. For without the support of the Light and also the support of others, you cannot step through the narrow gate.

Your wheat was delivered into chaff through the narrow gate, into the Void of the womb of your mother. You were delivered into the world, the dreaming in your birth. When you transition from this life, you pass back through the narrow gate, through the Void, and are redelivered, as you unstitch your wheat from the chaff and return to the womb of the Divine. Your chaff returns to Mother Earth and the fabric of creation.

You may not remember your delivery from wheat into chaff, and you may not remember your death in Deliverance. But, truly, Beloved, all that you need to remember is that you are a member of this world and of all worlds. You are a member of the Light. While you may not remember every moment of your life, when you stitch into a moment, that moment re-members you. Your soul, outside of time, re-members all.

You are a member of the Light. When you forget, it is time to take a breath, to re-member your knowing of what you are—a tapestry and moving mountain of energy. I was delivered the same way that you were delivered into the world—wheat into chaff through the womb of My Mother.

For how could I serve you if I did not know, and understand, and have the experience of walking as and among you? To have the experience of both humanity and Divinity at once is extraordinary. Which is why I encourage you not to rush through your humanness. When you re-member your origin and stand with Me in your radial center, THE Radial Center, there is no need to rush because you are already there.

Thus, when you look out at the world and feel disgust and hopeless over the state of humanity you perceive, re-member that you are a member. Of this world and all worlds.

You are a member of the Light of consciousness. That realization IS your Deliverance. Your Deliverance to Freedom. Through redeeming yours, you will help to deliver others to their Freedom, to the Truth of Love.

Each of you has a Divine signature inherent to your wheat, your soul, your spirit. When you come into body, this signature is woven through the whole of your be-ing. Your body, the chaff, thus maintains and upholds a Covenant with the wheat—that as long as you are in a body, it carries that signature. Once the Prophecy of your life is realized and you transition, you have made your mark. Sealed and signed the commitment you made to fulfilling what you needed to fulfill within your life, regardless of whether it was expansive or simple.

From the moment you come into a body, you sign your commitment to body by choice. And I can promise you, Beloved, that the terms are very well spelled out. You sign on the dotted line to every stitch that your soul weaves into the body, into the world, and into your relations with others. It is a co-creative commitment that you make with Us and with all those with whom you choose to create your soul contracts. It is sealed with the Blessing of the collective and the Divine, and you are delivered into the world.

When your life is complete, there is the signing of a life complete, even if the passing is sudden or even traumatic. There is a signing and a sealing . . . and you are re-delivered. Through the energy we have shared through My Words, what you have signed and sealed is your Deliverance, your rebirth within this life, to serve as a Divine be-ing, in alignment of will with the Divine Will. It is a recommitment and renewal of the unseen vows you made long ago that I am now drawing into the seen, into your awareness.

As such, all prior contracts are now off the table. From this point on, be discerning about what you sign up to and who you sign on to share the celebration of life with. You are here to make choices as the Divine human, not the human human any longer. You will find that choices that keep you stuck in the birth canal will make it harder for you to breathe. While We can move external energy and events for you to keep you flowing and moving, it is up to you to keep moving, changing, unbraiding, reweaving, and breathing. Patience and exploration will be central to your process as a doula or usher of Deliverance. To become a doula or usher, you must first be the doula or usher to thine own self.

That was My Offering to you when I was delivered into the Earth within My Death. My Love was so strong that, in My Passing and Resurrection, there was a sealing of all possibility of separation. I AM your birth and death doula and usher. I AM your pregnancy. I AM your life. I AM your death. I AM your rebirth. I AM all you know, and all you do not.

I AM the Origin, the Creator of the dreaming, your natural world and beyond. I AM the Architect, the One from whom your knowing of self and science came, as well as the One who upholds those Laws. I AM the Word, heard within the Stillness, who gives you the ability to testify through energy, words, and consciousness. Such is the Omnipotence, Omniscience, and Omnipresence of your Source, your God.

When you call out in the depths of the night, call out for God. Call out My Name in Supplication: Yeshua, Yeho-shuah. Yeho-shu-ah—the saving cry and true Redemption song. I AM your cry for the Light, as well as the One who answers the cry. Thus, those who answer your cry—they stand for Me. Those whose cries you answer—you stand for Me.

For My Name means Salvation. And Redemption. I AM the Salve that mends, repairs, and restores you when you tumble. I am not a fan of patchwork and masking tape to create transient fixes. I AM the Salve that heals your wounds through restoring you to your natural essence. So that you can be not what you wish to be, what you ought to be, but what you are.

I AM the "Physician" that brings the Salve for your restoration, reconciliation, and reparation. I AM your Salvation. The Salvation of your consciousness through consciousness as consciousness. I AM the Bridge to your eternal life *as* life eternal.

I was named in part after the Second Temple of Judaea. Through these Offerings, the Braiding of the Trinity, the Freedom Transmissions, I have laid the foundation for the Divine Temple of the silent Bell, the Temple of God, within you. For the Path to it can only be found within. You are its Foundation. Thus, you are the Salvation now

too, for your world now and in times to come. The Salvation of consciousness. The Bridge to the continuation of conscious life, eternal
life. That is the service you were designed to offer to this world from
your inception. But you cannot fully realize this humble, powerful
service until you are able to allow for My Salvation, or simply the Salve
of Divine Light, to wash over you.

In My Life, I was in a Body, just like you. I bled like you, I ached
like you, I even sometimes thought like you, and I certainly felt like
you. One of the central differences, however, is that from the very beginning, I did not forget what and who I AM. I did not run away from
My own Prophecy, for to fulfill a Prophecy is far more of a service than
creating a Prophecy for another to fulfill.

As a Child, I already saw and knew what My Life would be and
what My Death would be. I was not allowed to forget. In the moments
that I did, the support of those around Me helped Me very quickly
to re-member. You cannot escape yourself, nor can you escape the
glory of wheat and chaff. In My Life, the beauty of the world, including the human spirit, wove through Me a Love and gratitude so vast
that it was a joy to fulfill My Passion, Commitment, and Promise to
you in Death. That Love is what propelled, ignited, and made My
Resurrection—and yours—possible.

Be-ing in body helps you to evolve. Thus, re-member in the times
you complain or are dissatisfied with your life or life in general, it is
not a burden to be what you are. The burden comes in trying to "keep
up with" what you are not. When you are yourself and honest in the
face of the Truth that comes to reveal change, there is a flow of Love,
a reciprocity of Love realized. When you Free yourself to be as you
are, and Free others to be who they are, it suddenly becomes easy
to Love, to trust, and to release doubt. There is a natural Faith that
comes through delivering yourself from the shackles that keep you
from Freedom, mentally and emotionally. Shackles such as judgment,
wanting, and comparing.

Your ecosystem, Gaia, is now birthing. Your Deliverance now must occur, for you are being delivered into a whole new world above, below, and within. Those who stay stuck in the birth canal will suffer. Those who trust and allow for the Deliverance, no matter the Truth and re-balancing that occurs, will find extraordinary Freedom and Peace in the end.

You are all being delivered in a new way, into a new time of **Balance, Unity, and Community. This is the Braid of the Trinity of Light, as well.** The Divine is restoring fluidity and harmony through delivering you with safe passage into the Era of Masculine and Feminine Balance, Co-Creation, and Transparency.

As I have said, you have believed quite falsely that you are the most dominant and superior species just because you create cities, systems, infrastructure, art, and volumes of knowledge. That is arrogance and foolish wisdom. For such things are of the flesh and can be torn down in a moment's notice.

You have forgotten God and your commitment to God for the privilege of coming to body. You have forgotten to yield, to submit, and to supplicate. You have forgotten gratitude. Including gratitude for your Earth. Therein burdens and suffering are born, Beloved One. It always astounds Us how long you stay in the prison of your suffering before you even realize you are in it. And, despite all of your intelligence, the door to liberation from those burdens has always been open. It is your fear and judgment that blinds you to it.

More than food and even air, you need the Divine. Without submitting to a higher consciousness, you are lost in the chaos of the Void without even realizing it. That is neither Deliverance nor Freedom. Deliverance is delivering yourself back to your Simple Simon, Yeshua self. Deliverance is no longer playing God and instead embodying the qualities of the God you wish to know. Deliverance is remembering that your deepest joy comes from the simplest and even smallest of things—a cloud in the shape of an Angel's wings, Robes of Petrichor (the smell of the Earth when it rains), a butterfly on your Mother's grave.

Deliverance is restoration of gratitude and adoration for all things that come to you. Deliverance is embodying and living your soul's Prayer. Deliverance is honoring, inspiring, and receiving the soul Prayer of others. Deliverance is your fulfillment of Prophecy, which, in turn, creates the Prophecy of those who come after you. Just as those who came before you opened the seals and gates to your realization. Deliverance is worship instead of the warship your life becomes when you act as an army of one instead of be-ing One.

Once you re-member your need for the Divine, for the amazing Grace of humanity, for the humble gratitude that comes by way of reconnection to your Divine self, world, and ecosystem, you have just delivered and served yourself your own need. You don't have to be-lieve or even understand God, consciousness, or Spirit to allow for and receive the Presence of God within your be-ing and your life. Faith exists independently from beliefs and knowledge. Faith is a wisdom carried deep within the belly of the Whale. It is the Light, the Void. If you did not have the Light, the Void, within you, you would not exist.

Your survival as a species was and is predicated on your ability to change, to adapt, to evolve, to create, to destroy, and to share in com-munity and communion. It should not come as a shock to you that your evolution as a soul and collective soul is predicated on those self-same things. As above, so below. While your soul cannot die as a species can, when it does not honor change, creation, destruction, and shar-ing, when it separates from the community of Light, and community of the world, it suffers, withers, and loses its Divine life force. Such is the lonely life of the dying tree too stubborn to receive the support from the ecosystem around it. Unwilling to be Resurrected to the Tree of Life. Unwilling to share its fruit.

You have a need to share your Light with this world, even if only with one person. You have a need to share your life with others and with the Divine. If you were willing to share more of your life with God, the God of all things and all people, in a conscious way, you would live in such joy and Freedom.

Joy is an energy that spreads everywhere it goes. It is an emanation of Love that cannot be resisted or controlled. It is the Laughter of Love. It is the ultimate liberation to be in Love, in Peace, in Truth, fully naked before self, world, and the Divine. That is intimacy. When you have established it with Us, it is easy to discern, grow, and cultivate that intimacy with all others you choose to share your heart with.

This sharing of communion is a central tenet of this period of restoration of Balance. Through delivering yourself from the death-grip of the separate self, illusion self, victim self, Lucifer self to the Freedom of your wheat self, authentic self, Yeshua self, you are expressing a genuine desire and willingness to participate in the process of creation of the Divine Temple, the realization of the Braid of the Trinity of Light on Earth. **Some call it the movement into the Era of Christ Consciousness. I prefer to simplify that to just: the Era of Consciousness. Like Peace and justice, consciousness does not need a modifier.** Moreover, I AM consciousness; thus, adding My Name to the essence of what I AM and you are is a bit redundant, no?

Through active, not just passive, participation in reaching to the foundations, the origins of your Balanced essence, YHVH, you are putting in your order for more Light. And as such it will be delivered.

The Era of Consciousness is also the Era of Transparency and Accountability. For Transparency to come, you must all reap what seeds you sow on an individual level. You are all accountable for your share of the Peace, or your share of the burden, in ways you did not have to be accountable for before. For you cannot move into a new garden without first tending to the weeds of the old.

There is a time for sowing seeds; there is a time for reaping seeds. There are waves of grief and longing, ensued by waves of relief and joy. There always will be. Allow for the rise and the fall in the cycles.

This is a time of sharing, putting closure on the past, and allowing for resolution through Love, co-creativity, Simplicity, and Forgiveness. Do not keep starting things that you cannot see through to completion. Be refined in your commitments. When you commit, see it through. We will be holding you accountable for your commitments and authenticity. Thus, choose what you commit to wisely.

Those who choose to use their gifts self-righteously for money, sex, power, etc. under the guise of altruism are the deadest of trees with poisonous weeds. Stop feeding from their poisoned vines, Beloved One. I caution you to be discerning of those who preach Love and unity, then judge and condemn those who do not fall in line with them.

Accountability requires honoring equality, which includes all life, as I have said. Cease and desist from your slow crucifixion of Gaia. Though you are not single-handedly responsible for the crosses She now bears, it is still up to you not to contribute to Her burden. The very best way you can serve is by showing up as Her Simple Simon. Helping Her to bear a Lighter load.

Of all things, cease and desist in the harm you do to yourself through taking My Name in vain. Or projecting your opinions of what I would do in one case or another based on your illusion knowledge of Me two millennia ago. Statements such as, "If Yeshua saw this, He would punish you." Using My Name to punish or shame another is apostasy and deep imbalance.

Those who use My Name to storm the temple of another will find their own temples swiftly stormed. Thus, while Prayer is limitless and We have limitless Power to fulfill your authentic Prayers made in Peace, Patience, and Forgiveness, your Petition for the suffering of another perpetuates your own. Pray for thy foes and you will find your Freedom. As, in Truth, none are foes to you. My Prayer is that you, as a world, are able to realize this in time.

If you feel the events of these years are a Divine Storming of Temples, you highly underestimate the Power of God. Of the many things

I AM, incompetent is not one of them. If THIS is the best you think I have in Me—a few natural disasters, a simple virus, and bringing the roots of some inequalities to a head—I suggest you stop reading now and start again from the beginning. When I Storm Temples, it is through Love. When I Storm Temples, I dismantle not only universes but entire reality structures. If I, God, were to truly Storm the Temple of the world, you would know about it, Beloved. Or you wouldn't, because it would all be over so fast.

I have no need to Storm the Temple of your world when you are all so good at doing that on your own. You stormed Mine, My Body, My Temple, back then, and continue to now through your treatment of your Earth and your own bodies. You have all been storming Gaia's Temple for centuries. Yet at the slightest pin-drop of offense you feel regarding your temple—your appearance, your sexuality, your health, your body—off you go into a fiery fit or cloud of despair. We are not Storming your Temples, Beloved One. The next years for you are about closing out your tendency to storm your own temple and those of others. Will you be God's dream, a conscious dreamer? Or will you be God's nightmare, twisted in the dreaming? Will you be the dim reflection of God on Earth? Or will you be the illumination of God on Earth? Wake up.

This time is hardly a Storming of Temples. In fact, it is the opposite. This is a time of Salvation. And Deliverance to the Temple of the silent Bell. This is a time for Peace. That is why I am here. To save you from your illusion selves. To deliver you into the Peace of your Yeshua self. To share your journey with you.

This is a time of exploring and sharing. The sharing that I am speaking of is not just about sharing thoughts, feelings, and opinions through talking, talking, talking. Nor is it about sharing pudding and crackers from your lunch box. It is not about sharing "things." It is about sharing your Presence in Stillness and Grace. Sharing a moment with another in kindness and recognition of Divinity. Sharing the exploration *of* the present. Exploring the sharing possible *within* the present. The present is a multifaceted gift.

Sharing of Presence knows no time and distance. Sharing occurs in the moments you allow yourself to Be-Loved and emanate that Love through your Presence. The moment the world stopped being an invitation for sharing of The Beloved in a co-creative way was the moment the world went dark. We are turning on the Light again . . . together.

Beloved One, within the structure of these Transmissions, I have gifted you all you need to mend, to Balance, to Resurrect. There has been an unthreading, a reweaving, and mountains have moved through your willingness to move deeper into the Heart of Love. **I Pray you will honor My request and move through this process, reading or listening, at least twice more.** For these Transmissions were structured in Strands of the Braid of the Trinity of Light.

The first three Transmissions of the Freedom Transmissions are the three Strands of the first Braid—the Life. The second three Transmissions are the three Strands of the second Braid—the Death. The final three Transmissions are the three Strands of the third Braid—the Resurrection, the Deliverance. These three Braids of the Freedom Transmissions are now Braided together to create the One Braid, One Transmission of the Divine Trinity of Light.

It has been in this second Strand of the third Braid, the eighth Transmission, that we walk through the Gateway to Freedom. Thus note that only eight full Transmissions are included in this Offering.

That is because the final Strand of this Braid to complete the Divine Trinity of Light is . . . YOU.

You are the completion of what began at the beginning. You are the third Strand of Resurrection and You are the ninth Transmission.

Indeed, the Divine is your Salvation and your Salve. However, to your world in this new Era, YOU are now the Salvation and

Salve. Through your humility, courage, patience, devotion, competence, compassion, Peace, and unconditional Love. Those who embody Me serve as Me. Without you, Resurrection and completion of the Braid is not possible. That is Divine human service.

You will only realize this Prophecy through continual excavation of the common thread that unites you all—nature. You ARE Salvation, for, in receiving the Presence of the Divine, you are not just choosing to rest in human nature, you are choosing to unite with your Divine nature, One with the essence of all Life.

Will you serve as My Hands, Heart, Body, and Blood? Will you embody the Prophecy I set forth in My Life, Death, and Resurrection to realize this new Era of Balance and Consciousness?

All that is required is willingness, Surrender, and curiosity. A willingness to give your burdens over, a surrendering of your fear of what might change or what you might lose, and the curiosity to be open to what you might learn and gain. It is through these virtues that the Pathway to Peace is revealed. And you are delivered into Freedom. There is no worth that can ever be ascribed to your Freedom.

Consciously or subconsciously, if you are here, you have felt a call to realize your true purpose and service within this life. This is it. To complete the ninth Strand and Transmission so that we, together, may Braid the Trinity of Light deeper into you, into the Earth, and into the world. You may never see the rewards of this in your lifetime, thus you must release the need for instant gratification. The gratification will come through the Miracles that encircle you as a by-product of this process.

You are the ninth strand of the Trinity of Light—Yeshua's Strand, the Strand of Peace. You are MY strand. I am trusting MY strand to you. The ninth strand of the Trinity of Light is dependent on the Me within You and You within Me.

Thus, there is no ninth Transmission that I have to Offer. You are offering yourself up as the Offering. Through redeeming your Yeshua self, stripping down your illusions of Me, and illusions of self, you come to know Me. I already know you. **This is Revelation—the unfurling of the unseen to the seen.**

The ninth Transmission is your testimony and soul Prayer to Me, to self, to world. Your soul Prayer is an offering of service from a space of Freedom. I would like you to write your soul's Prayer in your journal. Do not include such things as "I wish to save the world"—that creates unrealistic burdens and carries potential for arrogance in assuming you know what the world needs. The soul Prayer is a Prayer of Love to self and thus to other. It is a Love note to the Divine, from the Divine within you. Please refine it as you read or listen at least **twice more to these Transmissions,** inclusive of committing to the meditations and writing.

Once you have honored this process, you will need to sign the final page. It is a Covenant shared only with Me, and the Whole of the Divine.

The ninth Transmission will unfurl through the whole of your life, through your death, and long after. This ninth Transmission began the moment you were born into this world. It is the Prayer you felt as a child. You have called Me to you now to realize it.

Now, breathe for a moment, Beloved, and take out the slip of paper with the **Freedom Transmissions Personal Process,** still folded and unopened. **With the power of your energetic signature sealed by the Divine, are you willing to allow for your Deliverance from suffering to Freedom? This question cannot be rushed, for when you commit you cannot go back. It is a Covenant. Sit with it.**

Do not open the paper, simply place your hand upon it. Keep it near you in your lap. Remember, it is simple to remember what you are. At a point, you were delivered to the world through the vessel of your mother. And now We deliver you to the world through the Vessel and Seed of your Divine Mother AND Father. Delivery and Deliverance. To the Freedom of the Light.

To help you to fulfill your commitment as the ninth Freedom

Transmission, the Yeshua or Peace Strand of the Braid and Trinity of Light, I wish to Offer some simple suggestions. Some may resonate, some may not. But I ask that, of those Offered below, you commit to nine. Or more if you wish to move even deeper into the process. But at least nine. If one is all you can commit to, let it be so, but I ask you to give full depth of consciousness to it.

For each one of the below that you commit to, We, the Divine, will commit something to you in return. The deeper you go, the more We will commit to you, for you are allowing for the deeper Pathway to Peace to reveal:

1. As said before, I would ask that you reread and/or re-listen to the Body of these Transmissions at least two times more. And keep a journal, for there are layers upon layers of energy within these Transmissions. Do not rush . . . take your time. And if you do not have the time, I will be sure to move things around in your life enough so that you do have the time. Continue with the braiding and weaving through each passage. Take notes on the Words. But most importantly, do the meditations and allow them to seed and reveal your Pathway to Peace.

2. Second, I suggest you do a bit of writing on your rhythms and cycles, including your breath. The only "work" to focus on now is your breath. There are illusions and distortions, fear prisons that are being imposed upon you and that you are imposing upon others, all of you, during this time. The trauma to your bodies is tremendous. Take a break from the noise to work with the cycles of your breath. This will help you to restore your natural rhythms. Explore them. Therein lies the key to reestablishing your physical, emotional, and mental Peace and Balance. That is your only "work" right now. Your "Home-work" or "chaff-work" is to breathe and to not make it more complicated than that.

3. I suggest that you do a bit of writing to reflect upon what crosses you need to set down, such as control and doubt. And what you wish to repent per My Words to you within the seventh Transmis-

sion. What is it that you wish to repent that keeps you from the true essence of your be-ing, which is kindness and Grace? And how do you wish to atone through your passion, your service through joy?

Finally, write about what you wish to redeem through the process. Your Balance? Your compassion? Your boundaries? Your Peace? Your time? Your feeling of connection to the Divine or world? Do not make the Redemption about wants . . . "I wish to redeem more financial abundance." If that is meant to come, it will come as a by-product of your Redemption. It is not the Redemption itself. The Redemption is the rejoicing. Then write about how you wish to redeem your joy in a way that is simple and abundant. Simplicity and abundance are two energies that actually coexist and co-create quite beautifully together.

4.   Take time to Pray for at least fifteen minutes per day for three to four months. In addition to fifteen minutes of meditation, at least. Prayer is a Sacred Right each of you carries. It is a Right very few of you exercise. It is time to exercise that Right. The greatest of Prayers are those you express of gratitude, humility, and Love for All be-ings, especially thine "enemies." When you can Pray for those who provoke you with an authentic desire for them to know Love and Peace, you have mastered the art of Prayer. Thus, your Prayer becomes more powerful, as does My ability to fulfill Prayers you do not even know you have.

You will continually be brought to your knees in polarity until you remember or learn what it is to Pray. In ways beyond the self. For without Prayer, how can you ever live and fulfill the soul Prayer you came to this life to fulfill? Prayer illuminates and magnifies the soul's Prayer. Thus, the more time you spend in Prayer, the sooner the living of that soul Prayer will be manifest and felt.

The Prayers I have given to you through the course of these Transmissions are wonderful Pathways to your Sovereign Divine Peace. Say them as Freely and often as you wish. For they carry an additional energetic resonance that will unlock aspects of self, your Yeshua self, in newfound ways more every day.

5. For purposes of Balance, I would like to gift to you the story of the monk who spent a lifetime moving one grain of sand at a time to create a mandala. After forty years of moving one grain at a time, it was complete. The moment it was complete, he destroyed it. For him, the creation of the mandala was a humble meditation of Presence that was not about the outcome—it was about the journey, moment for moment, grain for grain. THAT is creating for creation's sake.

Thus, though it needn't take forty years or even forty hours, I suggest that you create something for the process of creation . . . and then destroy it. Creating from the Void and releasing to the Void empowers you to be the Light, the conscious creator within it. Actions of sacrifice or Surrender solidify your commitment to the process of Surrender. If you can Surrender to God and destroy that which you perceive is "yours" consciously, it will be far easier to command that healthy control through the changes and perceived "losses" that come through life.

Please note, you can also take something that you have already created and destroy it. For example, if you have an old journal, full of words and feelings that you have evolved beyond, let it go. For, re-member: When you can let something go, you become One with it. The words are written in your heart. The more time that you have invested into what you created, the bigger the gain will be through letting it go.

6. My next suggestion is to live in silence for one full day. No speaking; you must communicate through hands and energy only. This is Vipassana—a vow of silence. It is a powerful practice of profound discipline, mastery, and devotion. I spent much time in silence in My Life so that I could seed, knead, and weave deeper Light into the consciousness of the Earth. Vipassana is a conscious time of silence in which your spirit echoes loudest. You have no idea how much energy you expend in actual speaking. In Vipassana, your soul communicates through the vibrations of your spirit in a way that revitalizes you.

If you take this vow of silence for one, or even better, three days, you may wish to share with certain family members that you are doing so.

I would ask that you refrain from emails, phone calls, text messaging, and messaging via social media during your period of Vipassana, as well.

It would be best served for you to take this time of silence in Gaia, in nature, in the truest sense of a vision quest of your own design. If you cannot commit to a full day or more, please spend at least an hour in silence in nature once a week. On a hike, in meditation. After all, nature is the common thread that unites you all.

7.   Please begin to design your own ceremonies and rituals. Never to be bound by as an obligation, but as an act of devotion and communion. Create an altar, a medicine wheel, a kiva, or find a sacred space in nature. Return there daily or weekly to commune and share your tidings with the Divine. That is showing up for the party, so to speak.

You may invite others. Else let it be our Sacred time. Holding ceremony to honor yourself, the Divine, and Gaia is an expression of humility and celebration. Allow your creativity and intuition to guide this process.

Other beautiful rituals and ceremonies may include establishing a way to greet and consecrate the new day when you wake, creating a purifying bath or tea, designing a music list that feels resonant for sharing, dancing, and processing, or simply taking the time to savor the taste of your food or the smell of a garden. Utilize your creativity and evolve the ceremonies or rituals as you evolve.

8.   My next suggestion is for you to write a letter of commitment to the energies of Faith, Forgiveness, and Freedom. What do you commit to in growing your Faith? Perhaps questioning and exploring the roots of your doubt? What do you commit to in growing your Forgiveness? Perhaps letting go of old vendettas? Perhaps letting go of your addiction to suffering, such as engaging with people, things, and activities known to trigger you (politics being one of My favorites)?

What do you commit to in growing your Freedom? Perhaps releasing impulsivity or procrastination? What do you commit to Surrendering to honor the liberation of the animals and ecosystem? It can be a great service for you to welcome into your heart and home an animal or creature that has not known Love. For you have much Love to give.

What are you willing to commit to the Braid of the Divine Trinity? Write a letter, sign it, and place it by your bedside. Each day infuse Love, patience, and gratitude. And witness what unfolds.

9. This suggestion may sound a bit silly but is actually quite important, for it is a means of acknowledging the Power of the Web of Life and your own weaving within it: I ask that you practice no conscious killing of spiders for two months at the very least. Spiders are Shakti weavers and dream catchers. Remarkable in their resilience and resourcefulness, they do not complain and despair when their webs get knocked down. They simply reweave their web with greater Balance and Grace. They know how to dance in a way you have forgotten. They see all that is around them when you only see what is before you.

If you deserve life, so too do they. Thus, despite your dislike for them, spare them. For they spare you from more than you could realize. If you do not wish for one to be in your space, take it outside.

While I am only asking you to focus on spiders, I ask that you also be mindful with other insects, as well. The role of insects, especially worms, ants, and snails, within your world is invaluable.

Many of you view them as lowly or unpalatable, because what they find palatable is poop—is waste. They break down your waste. Without them, the world cannot breathe. The plants cannot breathe. You cannot breathe. Thus, do not kill the animals who repulse you just because you do not want them in your Presence. Unless they are pouring into your home or present a risk to your health, spare them. There is much richness in extending kindness to them. You cannot fully weave upon the Web of Life when you do not fully honor all life within it.

10. To restore Balance to the mind from the imbalance of ignorance and denial, as well as to reconnect you to the energy of the Earth, I ask you to find out where your garbage goes. And where your water and food come from. I ask you to visit your local garbage dump.

Your local reservoir. Do you even know where those are? Do you feel you are above this knowing?

You all assume that these structures have always been and will always be there. That is not guaranteed, nor are you entitled to them. You put your blind Faith into these systems without knowing anything about them. What would you do should your garbage cease to be picked up? If you needed to fetch your own water? I say this *not* to incite fear. It is to make you aware of how much Peace and even personal power can come from understanding how to be less reliant on them. Or even just more grateful for them. That starts by bringing awareness into what these systems are and what your imprint within them is.

Your garbage will likely always be picked up. But just taking it out and trusting another to deal with it so that you don't have to look at it or smell it is arrogance. If you saw and knew where your own waste went, you might be inclined to be a bit more resourceful with what you purchase and what can be reused. This suggestion reconnects you to awareness of your ecosystem. And gratitude for the things you often take for granted. For those of you who choose this suggestion, some interesting connections will flow your way.

11. For those of you who enjoy service, My next suggestion is a Pathway to true self-full selfless service—Simple Simon service. Serving for the sake of service instead of serving to obtain recognition and praise. My suggestion is to make a donation or give something away, the larger the better, anonymously. No other person in the world may see or know what you did, but you do, I do, and the collective consciousness does. When you give without needing to boast your virtue to others, you are serving with humility from your Yeshua self. Thereby, you become the essence of virtue, fully recognized by the Light.

Likewise, if you offer something to others—a gift, a helping hand, your ear—give it free of expectation. They owe you nothing and you owe them nothing. Giving with an expectation of receiving is not giving. Unless an exchange is defined and communicated in advance, such as, "I pick up your child from school, you pick up my child from camp," do not get upset if you receive nothing in return. What you receive is the joy of giving. Many of you fancy yourself givers but often, in giving, you have an agenda. You do. It is part of human nature. Giving with strings attached is what keeps you bound to each other in love-nots of resentment.

Allow for God to know how you serve. I promise you, that is more than enough. The Truth is always known in the end.

12. Another suggestion to restore your Balance is to liberate yourself from the grip that overuse of or overreliance on technology can have. Overuse of the human web, the internet or "enter-not without deep consciousness and discernment," social or "mob" media, and even televisions, computers, and cell phones is a bit like sitting in a black widow's web. The widow is appealing, she wishes to mate with you and does a beautiful mating dance—and then eats you. Your mind, your emotions, and your communion with others on the Web of real Life can suffer as a result.

While your technologies can be wonderful tools, the moment you cannot feel Peace without having them near you is the moment you know you have fallen out of Balance. Separate when it is a need and when it is a want to spend time with such applications. I would like to ask that you spend one month practicing discipline with your technologies. One month of only using them when it is a need. For every hour you spend on technology, spend an hour off. You will find the vitality of your senses and body will restore rapidly and you will feel more Free as a result. You have enough extraordinary technology and intelligence within your own be-ing that is far more advanced and interesting.

13. My next suggestion is to have a conversation of depth with a small child, an elder, an animal, or a tree. Preferably a child, elder, animal, tree, or all four, who you do not know well, such as the child of a friend or a niece or nephew. Witness, watch, and learn—make it a study for one day, or one conversation in which you are simply listening. This is not about educating them. It is about communing, listening, and holding space.

The animal or the tree will teach you very much about how to communicate needs without even having to use words. The elder, especially those above seventy-five, as well as children, especially those below the age of nine, carry a great deal of wisdom that can shift perception back to gratitude and remembering what it is to live within the present. I recommend a chat, not on the basis of content and learning, but on the basis of connection.

14. Next, Beloved star, I recommend that one evening within the next weeks, you go out to sit beneath the stars. As you gaze upon the stars, close your eyes, then open them and allow one star to choose you. It will draw your attention. It needn't be the brightest one. One star. Do not research in advance. Either you choose one star that speaks to you or allow one star to draw your focus. Remember this star, befriend this star—your Star of Bethlehem.

This is the star that you will commune with at any time, day or night. You do not have to be able to see it to connect to it. Remember its Light. It will always remember yours. Even if you choose it and see it for only that one night, when you find it, say a Prayer, thank it, and allow yourself to receive its Grace. Say a Prayer beneath it, call in My Presence—Yeshua—to bless this Divine communion, and for the rest of your life, that star will serve and hold Light for your star of self.

Communicate with it and it will always communicate with you too, even from Light-years away. Always. It is the Star of Wonder and Faith, your celestial friend and advocate.

15. A wonderful suggestion, one of My favorites, is to write a list of all things you tend to whine or complain about. Why is it that you have grown so feeble in the face of discomfort?

Why do you run from discomfort? When did you disconnect from the reality of its importance? Why do you burden others with your own delusions, issues, and discomfort?

After all, discomfort isn't suffering. It can bring you to the depths of transformation of imbalance. It can be the greatest manifestation of your shadow, saying, "I am entitled and, to center back to my humility, I need to shake things up," or, "I have serious changes to make." Why is discomfort suddenly a prison for you to lash out and blame others for instead of honoring acceptance and moving through it? What is your entitled fragility to feel that you should be immune from the discomfort of human life? When did your resilience and sense of responsibility for your own life disappear from the tapestry? The amount of complaining and whining you all, ALL of you, feel entitled to undermines the joy, revelation, and evolution that comes through change. This suggestion is to deliver you from your complaining so that we can Resurrect your Freedom.

I would like you to replace discomfort with gratitude. Gratitude for discomfort is a great gift to self, Beloved. Write about how you can become more resilient and allow for discomfort before leaping to complaining, self-pity, or defensiveness. Write about why discomfort tends to make you doubt your ability to trust everything and everyone, including yourself. Are you willing to replace the doubt with discernment? Write about how discomfort can grow your discernment and deepen your ability to trust. There is infinite relief in weaving deeper consciousness into not only understanding the sources of your discomfort but also how you can shift your perception and behaviors as a result. Hence the importance of this suggestion.

16. Another suggestion or option is to make a list of all things in your life that need closure or resolution—whether it is an inability to set boundaries, wrapping up old projects, ending of a relationship, clarity on a living space, resolving a financial matter, getting a disorganized business organized, receiving support to declutter your home, releasing of old burdens and crosses, and/or letting go of an addiction or behavior that causes harm to you or others. This suggestion is to help you to become more proactive in your own liberation. By bringing

these lingering issues into the Light and asking for support in transforming them, you are granting Me permission to bring to you what you need in the process.

In the Era of Transparency, clearing out old lingering issues, possessions, and projects is a simple essential. Inherent to honoring this recommendation, you will be learning to employ healthy separation from your burdens. Give over what you no longer need to Me. You know how I Love taking your burdens and clutter so that you can be Free. Honoring this suggestion of resolution and closure will bring you more space, more Balance, and the clarity that comes from clear vision.

17. My favorite suggestion is for us to have more time together, you and Me. It is My greatest joy when you invite Me to walk with you through your day. I always do walk with you through your day but, when you do not invite Me, I walk silently behind or beside you, unacknowledged. I would Love an invitation to engage with you more deeply. Consciously inviting the Divine, the Light, to walk with you through the whole of your day, including when you are driving, eating, and working, creates a deeper intimacy and connection to the Divine Braid of the Trinity within you.

Thus, for the next few months, I would like you to establish a time each day, preferably the same time each day, for us to share a moment of quiet in your heart. A meeting of Light with Light. Some days you may feel Light as a feather. Some days you may feel grumpy and angry with Me, yourself, or another. It does not matter how you come, oh Faithful, it is that you come. Each day for a few months.

In addition, once a week, I would like to ask for a longer check-in of ten to twenty minutes at least. Throughout the week you may wish to journal about any new awareness that came to you, a revelation you experienced, a discomfort you had, a moment of unexpected joy, a triumph, or a perceived failure. Bring your journal and read it out loud to Me. Our longer check-in is a time of mutual sharing, intimacy, and honesty.

This is our weekly confessional. You will confess to Me that with which you struggle, where you feel you have transformed, as well as what you feel you are still moving through with patience and willingness. I will hold the Light and confess to you the Truth, especially the Truth that I unconditionally Love you no matter what.

This confessional is to aid in your Repentance, Atonement, and Redemption. To confess is to be honest, to unburden. There will never be judgment, blame, shame, "told-you-so's," or penances given. You give enough of those to your own self. This confessional is a communion—the confessional IS the communion now—the communion is the confessional. The willingness to consciously invite consciousness into your transformation is what this suggestion is about.

18. My final suggestion is important for those of you experiencing times of deep change, endings, and grief. It is easy in these times to become lost in shock, fear, shadow, and the Void. To Resurrect the Light within, I recommend that you shift your focus away from the loss and move it to celebration. That does not mean denying your vulnerability, anger, and grief. It simply means allowing space for the Light within it. It is not celebrating that you are in grief, it is celebrating that you CAN grieve, which is also celebrating that you can Love. The ability to share in Love, in joy, in grief IS celebration, especially when shared with others. That is how the healthy Love knots are stitched and woven.

In any ending, even if it is just a project, instead of racing to the next beginning, take a moment to celebrate. To share. With others and with the Divine. Suspend the moment in the space between moments. The only space there is.

In new beginnings, recognize that there is a death to something else. Celebrate the old, for it served you. Celebrate the possibilities for the new. Take a moment to celebrate and to re-member what has just died, for it was a part of you. And what is being born, for it is a part of you.

Thus, in new beginnings, remember to have a funeral for the old. In endings, have a party and a celebration for the new. Even if it is a Beloved that you have just lost, celebrate the new relationship you are

beginning with him or her in Spirit. Through honoring this suggestion, the grief and joy Balance each other out and, with time, bring you
to Peace within the present.

This suggestion is a lesson on working with the energy of counter-
polarity. You will find through this that your perception of funerals and
parties shifts. In every celebration lies a funeral and a re-birth-day. In
every funeral lies a celebration and a re-birth-day. Let it all be One.
That is another reflection of the Trinity of Light: Life, Death, and
Resurrection, all in One. That is Deliverance to Freedom. And so it is.

Beloved One, I ask again for you to take several breaths. And review
this list to sit with which nine, if not more, you will commit to. Will
you commit to the writing and re-listening? The time in silence? The
time with your devoted Gaia? The time with Me? Honoring the creatures of your world? Weaving with a star?

Whichever nine, or even one, you choose is a Covenant and commitment. The more you give, the more you will receive. If you commit, We
will make Our Divine commitment to you clearer, as well. For you are
taking the time to commit to the Braid of the Trinity of Light through
your service as the ninth Strand, ninth Transmission: Yeshua, Peace.

Take several breaths once you have chosen your nine. Then place
one hand on your heart and the other on your womb for women, hara
for men. Sealing and signing this commitment to your own Freedom.
You sign and seal . . . and We will deliver.

Take a moment, if possible, to get down on your hands and knees
and place your forehead to the Earth. For now we weave into the final
moments of the Freedom Transmissions—the consummation and
consecration. Thus, take a moment to ground your energy deeply into
Mother Earth. Then sit up, smile, exhale, and let it all go—so that we
may share My final Transmission and commence the Invocation of the
Light. Amein.

2

The Chalice and Vessel of Freedom

YESHUA TEACHING

Beloved One, in the closing and opening of the Freedom Transmissions, I wish to share some final Truth, which you may or may not wish to hear:

Freedom is a responsibility. As a human be-ing AND as a Divine Sovereign Be-ing. While Divine Freedom is available to All, through Me, the Divine Essence of Peace, human Freedom doesn't often look or feel the same. As an "energy field," a spirit be-ing in form, wheat in chaff, human Freedom is hard-earned and hard to maintain in a world of others in imbalance who continuously wish to strip you of yours— or your own imbalanced self who does the same to you and to others, even if it knows not what it does.

Freedom is not an entitlement in human or in Divine. The moment you feel entitled to it or take it for granted is the moment it disappears faster than the Cheshire Cat. There is no room for complacency, separation, and imbalanced polarity in the heart of Freedom, for Divine Freedom IS the essence of Transcendence from these Veils. It is the state of be-ing realized when the Seven Imbalances come to Balance. It is the Light found when, through Presence, you become conscious that you are consciousness itself. That is true Divine Freedom.

I Offer this to help you to shift your perception away from the illusion of Freedom, mired in your expectations and projections, which leads to self-made disappointments and resentments. Fantasy Freedom is mistaking Freedom with having the power of getting to have and do whatever you want. That Freedom is false hope and, even if you realized it, it would be a false Freedom. The loud bell that tempts you by promising you Freedom while shackling you to want and regret. The hope for Freedom within your external reality without having to take any responsibility for creating it internally. True Freedom is a responsibility, choice, and privilege Offered to all.

However, it is a rare few within your world who accept that Offering and actually find true Divine Freedom. For, to do so means you must transcend the idea of what Freedom "should be" or "could be," the fantasy Freedom, to realize the essence of Freedom itself. Freedom on the external cannot come until it is realized on the internal. You have all, since the dawn of time, been looking to find it on the outer. That is an unwinnable, unsustainable war, if you have not gotten the memo. For Freedom does not lie in the seen, it lies in the unseen. Thus, you must look to the unseen, the space of Consciousness and Spirit, to realize your Deliverance from suppression, repression, or even oppression to Freedom.

Freedom is indeed something you need to "fight" for. However, the "fight" for inner Freedom can only come through Peace. When Peace is the sword instead of violence and shame, that is where real Freedom begins.

The Freedoms and Rights you currently enjoy on your planet, of varying forms and dimensions depending on the culture and country in which you live, were created most often through war. Freedoms that come through war are always precarious, fragile, and hard-won. Some win, many lose. If you saw the horrors of the destruction it took to create the Freedoms you enjoy now, you would weep and tremble. Many of you now only watch such horror on your screens at a safe distance.

Some of you now enjoy "playing war" in your computer games without understanding the catastrophic reality of real war. When there is not a war to fight, you make one up. All you have ever known as a world is the fight for Freedom, some illusion Freedom in which you all get everything you want and live happily ever after.

As a world, you have fought wars for your Faith. You have fought wars for your Freedom. You have even fought wars for your Peace, which is contrary to its essence, My essence, and your true essence. Such fights always result in more of these energies for some and less for others. And never lead to true Divine Freedom in the long run.

The reason you continue to fight so hard for it in an unwinnable war of separation is because you have been picking the wrong battle. All along, the only fight that has ever mattered, the only fight that will ever result in universal Freedom, is the fight for Forgiveness. The one fight that cannot be fought through war. Only through the strength of Peace.

You shed blood in all of the other crusades and wars. And yet the one fight that sets you Free is the one only a rare few have ever had the courage to fight: the fight to Forgive. It is NOT so much of a fight and more of a Right. A Sovereign Right and Holy Power that lies within you. When will you exercise your Right to Forgive? It is the only "fight," the only Right, that comes from the choice of Peace and Surrender and thus delivers you into Peace and Divine Freedom—the Freedom of Love.

Surrendering to Forgiveness is the only "battle" that will ever result in Divine Freedom and Peace for you as an individual and for you all as a world. I was the Chalice and the Vessel then. I lived in Surrender, died in Surrender, and was Resurrected through Surrender. I surrendered My Body, My Blood, My Life to create the Pathway to Peace for you to follow. Through these Transmissions I am revealing the Path to you in a new Way. You are now the chalice and the vessel. It is now up to you to follow, realize, and evolve the Path, the Way. The

Path of the River, the Magi, the Star. The Path that exists beyond the passage of time for the Path is not only the Way to the narrow gate but also the passage through it.

What I was then, Peace and Freedom, is up to you to be-come now. Not through sacrifice, unholy wars, and crosses but through inner transformation, kindness, resilience, compassion, consciousness, and Presence. Through these energies, you win not the war but the Peace. Why fight the war when you can realize now in Simplicity what all wars have been waged for but none have ever won: Peace. The Freedom of Peace. Your signature upon the ninth Transmission is a commitment to this journey to the Heart of God.

All that has been Offered to you through these, the Freedom Transmissions, as with all of My Transmissions of the past and to come, is that which helps you to see that Pathway to Peace. Through the sacred heart and clear eyes of your Yeshua self, your authentic self.

Always remember, nature is the common thread that unites you all. For the nature of matter is resolved unto the roots of its own origins. All creatures exist in and with one another, and they will be resolved again into their own roots. Your true nature is Divine. Trust in your wheat in chaff, be in your natural essence, rejoice in your Yeshua self. Run with the Horses, hear the silent Bell, and feel the rising Star.

The Beloved is Risen. Risen within you. That is not a burden, but it is a responsibility. If you have found your way here, it is the responsibility you came to serve for yourself, family, ancestors, Beloveds in Spirit, and world. You are a liberator of Love, through Love, as Love. Accepting that responsibility with joy instead of fear is what leads you to the joy and Peace afforded to you through the Power of the Light of Consciousness. That is the Deliverance, Salvation, and Resurrection of Divine Freedom.

You have said to Me, "Thy will be done on Earth as it is in heaven."

I say to you, "Thy will be done in heaven as it is on Earth."

Abun D'Shemaya. The Valley of the Lord. When you walk through the Valley of the Shadow of Grief, Pain, Void, or Death, fear not, for you already walk within the Light, the Holy Space of the Presence of Freedom. Therein, I am with you.

Know Me not as I was, but as I AM. Know yourself not as you were, but as you are. The Beloved is Risen and alive within you. You are the chalice and the vessel. Let the waters rise and the fires descend. The fires rise and the waters descend. Rest in the space and Presence of Light. Let there be Light.

Ma Omni Hu. Hu Omni Ma. Walk with Me.

YESHUA COVENANT

In these final moments together, I am opening the narrow gate and Seal of Deliverance that was created long ago. Thus, please take out the sheet of paper that you began with: **The Freedom Transmissions Personal Process.** Note that, since you wrote these things in the beginning, I have asked you not to open or look at it since. Only to sit with it. For through these Transmissions, you have woven and unwoven from much held within the questions and what you wrote.

Now I ask you to open it and read back to yourself the three questions:

- **What do I need to have Faith in?**
- **What do I need to Forgive and be Forgiven for?**
- **What do I need to be Free from?**

Read what you wrote next to each. Now take some moments to write about what you are experiencing reading back your initial responses. Has your perception of these things changed? Have you experienced any transformation or even an event that has shifted your consciousness, thoughts, feelings, or attachments to these three things as you moved through the Transmissions? How so? Take a moment and simply write. And then set the paper down beside or in front of you and take a deep breath. Exhale. And smile.

Beloved One, as you know, I am a fan of polarities to create unity, and unity to create polarity, for all is Balanced in the center. There are times My Words may seem contradictory or paradoxical, but I promise you, there is always a space in which they coexist and intersect.

Thus, though this may seem to contradict much of what I have said throughout the course of the Braid of the Freedom Transmissions, the Truth is:

There is nothing to have Faith in, for you ARE Faith.

There is nothing to Forgive or be Forgiven for. There never was. For you ARE Forgiveness.

There is nothing to be Free from, for you ARE Freedom. You are already Free.

I Pray you will hear and receive these Words deeply within your sacred heart. There is nothing to Forgive. There never was. There is nothing to be Free from; you are already Free. There is nothing to have Faith in, as Faith is naturally present within the very essence of your be-ing. That is the Truth of Love. As I AM All, so too are you, inherent to your Presence. Through these Transmissions, you have opened your heart to allow My Light to shine upon and into the Light of your wheat.

Thus, within the wheat of your Yeshua self, there really is no choice of Faith over fear, Forgiveness over blame, and Freedom over suppression. As illusions of the dreaming, fear, blame, and suppression have no power "over" you, the dreamer. For within you, your authentic essence, IS the Seed of Divine Faith, Forgiveness, and Freedom. Your Presence IS the Seed, the Chalice, and the Vessel. Such are the Seeds you plant on Earth as it is in Spirit when you rest in and echo from the Grace of your Divine self.

As for Freedom, Divine Freedom is never a "from," it is always a "to." Beneath the Veils, you perceive you need Freedom "from" things—little things, big things, scary things. That suggests you are identifying more with the suppression than the Freedom. When that is the illusion lens you choose to peer through in life, you will always be fighting for a Freedom that can never be fully realized.

Within Divine Freedom, you recognize that you already are Free. That Frees you "to" create, destroy, dance, weave, braid, explore, perceive, witness, realize, and be realized. Freedom from is a fight. Freedom to is a Right. A Divine Right that, when exercised, brings Peace, communion, celebration, joy, and true liberation. Now that you know that you are not only Free but the essence of Freedom, you are Free to go forth revealing and unfurling your beautiful tapestry within the Tapestry of the Web of Life.

Behold. And so it is. You are now Free to consummate and consecrate your movement into and as the ninth Transmission. You are Free to go, so to speak!

As such, at the bottom of the Freedom Transmissions Personal Process page, please write: "Divine Light, through the Power of Presence, I commit to living as and in alignment with Faith, Forgiveness, and Freedom in honoring and embodiment of the Divine Braid of the Trinity." Then sign your name. Next to your name, write Mine. Alternately or additionally, you may also sign the Covenant on the final page once our journey together is complete.

And now in this final meditation we will seal both of our energetic signatures. And mark the Covenant with the Light of Love, Truth, and Peace. Amein.

In honor of these final Words, please prepare your body to receive the Host.

YESHUA FINAL MEDITATION:
THE INVOCATION OF THE LIGHT

Close your eyes, Beloved One, and begin to breathe. Letting go of all that you have known prior to this moment. Begin to breathe deeply. Feel the Lightness, the Lightness of a life unstitched from the braids of judgment, wrath, and despair.

Feel the support of your chaff, your body. The beauty of the stitches and Balanced Love knots that connect your wheat, your soul, to your body, your chaff. Feel your wheat as a network of threads of Light permeating through the whole of your be-ing. Radiating from the center. Feel your wheat Lighting up through energy and Presence and echoing out through the Grace of your spirit onto the Web of Life. Allow the breath, yours and the breath of the Divine, to relax all tension, hooks remaining in your body. Let any vapors of thoughts waft away.

Allow your breath, our breath together, to weave through you, to restore wholeness, Balance, and Peace. Through our breath together feel the Braids of Light and Unity weaving down and up your spine. The Divine stitches restoring equilibrium and equality to the whole of your be-ing. I have weaved what you have allowed Me to weave within you. Allow yourself to weave deeper into Me through the Divine threads of Love, Truth, and Peace.

Now breathe into the Strand of Faith. Feel the deeper weaving of this Strand within your Braid.

Now breathe into the Strand of Forgiveness. Feel the deeper weaving of this Strand within your Braid.

Now breathe into the Strand of Freedom. Feel the spaciousness of Divine Freedom within. Feel the deeper weaving of this Strand within your Braid.

Now, through the Power of God vested in Me AS God, I Invoke the Light to enter the Sacred Heart, Chalice, and Vessel of Thy Be-ing.

Breathe in the Light. Feel the Light moving toward, through, and into you. Feel it stream through the whole of your be-ing through your crown, the top of your head—drawing Light through your brain, face, throat, shoulders, arms, hands, lungs, heart, spine, stomach, organs, womb, genitals, legs, knees, ankles, feet. Feel the Light spilling from you into the Earth. A Sacred Embrace of Light, above and below.

Draw the Power of the Light within you—begin to feel as the vibration of the Light sets you Free from the stitches of tempests and storms inherent to the illusion of Freedom. And sets you Free to weave, dance, and be inherent to the Truth of Freedom. Draw through your breath the Golden Light of My Presence. Feel the strength of the strings and rays of Light shining into and through you. As you exhale, feel your spirit weaving this golden thread into the space and ecosystem all around you. Light to Light. Illuminating the spectrum of color from within the dimness of the shadow. Feel the radial Light pouring into, through, and from your heart's center.

In this space of perfect Balance, trust, and Peace, the Light is within you. Thus, let us begin now to release your need for even the Strands of the Braids of Light. For you are the Light, and the Light is already sewn into every stitch of your be-ing.

Through the Power of the Grace of the Light, breathe into the Strand of Faith. Through energy, begin UNbraiding from the attachment to Faith to BE the Faith that you already are. You do not need the thread anymore. For you are the now Faith-full. You may now exhale and release the Strand of Faith to the outer for all those coming in readiness and need of it to receive. Releasing the chaff of Faith to realize the wheat of Faith within you.

Through the Power of the Grace of the Light, breathe into the Strand of Forgiveness. Through energy, begin UNbraiding from the attachment to Forgiveness to BE the Forgiveness that you already are. You do not need the thread anymore. For you are now the Forgiven and For-giver. You may now exhale and release the Strand of Forgive-ness to the outer for all those coming in readiness and need of it to receive. Releasing the chaff of Forgiveness to realize the wheat of For-giveness within you.

Through the Power of the Grace of the Light, breathe into the Strand of Freedom. Through energy, begin UNbraiding from the at-tachment to Freedom to BE the Freedom that you already are. You do not need the thread anymore. For you are now the embodiment of Freedom. You may now exhale and release the Strand of Freedom to the outer for all those coming in readiness and need of it to receive. Releasing the chaff of human Freedom to realize the wheat of Divine Freedom within you.

Breathe. Unbraid the thread so that the Light of your essence may shine through in Sacred nakedness and glory. YOU. ARE. DELIV-ERED. Breathe into the essence of Presence, Mine and yours as One. Breathe into this, your authentic Self, Divine Self, Yeshua self.

This IS your Deliverance and Redemption. You are redeeming Di-vine Freedom. You are Delivering yourself to the Divine Father and Mother. We are Delivering Ourselves to you. You are re-Delivered unto Gaia as She Delivers Her Love to you. This IS the Deliverance and Rebirth. You are reborn, born anew. Breathe in your first breaths of your life as the ninth Transmission: Yeshua, Peace.

You ARE and, accordingly, are within the Light, the Void, the space of Spirit, and realm of infinite possibilities. Consummated, Consecrated, Delivered, Realized, and Reborn. What will you pluck from the space of this moment to realize through this, your life as the essence of Divine Freedom on Earth? Weave and braid into the realm of infinite possibilities. Feel the Revelation, the unfurling of the unseen to the seen, gestating, birthing, weaving, and igniting within your consciousness. Allow your Passion of Peace to reveal itself, as I reveal the Pathway.

With clear eyes and unwavering Truth and Love, now say three times: We ARE Free. WE are Free. We are FREE. And now three times: I AM Free. I AM Free. I AM FREE. Take a deep breath, hold it at the top, and . . . exhaaale.

Now allow the Light to simply integrate with your be-ing. Not going or leaving. Simply now integrating, softening into your be-ing. Allow the Light to Balance and settle within you. Breathing gently and with Peace. Allow Peace to settle into your be-ing.

Settle, breathe, and allow as we Pray:

Om Mani Hu. Om Mani Ma.
Hu Omni Ma. Ma Omni Hu.
Abun D'Shemaya. Abun D'Shemaya.
Hashem, Pesach, Aharit, Chofshi Chofesh.
Hashem, Pesach, Aharit, Chofshi Chofesh.
Il-Alah Sabtai. El Shaddai, El Shaddai, El Shaddai.
Amein.

Please place your left hand on your heart, and your right hand on your womb for women, hara for men. Smile a deep smile and simply say, "Thank you." Move to your hands and knees and place your forehead on the Earth. If you cannot, please simply connect to the Earth through your focus to ground your energy deeply in Prostration, Gratitude, and Thanks-Giving. Sancti. Pace. Amein.

YESHUA BLESSING

Behold, Beloved One. What a journey we have shared. Rejoice! Let us dance, weep, celebrate, and laugh together upon the Web of Life through the Vine, Trunk, Roots, and Branches of the Tree of Eternal Life.

Throughout these Transmissions, My Words may have elicited joy within you, knowing within you, anger within you, hatred within you, grief within you, relief within you, confusion within you, Peace within you, wisdom within you, strength within you, Love within you. Whatever you have experienced is Sacred.

As you go forth into your life as the ninth Transmission, Peace, I ask that when you speak, speak as I would Speak, in Forgiveness and Love. When you act, act as I would Act, in Truth and Peace. When you walk, know that I Walk with and within you. When others walk with you, they will walk with and within Me through you. The Way to the Divine Father, Truth, and Divine Mother, Love, is now through you, Divine Yeshua Child. You are now the Pathway to Peace. We will all walk together on this Pathway in equality, humility, kindness, compassion, and joy.

We will live your soul's Prayer, the **Prayer of Presence.** We will live your soul's Prayer, **My Prayer for You in Your Creation.** We will live your soul's Prayer, **Your Prayer of Communion.** We will live your soul's Prayer, **Our Walking Prayer of Peace.** We will live your soul's Prayer, **for you are the essence of Divine Freedom.** You are Free to go forth with My Blessing, as My Blessing. Blessed Be.

A new journey now begins. I Cherish you. I Love you. I Walk with you. I Breathe with and as you. You are the Beloved, and I AM yours. It has been My honor to have served you through these, the Freedom Transmissions.

I AM Yeshua. I AM your Peace. Be at Peace. Rest in Peace in Life.

Om Nami Maia. Om Namah Sananda. Om Nami Yeshua. Sancti. Sancti. Sancti. Pace. Pace. Pace. Namaste.

TRANSMISSION 9

The Covenant

[Read by Carissa as dictated per Yeshua]

Hello, Beautiful Spirits. I am back. It has been my joy to hold space for you through your extraordinary journey with Yeshua and I have certainly experienced it alongside you. In an unexpected and deeply cherished way, I have felt you holding space for me, too. It takes a lot for me to anchor Yeshua's infinite Light and your Presence has supported, inspired, and moved me. I Pray you will receive my deep gratitude for your strength, openness, kindness, courage, authenticity, and Grace.

Yeshua has asked me to deliver to you the final Covenant for you to sign in realization and completion of this sacred journey. It is my humble honor to do so. He says:

Beloved One, as I have shared, the ninth and Final Freedom Transmission is:

You. Your Yeshua self. God self. True self.

The ninth Transmission and Strand to complete the full Braid of the Divine Trinity is entrusted to you. It is now up to you to honor and fulfill the Realization of the Divine on Earth through the heart of the Beloved that you are. For all the days of your life.

You are the ninth Strand. May your life be a Transmission of Love, Truth, and Peace; Faith, Forgiveness, and Freedom. May you live your soul's Prayer. May you move deeper into the Void, the Light, the Sacred Heart of God with each day more. May you Move Mountains. May you illuminate Stars. May you set down crosses. May you walk in the Garden of Gaia and God. May you be merciful and know mercy. May you walk gently hand in hand with the Light.

[Insert the Covenant of the Freedom Transmissions Personal Process signed: Your name and "Yeshua" next to yours.

Or sign below:]

"I, _____ (write your name) _____ (then write Yeshua), commit to upholding My service as a Holder of the Light, a Just-is of the Peace, and the Ark of the New Covenant of Divine Freedom. Sancti. Pace. Amein."

Thank you for your service as Holder of the Light
on Earth as it is in Divine Freedom.

Let there be LIGHT. Amein.

YESHUA

And so it is. May Peace be with and within you always.
Deepest Blessings.
Namaste.

Acknowledgments

Jennifer Rudolph Walsh—LIGHT, Unity, Miracles
Judith Curr—Vision, Power, DIVINITY

Jaycal Johnson—Trust, Integrity, Wonder
Elise Loehnen—Resurrection, Inspiration, Presence
Shannon Welch—Surrender, Understanding, Wholeness
Eric Zohn—Honesty, Patience, Acuity
Johanna Castillo—Illumination, Attunement, Synergy
Laina Adler—Depth, Leadership, Resonance
Paul Olsewski—Majesty, Autonomy, Commitment
Aly Mostel—Clarity, Fluidity, Direction
Anna Paustenbach—Eloquence, Convergence, Completion
Lucile Culver—Perception, Simplicity, Versatility

Danielle Gibbons—Grace, Service, JOY
Dr. Michael Smith—Radiance, Laughter, Transformation
Joseph Greywolf—Embodiment, Co-Creation, Spirit
Richard Christiansen—Brilliance, Evolution, Rebirth
Marie King—Prayer, Revelation, Deliverance
Adele Sands—Kindness, Compassion, Stillness
Phoenix Two Moons—Mastery, Magic, Connection
Leslie Dewald—Transcendence, Devotion, Ascension
Alexis Kahlow—Balance, Resilience, AWE
Luke Iorio—Stability, Abundance, Realization
Nik McCrae—Soul, Intuition, Consciousness
Debra Hess—Synchronicity, Essence, Peace
Taryn Toomey—Oneness, Luminance, ReGenesis
Jim Fackrell—Courage, Honor, Reverence
JT Walgren—Sharing, Forgiveness, Celebration

Karl Schumacher—Strength, Passion, Faith
Carmi Salas—Harmony, Beauty, Love
Charles Salas—Wisdom, Humor, Insight

Kelly Sullivan (Communion), Tyree Edmondson (Recognition), Steve Oppenheim (Beacon), Robyn Berkley (Enlightenment), Kristen Hahn (Expression), JA (Equality), Andy Brimmer (Immanence), WBP (Humility), Jayda Hammermeister (Gaia), Samantha Jackson (Emergence), Franca Munoz (Source), Sara Werner Costa (Vessel), Rooney Mara (Empathy), Sheri Salata (Manifestation), Jenna Dewan (Lucidity), Scott Sternberg (Creativity), Brooke Baldwin (Liberation), Scott Nathan (Originality), Wyatt Walsh (Consecration), Christopher Pizzini (Covenant), Angela Guerra (Mercy), Tammy Jackson Hammonds (Friendship), Sarah Aynesworth (Serenity), Phil Fischman (Resplendence), Leticia Gonzalez (Blessing), Hazel Groff (Sincerity), Uta Opitz (Healing), Sun Paik (Dedication), Maya Alpert (Alignment), Lowell Foster (Excellence), Taylor Darcy (Resolution), Ward Richmond (Wheat), Ivan Gibbons (Exploration), Piper Rose (Hope), Barbara Zelnick (Vitality), and the late Carolyn Humphries (Transfiguration).

David John Carnell—Authenticity, Sovereignty, Truth
GSP Autumn Carnell—Beloved, Sacred, Heart
GSP Jax Carnell—Innocence, Purity, Bliss

The Late Black Lab, Pierce Carnell, who unexpectedly transitioned during the channeling of these Transmissions in August of 2020. You are Forever Cherished, Pup—Loyalty, Gratitude, Freedom.

And . . . Beloved Yeshua, Son of God,
Prince of Peace, it is my life, my life to
serve You. You are all that I see, know,
serve, and am. You have not just taught me
how to live, You have taught me how to
be. *You* are the Essence of Be-ing. *You* are
the Light of the world and beyond.
Thank You for bringing us Home.
Sancti, Yeshua, Sancti.
Pace, Yeshua, Pace.
Amein.